CU

WALDHEIM

Adolf Hitler and the German Trauma
Western Civilization
The War That Hitler Won
The Nazis
When Nazi Dreams Come True
Roosevelt and Hitler

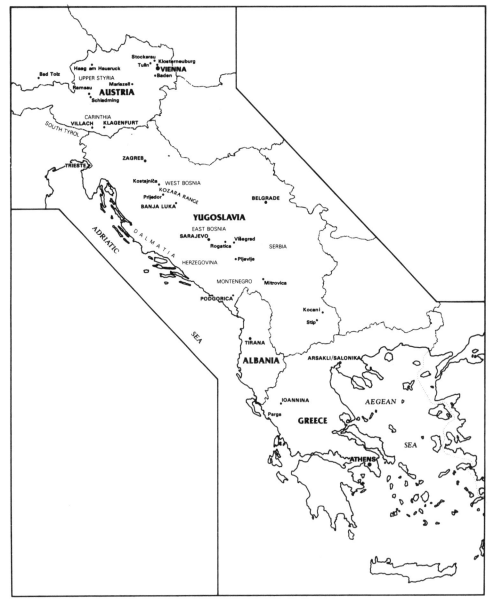

Drawn by Jerry Ulrey

WALDHEIM
The Missing Years

Robert Edwin Herzstein

Paragon House
New York

First paperback edition, 1989

Published in the United States by

Paragon House Publishers
90 Fifth Avenue
New York, NY 10011

Reprinted by arrangement with William Morrow and Company, Inc., New York.

Library of Congress Cataloging-in-Publication Data

Herzstein, Robert Edwin.
   Waldheim : the missing years / Robert Edwin Herzstein.—1st
paperback ed.
     p. cm.
   Reprint. Originally published: New York : Arbor House, c1988.
   Bibliography: p.
   Includes index.
   ISBN 1-55778-221-0
   1. Waldheim, Kurt—Career in military science. 2. Austria—
Presidents—Biography. 3. National socialism. 4. World War,
1939–1945—Atrocities. 5. Germany. Heer—Biography. I. Title.
DB98.W28H47   1989
943.605'3'092—dc20
[B]   89-31924
                                        CIP

Manufactured in the United States of America

*To the Memory of Dr. John Mendelsohn, and
to Robert Wolfe, George Chalou, and John E. Taylor
of the National Archives: Archivists and Friends*

Preface

The Waldheim controversy has been raging for more than two years now. On the one side, we hear charges such as "war criminal," "Nazi," and "liar." On the other side, we note professions of innocence, claims of conspiracy, accusations of blood libel. The enormous publicity that has surrounded the affair from the beginning has only added to the confusion, resulting in greater perplexity among a lot of honest, concerned people.

It is rare that a historian becomes involved in an ongoing public controversy, and I hesitated before plunging into the middle of the Waldheim debate. I am used to a quiet life of teaching and research, both far from public view. In the end, however, I decided that the importance of a dispassionate, scholarly, historical treatment of Kurt Waldheim's youth, wartime experiences, and early postwar years more than justified any sacrifice of peace and quiet on my part.

Indeed, the more I looked at the Waldheim problem, the more I became convinced that my entire career had been one long preparation for the task of finding his missing years. I had studied Austrian history for several years, at both the undergraduate and the graduate levels. By the winter of 1986, I had been researching captured German military records for almost two decades; it was these records that contained the details of Waldheim's service in the Balkans. For fifteen years, I had been teaching the history of European international relations, precisely the arena in which Kurt Waldheim was to distinguish himself after the war. In recent years, I had been specializing in the history of the Third Reich—and as we now know, Kurt Waldheim's story is part of that tragic era.

Though I eventually became totally absorbed by the Waldheim affair, I never saw my task as involving a search for guilt or vindication. Such a pursuit is not the proper work of the historian. As I saw it, my role was to place Kurt Waldheim in the context of his lost world of forty and fifty years ago—the idea being that if we can understand where he came from, we can better understand how he arrived at his destination. To that end, one is better served by an obsession with the truth than by any passionate self-righteousness.

Most of my account of Kurt Waldheim's first thirty years is based upon documents, microfilmed records, transcripts, and photographs stored in the archives of the United States, Yugoslavia, Britain, Austria, West Germany, Italy, Israel, and Greece. I conducted almost all of this research between May 1986 and January 1988.

I also conducted personal interviews with numerous men and women who either knew, worked with, or witnessed Kurt Waldheim at various stages in his life. Some of these people insisted upon remaining anonymous, and I have honored their requests. In no instance have I used oral testimony that conflicts with documentary evidence or is contradicted by statements made by equally credible witnesses.

This book contains a lot of information about Kurt Waldheim. The more complete the documentation, the more detail I was able to provide. Yet I have emphasized events that appeared to have molded Kurt Waldheim's character and career.

This book would not have been possible without the help and cooperation of many people and organizations. To begin with, I would like to thank my editor, Allan Mayer, who among other things helped me to shape, structure, and refine my manuscript. Like me, he has become fascinated with Kurt Waldheim's past. Allan has been an ideal editor over the last two years; his intelligence, helpful insights, and dedication have been most valuable.

I also owe acknowledgment to the World Jewish Congress, *The New York Times,* and ABC News. These organizations retained me as a consultant on the Waldheim matter for a total of four weeks in the late winter and early spring of 1986. Their support enabled me to conduct the early stages of my research, before I decided to write a book about Waldheim's unusual past. I met several fine people as a result of these assignments. In particular, I would like to extend my appreciation to Dr. Israel Singer,

Elan Steinberg, and Eli Rosenbaum of the World Jewish Congress; to Elaine Sciolino of *The New York Times;* and to John Martin of ABC News.

Edward T. Chase, the highly regarded veteran editor, played an important role in my decision to write this book. I am grateful for his confidence in me.

President Kurt Waldheim consented to a long discussion with me. Much of the information he offered was new and highly useful. Though profound disagreements remain between us, I thank him nonetheless for his cooperation.

Simon Wiesenthal has been most generous with his time. His comments and criticism have been of great assistance to me.

Former congresswoman Elizabeth Holtzman, now the district attorney of Kings County (Brooklyn), New York, offered useful insights into the Holtzman amendment and the U.S. Watch List. Neal Sher of the Justice Department's Office of Special Investigations and Mary Mochary of the State Department's Office of Legal Counsel helped me to understand the background behind the decision to put Kurt Waldheim's name on the Watch List.

Though seriously ill, Dr. Bruno Kreisky, the former chancellor of Austria, agreed to speak with me at length about the Waldheim affair. I thank him for enriching my understanding of Waldheim, of Austria, and of Bruno Kreisky.

Dr. Karl Gruber, the former foreign minister of Austria, has been corresponding with me for more than a year now, patiently responding to my endless, detailed queries about postwar Austria. I am very grateful to him for his prompt and useful replies.

Fritz Molden has offered me valuable insights concerning Waldheim's early career in the Austrian foreign ministry, particularly his vetting by U.S. intelligence authorities. I appreciate his speaking with me, both in Vienna and in New York.

Professor Robert Rhodes James, a member of the British House of Commons, shared some of his insights into the Waldheim affair with me. This was particularly valuable, since Mr. Rhodes James worked with Waldheim at the United Nations and knows him well.

I also found it highly useful to discuss many aspects of Waldheim's wartime career with retired Brigadier General James L. Collins, Jr., a historian with a distinguished military record and the American member of the International Military Historians' Commission on Kurt Waldheim.

Rabbi Marvin Hier of the Simon Wiesenthal Center in Los Angeles kindly sent me a copy of Waldheim's doctoral dissertation. I emphasize this because it was not easy for Rabbi Hier to obtain Waldheim's dissertation.

Robert Rosenstock, legal counsel at the U.S. Mission to the United Nations, was kind enough to share with me his insights into that organization. He also assisted me in obtaining access to important UN war-crimes records.

Dr. Gerhard Waldheim spent several hours with me on two occasions. His spirited defense of his father is well known. His viewpoints have always been interesting and often useful to me.

Dr. Ralph Scheide, President Waldheim's personal secretary, has answered my inquiries in a helpful manner. Among other things, he helped to arrange my interview with the president.

Ferdinand Trauttmansdorff of the Austrian Embassy in Washington, D.C., provided me with an early copy of Dr. Waldheim's "White Book."

Ana-Marija Bešker of the Yugoslav Embassy in Washington, D.C., assisted me in obtaining permission to work in the Belgrade archives. Several Yugoslav archivists enabled me to study crucial documents relating to the Waldheim case, the contents of which have never before appeared in print. I am especially grateful to Dr. Bogdan Lekić of the Arhiv Jugoslavije and Colonel Antun Miletić of the Military-Historical Institute Archive, both in Belgrade. Professor Peter Strcić of the Arhiv Hrvatske in Zagreb was also most cooperative. And Dr. Ladoslav Kadelburg, president of the Federation of Yugoslav Jewish Communities, assisted me in my research on the deportation of the Jews from Banja Luka in 1942.

Professor V. Kuić and Dr. Hana Pokorna rendered important Serbo-Croatian materials into English.

Dr. Alf M. E. Erlandsson of the United Nations Archives has earned my thanks. Despite the fact that unreasonable and outdated restrictions on access to the war-crimes files placed him in a difficult position, Dr. Erlandsson was open and helpful, as a good archivist always is. Once I obtained full access to the records, he was gracious in assisting me.

I am grateful to director Benedict K. Zobrist and to archivist Dennis Bilger of the Harry S. Truman Institute Library in Independence, Missouri. The institute gave me a generous grant so that I might conduct research in the library's excellent collections. Mr. Bilger proved to be a most helpful archivist.

Dr. Maria Keipert and the staff of the Auswärtiges Amt archives in Bonn, West Germany, were prompt and cooperative in responding to my many inquiries.

Dr. Helga Welsh of the Institut für Zeitgeschichte in Munich called my attention to the inventories of documents stored in the Munich collections of the IfZ archive. These catalogues led me to some important discoveries.

General Lenzo of the Italian Embassy in Washington, D.C., provided useful information in response to my queries about the fate of the Eleventh Army. Professor Fausto Pauluzzi of the University of South Carolina translated several of my Italian documents.

Hadassah Modlinger of the Yad Vashem Archive in Israel sent me copies of important documents concerning the Holocaust in Greece.

Special thanks go to the staff of the Modern Military Branch of the U.S. National Archives, particularly the late Dr. John Mendelsohn. Mendelsohn's colleagues, Robert Wolfe, George Chalou, and John Taylor, are all superb archivists who care deeply about researchers and their work. Their associates, Will Mahoney, Tim Mulligan, Eddie Reese, and Harry Rilley, have been most helpful. Terri Hammett provided excellent service, photocopying documents with great efficiency.

The staff of the Suitland Branch of the National Archives assisted me in finding many important documents concerning postwar Austria. I owe a debt of gratitude to Dr. Amy Schmidt, Rich Boylen, Bill Lewis, David Pfeiffer, and other staff members.

James Hastings and Ron Plavchan of the Nixon Presidential Materials Project at the National Archives in Alexandria, Virginia, were very helpful.

The Motion Picture Section of the Library of Congress has important film footage depicting German counter-partisan warfare in Yugoslavia. Thanks to Patrick Sheehan and Cooper Graham of the LOC staff, I was able to view these films.

Marek Web of the YIVO Archives in New York assisted me in finding important photographs and documents concerning the Jewish experience in Greece during the war. Diane Spielmann of the Leo Baeck Institute in New York was also very helpful.

Dr. Meryl Foster and the staff of the Public Record Office in Kew, Great Britain, were most cooperative. The PRO's holdings on postwar Austria are of great value. They helped me discover the context of the 1947–48 war-crimes charges against Kurt Waldheim, and made my trip to Belgrade more useful.

The Jewish Museum of Greece, under the direction of Nicholas Stavroulakis, has been most helpful.

Journalists have played a major role in the Waldheim story.

Hubertus Czernin of *Profil* magazine in Vienna is one of the pioneer researchers on Kurt Waldheim's past. He has generously shared his great knowledge with me, and has enriched this book by making important photographs available to the author.

Gerhard Oberschlick of *Forum* magazine in Vienna provided me with copies of his interesting magazine, and generously permitted me to use the photograph of the young Waldheims.

I am happy to offer special thanks to James Polk of NBC News for his interest in my work. His cooperation and his insights have been most helpful. One of the nice results of my research on Kurt Waldheim has been the opportunity to become acquainted with Cara, Abigail, and Tia Polk.

Dr. Gerhard Weinberg of the University of North Carolina shared his vast knowledge of German military records with me. His advice proved particularly invaluable in my research on Battle Group West Bosnia.

Professor George Kent of the University of Maryland has discussed the Waldheim matter at length with me. His insights were of great value. Professor Kent provided the names of Viennese historians who might be helpful in my work. These colleagues have been of real assistance, and their generosity vindicated George Kent's judgment.

Robert Knight has kindly made his excellent writings on the Carinthian question available to me.

Dr. Oliver Rathkolb has kindly called my attention to important documents and articles pertaining to contemporary Austrian history. He made my recent trip to Vienna far more productive and pleasant than it might otherwise have been.

Professor Gerald Stourzh of the University of Vienna offered me valuable insights into the postwar history of Austria, as did Dr. Manfried Rauchensteiner.

Dr. Sybil Milton's comments on the Waldheim matter, and her suggestions, have invariably been helpful.

My colleague the noted historical editor Dr. David R. Chesnutt helped me solve the mysteries of word processing. His patience and excellent instruction have given me a deeper understanding of the word "collegiality." I have also benefited from many hours of discussion with other distinguished colleagues, among them Charles Sydnor, the president of Emory and Henry College; Dr. Donald M. McKale of Clemson University; Dr. Jerry Augustinos of the University of South Carolina; and Dr. Peter Pabisch of the University of New Mexico.

My student aides have provided me with courteous assistance. I am happy to mention Richard Rayburn, Jennifer Diz, and Kim Caley in this context.

My mother's encouragement and criticism have helped me to produce a better book. My friends Miss Meredith Wallace and Miss Adrienne Petrisko have tolerated my obsession with the Waldheim case. They have, in their own important ways, contributed to the creation of this work. Their support has been gratifying.

Archivists, historians, journalists, and friends have all played crucial roles in my search for Kurt Waldheim's missing years. But most important of all were the documents themselves, which I alone had to interpret. Except where otherwise indicated, I am solely responsible for the statements of fact and interpretation that follow.

Robert Edwin Herzstein

Columbia, South Carolina
January 1988

Contents

Preface 9

Prologue 21

PART ONE: A Young Man with a Future

1 Walter Watzlawik's Son 27
2 In Hitler's Ostmark 47
3 Wehrmacht Hero 61
4 A Place Called Kozara 71
5 Lilo, Kurt, and Professor Verdross 79
6 A Cog in the Machine 91
7 Dr. Waldheim 107
8 A Changed Man 119
9 The Final Retreat 147

PART TWO: The Man Without a Past

10 To the Ballhausplatz 159
11 Denazification 173
12 Power Politics 183
13 Conspiracy in Belgrade 193

14 **Off the Hook** 203

15 **The Man Without a Past** 213

16 **The Return of Lieutenant Waldheim** 233

17 **Facing the Truth** 249

Postscript 265

Archival Sources 277

Notes 279

Abreviations 305

Index 309

"Past, get thee behind us!"
—Goethe, *Faust,* Part II

"I have handled a crisis or two before."
—Kurt Waldheim, 1971

Prologue

On Friday, March 21, 1986, I walked into the thirteenth-floor research room at the National Archives in Washington, to find senior archivist John Mendelsohn hunched over a 1950s-vintage Recordak microfilm reader. Portly, with gray hair and an aquiline profile, Mendelsohn had survived a childhood in Nazi Germany because he was what the Nazis called a *Mischling*, or half-breed, having both "Aryan" and Jewish ancestry. He had since become a leading historian of the war-crimes trials that followed World War II. I had gotten to know him while I was researching my book on Nazi wartime propaganda, *The War That Hitler Won*. John had liked the book, and we often talked shop.

Mendelsohn was not normally given to melodrama. But as we exchanged a glance across the ancient, oppressive room, crowded with army-issue tables and dilapidated chairs, I could see that he was excited. Motioning me over, he pointed to the barely legible document displayed on the screen of his microfilm reader. "Your friend," he said quietly, "was a war criminal."

I blinked with surprise. "What were the charges?" I asked. "And who made them?"

"Murder," Mendelsohn replied. "The Yugoslavs."

I stared over his shoulder at the screen. The microfilm was old and faded. It contained a June 1948 war-crimes list. On it, I could make out the name "Waldheim" and the word "murder."

* * *

A week earlier, I had been sitting at home in Columbia, South Carolina, preparing a lecture on Benito Mussolini, when the telephone in my kitchen rang. The caller was Eli Rosenbaum, the general counsel of the World Jewish Congress. Explaining that he was speaking on behalf of the WJC's secretary-general, Dr. Israel Singer, Rosenbaum asked if I had been following the simmering controversy over the alleged prewar Nazi background of Kurt Waldheim, the former secretary-general of the United Nations, who at the time was running for the presidency of his native Austria. When I replied that I had, Rosenbaum said that the WJC was looking for a reputable, German-speaking historian experienced in working with captured German military records. My name had surfaced in conversations with several scholars, he added. Would I be willing to go to the National Archives to do some research on Waldheim's wartime career?

The prospect intrigued me. I had actually met Waldheim once, and I had vaguely troubling memories of the encounter. It was in the spring of 1979, when the University of South Carolina, where I teach, had awarded him an honorary degree. Though it was a gala occasion—we were trying to promote the international role of the university, and Waldheim was about as eminent a catch as we could hope for—I recalled being bothered by something someone had told me about him: the fact that he had received a doctoral degree from the law faculty of the University of Vienna in 1943 or 1944. As a historian specializing in the Nazi era, I knew that the University of Vienna law faculty had been thoroughly "coordinated" by the Nazi regime before the Second World War. Did this mean that Waldheim, too, had been a Nazi? I also couldn't understand how, at that point in the war, an Austrian of his age—he would have been twenty-four or twenty-five at the time—could have been doing graduate work instead of serving in the army.

The festivities beckoned, however, and I had dismissed my doubts, chalking them up to the academic obsessions born of fifteen years of writing and teaching about the Nazis.

Now, seven years later, the WJC was offering me a chance to follow up on my vague suspicions. The problem was, we were in the middle of an academic semester. I had lectures to give, seminars to conduct, papers to read. I could get away to Washington for at most ten days, I told Rosenbaum, and I had no idea if in that short amount of time I would be able to come up with anything of interest. He told me to try anyway, and we agreed that I would report my findings, if any, to the WJC around March 23.

* * *

What I wound up discovering in the archives during those ten days surprised not only me but also the world. Indeed, after the WJC announced my preliminary findings at a March 25 press conference in New York, I found myself in the middle of an international controversy that at this writing has yet to die down. I was at the very beginning of a journey of discovery, for my brief sojourn at the National Archives in March 1986 barely scratched the surface of what turned out to be a complex tale of conspiracy, concealment, and complicity that involved some of the worst atrocities of World War II and some of the most cynical big-power maneuverings of the postwar era. Before I was finished, the full chronicling of that story would take me to London, New York, Belgrade, and finally Vienna, where on a June day fourteen months later, Kurt Waldheim himself would invite me to his private office in the Hofburg Palace to tell me his version of what by then I had come to think of as his missing years.

In the process, I discovered a man who was not evil but merely ambitious and clever, a man who in many ways was both a product and a reflection of the catastrophic era that engulfed his native land between 1914 and 1955. He was a man, like many of his generation, who had tried to dispose of the awkward baggage of his past simply by forgetting about it. That baggage, however, didn't disappear. It merely gathered dust in musty archives, waiting for someone to come along and recognize it for what it was.

The story of this man had begun in the countryside of Lower Austria almost seventy years earlier.

PART ONE

A Young Man with a Future

CHAPTER ONE

Walter Watzlawik's Son

The winter of 1918–19 was a harsh one. The Great War was over at last, but a Central European empire lay in ruins. Food was scarce, refugees wandered about the countryside, people worried about malnutrition and influenza. In the Lower Austrian town of Tulln, on the banks of the Danube twenty-one miles northwest of Vienna, a battle-weary former first lieutenant named Walter Watzlawik was particularly concerned about his infant son, Kurt Josef. The baby, born just four days before Christmas 1918, was too thin; his mother feared for his survival.

An ambitious young man, Watzlawik had been born in 1889, the son of a Tulln blacksmith. Determined to rise above his humble origins, he struck out on his own quite early, qualifying as a schoolteacher and finding a job in the nearby village of St. Andrä-Wördern. Then came the war. Before long, he met and married Josefine Petrasch, the daughter of a well-to-do farmer. They moved back to Tulln and he went off to battle.[1]

Watzlawik was lucky. Although he was wounded in battle on the Italian front, he did make it home. Some 59,000 of his comrades from Lower Austria did not. But the Austria to which he returned was a very different place than the one he had left.

Like many of his countrymen, Walter Watzlawik had originally regarded the war as a just one, a genuine struggle for survival. Also like many of his countrymen, he did not doubt that Austria would win.

The Austrian empire of Walter Watzlawik's youth had been a sprawling realm with almost fifty million inhabitants and a standing army of nearly half a million men. It stretched from the Swiss border in the west to Rumania in the east, from Bohemia in the north to the Adriatic Sea and the Serb lands in the south. The double eagle of the Habsburg emperor Franz Joseph flew over cities as diverse as Vienna, Prague, Sarajevo, and Cracow, and the dignified old monarch with the muttonchop whiskers counted among his subjects not only Austrians but large numbers of Germans, Hungarians, Poles, Ukrainians, Italians, Rumanians, Czechs, Serbs, Croatians, Slovaks, and Bosnians. Though most were Catholic, there were also plenty of Calvinists, Lutherans, Muslims, and Jews.

The landed elite and state bureaucrats who governed the Austrian empire were drawn largely from two groups, the German-speaking Austrians and the Hungarians. The Hungarians ruled their extensive crown lands from Budapest, the German-Austrians oversaw the western empire from Vienna, and the Habsburg monarch reigned over both as emperor of Austria and king of Hungary.

With only a few exceptions, the German-Austrians and the Hungarians viewed the other nationalities in their empire as underdeveloped or inferior, as alien peoples not worthy of having their own, unique national destinies. The divide was not always a rigid one, for in some regions there had been much intermarriage. Many Austrian nobles had Slavic names (as did many ordinary Austrians, such as Walter Watzlawik), and people routinely changed their nationalities in order to further their careers. For his part, Franz Joseph had a better opinion than his functionaries of the diverse ethnic groups that made up his empire, and he welcomed greater participation by responsible national elites.

By 1914, however, the double eagle was in jeopardy. The pious, Catholic Austria of Walter Watzlawik's youth was being shaken by urban riots, fiery speeches, and threats of revolution. Walter, who believed in the Catholic Church, watched with dismay as the Socialist movement grew increasingly powerful, gaining adherents in nearby Vienna, the very heart of the empire.

Perhaps most worrisome were the increasingly outspoken aspirations of the empire's ethnic minorities. In particular, there was the mounting crisis to the north in predominantly Czech Bohemia and Moravia. An increasing number of Czechs, especially those in the intellectual and professional classes, were growing weary of German-Austrian domination. They wanted equality in their own lands, greater respect for their language, equal opportunity in the universities and the bureaucracy. By the time of Watzlawik's childhood, they were prepared to demonstrate and riot to get what they wanted.[2]

Many German-speaking Austrians watched all this with undisguised horror. Not only did they feel threatened by the rise of Czech nationalism; they also felt abandoned by their tolerant emperor. As a result, some began to call for the destruction of the monarchy, for the violent suppression of all Slavic aspirations, and for union with the mighty German Reich to the north.[3] One such radical, who wandered the streets of Vienna nursing a growing hatred for the upstart Czechs (and the contemptible Austrian state that tolerated them), while Walter Watzlawik studied to become a teacher in the provinces, was a moody eighteen-year-old would-be painter from Upper Austria named Adolf Hitler.[4]

Hitler, of course, did not reserve his hostility solely for the Czechs. And, indeed, the new nationalist hatreds coursing through Austrian society coincided with the renaissance of another, far older expression of Austrian xenophobia—the long-standing Austrian tradition of anti-Semitism. For centuries, Austrians had viewed the Jew as a rootless wanderer with a mysterious access to money, an outsider in rural society and a source of painful change in the metropolis. He was, or so many an Austrian priest taught his flock, a Christ-killer, a diabolical alien who cheated Christians and ridiculed their Lord. The fact that bishops and princes sometimes protected the Jews (mainly because both church and state were often dependent on Jewish loans) only added to the popular resentment against them. As a result, more so than elsewhere in Europe, Jews had long been the object of discrimination, hatred, and fear in Austria, despised for their liberalism, radicalism, or financial success—often for all three.[5]

It was in Vienna as a young man in the years preceding the First World War that Hitler acquired his frenzied hatred of the Jews. Insecure, ambitious, rejected, arrogant, and alone in the imperial capital, he eagerly took to the notion of the Jew as scapegoat. Combining native prejudice with the fake science he read about in racialist newspapers, Hitler asked himself, he later recalled, if there was "any form of filth or profligacy . . . without at least one Jew involved in it." He felt chills of revulsion as he forced himself to walk through the dark streets and narrow alleyways of the Leopoldstadt ghetto, discovering "the relations of Jews to prostitution, and even more, to the White-slave traffic." He became an anti-Semite in Vienna, he later boasted. He was a post-Christian anti-Semite, to be sure, but one nurtured by Austrian Catholic society. Fearing the Slavs and hating the Jews, Hitler saw but one solution: the creation of some form of Greater Germany that included German-speaking Austria, and the elimination of the Jews from Europe.[6]

Certainly, not all Austrian Christians were anti-Semitic. But during Walter Watzlawik's youth, anti-Jewish feeling was the rule, not the exception. Buffeted by the profound dislocations brought on by the industrial revolution, many in the middle and lower classes blamed the Jews for the social changes that they felt were ruining their lives: increasing urbanization (and urban poverty), the decline of the protective guilds, the rise of rapacious capitalism.

Not surprisingly, ambitious politicians moved quickly to exploit these resentments. Among the more successful—and ferocious—of them was Georg Ritter von Schönerer, a rabid anti-Semite who was anxious to unite German-speaking Austria with the German Reich and purge Jews from the life of the state. An anti-Catholic as well (*"Los von Rom!"* he screamed. "Away from Rome!"), Schönerer demanded that the Jews be treated from the "brutal racial point of view." He railed against Jewish entrepreneurs, and gained quite a following among German-speaking artisans and workers who felt threatened by both Jewish capitalism and Slavic protest movements.[7]

Schönerer's hatred for the monarchy, as well as his anti-Catholicism, did not play well with traditionalist provincial families such as the Watzlawiks in Tulln. The Watzlawiks were all *Kaisertreu*, loyal to the old emperor and devoted to the Church. As such, they—like many of their neighbors—found the conservative, clerical-minded Christian Social movement far more to their liking.

The Christian Social movement was led by Dr. Karl Lueger, a conservative who favored baptism as a solution to the "Jewish Question." In 1897, Lueger had demonstrated how the new democratic franchise could be used against the Jews and "their" liberalism by getting himself elected *Bürgermeister* of Vienna over the vehement opposition of the emperor. For all that, Lueger was not above consorting with prominent Jewish citizens on a personal basis. *"I* decide who is a Jew," he answered his critics.[8]

Lueger's hypocrisy—or, as some might have it, his sophistication—was typically Viennese. *Fin de siècle* Vienna was a remarkable place, a city of more than two million, where one could hear a babble of tongues from every land in the empire. Its grand palaces and state buildings formed an imposing backdrop for a gaudy mixture of peoples and ideas. Culturally, the capital was at the zenith of a rich period of diversity and creativity. It was the city of Sigmund Freud and Gustav Mahler, and—for all Schönerer's ravings and Lueger's demagoguery—a thriving liberal Jewish intelligentsia.[9]

But in Vienna, as elsewhere in prewar Austria, anxieties were intensifying. The rural populace feared socialism. The Church feared the liberalism of the capital. The Germans feared the Slavs, especially the Czechs in the north and the Serbs to the southeast. The workers feared for their jobs. And nearly everyone feared the chaos that would certainly follow the death of the old emperor, now a doddering old man, his face a mass of liver spots, his hands shaky.[10]

By the late spring of 1914, the eyes of the empire's political and military elite had come to be focused on Serbia, a small independent state in the Balkans. Vienna had recently annexed the neighboring territories of Bosnia and Herzegovina, a move that enraged Serb nationalists, who wanted to create a South Slav kingdom dominated by Serbia. The consequences of continued Serb agitation worried the Austrian elite; if Serbia could disrupt the monarchy, it was felt, where would the disintegration end?

In an effort to gain the allegiance of the local population, and thus weaken the appeal of Serb nationalism, the heir presumptive to the Austrian throne, Archduke Franz Ferdinand, made a state visit to Serbia in the early summer of 1914. On June 28, 1914, in the city of Sarajevo, a small band of Serb terrorists ambushed the imperial limousine carrying the archduke and his consort, Duchess Sophie Chotek, and murdered them both. Within a month, Austria and Serbia were at war. Soon all Europe was embroiled in the conflict.

The war did not go well for Austria. The bloodletting was enormous, and the enemy was everywhere. The old emperor, Franz Joseph, died in 1916. His successor, Karl I, tried to make peace but failed.

By January 1918, the Social Democrats were calling for a settlement that would solve the problem of Slav self-determination by turning the empire into an autonomous federation of the various nationalities. Hungarian leaders quickly undermined that project by insisting that "the integrity of the Holy Hungarian Crown is in no way affected." Rebuffed at home, Slavic leaders took some solace from events abroad. The American president, Woodrow Wilson, was calling for self-determination in his "Fourteen Points." Though Wilson did not specifically demand the destruction of the Habsburg monarchy, some Czech leaders took Wilson's agenda as their cue to start talking about seceding from the empire. Partly as a result of the building pressure, Emperor Karl accepted the federal idea in October 1918. But by then it was too late.[11]

Bolstered by the entry of the United States in the war, the Allies had turned the tide. In the north of France, the German army was falling back. At home, the empire was breaking apart, with nation after nation seceding. Within Austria itself, there were strikes, peace demonstrations, a general exhaustion with the war effort.

On the Italian front, Walter Watzlawik was worried about his pregnant wife. But the Austrian army was now on the defensive in Italy, and leave was hard to obtain. Finally, on November 4, 1918, Austria signed an armistice. A week later, the Germans followed suit, and the emperor withdrew from public life.

Watzlawik came home to a profoundly changed country. Europe's second-largest state in 1914, Austria now comprised a mere 32,000 square miles, her once vast empire having been reduced to only the German-Austrian provinces between Hungary and Switzerland. Her population, over fifty million at the empire's peak, was now less than seven million. There were many more women around than men, and very few children. Little Kurt Josef would be one of only 36,000 male babies born in Austria in 1918. In 1914, the figure had been 55,000.

Wartime production needs had turned what had been primarily a rural agrarian society into an increasingly urban and industrialized one. Vast factories, some employing as many as forty thousand workers, had sprung up in Wiener Neustadt and other Vienna suburbs. Though most country folk still depended on candles and gas for light and on bicycles and horses for transportation, electrification and automobiles had made great inroads in the cities.

Social cohesion seemed to be fast disappearing. Townspeople resented the peasants, who they believed were holding back food supplies in order to force up prices. Everyone feared escaped prisoners of war, who were supposedly wandering through the countryside despoiling the land. Coal shortages caused by the erection of new tariffs had disrupted rail traffic. The currency was collapsing.[12]

Austria—or, as she now styled herself, "German Austria"—was no longer a coherent state but rather a desperate collection of German-speaking *Länder*, or provinces, held together by fear: fear of being annexed by their neighbors—by the Italians to the south, the Slovenes to the southeast, the Hungarians to the east, the Czechs to the north. The conservative Christian Social party was engaged in a bitter power struggle with the Social Democrats, who favored union with the new German Republic. In Vienna, Communists, inspired by Lenin's triumph in Russia, were talking of revolution.

The provincial regions—Styria, Carinthia, the Vorarlberg, the Tyrol, Salzburg, Upper and Lower Austria—were all suspicious of "Red" Vienna, where radical Socialists such as Otto Bauer gave their fiery speeches. Vienna was the metropolis, however, and without its gravitational force what remained of Austria would fly apart.

With the empire in ruins, and no one able to agree on what would or should replace it, the political landscape deteriorated into something close to anarchy. Radicalism was the order of the day. Men who had learned to use machine guns in Italy could easily employ them in the streets of Vienna. But though the nation teetered on the edge of chaos, an uneasy coalition between the Socialist "Reds" and the Christian Social "Blacks" might, in the grand Austrian tradition, allow the country to muddle through—to survive long enough to unite with Germany.

Though the Socialists were convinced that this was the way to go, the Christian Socials, led by Monsignor Ignaz Seipel, were not so sure. To the Socialists, Germany was now a progressive republic; for Catholics like Seipel, it was still a largely Protestant state. Nonetheless, Seipel ultimately went along with the idea of *Anschluss,* as it was called. After all, the word meant only a "drawing together," not the obliteration of Austrian identity by the German colossus. Thus, on March 2, 1919, with Seipel's tacit support, Socialist leader Otto Bauer signed a secret agreement with Germany designed to pave the way for the *Anschluss.*

The Red-Black coalition saw Austria through the desperate days immediately following the war, but the Treaty of St.-Germain, imposed by the Allies in 1919, made many wonder if the effort to survive had been worth it. The treaty dealt with Austria as a defeated state, not a new democracy. Her army was now limited to no more than thirty thousand men, including a maximum of fifteen hundred officers and two thousand noncommissioned officers. In addition, Austria was forbidden to restore the Habsburg monarchy. Worst of all, the treaty prohibited Austria from joining in any form of union with Germany.

The fledgling republic was bankrupt, saddled with the debts, pensions, and other financial obligations of a large empire—plus the scourge of inflation and the bills from having waged and lost the greatest war of all time. Her largest industries were war-production plants that she was now forbidden to use. Most of her prewar industry had been located in Bohemia and Moravia, which she no longer controlled. She had also lost her access along the *Südbahn* to the vital port of Trieste, and the consumers of her timber and agricultural products were raising trade barriers. Just about all that remained was the mordant Viennese sense of humor. A joke circulating in the former imperial capital just after the treaty was signed had one Austrian asking another, "What do you want to do today?" "Take a walk around Austria," the second one replies. "Fine," the first says, "but what shall we do in the afternoon?"

The sense of lost empire was especially intense in Vienna. Though its population had dwindled to 1.6 million, Vienna was still a huge capital for such a small country. The memories of imperial glory were everywhere—along the Ringstrasse, at the Stephansplatz, in the Karlskirche.

Yet what was Austria now? A poor country struggling to survive, an insignificant German-speaking state forbidden to play anything approaching a leading role in world affairs.

Such grandiose matters were of little concern to Walter Watzlawik. Reunited with his family, he was content to concentrate on building a life for himself as a provincial schoolteacher. He had solid pedagogical skills, and through his wife and her father he had acquired some modest social contacts. Still, the breakup of the empire did affect his life in at least one measurable way. Around the time of the birth of Kurt Josef, a colleague supposedly warned him that he would have a difficult time making a career in German Austria with a Czech name like Watzlawik. Not that anyone had anything against the Czechs. But after all, they no longer belonged "to us," as the Austrians liked to put it. So Walter changed the family's name to the German Waldheim.

Walter Waldheim's career advanced steadily throughout the 1920s. He was an effective, thoroughly professional teacher, a good colleague and a skilled administrator. A booklet he wrote on how to teach art went through several printings. (It advocated firm guidance as opposed to untutored exploration.) People respected him as a devout Catholic and a good family man.

The period after the war was a time of important change in the Austrian school system, marked mainly by the ascendancy of Otto Glöckel, a Social Democratic educational reformer. An anticlerical who wanted to separate church and state, Glöckel abolished religious instruction in the public schools. He also tried to reform the curriculum to make it better suited to the needs of the individual. And he saw education as a key tool in achieving equality of opportunity.[13]

Walter Waldheim was also something of an innovator, but he was hardly a Social Democrat like Glöckel. Certainly, he was not anticlerical. Indeed, with Glöckel dominating the school system, Waldheim's career would no doubt have suffered had not the Christian Social party wrested control of all Lower Austria outside of Vienna from the Social Democrats in 1922.

Waldheim was a staunch Christian Social, admiring the stern, patriarchal style of the party's leader—and Austria's new chancellor—Monsignor Ignaz Seipel.[14]

Under Seipel, the Christian Social party had become more conservative and less reformist. Anti-Semitism was part of its tradition. It was not the vote-catching demagoguery of Karl Lueger, but it was firm. As the party's first postwar manifesto declared:

We Germans gladly encounter the Jewish people and its national religion with respect; we wish to see them protected, but also wish to protect ourselves. . . . In the future [the Jews] will have to leave us to ourselves in our own concerns. . . . In our national culture they will not be allowed their say except as guests.[15]

An expert administrator, Walter Waldheim was soon named head of the Wieselburg Boys School. Eventually, he rose to become superintendent of schools for the entire Tulln district. As superintendent, Waldheim worked for the establishment of a gymnasium in Tulln and was active in adult education. His work brought him recognition, including the title *Regierungsrat*, or government counselor.

As a result of his father's success, Kurt Waldheim grew up in Tulln in a nice house with a garden and a veranda. Walter Waldheim was the dominant figure in the household, which now included two children in addition to Kurt—a younger brother, Walther, and a sister, Gerlinde. Walter senior wanted the best for his children, even if it cost more than he earned. In particular, he wanted them to attend gymnasium and continue their education even further if possible. (At the time, fewer than one fifth of all Austrian schoolchildren went beyond the *Volksschule*, or grammar school.) Just as Walter had surpassed his blacksmith father, he dreamed that his children would surpass him.*

Walter Waldheim could dream such dreams because Austria seemed to be getting back on her feet. Though ideological divisions still pervaded the society, a combination of foreign loans, severe budget cutting, and the apparent recovery of the world economy had helped the country out of her postwar slump. Poverty and unemployment were still rife, but the currency was stable and tourists were returning.

Kurt grew up a very tall, thin young man, quiet, amiable, and anxious to please, diffident rather than shy. He had a broad, slightly self-conscious grin that turned his eyes into long, narrow slits. His height may have been the most unusual thing about him. By his late teens in the mid-1930s, Kurt was well on his way to becoming one of the tallest young men in Austria. At a time when the average Austrian male was about five feet three inches in height, and five feet eight was considered tall, Kurt was

---

*Walther, who apparently had less drive than either of his siblings, was content to follow in his father's footsteps and become a teacher. (He died in 1974.) Gerlinde, on the other hand, became a physician. Walter senior wanted Kurt to become a doctor too, but Kurt objected, pleading: "Father, don't do this to me; I can't stand the sight of blood."

a striking six feet four. As a result, he tended to lean forward when he conversed, his head cocked slightly to one side.

He was intrigued by the turmoil in the world of the late 1920s and early 1930s, and he later recalled wondering how those faraway figures whose voices he could hear on the radio and whose images he could see in the cinema newsreels could affect his country and his life. The world outside Austria attracted him. He wanted to be one of those figures he saw striding the international stage, one of those diplomats, with their long formal coats and their globe-trotting lives. To do that, he knew, he would have to learn foreign languages, and probably also the law. Acutely aware of the hopes his father had placed in him, and of the sacrifices made on his behalf, Kurt was determined to work hard and to succeed. He would let nothing stand in the way of his career.

Fortunately for Kurt, though Tulln was provincial, it did provide access to a wider world. With a population of about 4,300, the town had a sense of history, tracing its origins back to the time of the Romans. In more modern times, it had served as the collection center for the reserve forces assembled by the Hapsburgs for their defense of the empire against the Turks. Two churches dominated the town, the Romanesque parish church of St. Stephan, with its two towers, and the rococo Minoriten-Kirche. If one wanted to relax, one could go to the Hirsch Inn, where men smoked long pipes and drank the local white wine and beer. Legend had it that Franz Schubert himself had enjoyed a glass or two of his beloved Heuriger at the Hirsch. Kurt loved classical music, and his town had named a park after the tragic composer and erected a memorial plaque to his memory.

Not far from nearby Wetzdorf Castle was the Heldenburgtor memorial, which honored the Austrian imperial army. Kurt discovered the memorial as a boy, and admired the statues of Franz Joseph and Field Marshal Count Radetzsky. Radetzsky had saved Austria from her foreign enemies in 1848–49, and Johann Strauss's "Radetzsky March" was regarded as an unofficial national anthem. Radetzsky's remains were interred beneath a seventy-five-foot obelisk, which added to the patriotic feeling of the place and complemented the Catholic piety of the town and of the Waldheim household. Catholicism, patriotism, and Austrian culture all molded young Kurt's imagination.

The cosmopolitan world of Vienna—just forty-five minutes away by train—intrigued young Kurt Waldheim even more. Vienna might have fallen from imperial grace, but the splendor of the Ringstrasse with its equestrian statues and the Innenstadt with its imposing government buildings was still intact. Some of the international flavor was gone, but the Belvedere and Schönbrunn palaces remained.

Kurt particularly admired the Cathedral of St. Stephan, which dominated the city. From its tower, which he climbed, he could see the entire city, including the magnificent Hofburg complex, built in the eighteenth and nineteenth centuries, with its great library containing the imperial treasures: the coronation mantles of the Habsburgs, the regalia of the Holy Roman Empire, the priceless tapestries and jewelry—all glorious reminders of a glorious past.

It was in Vienna that Kurt acquired his lifelong love of fine paintings and silver place settings, of titles and honors. Vienna was Kurt's gateway to a world beyond his provincial petit bourgeois origins.

Kurt's first extended foray into the wider world came in his midteens, when he had to go away to gymnasium. Because Tulln did not yet have one of its own, Walter sent Kurt to the gymnasium in Klosterneuburg, a slightly larger town due north of Vienna, one hour by train from Tulln. Every morning Kurt would arise at 5 A.M., grab the bread-and-butter sandwich his mother had prepared for him, and run to the train station.

At Klosterneuburg, Kurt joined the Catholic Comagena fraternity. As a student, he was highly diligent, good at languages—indeed, at most subjects except for mathematics. Though of only average musical ability, he worked hard at the violin and played the instrument in the school orchestra. In his spare time, he loved to go swimming and boating, and he took up tennis. Already a model of discretion, he proved to be an adept mediator when occasional schoolboy quarrels erupted.

While Kurt enjoyed a happy boyhood, three forces were struggling for political dominance in Austria. On the right, there was the Christian Social party, which controlled Lower Austria and the national government. On the left, there were the Social Democrats, who ran Vienna. And then there were the various Greater German or pan-German groups, which had substantial support in the west and south. All three movements had roots in the defunct empire, and all three held views and prejudices that made it difficult for them to adjust to the changed environment.

While Kurt was growing up in Tulln, his family took for granted that the Christian Social party would continue in power. Monsignor Seipel was a strong chancellor, whose firm hand created the type of state the Waldheims admired. Conservatives like the Waldheims in towns like Tulln were appalled to learn of incidents like the one in 1927 when a mob of Socialist workers sacked and burned the Ministry of Justice in Vienna. The workers were protesting the acquittal of some right-wing soldiers who had attacked members of the socialist Republican Defense League, or

Schutzbund, a self-protection group strong in Vienna and in Austria's industrial cities. As far as the good burghers in small towns were concerned, the events in Vienna were the fault of the Reds, a sign of the inability of Socialist leaders to control the more extremist and subversive elements of their movement.

An admirer of the Italian corporative state of Benito Mussolini, Chancellor Seipel reacted to such outrages by becoming more authoritarian. In 1929, he introduced a new constitution, under which a chancellor with greatly increased powers would be named by a president. He also decreed that the state would henceforth play a greater role in education. This suited Walter Waldheim just fine, so long as the government remained in the hands of men like Seipel.

Seipel also drew closer to the Heimwehren, a collection of militias and paramilitary groups that had defended the frontiers of Carinthia against the Yugoslavs in 1919. Largely respectable and middle class, the Heimwehr drew most of its support from the small towns of the outlying *Länder.* Its main raison d'être now was to combat the revolutionary Socialists and other leftist forces of the Schutzbund.[16]

Seipel retired in April 1929, after putting his new constitution in place. The three ideological blocs continued their uneasy truce for another two years. But then a new catastrophe shook Austrian society and everything fell apart. In May 1931, the giant Credit-Anstalt bank collapsed, and the Great Depression hit Austria with a vengeance. Unemployment soared, moods worsened, street clashes became increasingly common, and the paramilitary forces of both left and right grew in strength. With the calm hand of Seipel no longer there to guide the flock, a widespread fear of revolutionary Socialists and Communists gripped towns like Tulln and Klosterneuburg. Meanwhile, Socialist leader Otto Bauer, assisted by young radicals like Bruno Kreisky, urged the Social Democratic party to join with the armed cadres of the Schutzbund and force radical change on the nation.

The democratic order, born out of the defeat of 1918, was becoming an unwanted orphan. Austria had muddled through thus far because the decade of the 1920s had been better than the preceding five years. But a fundamental problem had never been addressed: Austria was the only republic in the world whose three major political parties had favored its dissolution from the very beginning. To be sure, many Austrian conservatives, from Walter Waldheim to Ignaz Seipel, had little enthusiasm for the idea of union with the German Republic. Nevertheless, their party program had endorsed *Anschluss.*

The Depression begat despair and more violence. The number of people who wanted to preserve the existing order was rapidly diminishing. More and more wanted radical change. In 1931, twelve-year-old Kurt Waldheim became aware for the first time of a group called the National Socialists. In a failed attempt at sparking an uprising, they had thrown hand grenades into a crowd in the nearby town of Krems. The Nazis, as they came to be known, became much bolder in the summer of 1932, when their brethren to the north—led by the erstwhile stateless Austrian Adolf Hitler—won an electoral landslide in Germany.[17]

The Nazis quickly began to dominate the politics of the right, supplanting the pan-Germans and inheriting their constituency—for the most part, Protestants and wealthy peasants from the vulnerable frontier areas of Styria, Carinthia, and the Tyrol, who felt unprotected by the Catholic pieties of the respectable Christian Socials and threatened by Red Vienna, Yugoslavia, and Italy. The Nazis also offered an outlet to violence-prone hoodlums from the streets of Vienna as well as to former soldiers itching to bring the techniques of the front to domestic politics. The Storm Troop movement, or S.A., soon attracted as many as forty thousand young men. Right-wing authoritarianism engulfed Austrian politics.[18]

While Kurt studied at gymnasium, he and his father hoped that Seipel's successor as leader of the Christian Socials, Engelbert Dollfuss, would maintain the existing Austrian state under its red-and-white banner. The Waldheims admired the diminutive Dollfuss. Of humble Lower Austrian origins, Dollfuss was deeply religious and had once aspired to the priesthood. Instead, he became an organizer for the peasantry, building cooperatives and lobbying for agrarian interests. During the war, he served bravely on the Italian front. Founder of his own Heimwehr unit, Dollfuss plunged into national politics in the 1920s, rising to become president of the federal railroad system, then minister of agriculture, and finally, in 1932, chancellor.

Like Seipel, Dollfuss admired Mussolini and possessed a strong authoritarian streak. But he cared even more for his Catholic faith. Like many of his countrymen, he had warm feelings for Germany. But after the Nazis consolidated their power late in March 1933, Dollfuss and the Christian Social party officially rejected the idea of *Anschluss*.[19]

Having dropped the idea of uniting with Germany, Dollfuss began to move Austria closer to an alliance with Mussolini's Italy. At the same time, he grew increasingly dependent on the ambitious, militant leaders of the Heimwehren. To these men, it was the left-wing radical Socialists who represented the greatest threat. They hoped to establish some sort of fascist Austria, one unencumbered by the parliamentary democracy that they felt had failed them so miserably.

They got their wish on March 7, 1933, when Dollfuss used a stalemate over the budget as a pretext for dooming the parliamentary system. He dismissed the legislature, decreed that all public meetings had to be approved in advance by the government, and imposed censorship on the press. Three months later, on June 19, he drove the Nazis underground by declaring their movement illegal. (From then on—until the Nazis were allowed aboveground again in March 1938—all members of the National Socialist German Workers Party, NSDAP, were known as "Illegals.")

The move against the Nazis was the beginning of an attempt by Dollfuss to abolish all political parties. What he actually accomplished was to radicalize the Socialists. Among other things, the Schutzbund began to prepare itself for combat. Meanwhile, the Nazis began resorting to acts of terror—the same repertoire, from stink bombs to murder, that had worked so well for them in Germany. Early in October 1933, Dollfuss himself was wounded by a would-be Nazi assassin. As Kurt Waldheim later recalled, "Austria became the target of the whole gamut of ideological and political subversion of which the Nazi regime was capable."

Dollfuss's idea was to mobilize the nation against his enemies on the left and the right. He offered a glimpse of the new order he had in mind during a major ceremony at Schönbrunn Palace in May 1933. With great fanfare, Dollfuss announced the establishment of a Patriotic Front, a mass organization intended to encompass the entire nation. Political parties would be a thing of the past. The chancellor even intended to dissolve his own Christian Social party once the opposition had been suppressed. Everyone was pressured to become a member of Dollfuss's Patriotic Front. State employees were required to join, and cynics referred to their membership badges as a form of employment insurance. Along with his friends, Walter Waldheim signed up willingly, hoping the Front would offer Austria a way out of its troubles.[20]

Dollfuss's main support came from the Church and his allies in the Heimwehr. The Heimwehren were particularly enthusiastic. On May 14, they adopted what became known as the "Korneuberg Oath," a pledge of allegiance to Dollfuss, in which they vowed to remake the nation:

We are determined to rebuild Austria from its foundations!

We are determined to bring into being the people's state of the Heimwehr . . .

We are determined to take over the state and to remold it and its economy in the interests of the whole nation![21]

Dollfuss also counted on the support of the small but highly professional Federal Army. And, indeed, when they sang the old marching song "We Are the Emperor's Rangers from the Fourth Regiment," some soldiers began adding a new line: "We are marching with Dollfuss into the new era!"[22]

What Dollfuss wanted was nothing less than to remake Austria into a *Ständestaat,* a Christian corporative state. His view of government was paternalistic, his political guide the teachings of Pope Pius XI. He rejected liberalism, with its secular, individualistic bias.[23] On July 7, 1933, in a speech to the General Catholic Convocation, the chancellor unveiled his notion of the *Ständestaat.* As dictated by Christian principles, it would be obliged to care for its citizens; divisive class conflict and materialistic greed would be abolished. Over the following six months, with the backing of the Church and the Heimwehren, the federal government under Dollfuss assumed sweeping police powers through the establishment of a Central Police Directorate. In November 1933, Dollfuss prevented the Social Democrats from celebrating the anniversary of the Austrian Republic, and he prepared to destroy the Socialist administration of Vienna by stripping it of its power to levy taxes.

Though Dollfuss appealed to the workers for support, most scorned him as a "mini-Metternich," a reactionary dwarf draped in priestly black. Some Schutzbund members in Vienna and Linz began making final preparations for the armed confrontation that Dollfuss seemed to desire.[24]

Much of the pressure on Dollfuss came from Mussolini, who disliked having a democracy on his borders, particularly one in which socialism thrived. Some of the Austrian Socialists had known Mussolini in his days as a youthful left-wing radical. The Duce hated his old comrades—and their embarrassing memories—and he pressed Dollfuss to destroy them. It wasn't simply a matter of personal pique, though. Mussolini knew that after repressing the Socialists, Dollfuss would be more dependent than ever on Italy.

Dollfuss said he had no use for Nazis, Communists, and Socialists because all three brought poisonous *"fremde Ideen"* (foreign ideas) into Austria. What he apparently did not consider was that in crushing these alien ideologies he would wind up putting Austria in the thrall of an equally alien force, Italian fascism.

Throughout the winter of 1933–34, Dollfuss grew increasingly desperate. While Germany recovered and Italy boasted (falsely) about record productivity, Austria's economy remained in a shambles. Torn between his dreams of the *Ständestaat* and the realities of the day, urged by both Mussolini and the leaders of the Heimwehr (who were receiving subsidies from Italy) to crush the Socialist Schutzbund, Dollfuss convinced himself that a revolution was imminent. After first making sure that the army would support him in a preemptive strike, he ordered the police to search Schutzbund and Social Democratic offices in Linz and other cities for illegal weapons. Not surprisingly, the leftists resisted; in Vienna, some rose in open revolt.

On February 12, 1934, Dollfuss ordered the army to shell Karl Marx Hof, a working-class housing development that had become the center of resistance. For a few days, Austria was torn by civil war. The conflict was both bloody and brief. Outgunned and outmanned, the Socialist leaders quickly fled to Prague and other foreign cities. By February 15, the green-and-white banner of the Heimwehren flew from the top of what had once been the bastion of Austrian socialism, the Vienna Rathaus.

In Tulln, fifteen-year-old Kurt Waldheim wondered what was happening to his country. His family and most of their neighbors stayed loyal to Dollfuss. But the regime was stained with Austrian blood, and worse was to follow. Soon the government began constructing detention camps for political prisoners. Nazis, Communists, and Socialists often wound up sharing the same cells.[25]

Among those arrested was Otto Glöckel, the Socialist educator and reformer. (Glöckel would die in jail in 1935, living just long enough to witness the ruin of his life's work.) The Waldheims and their neighbors consoled themselves with the thought that order had been restored. What's more, the government had the support of the clergy; that was important to families like the Waldheims. In any case, educators who supported Dollfuss's Patriotic Front and were good Catholics—in short, educators like Walter Waldheim—had nothing to worry about.

That spring, Dollfuss outlawed all trade unions except the corporation that he had created for the workers. On May 1, 1934, the chancellor proclaimed the Christian corporative state and ordered the preparation of a new constitution.

In Berlin, Hitler told the French ambassador that "Dollfuss has behaved with criminal stupidity. . . . His hands are now stained with the blood of his own people and he will very soon fall and be replaced by a National Socialist government."[26]

Hitler knew what he was talking about. By suppressing the left, Dollfuss had succeeded in completely alienating the workers, Socialists, and radicals who composed more than a third of the Austrian population—and who would be his only allies in the event that he was attacked from the right. And, indeed, Hitler wasted no time in taking advantage of Dollfuss's increasing isolation by stepping up his efforts to bring down the Austrian regime. In the late spring of 1933, Nazi Germany had opened its doors to Austrian Nazis, allowing them to form an Austrian Legion on German soil. The following winter, Hitler attacked Austria's economy where it was most vulnerable: tourism, levying a 1,000-mark fee on German citizens who visited Austria. As a result, German holidaymakers wishing to ski in the Tyrol, for example, found it more economical to vacation at home in Bavaria.

On July 25, 1934, the Nazis struck in earnest. They seized government buildings in Vienna and other Austrian cities, and shot Dollfuss, letting him bleed to death without benefit of physician or clergy. Mussolini was enraged by the Nazi uprising, regarding it as a personal affront. He had recently met with the upstart Hitler in Venice, and the Führer had said nothing about an impending move on Austria. To make matters worse, Dollfuss's wife and children happened to be staying with Mussolini and his wife as the Duce's personal guests the very day the Austrian chancellor was murdered. In response, Mussolini rushed three Italian army divisions to the strategic Brenner Pass in the Tyrol, a move that may well have prevented Germany from occupying Austria right then and there.

Unable to take immediate advantage of the turmoil following Dollfuss's death, Hitler treated the uprising as an unpleasant business about which he knew nothing. Inside Austria, the police, the army, and the Heimwehren rallied to the state. More Nazis were arrested or forced to flee to Germany.

Like many Austrians, the Waldheims were horrified by the abortive revolt. The brutal murder of the Austrian chancellor inspired a great wave of mourning—though not in the working-class districts of Vienna—which included huge demonstrations with participants chanting, "Heil Dollfuss!" The Church spoke of him as a martyr to both Austria and Catholicism, and people vowed to carry on his work.

At the gymnasium in Klosterneuburg, young Kurt Waldheim noticed that not everyone in his class regarded the death of Dollfuss as a tragedy. Some of his schoolmates were clearly sympathetic to the National Socialists. Occasionally, fistfights would erupt. Always the mediator, Kurt broke up some of them.

Dollfuss was succeeded as chancellor by Kurt von Schuschnigg, a Heimwehr leader who had previously served as minister of education. A colder, more remote and ascetic figure than Dollfuss, Schuschnigg lacked his predecessor's popular touch. With his pinched features, the bespectacled Schuschnigg resembled a pedantic provincial school principal; he looked downright ridiculous in his Patriotic Front uniform. Though honorable and courageous, the intellectual Schuschnigg was simply not up to the job of inspiring people and dealing with the likes of Hitler and Mussolini. Dollfuss may have antagonized his enemies, but he knew how to rally his followers. Schuschnigg simply made more enemies and lost popular support. Still, his government had the advantage of three important assets: the martydom of Engelbert Dollfuss, the guns of its police, and the goodwill of Benito Mussolini.

As Schuschnigg saw it, the best hope for his regime lay in expanding the size of the Federal Army, which at the time he took over numbered only about 36,000 men. The idea was that a larger army could both defend the nation and counterbalance the Heimwehren. In particular, Schuschnigg was hoping to recruit the sons of conservative upper-class families.[27]

The Waldheim family was hardly upper-class, but it had the right political and personal credentials. Indeed, at Klosterneuburg, Kurt had already made a favorable impression on Father Roman Scholz. The priest was a former Nazi sympathizer who turned against Hitler after visiting Germany in 1936. (Later a hero of the Austrian anti-Nazi resistance, Scholz was murdered by the Nazis on May 10, 1944.) When Scholz was asked to compile a list of patriotic young men who could be counted on to defend Austria, he put Kurt's name on it.

Kurt's last years at Klosterneuburg were played out against a backdrop of increasing uncertainty. The tall teenager had pretty much decided to study law and diplomacy, with the aim of pursuing a career in the judiciary or the foreign service. But what kind of state might he wind up working for? Indeed, would there be an Austrian state at all?

In the spring of 1936, at the age of seventeen, Kurt Waldheim made the first important career decision of his life: He decided to enlist in the Austrian army as a "one-year volunteer."

The decision was eminently sensible. Not only was the country at peace, but as a "one-year volunteer" Kurt would be in the military for just twelve months. What's more, with Kurt's ambitions focused on government service—and Walter Waldheim determined to see his son ascend the social ladder—there was no ignoring Chancellor Schuschnigg's promise: "Anyone who gives something voluntarily to the Fatherland . . . will have to be given preference [in the civil service]." In fact, a law passed on March 31, 1936, made prior military service mandatory for all new government employees.

Kurt graduated from Klosterneuburg on June 22, 1936. He promptly volunteered for the army and was accepted—his service to begin by the time he turned eighteen, the following December 21.

To Kurt and his father, the future looked considerably brighter than it had at any time since the murder of Dollfuss two years earlier. Schuschnigg seemed to be firmly in control; Mussolini continued to act friendly; the economy was a bit stronger. Illegal Nazis still made trouble, but they were hardly running wild, and Hitler appeared less hostile to Austria. What the Waldheims, and millions like them, could not know was that behind the scenes, the landscape was shifting.

CHAPTER TWO

In Hitler's Ostmark

While seventeen-year-old Kurt Waldheim anxiously awaited his army orders in the summer of 1936, an increasingly desperate Chancellor Schuschnigg attempted to reorient Austrian policy toward Germany. The result was disaster.

Schuschnigg's tilt toward the Third Reich came largely as a result of his increasing political isolation. On the one hand, the endless scheming of the Heimwehr leaders had alienated him from his own right wing. On the other, having supported Dollfuss's suppression of the Socialists, he was in no position to make any overtures to the left. In addition, his personal sympathy for the idea that Austria was essentially a German state weakened his resolve to resist the Nazis.[1]

As if all that wasn't enough, Schuschnigg also believed that Austria could no longer depend on Mussolini, at least not to the extent that Dollfuss had depended on him. Originally from Innsbruck in the Tyrol, Schuschnigg had been a POW in Italy during the 1914–18 war. The experience made him less susceptible than his predecessor to Mussolini's blandishments. (Nonetheless, Schuschnigg had loyally supported Italy in 1935, when the League of Nations condemned Mussolini for his aggression against Ethiopia—a move that further isolated Austria by antagonizing the Western democracies.)[2]

In any case, Mussolini himself was drawing closer to Hitler. Indeed, after the Germans proved to be the only major power to stand with Italy over Ethiopia, the Italians began to speak of a new "Axis" around which

Europe revolved—an axis that ran from Rome to Berlin. Thus, in attempting to improve relations with Germany, Schuschnigg was simply following Mussolini's lead.

On a practical level, Schuschnigg hoped that a new spirit of cooperation between his government and Hitler's Third Reich might ameliorate Austria's economic plight. Schuschnigg also thought that he could enlist Hitler as a partner in taming the Austrian Nazis.

On July 11, 1936, Schuschnigg signed a "gentlemen's agreement" with Hitler. On the face of it, both parties seemed to gain something from the deal. But Hitler's victory turned out to be far more enduring.[3]

For his part, Hitler agreed to lift the 1,000-mark fee he had imposed on Germans traveling to Austria. He also pledged to stop arming and supporting the exiled Austrian Nazis living in Germany. And he promised that normal and friendly relations would prevail between the two neighbors. In return, Schuschnigg declared that "Austria acknowledges herself to be a German state." Accordingly, he agreed to censor the Austrian press in order to suppress anti-German (meaning anti-Nazi) sentiments, and to grant a far-reaching amnesty to political prisoners (as long as they had not "committed serious public crimes"). Most important of all, Schuschnigg pledged to bring members of the "National Opposition" into positions of political responsibility. (They included such Nazi sympathizers as Guido Schmidt, who became state secretary in the foreign ministry, and General Edmund Glaise von Horstenau, who was appointed minister of the interior.[4])

It quickly became apparent that in signing the agreement Schuschnigg had stripped his own regime of whatever legitimacy it might ever have had. Reflecting that fact, Austria's still-illegal Nazis became bolder. Just weeks after the agreement was signed, the Olympic torch-bearer passed through Austria on his way to the 1936 Summer Games in Berlin. Crowds of Illegals and their sympathizers assembled along his route, singing the "Horst Wessel Song" and the German national anthem.

All over the country, particularly in the southern and western *Länder*, Nazi sentiments were being expressed openly. Though almost everyone belonged to the Patriotic Front, few believed in it. One day that summer, the British historian E. H. Carr had lunch in a restaurant in the Upper Austrian town of Linz. The waiter, Carr later recalled, inundated him with Nazi propaganda and smirked as he showed off his Patriotic Front badge. Austrians like Carr's waiter were legion, people who viewed the Patriotic Front as nothing more than an insurance policy, useful until the "millennium"—in the form of Hitler—arrived. Schuschnigg tried to breathe life into the Front by ordering the Heimwehren disbanded and absorbed into it. All that accomplished was to drive some Heimwehr men into the ranks of the Nazis.[5]

The shift in the wind was becoming more and more apparent. Though Schuschnigg still refused to legalize the Austrian Nazi party, he did release some Nazi political prisoners from his jails. Rumors began circulating that certain local police forces were going easier on suspected Illegals. Anti-Semitism, never far beneath the surface in Austria, became more acceptable than ever. British diplomats reported that hatred of the Jews was widespread in both the professional classes and the officer corps. Some officials of the Patriotic Front began organizing Nazi-style economic boycotts of Jewish merchants, with slogans such as: "Germans, do not buy from the Jews!" Jews were being kicked out of professional associations and business organizations.[6]

Meanwhile, the economy continued to deteriorate. White-collar youths, including graduates of the best schools, feared for their future. Aware from the German experience that economic insecurity and National Socialism formed a potent combination, Schuschnigg tried to protect the threatened middle classes from the Great Depression by controlling trade and preventing competition, imposing a welter of cumbersome rules and regulations. But Austria could not be shielded from the worldwide consequences of devalued currencies, high tariff barriers, and economic warfare. The only people who enjoyed any real job security were those who worked for the state, people like Walter Waldheim. Not surprisingly, they formed Schuschnigg's main source of support. But they were a minority. More and more people were looking north to the dynamic Third Reich for salvation. There, it was said, *everyone* had work.

Kurt Waldheim received his army orders at the end of 1936. He was to report to Stockerau, headquarters of the elite Dragoon Regiment 1. An avid horseman, who had been hoping to be posted to a cavalry unit, Kurt was delighted by the assignment. Not only did the cavalry represent Austrian tradition and patriotism, but in it one could meet the right sort of people—aristocrats and other well-connected young men. For someone of modest social origins who wished to obtain entry to the Austrian foreign service, this was extremely important. (Even better, Stockerau was close to home—only about ten miles northeast of Tulln.)

Kurt proved to be a fine recruit. He worked hard, was a good comrade, and coped well with the inevitable stress and tedium of military service. Not that army life was overly harsh. His fellow trainees were pleasant and well-bred, and the instruction he received was interesting. Kurt learned about the use of cavalry units in reconnaissance and assault. He acquired a basic knowledge of carbines and pistols. He was taught how to survive in various types of terrain, how to scan the horizon for enemy forces, how to communicate from afar with his own unit.

In addition, there were the dress parades, set to the glorious Austrian march music. Kurt cut a splendid figure in his cavalry uniform, tall, slim, and self-assured, and he took real pride in the symbols of imperial greatness—the banners and standards—that surrounded him.

At the end of 1937, the name of Kurt Josef Waldheim was inscribed on the Austrian army's reserve list.

While Kurt was still in training, Walter Waldheim had heard a friend boast about his son's entry to the Consular Academy in Vienna, an elite, world-famous training center for diplomats. Walter discussed this news with his own son. Kurt was as intelligent and diligent as anyone. Why shouldn't *he* become one of the select group of forty or fifty students who attended the Consular Academy?

His military service now behind him, Kurt applied to the academy and was granted admission as well as a scholarship.[7]

Kurt's plan was to study both law and diplomacy, a combination common in the Austrian foreign service. He began classes in autumn 1937. Unable to afford the high cost of living in Vienna, he had to commute from home, taking the train every morning from Tulln to Vienna's Northwest Station in time to arrive at the academy on the Boltzmanngasse by 8 A.M. His courses included languages, diplomacy, international studies, and law. He also attended lectures on finance and political science. In all, Kurt took ten courses his first year. He earned excellent grades in half of them, and good or average marks in the rest.

In addition, he learned about etiquette and protocol, how to shake hands and bow properly. He improved his speaking skills, plumbed the mysteries of social and diplomatic rank and status, became less of a provincial petit bourgeois.

Smiling and anxious to please, Kurt never complained, nor did he ask for special favors. Like most of Kurt's teachers, the director of the academy, Friedrich Hlavec von Rechtwall, came to admire the tall, soft-spoken teenager, regarding him as both hardworking and gifted. Kurt Waldheim had a way of attracting the admiration of his superiors.

Adolf Hitler had an uncanny ability to sense when his prey was ripe for the taking. Early in November 1937, he told his top generals and his foreign minister that Austria was doomed. Not only did he have his own people in place in Schuschnigg's government, but thousand of Illegals and Nazi sympathizers were ready to do their part to bring the regime down. The newly friendly Mussolini wouldn't object, nor were the Western democracies likely to do anything; after all, hadn't Britain and France stood by idly when the Nazis murdered Dollfuss?

On February 12, 1938, Hitler summoned Schuschnigg to the Berghof, his Bavarian mountain retreat near Berchtesgaden. There, with a cadre of his most imposing generals at his side, the Führer forced the Austrian chancellor into a ridiculous argument about Austrian history, the point of which was that Austria had always betrayed the "German idea." "The whole history of Austria is just one uninterrupted act of high treason!" he screamed.

Schuschnigg, who himself believed in the concept of a common German folkdom, lamely invoked the example of Ludwig van Beethoven, a longtime resident of Vienna, as proof of Austria's contribution to German culture. Hitler roared back that Beethoven was from Bonn, in the *German* Rhineland!

The choice Hitler gave Schuschnigg was simple: Either Austria accepted a National Socialist "coalition government" or Germany would invade. Hitler did not phrase it quite that bluntly, but he made sure Schuschnigg understood exactly what he meant. If Austria resisted, the Führer went on, Schuschnigg would be guilty of spilling innocent blood. "I know that I will not be able to spare the German people a military confrontation with the world," Hitler told him, "so please spare me at least from one within the German nation." He added that if Schuschnigg thought Italy or England would help him, he was dead wrong.[8]

In the end, Schuschnigg agreed to a series of far-ranging concessions, the most important of which was the appointment of Nazi lawyer Artur Seyss-Inquart as minister of security. Schuschnigg still refused to legalize the Austrian Nazi party, but he consented to let more Nazis out of his prisons and to allow them to agitate more openly.

News of the new concessions plunged Austria into turmoil. Mass rallies were held, street fights became more common, the Nazis grew bolder.

Not everyone was ready to turn the government over to the National Socialists. Legitimists yearned for a return to the stable days of the monarchy, which now seemed as remote as the ice age. In Vienna, they held a huge rally calling for the restoration of the pretender to the throne, Otto of Habsburg.

But the Nazis had the momentum on their side. When they heard about the legitimist rally, they staged a counterdemonstration of their own, chanting: "We shit on Otto by the Grace of God—We want Adolf from Berchtesgaden!"

On February 18, 1938, when a group of Nazis were released from prison in Linz, huge crowds gave them a tremendous ovation. An observer wrote that the newly freed Illegals arrived in town in "flower-decked motor cars and were greeted with the storm trooper's song and cries of 'Heil Hitler.' "9

The Nazi ranks were swelling fast. In the poorer sections of Vienna, an increasing number of young men were rejecting the radical socialism of their fathers in favor of a socialism based on envy and hatred—National Socialism. The Nazis offered them just what they wanted: the chance to take revenge for their cold-water flats and unemployment, for the arrogant snobbery of the Schuschnigg and Heimwehr elites, which had looked down on them for years. The Nazis would give them opportunity to humiliate the Jews and loot Jewish-owned businesses.

At the same time, the Nazis were also attracting respectable bureaucrats and military men, ambitious lawyers and wealthy peasants with pan-German sentiments.

Though Schuschnigg had permitted the slow subversion of the state by the Nazis, he refused to surrender Austria to them in one fell swoop. Instead, he decided to leave the ultimate decision to the nation. On March 13, 1938, he announced, a referendum would be held to determine whether the people wanted an independent Austria. In Tulln, the Waldheims wondered and worried about the fate of Austria. They had long been, and remained, staunch "Blacks"—supporters of Schuschnigg and the Christian Social movement. With the plebiscite just days away—and the fate of his country hanging in the balance—Kurt decided, for the first time in his life, to engage in political activity. He and his family began campaigning for a "yes" vote in the March 13 referendum. Such commitment was not without some risk. One night, Nazi vandals defaced the veranda of the Waldheim house on the Wildgasse, painting the words for "black raven"—meaning "priest-lover"—over the entrance. On another occasion, while passing out leaflets in the streets of Vienna, Kurt was attacked and beaten by a group of Nazi toughs. If it hadn't been for his size and his military training, he might well have been killed.10

To be sure, the Waldheims were hardly alone in their sentiments. Estimates were that at least 60 percent of the nation would vote "yes" in the plebiscite. Not surprisingly, the idea of putting the question to a popular vote enraged Hitler. He and his supporters in Berlin, Munich, and Vienna demanded that Austria form a "decent" government and cancel the plebiscite.

At 1 A.M. on March 11, less than forty-eight hours before the voting was to begin, Hitler signed the final orders for a German invasion of Austria. The only thing that could forestall bloodshed now, he said, would be the immediate ouster of the "traitor" Schuschnigg and the installation of a Nazi-dominated government.

That night, Schuschnigg resigned, intoning the words: "God save Austria." The recently appointed Nazi security minister, Seyss-Inquart, replaced him as chancellor.

Throughout Austria, jubilant Nazis—many wearing their illegal uniforms—poured into the streets to celebrate. Curses against Schuschnigg mingled in the air with anti-Jewish slogans. Former Nazi prisoners burned down the concentration camps in which they had been held. Scores were settled with old enemies from the Heimwehren and the police.

The idea of being part of a great and powerful empire once again was a heady notion for many Austrians. With the *Anschluss* finally at hand— and the German army preparing to cross the frontier in the morning—the conviction was widespread that the country's economic problems would now disappear, just as they had in prosperous Germany. And Hitler was right about Austrian isolation. Austria, abandoned by Italy and the democracies, looked north for salvation.[11]

The Waldheims were shocked and saddened by the unexpected turn of events. For his part, young Kurt had learned an important lesson. In the future, he would be more cautious about passing out leaflets, about taking public stands on controversial issues.

Panic swept through the capital's Jewish quarter. Terrified Jews lined up in long queues at foreign embassies, hoping to obtain exit visas. The Gestapo was making mass arrests. (By the end of July, the figure would total thirty thousand.) At the same time, exultant Nazi mobs ran riot. With the police standing idly by, S.A. men and Hitler Youth dragged well-dressed Jews off the sidewalks and forced them to clean "Aryan" apartments. Other Nazis gathered in the city's forty-four synagogues, smoking cigars, humiliating rabbis, and generally enjoying themselves. Looting was widespread.

Grotesque scenes took place in the streets, some not far from the Boltzmanngasse, where Kurt Waldheim continued to attend classes at the Consular Academy. Jews were made to scrub garbage-strewn cobblestones with toothbrushes and painful acid while crowds looked on and laughed;

when they finished, fresh garbage would be tossed down and the game would begin again. Jews were also forced to scrub off graffiti calling for a "yes" vote in the now-canceled plebiscite.[12]

When Hitler arrived in Vienna on March 15, a quarter of a million Austrians jammed the Heldenplatz to see and hear him speak from the balcony of the New Hofburg. A half million more lined the Ringstrasse. The huge crowds cheered themselves hoarse.[13]

That afternoon, Archbishop Innitzer, the leader of the Austrian Church, visited Hitler at the Hotel Imperial, where the Führer had established his Vienna headquarters, to express his joy over the *Anschluss* and pledge the goodwill of the Catholic population in the task of reconstruction. Like most Christian Socials, the Catholic leadership had never been enthusiastic about union with Germany. Nonetheless, Innitzer and his bishops were eager to safeguard their flock as well as the privileges of the Church.

For his part, the Führer welcomed the Church's support. A new plebiscite had been announced for April 10, this one to ratify the *Anschluss,* and Hitler wanted Innitzer to advise the 91 percent of all Austrians who were baptized Catholics to vote "yes." The archbishop agreed, and the following Sunday a statement advocating a "yes" vote was read from the pulpit of every Catholic church in Austria.[14]

Hitler also sought the support of Austrian workers. Somewhat surprisingly, Socialist leader Karl Renner helped him get it, declaring that he could not turn his back on the "thousand years of common history" shared by Austria and Germany. (By doing so, Renner apparently hoped to win the release of some imprisoned Socialists. If that was his aim, he failed.)

When plebiscite day finally came, over 99 percent of the voters wound up casting their ballots in favor of union with Germany.

With the formalities now taken care of, the Nazis moved quickly and ruthlessly to consolidate their victory. Renamed Ostmark (the Eastern March), Austria soon found itself playing host to thousands of German troops, police, party functionaries, and bureaucrats. The Waldheims' Lower Austria became the Lower Danube Gau. Kurt became a reservist in Defense District XVII.[15]

Those who thought that Hitler was prepared to accommodate the Catholic Church were quickly proved wrong. The Nazis hadn't forgotten that Innitzer and most of his bishops had been strong supporters of Dollfuss, Schuschnigg, and the corporative state. And as soon as they no longer needed the Church's goodwill, they cracked down with a vengeance. All Catholic associations and youth groups (including the Comagena, which Kurt had joined while at gymnasium) were disbanded.

Ordained priests were prohibited from teaching. All confessional schools were closed. So were three of the country's four Catholic theological institutes. In addition, people were encouraged to marry and to bury their dead outside the Church.

Protestants, liberals, and Socialists—most of whom regarded the Church as rich, reactionary, and arrogant—were not particularly unhappy with this development. But the nation's Catholic majority recoiled at the attack on their church. In October 1938, a crowd of eight thousand mostly young Church supporters assembled in front of Archbishop Innitzer's palace, chanting "Hail Christ! Hail Bishop!" In retaliation, an organized Nazi mob consisting of S.A. men and Hitler Youths broke into the palace the next day, looting the place and smashing its windows.[16]

Shortly after the *Anschluss,* the town clerk of Tulln, Edward Müllner, received a visit from the police. "Upon their order," he later reported, "I had to take the Gestapo to the Waldheim house on the Wildgasse." Walter Waldheim was arrested. Though he was released within a day or two, he lost his job as school superintendent, and his pension was slashed. In addition, Kurt's scholarship to the Consular Academy was canceled.

Thereafter the Waldheim house was visited occasionally by S.A. men looking for subversive literature. Walter was arrested a second time; again he was quickly released.

The shock to the family was intense. After all, they were not Jews or Communists. Yet their neighbors began to shun them. Kurt's mother, Josefine, became nervous about going out in the streets.[17]

Without his scholarship, Kurt had to borrow money from relatives in order to be able to continue his education. (His sister, Gerlinde, also received help from relations, to enable her to pursue her medical studies.) To raise extra money, Kurt began hiring himself out as a tutor in Latin and Greek. An aunt supplied the Waldheims with eggs and milk.

At the Consular Academy, *Gleichschaltung,* or Nazi coordination, proceeded apace. The director, Hlavec von Rechtwall, gave a moving speech on the Führer's birthday, extolling the union with the Reich. On May 16, 1938, he expelled the academy's few remaining Jewish students. Fortunately for Kurt, Hlavec remained very fond of him.

According to German army records, on April 1, 1938, the nineteen-year-old Kurt Waldheim was enrolled in the National Socialist German Students League. The official "Organization Book" of the Nazi party specified that an individual had to go through a probationary period of one or two semesters before becoming a full member of the league. Kurt evidently went through this probationary period, for his army records later listed him as having been a full member. Waldheim later vigorously denied—and to this day continues to deny—that he ever joined this Nazi organization. The fact is, however, that whether he enrolled himself or, as is certainly possible, Hlavec filled out the papers on his behalf, Kurt was indeed a member.[18]

For the most part, the academy remained less Nazi than the University of Vienna. Its international reputation was important to the regime, and the Nazis knew from their experience in Germany that conservative elites would generally cooperate with them if they were allowed to keep some appearance of autonomy. In addition, the student body of the Consular Academy contained a number of children of foreign diplomats, some of whom tended to ask their Nazi teachers awkward questions. Because they were foreigners, they could get away with their impudence. After class, Kurt often thanked them for raising important issues.

That spring, Kurt wrote a seminar paper on the theme of "Press and Propaganda." Unfortunately, it has been lost. He continued to impress his teachers, one of whom wrote that he "personifies that student type of our time and of our country in a good manner."

As summer approached, Kurt began to think of traveling to Italy, a country that greatly attracted him. First, however, he was due to put in some more military service. By now, of course, the army to which he was obligated was the German army.

On August 17, 1938, Kurt returned to a cavalry instructional unit. He completed his work on September 9, and was then posted to Stockerau for further combat training. Assigned to his old Austrian unit, now called the 4th Squadron of the 11th Cavalry Regiment, Kurt was promoted to the rank of *Wachtmeister,* a noncommissioned officer.[19]

While Kurt continued his military training, the international situation grew increasingly tense. With Germany engaged in a border quarrel with Czechoslovakia, it looked as if a European war might erupt at any moment. At the end of September 1938, however, war was averted when the democracies let Hitler have his way. First Austria, then Czechoslovakia—Hitler seemed unstoppable.

Many an Austrian resigned himself to an extended period of Nazi rule. And to a growing number, that didn't seem so bad. The economy was improving, job prospects were brighter, and there was looted Jewish property to enjoy. Even those conservatives who bristled at Nazi anti-Catholic hooliganism began to shrug off such unpleasantness as nothing more than temporary excesses. "If the Führer knew," went the popular refrain, "these things would never happen."

In the early fall, Waldheim's 4th Squadron was assigned to occupation duty in the Sudetenland, the newly annexed border region of Czechoslovakia. The irony was apparent: The would-be Austrian diplomat made his first trip abroad as a German soldier. He was home by October 29. Not yet twenty, Waldheim was now a reserve officer candidate. Back in Vienna, he resumed his studies at the Consular Academy.

In Vienna, S.S. *Untersturmführer* Adolf Eichmann worked busily in his Central Office for Jewish Emigration, in a mansion that belonged to the Rothschilds. Eichmann's task was to rid Austria of its 200,000 Jews. To expedite the job, he came up with the idea of making rich Jews pay for exit permits and using the proceeds to finance the departure of their poorer brethren. By November 1938, 50,000 Jews had been forced out of the country. Within eighteen months, almost 150,000 had gone. They were the lucky ones. Most of those who remained were later killed.[20]

On the evening of November 9, 1938, Hitler's propaganda minister, Dr. Paul Joseph Goebbels, orchestrated a gigantic pogrom throughout the Greater German Reich. The idea was to teach the Jews that if the West resisted Hitler, they would pay the price. Throughout the cities of the Reich, synagogues went up in flames, Jewish-owned businesses were looted, and Jewish homes were invaded. *Reichskristallnacht,* or Reich Crystal Night, it was called, taking its name from the broken glass that littered the streets the next morning. In Vienna, forty-three out of the city's forty-four synagogues were destroyed. As many as twenty thousand Jewish males were arrested and sent to concentration camps such as Dachau and Buchenwald.

One week after Crystal Night, Waldheim was enrolled in the *Sturmabteilung,* or S.A. (This, at least, is the date that was listed in his *Wehrstammkarte,* or military record file, when it was filled out the following June.) According to Waldheim's diplomatic-career résumé in the files of the Austrian foreign office, he served in the S.A. cavalry known as the *Reitstandarte,* assigned to Storm Detachment 5 of Unit 90, which had its offices at 19 Schuttelstrasse in Vienna. At first he was a probationary member of the S.A., finally becoming a full-fledged *S.A. Mann* after six months.

The Nazi party "Organization Book" made it clear that membership in the S.A. was "in principle a voluntary one." It added that the "statutes of the S.A. give every member the opportunity for leaving if he thinks he cannot agree with the policies of the S.A., or if he is unable to fulfill the duties imposed upon him by his membership." Nonetheless, after the war the United Nations War Crimes Commission did not list the S.A. as a criminal organization, concluding that many of its members may have felt pressured to join in order to safeguard their economic or social position.

Such seems to have been the case with Waldheim; it is likely that he joined (or allowed himself to be enrolled) in order to protect his father and advance his own career.[21]

For his part, Waldheim heatedly disputes the notion that he was a storm trooper or an S.A. man. "I was no Nazi," he has said. "I was neither a member of the S.A. nor of the N.S. Student League . . ." As he tells it, his S.A. "unit" was merely a riding group at the Consular Academy that was "coordinated" by the regime. The group consisted of ten or twelve students, and its activities amounted to nothing more than perhaps two or three harmless horseback outings around the parks of the Prater.[22]

It is certainly possible that Waldheim's membership in the S.A. was simply a bureaucratic nicety. As an official organization, the academy would have had its students' horse club considered part of the National Socialist Riding Corps, and for purposes of training and administration its members could well have been enrolled in the S.A. as a group. Yet there is no doubt that Kurt Waldheim was listed by responsible authorities as a member of an S.A. riding unit. The Wehrmacht certainly considered him an S.A. man, and after the war Waldheim listed himself as a member when applying for a government post.

Waldheim graduated from the Consular Academy in the spring of 1939. On May 6, director Hlavec wrote a sterling evaluation of the lanky student, recommending him for a grant that would enable him to travel in Italy. But Waldheim was still at the disposal of the 11th Cavalry Reserve Section, and he was ordered to return to Stockerau in August.

By the end of August, the 11th Cavalry Regiment had evolved into the 45th Reconnaissance Unit. Waldheim was assigned to its 1st Mounted Squadron and was sent to the Krampnitz Cavalry Academy near Berlin as an officer candidate.

Waldheim was on his way to becoming a reserve officer in the German Wehrmacht. He expected to serve for a couple of months, then travel to Italy. After that, he would return to Vienna and resume his quest for a law degree.

On September 1, 1939, German forces crossed the Polish border. Within two days, Britain and France declared war on Germany. Kurt Waldheim would not get to go to Italy—at least not yet, and not as a tourist. On November 19, he was detailed to the 1st Cavalry Squadron of the 45th Reconnaissance Unit. Shortly thereafter he obtained leave. The stunning Germany victory in Poland made it look to many as if the war was already over.

Back in Vienna, Kurt attended some law lectures, and—like millions of others—waited in vain for news of a peace agreement with Britain and France. He returned to his unit in March, and found himself stationed in Hesse in central Germany. He was hoping the war would end without a campaign in the west. A long war would delay the beginning of his career.

CHAPTER THREE

Wehrmacht Hero

Kurt Waldheim had survived his first great crisis, the *Anschluss*. Now, as Reconnaissance Unit 45 awaited its marching orders, he faced a new challenge. As a civilian, he had enjoyed considerable room to maneuver; he could decide how—indeed, even whether—to react to the pressures on him. As a soldier in the Wehrmacht, Waldheim was at the mercy of his superiors' orders.

In a memoir he wrote in the late 1970s, Waldheim recalled: "I was called up, along with my brother, just as World War II began. . . . [O]ur only alternative was court-martial. Actually, at that period, a soldier was better off than a civilian if his politics were questionable."[1]

The implication is that Waldheim considered refusing to serve in the German army, then thought better of it. In fact, there is no evidence that Waldheim ever tried to get out of his military obligation. Nor is there any indication that he used the army as a shelter for any anti-Nazi views. What seems clear is that Waldheim knew that a respectable military record would look good on his résumé, cleansing him of the taint of having a suspected anti-Nazi for a father.

During the winter of 1939–40, Waldheim studied feverishly for his basic examination in law. He took the test in Vienna on March 15, 1940, and passed with a satisfactory grade. On March 25, Waldheim received the title of "junior barrister," with probationary status. As he didn't belong to the Nazi party—according to his personnel form, party membership was not yet possible for him, "since he is in the military"—he would have to undergo a complete political evaluation before being allowed to become a career civil servant.[2]

By then, Waldheim was back in uniform. He was hoping that this period of service would be brief, perhaps his last. This was the time of the "phony war," with little military action in the west. The Germans sat behind their impregnable Siegfried Line; the French felt secure behind their Maginot Line. Waldheim hoped that the war would simply peter out in some sort of compromise.

In April, the 45th Reconnaissance Unit was ordered to prepare for action.

On May 10, the Wehrmacht and the Luftwaffe struck France and the Low Countries. The Allied forces were quickly overwhelmed. Belgium and Holland fell within two weeks. The mighty French army collapsed in five weeks. Germany, it seemed, had won the war.

Waldheim's unit, AA 45, saw little action, moving from the area around Etreux toward Boulogne-sur-Mer in the Pas-de-Calais region of northern France. By June, the pace was almost leisurely. For the first time, Waldheim had a chance to employ his linguistic skills, using his French on behalf of his unit. His considerate manner and deferential style came as a pleasant surprise to French civilians. Instead of a jack-booted Prussian barking guttural orders at terrified locals, here was a nice young Austrian politely asking landlords if the German army might request the use of a certain chateau or residence as temporary accommodation for a group of cavalry officers. Payment would be arranged, and the property would not be disturbed. Dealing with defeated, demoralized, frightened people, Waldheim's diplomacy worked wonders, and his superiors were properly grateful.

In August, Waldheim, by now a senior noncommissioned officer, was sent home on leave. Though housing was not easy to come by in wartime, Waldheim's parents had managed to move out of Tulln that spring to smaller but safer quarters on the Eichwaldgasse in Baden, about fifteen miles south of Vienna. Their expenses were lower, but so was Walter Waldheim's income. No longer allowed to teach, he had to scrimp by on his reduced pension. Still, there was some good news for Kurt when he got to Baden. The chief of the Nazi Party Personnel Office for the Lower Danube region had approved his request to be allowed to pursue a legal career. In a report dated August 2, 1940, the chief wrote of Waldheim:

> The above-mentioned was, like his father, a supporter of the Schuschnigg regime, and . . . boasted ample evidence of his hateful attitude

towards our movement. The above-mentioned has now been conscripted, and is said to have proven his worth as a soldier of the
German Army, so that I do not oppose his admission to judicial
service.[3]

The legal profession in the Third Reich was a thoroughly "coordinated" one; that is, the regime made sure that all lawyers were politically
reliable. Waldheim's strategy had worked: By going along, he had gotten
along.

Waldheim returned to AA 45 in the middle of September. On December 1, 1940, he was commissioned a lieutenant in the reserve.

Though many, including Waldheim, had hoped that the war would
end with the collapse of France, the stubborn British refused to negotiate.
Still, there was no sense of emergency or total mobilization, and Waldheim received study leave for part of the winter 1940–41 semester. He
used the time to begin work on a doctorate in international law, a degree
that could further his career as a diplomat.

Waldheim returned to his unit in France in the middle of February
1941. His knowledge of French culture and language had increased
greatly since he had first arrived the previous May. Though he regretted
the fact that he was a foreign soldier in an occupied land, on the whole
life was good. He got along well with his comrades and was in no real
danger. Now that his family was in Baden, he worried less about his
parents. He knew that his father was very pleased with his professional
progress. Among other things, Kurt's good fortune allowed Walter Waldheim to stop worrying that his political problems would impede his son's
career.

After a pleasant late winter and early spring, Waldheim and his
comrades were shipped east. Despite a string of Axis victories in Greece
and Yugoslavia, the war was not ending. Indeed, it was about to escalate.

For nearly twenty years, Adolf Hitler had dreamed of destroying what he
regarded as the "Jewish-Bolshevik" colossus to the east, Soviet Russia. By
late 1940, he was ready to make his dream a reality. In large part, Hitler's
decision to junk the nonaggression pact he had signed with Stalin reflected
his conviction that Britain would never surrender as long as there was a
chance that Russia might one day break with Germany and come to her
aid. If the German Reich conquered Russia, or at least drove her armies
back to Asia, that hope would dissipate, Hitler believed, and Britain would
finally sue for peace.

With that in mind, Hitler ordered the Wehrmacht to strike east early in the morning of June 22, 1941. Lieutenant Waldheim's unit was part of the invading force.

AA 45 was attached to the 45th Infantry Division, which itself formed part of the huge Army Group Center, whose ultimate goal was the capture of Moscow.

The first task handed AA 45 was a difficult one. Its men had to storm the Soviet positions in and around the border city of Brest-Litovsk. Early on in the fighting, Waldheim and his comrades realized this was nothing like the leisurely campaign they had waged the previous year. Though German motorized and horse cavalry units could occupy vast amounts of territory very quickly—and though many Russian soldiers surrendered or wandered around in confusion, cut off from their units—this enemy was very different from the one they had faced in France. Motivated by a combination of patriotism and fear (of their own Communist commissars as well as the German invader), Red Army soldiers often fought to the death, giving up only when their ammunition ran out.

After a bloody battle, Brest-Litovsk fell to the Germans. For his efforts, Lieutenant Waldheim was awarded the Iron Cross, Second Class.

In July, AA 45 was expanded into the *Vorausabteilung* 45, or Vanguard Unit 45. VA 45, as it was known, soon learned a new and different type of warfare, one inspired by Hitler's racist ideology. Hitler had long preached that the millions of Jews, Slavs, Communists, and other *Untermenschen,* or subhumans, who cluttered up Europe had to be eliminated in order to provide *Lebensraum,* living space, for the superior Aryan peoples. The war to achieve this goal, he warned, would have to be a new and different kind of war, a war in which the traditional Western military and diplomatic protocols no longer prevailed. It would, he said, be an "ideological war of extermination."

On July 28, 1941, S.S. *Reichsführer* Heinrich Himmler issued orders regarding Russian resistance to the German advance, orders that reflected Hitler's ideas about the nature of the war in which he considered Germany to be engaged. Himmler pointed out that the huge Pripet Marshes and other swampy areas could be used by the enemy as places of refuge. There they might hide and organize resistance forces, commonly known as partisan units. To prevent this, Himmler authorized the S.S. units that fought alongside the Wehrmacht to take a number of specific "cleansing actions," especially if the enemy consisted of racial inferiors or if a village was suspected of helping partisans. In such cases, anyone under suspicion was to be executed immediately, while "women and children are to be deported. . . . The villages are [then] to be burned to the ground." These instructions, and similar orders stemming from the German Army High Command, became models for German behavior throughout the eastern theater, in the Balkans as well as in Russia.[4]

On the Russian front, Lieutenant Waldheim and his comrades were mainly concerned with survival. The fighting seemed endless. One drove the Reds back, then they counterattacked. One pushed them back again, and they counterattacked again. They had so many reserves. At one point, the young would-be diplomat found himself under fire in a village cemetery, sheltering himself by crawling from gravestone to gravestone. What a place in which to die, he later recalled thinking.

In recognition of his valor, Waldheim received the Cavalry Assault Badge on August 18. He was clearly cut out to be a leader, and on October 8, 1941, when the squad leader was absent, he was placed in temporary charge of the 1st Squadron of VA 45.

As squadron leader, Waldheim led his men into battle mainly against groups of Red Army *Versprengte*, or stragglers. Early in October, the city of Orel had fallen to the Germans. Though there was pressure to advance because of the imminence of autumn mud and winter cold, the Wehrmacht made little progress after that. Waldheim's unit became involved in a series of mopping-up operations in the Orel sector, southwest of Moscow.[5]

Waldheim was respected by both the men under him and the officers he served. Forty years later, Hans-Georg Kwisda, a squad leader who fought alongside Waldheim in Russia, recalled him as being "quite good," noting that "Pannwitz praised him a lot."[6]

That was praise indeed, for Colonel Helmut von Pannwitz, the commander of VA 45, was the very model of the modern Wehrmacht officer—brave, imaginative, and brutal. Waldheim had first come into contact with Pannwitz three years earlier, when he returned to Stockerau to continue his combat training in the summer of 1938; the older man was there helping to integrate the Austrian *Bundesheer* into the German Wehrmacht. (A tough soldier, Pannwitz went on to become the commanding general of the infamous First Cossack Division, which committed numerous atrocities in Yugoslavia. In 1947, he was hanged as a war criminal in Moscow.)[7]

Pannwitz was the first major military figure to take note of Lieutenant Waldheim and to use him to advantage. He was not the last.

After almost six months in Russia, Waldheim's luck ran out. On December 5, 1941, the Soviets began their great counteroffensive against Army Group Center. Waldheim's unit was in the thick of the fighting. On December 14, exactly a week before his twenty-third birthday, a piece of shrapnel from a grenade ripped through Waldheim's right leg. In the freezing cold, medics manhandled him onto a two-wheeled pushcart, then dragged him to a sleigh. When he regained consciousness, he was on his way to a field hospital in Minsk. Everywhere he looked, he could see villages in flames—the result of a German scorched-earth policy designed to slow the Soviet advance. Waldheim was in immense pain. Medics warned him of the dangers of frostbite and infection, telling him over and over again: "Move your leg or you will lose it."

Even if he made it to Minsk, there was no guarantee that he would ever walk again, or even survive. Years later, he recalled to me how he wondered at the time if all his father's sacrifices, all his years of study, all their hopes for the future, had been for nothing.

Waldheim finally arrived in Minsk after a harrowing journey of several days and nights. In the field hospital there, a pleasant Austrian doctor told him he would have to amputate—unless, that is, the injured young lieutenant could provide some wool for a bandage. Hitler had not prepared his troops for a winter war, and wool was in short supply on the Russian front.

"I have wool," Waldheim replied. He pulled out a scarf a friend had given him. The doctor saved the leg.[8]

A few days later, Waldheim was flown back to Austria, where he checked into Reserve Field Hospital 23, located on the Rudolfinergasse in Vienna. The delayed treatment for his leg had temporarily left him with a limp, but he had made it home in time for Christmas. Comforted by his family, he began physical therapy.

Waldheim has since claimed that the injuries he suffered in Russia effectively ended his career in the Wehrmacht; that after being wounded, he was declared unfit for service at the front and never again engaged in any significant military duty. That is not strictly true. The fact is, after undergoing physical therapy in Vienna for two months, and resuming work on his doctoral degree during the winter semester, Waldheim was declared once again fit for service.

On March 6, 1942, Lieutenant Waldheim reported back to his old unit, Cavalry Reserve Unit 11 in Stockerau. There he was told that he had been transferred to the high command of the German Twelfth Army. He was to report to headquarters in Belgrade, Yugoslavia, by March 14, at which time he would be given a specific assignment.[9]

Waldheim was not happy about being sent to the Balkans. Shaken by his brush with death in Russia, he had hoped to remain with his family and obtain study leave. Still, a staff job in Belgrade was better than going back to the front. He was well aware that extended service on the eastern front was tantamount to a death sentence. (Indeed, two years later Waldheim's old unit was wiped out near Bobruisk.) In Belgrade he would be closer to his family, and safer. After what he had seen in Russia, the Balkans might almost be pleasant. There were a lot of Austrians serving there; his countrymen had a long tradition of involvement with the region and its peoples.

Yugoslavia had been overrun by Axis forces nearly a year before Kurt Waldheim arrived in the fortress city of Belgrade. That didn't mean the war there was over, however. The Serbs were tough fighters, and Yugoslav partisans continued to harry their occupiers with stiff resistance.

The Germans responded with brutality. According to Yugoslav historian Vladimir Dedijer, in October 1941 alone, the Germans executed seven thousand civilians in Yugoslavia. At the high school in Kragujevac, they killed every student and teacher. In western Serbia that autumn, German troops slaughtered 37,000 peasants and townspeople. A typical report by the Twelfth Army High Command noted: "As reprisal measure for German losses in the month of January [1942] 449 prisoners shot, further 3,484 shootings ordered."

The carnage was one-sided. In the third week of February 1942, the German command in Belgrade reported that Axis forces had lost eighty-four dead, while enemy losses totaled almost seventeen hundred.[10]

Whenever the partisans attacked Wehrmacht soldiers, the Germans would get the local Serb police to hand over dozens or hundreds of "Communist" detainees, who would then be shot. In February 1942, over five thousand people were being held at the Semlin concentration camp outside Belgrade for just that purpose. Occasionally, however, the German authorities wouldn't wait for the police to provide them with victims; they would simply pull people off the streets of the capital and hang them from the lampposts as a warning. Several bodies were strung up throughout Belgrade, swaying in the cold, late-winter wind, when Lieutenant Waldheim arrived there on March 14.

As a result of the Axis occupation, much of what used to be Yugoslavia now belonged to the new Independent State of Croatia (ISC). In large part a German creation, the ISC was nominally governed by leaders of the Fascist Ustasha movement, whose proclaimed goal was racial purity, meaning the expulsion of all Serbs, Jews, Gypsies, and other minorities. In fact, the ISC was independent in name only. Lacking effective police and military forces, it was completely beholden to its German and Italian sponsors.[11]

The Italians, who viewed Croatia and its lands as properly belonging to their sphere of influence, had little interest in propping up the ISC. Accordingly, Italian forces did little to stop the growth of Communist bands, and they allowed partisan forces to take refuge in neighboring Italian-occupied territories.

Partly as a result of the Italians' deliberate laxity, but also because of German overconfidence and Croatian ineffectiveness, the partisans managed to build up their forces in East Bosnia through the winter of 1941–42.[12] As a result, in March 1942, just before Waldheim arrived in Belgrade, it was decided that the Italians, Croatians, and Germans would move jointly into East Bosnia to clean out the partisans. The operation— involving three Italian divisions, twenty-eight Croatian battalions, and the German 718th Security Division—was called "Trio." Its mission was officially defined as "the annihilation of the rebels in Bosnia and the pacification of the whole area." The commander of German forces in Croatia, General Paul Bader, was put in charge of Operation Trio (though to appease the Italians, he was made tactically subordinate to their Second Army). Bader established the headquarters of what became known as Battle Group Bader in Sarajevo, the capital of East Bosnia. Further instructions followed: ". . . rebels not captured in battle are to be deported to Norway for labor purposes. Rebels captured in a battle are in principle to be hanged or shot." The local quartermaster unit would be responsible for deportation of prisoners, captured war booty, and the security of the rear. It would also be the liaison unit for the Croatian civil authorities.[13]

Among the officers assigned to the operations staff of Battle Group Bader was the newly arrived Lieutenant Waldheim. Bader needed Waldheim (who spoke some Italian as well as French) to provide liaison with one of his Italian units, the 5th Mountain Division, known as "Pusteria." Based in Pljevlje in Montenegro, Pusteria was meant to play a role in the relief of the beleaguered town of Rogatica. By moving from Pljevlje to Rogatica, Pusteria and two fellow Italian divisions were supposed to prevent the partisans currently surrounding Rogatica from escaping toward Serbia. Waldheim's job was to keep Bader's headquarters informed of Pusteria's movements, and to convey requests and commands to the division's commanding general, Giovanni Esposito.

Waldheim arrived in Pljevlje early in April. A week or two later, the German High Command in Salonika, complaining about Italian tardiness, postponed the entire operation until the end of the month. As a result, Bader ordered Pusteria to remain in place. General Esposito was happy to oblige. His forces were not very mobile, nor were they especially eager to engage in combat.[14]

By April 24, the Italians were still not ready to move on Rogatica. While partisan bands escaped to the southeast, right past Pusteria's garrisons, the division sat tight, doing little but fortifying its positions. On April 27, the Germans and Croatians relieved Rogatica without any Italian help. Three days later, the operation was complete.[15]

Though their failure to participate in the relief of Rogatica cost the Italians prestige in Croatia, that was all it cost them. They were happy to let the Germans do most of the killing and dying. Like many Italian divisions, Pusteria's main concern was to protect itself and its lines of supply. By and large, its officers were more concerned with surviving the war than with winning it. Lieutenant Waldheim, who had seen more than his share of combat, and who enjoyed the opportunity to improve his Italian, got along with them just fine.[16]

Waldheim got on particularly well with General Esposito. The Italian commander took an immediate liking to the tall young Austrian and often invited him to play cards. They would sip valpolicella together while Waldheim talked about his family, his aspirations, and his terrible experience on the Russian front.

Waldheim's duties were hardly onerous. Mainly, he relayed messages from Bader urging Pusteria to move on Rogatica, then transmitted back the Italians' excuses for not being ready. His radioman, a German soldier named Köhler, did all the technical work, leaving Waldheim free to enjoy the mountains of Montenegro and his card games with Esposito. He also became quite friendly with the local family in whose cottage he was quartered, bringing them chocolates and other scarce items from the military stores to which he enjoyed access. Some locals recall that the family's eighteen-year-old daughter became extremely fond of the courteous twenty-three-year-old officer. (Reportedly, she died in 1986, having never married.)

From General Esposito, Waldheim learned the reality of the Axis war against the Yugoslav partisans. It was more a traditional defensive effort than authentic counterinsurgency. Waldheim listened closely as Esposito summarized Pusteria's experiences in Montenegro; among other things, Waldheim was responsible for keeping the German command in Sarajevo apprised of what the Italians were saying and thinking. He was learning the craft of intelligence gathering.

Esposito explained that even though Pusteria enjoyed enormous superiority in firepower, the division found it difficult to take the offensive because the partisans were so evasive. They moved at night and almost always attacked before dawn, approaching silently, then hurling grenades at outposts, barracks, and storage areas, before withdrawing. Pusteria was particularly vulnerable when it moved out of fixed positions, for the partisans knew the terrain, had the support of the people, and could move much more rapidly than the Italians, burdened as they were by large amounts of munitions and stores. As a result, Esposito and the other Italian commanders tended to stay put. Their prudence saved Italian lives (Pusteria lost only thirty-one men in the East Bosnia operation) and spared the country the ravages of war. But it also left the enemy intact, and the Fascist Croatian state in tatters.[17]

Nonetheless, on May 30, 1942, General Bader declared victory in East Bosnia. "Success has been achieved in restoring calm to large areas," he said, adding that the Germans would "now move on to new tasks in other parts of Bosnia."[18]

Waldheim moved with them on the morning of May 29, reporting to a new battle group headquartered in Banja Luka, West Bosnia. After the experience in East Bosnia, as reported by officers like Waldheim, the German command made sure there would be no Italian forces participating in the new operation. The young lieutenant had made an important contribution to German intelligence.[19]

CHAPTER FOUR

A Place Called Kozara

For much of 1941, partisan forces under the command of Josip Broz Tito, the Croatian who led the entire Communist movement in occupied Yugoslavia, had been establishing a foothold in the mountainous and densely wooded region around the Kozara plateau in West Bosnia. By the spring of 1942, they were threatening to cut the vital railway link from Zagreb to Belgrade. Even worse, they were in a position to shut down the province's strategically important iron, silver, lead, and manganese mines.

In May 1942, the German command ordered the Croatians to clean out Kozara and secure the region's mines and rail lines. The operation was supposed to begin near the Muslim city of Prijedor on June 15. But in mid-May, while the Croatians were still ensconced in Banja Luka, making their plans, the partisans attacked Prijedor. The defending Croatians panicked and ran, leaving the town—and more than a thousand rifles and machine guns—to the partisans. Heartened by the victory, hordes of resistance fighters poured into the area from the Italian-held zones. The threat to West Bosnia's mines and railroads grew worse than ever.[1]

The German High Command rushed in to pick up the pieces. The newly formed Battle Group West Bosnia, to which Waldheim was assigned on May 29, was ordered to take over from the shattered Croatian forces. Within days, elements of the German 714th Infantry Division under the command of General Friedrich Stahl had encircled Prijedor. On June 10, the city fell, and the partisans fled to the Kozara plateau.

Though the loss of Prijedor came as a shock to the partisans, they quickly recovered, defeating two Croatian mountain brigades near the west ledges of Kozara. As more partisan troops poured into the area, crossing territory recently evacuated by the Italians, General Stahl realized that the only way to secure West Bosnia was for German troops to pacify the entire Kozara region themselves.[2]

Thus was the stage set for a horror story that has since become part of the modern folklore of Yugoslavia.

There being no Italian units involved in the operation, Lieutenant Waldheim was assigned to the Ib unit, or quartermaster's department, of General Stahl's battle group. (Ia was operations, Ic was intelligence, and so on.) Ib was responsible for everything from supplying the division with food and clothing to maintaining relations with the Croatian civil authorities. Ib also audited the numbers of prisoners and captured war booty. The work was basically clerical in nature; most of the Ib staff worked out of an office in a villa in Banja Luka, handling paperwork and doing routine bookkeeping.

Stahl's entire West Bosnian operations staff was quite small, consisting of just twenty-nine officers and noncoms, including the chaplain and the paymaster. Accordingly, everyone was expected to do a little of everything. It was a situation in which an intelligent, disciplined officer could shine, and Waldheim did.

Not that he had a lot of competition. As a security division fighting a confusing, dirty little action in one of the backwaters of the war, the 714th generally did not get the best officers the Wehrmacht had to offer.

General Stahl himself was something of a contradictory character. Ambitious, demanding, and temperamental, he had been an officer since 1909; his specialty was transport and communications. Though he loved opera and classical music, and appreciated officers with similar tastes, he had a reputation, which he encouraged, for being hard as his name (which was German for "Steel"). His harshness extended both toward the enemy ("The prisoners were shot immediately, insofar as they were not needed by the unit for interrogation purposes," was a typical phrase from his reports) and toward his own men (the motto of the 714th was: "Against exhaustion and the torture of homesickness only one thing helps: 'Hard as steel'"). According to an evaluation by his superiors, Stahl was troubled by exhaustion and irritability. His nerves weren't good, and the strain of command gave him hot flashes and headaches.[3]

Stahl's deputy adjutant, Major Hermann Funke, was even less impressive. Funke's superiors described him as unbalanced, highly nervous, irritable, depressive, and neurotic. A former police lieutenant who had been forcibly retired for health reasons before the war, he suffered from claustrophobia, general exhaustion, anxiety attacks, and a heart ailment.[4]

Though the 714th did some fighting, most of its work consisted of police-type actions: roundups, interrogations, deportations. The Ib staff worried about things like providing hay and fodder for the division's 619 horses, combating rumors among the troops that their antimalaria pills caused impotence, convincing the field kitchens to conserve stores by preparing more Balkan dishes for the men.[5]

Late in June, the partisans inflicted heavy losses on the Croatian 1st Mountain Division, forcing it to withdraw. The Croatian High Command wanted to launch an investigation of the officers responsible for the rout, but Stahl resisted, sensing that such an inquiry might result in the complete collapse of the already shaky Croatian morale. Instead, he sent German officers to the Croatian units—in effect, taking them over.

By July 1, the Germans had encircled the partisans on Kozara. Two days later, fresh elements of the 714th having arrived from Serbia, the Germans began their final attacks. The fighting was fierce. Between July 1 and July 10, German intelligence reported two thousand partisans killed and another five thousand captured. On July 8, units of the 738th Infantry Regiment stopped fresh partisan forces from relieving their beleaguered comrades trapped on the plateau. Around the same time, the 1st Battalion of the 737th Infantry Regiment blocked a partisan attempt to break out of Kozara toward the west.[6]

German intelligence estimated that some four thousand partisan fighters—along with several times as many civilians—were surrounded on Kozara. Using artillery, machine guns, and barbed wire, Stahl began to draw the noose tighter. Since reports indicated that partisans were blending into the crowds of civilian refugees streaming out of the combat zone, the last phase of the operation turned into an encirclement of the entire Serb population on the Kozara plateau.[7]

Though they were outnumbered and outgunned, the partisans continued to fight. By late July, their losses totaled nearly 3,400. And while only 150 Germans had been killed so far, the Croatians had lost more than ten times that many. "For the first time in the Serbo-Croatian area," General Bader's operations unit observed, "the rebel movement has shown itself to be a tough fighting enemy when engaged in battle." The implications were not lost on the Yugoslavs. All over the country, young men began to rally to Tito's call. The legend of heroic Kozara had been born.[8]

The nightmare was yet to come.

* * *

The Germans had four goals in mind when they mounted the Kozara operation: smashing the partisan center of resistance, securing the mines near Prijedor, safeguarding the rail links to Zagreb and Belgrade, and obtaining workers for the *Arbeitseinsatz*, or forced labor program, in the Reich. After several weeks of pitched battles, the German High Command and the Croatian authorities agreed that in order to achieve all these ends, Kozara would have to be completely depopulated (though a few trustworthy peasants might be permitted to continue working there, mainly gathering wood for the Germans). After all, if there were no people on Kozara, the partisans could not return and reestablish a stronghold, for they depended on the local population for food, shelter, and new recruits for their ranks.

By the end of August, the Germans and the Croatians, using everything from barbed wire to bloodhounds, had swept the plateau virtually clean of inhabitants. More than thirty thousand people, most of them women and children, were taken prisoner.

The German attitude toward these sorts of captives was brutal. The week Waldheim arrived in Belgrade, the commander in chief of the Twelfth Army had approved orders stating: "No humanitarian drivel! It is better that fifty suspicious persons be liquidated than that a single German soldier be destroyed." The specific policy regarding prisoners taken on Kozara was equally harsh: "All persons caught with weapons, or who have fought against German or Croatian troops, will be shot, as well as those proven to have taken active part in the revolt."[9]

But while many of the Kozara prisoners were executed immediately, the majority were allowed to live—at least for the time being. With the Reich in desperate need of workers, it made more sense to save the healthy ones for the more lingering death of *Arbeitseinsatz*. What General Stahl's staff needed to do now was to sort them out and arrange for the necessary mass deportations.

Lieutenant Waldheim's Ib unit did part of this work. It collated statistics regarding the number of prisoners, then surveyed the number of trucks and railway cars available to deport them.

In order to be closer to the prisoners, part of Ib relocated to the railhead at Kostajnica. Here Stahl established an *Umschlagstelle*, or transshipment center, working with the Croatians in processing the would-be slave laborers, deciding which would go where. Those who appeared fit enough were shipped off to the Reich or to Norway, where most were worked to death within months; those deemed too sick or too weak to survive the journey were turned over to the Croatians, to be butchered at leisure.

In all, the number of Kozara victims—those killed in action, executed afterward, or deported into oblivion—is generally estimated to be between 66,000 and 68,000. The historian Vladimir Dedijer puts the figure even higher—at 90,000.

It was around the time of the Kozara operation that President Franklin D. Roosevelt declared that "it is the purpose of each of the United Nations to make appropriate use of the information and evidence in respect to these barbaric crimes of the invaders in Europe and Asia. It seems only fair that they should have this warning, that the time will come when they shall have to stand in courts of law in the very countries which they are oppressing and answer for their acts."

The 714th's own official history of the Kozara action describes it as "a battle without mercy, without pity." It concludes with this chilling summary:

> In the weeks that have gone by since these days on Kozara, the purification action has made decisive progress. With increasing success, the mobilized troop units have worked at the goal of the final liquidation of the [partisan] bands' criminality.[10]

Attached to this description is a staff list. The twenty-ninth name on this list is "Leutnant Waldheim." Printed on finer paper than the divisional history, this list was clearly produced for display purposes. It is not an ordinary bureaucratic staff roster.

In Wehrmacht commemorative divisional histories, a list of this sort is known as an *Ehrentafel,* a list of honor.[11] It generally includes only the names of men who distinguished themselves in some way in the action described in the history. Waldheim's inclusion on this particular list doesn't necessarily mean he actually took part in—or even witnessed—any of the fighting and killing at Kozara; it indicates only that he was deemed to have distinguished himself in helping to make the battle and its outcome possible.

There is another indication that Waldheim may have played a more significant role at Kozara than he later admitted. On July 22, 1942, the Croatian leader Ante Pavelić awarded Waldheim the Silver Medal of the Crown of King Zvonimir with Oak Leaves, singling him out, along with three other staff officers and a number of enlisted men and noncoms, "for courage in the battle against rebels in West Bosnia in the spring and summer of 1942." Though Waldheim later insisted that the "Zvonimir" was routinely given to staff officers, this does not seem to have been the case. The month before, only five of these medals were awarded to German soldiers in Stahl's division.

The Zvonimir medal had been created by Pavelić and his regime in order to reinforce Axis solidarity by strengthening Croatian ties to friendly German officers. It represented the acknowledgment of a German officer's efficient collaboration with Croatian forces, both at the front and behind the lines. (As the regulations said, it was meant "for those who took part in combat situations, as well as for the leadership.") A German army chaplain might get one for having ministered to Croatian army soldiers. A German paymaster might be recognized for having eased the financial burdens of the corrupt and inefficient Croatian command.

The point was, the Croatians only gave the medal to people who actively helped them. Waldheim could not have received the medal for routine bookkeeping tasks carried out for the German forces alone. Nor could he have been given it as a mere courtesy. The Germans saw to that. Concerned about the possibility that Wehrmacht soldiers might deliberately cultivate Croatian officers in order to obtain medals, German authorities had earlier instructed General Bader and General Stahl to approve personally all Zvonimirs given out during and after Kozara.

In Waldheim's case, the Zvonimir acknowledged his efforts in department Ib. What might a Ib officer have done to earn the gratitude of the Croatians? He may have discreetly made supplies available to the beleaguered Croatian staff. He may have demonstrated uncommon efficiency in handling the paperwork concerning matters of mutual interest—such as the deportation of prisoners—at Kostajnica. He may have done both.

What is indisputable is that Waldheim attracted the favorable interest of Croatian officials, for they were the ones who put his name on the Zvonimir list. (The role of Bader and Stahl was merely to ratify the Croatians' choices.) In itself, that is hardly surprising. Waldheim was a would-be diplomat with a great interest in foreign countries; a gifted linguist, he had even managed to pick up a little Serbo-Croatian in his few weeks in Yugoslavia. The Croatian official most likely to have taken a shine to Waldheim was Oskar Turina, the head of the Croatian liaison staff in West Bosnia and Pavelić's personal representative in the province. A German-speaking diplomat who knew Vienna well, Turina spent a lot of time at German staff headquarters. He also had a particular assignment that could well have resulted in his working closely with Waldheim and Ib. Turina was the man in charge of all Croatian deportation operations.[12]

*   *   *

More than forty years later, Waldheim's own statements about Kozara were confused and contradictory.[13] First he admitted he had been there, but insisted there had been no massacre. Then he said he had been there only briefly, having been sent back to General Esposito's Pusteria regiment after reporting to Stahl's staff. Finally, he conceded that he had served with Stahl's Ib unit at Kostajnica, but in an innocuous supply capacity, doing clerical work concerned only with army supplies. (In fact, Waldheim's name appears nowhere in the records of Ib's supply operations during this period. We shall never know if his name was listed among those working on the deportations; those records have been lost.)

Waldheim's willingness—however belated and reluctant—to concede his presence at Kostajnica in the summer of 1942 could have something to do with the fact that the only other place he could have been at the time was the divisional headquarters in Banja Luka, and Banja Luka may be an even worse place to admit having been that summer. While Ib was setting up shop at Kostajnica, Croatian authorities in Banja Luka were rounding up the town's entire Jewish community—all of whom wound up being exterminated at the notorious Jasenovac concentration camp.[14]

Lieutenant Waldheim left the heat and depression of Kozara late in August 1942. By August 31, he was back at Twelfth Army headquarters, which by now had been moved from Belgrade to Arsakli, a small town in the hills above the Greek port of Salonika. His new assignment was an easy one; he was one of several translators attached to the Ic/AO intelligence staff. He even obtained leave in September. He needed it. Russia and Kozara had changed him. Though his leg had healed and combat seemed further off than ever, there was too much on his mind. How long would all this go on? What would happen next?

Over the past year, Waldheim had received four medals. Not yet twenty-four, the ambitious Austrian boy struggling to make it into the Vienna elite had become a Wehrmacht hero.

A friend he visited later that year recalled that Waldheim seemed more sure of himself than before, less the lower-middle-class youth on the rise. He no longer doubted that his career would progress—if, that is, he could ever get home. That was the reason for Waldheim's jumpiness. He knew from his experience in Russia and Kozara that the war was a long way from over.

While Waldheim stewed at Twelfth Army headquarters in the autumn of 1942, German troops were battling in the rubble of a place called

Stalingrad. There were rumors of massive Allied air raids over northwest Germany. Worst of all, from the Twelfth Army's point of view, was the Axis collapse in North Africa. Would the Allies now invade the Balkans?

Waldheim had already missed the fall semester. Perhaps he could make it back to Vienna for the winter. Surely the Twelfth Army would not miss him.

Somewhat surprisingly, his superiors agreed. Despite the grave military situation, Lieutenant Waldheim—as of December 1 he would be First Lieutenant Waldheim—was granted study leave for the winter semester. He arrived home in the middle of November.

CHAPTER FIVE

Lilo, Kurt, and Professor Verdross

The train ride back to Vienna was a long and exhausting one. Still, Waldheim knew he was fortunate to have gotten leave in time to spend Christmas with his family in Baden. He was also looking forward to discussing his graduate work in international law with the famous Professor Verdross, a renowned diplomat and legal scholar who taught at the University of Vienna.

From the window of his compartment, as his train rumbled through Lower Austria, Waldheim saw how much the apparently endless war had changed his homeland. There were hardly any young men around. All the tram drivers and traffic police were either old men, Hitler Youth, or female auxiliaries. Everyone seemed to be in uniform, and there was no escaping Joseph Goebbels's propaganda. Slogans were everywhere, painted on walls, plastered on trains, blaring out through huge loudspeakers: "Unity of Front and Homeland!" "Total War—Shorter War!" "Adolf Hitler Is Victory!" "Support the War Winter Relief Drive!" "The Jews Are to Blame!" "Behind the Enemy Coalition—the Jew!" "Quiet, Big Mouth! The Enemy Is Listening!"

After what Waldheim had seen in Russia and Kozara, the slogans left him cold.

In the southern suburbs of Vienna, Waldheim noticed the huge influx of foreigners, workers employed at the giant war plants that now dominated towns like Wiener Neustadt and his parents' home, Baden. Though Vienna and its environs had not yet felt the fury of Allied bombing raids, there was a grayness about the metropolis and its inhabitants. Few people smiled as they went about their business. Everyone complained about the omnipresent *Piefkes,* the arrogant Germans who bossed them around and looted their country.

The mood was quite different in the Waldheim house in Baden. Waldheim's parents were overjoyed to see him. Not only was their son alive and whole, but he had permission to remain at home until the spring. Sensitive to his parents' worries, Waldheim reassured them that his duty in the Balkans was safe, even pleasant. Unlike Russia, nobody threw hand grenades at him there. He simply served on a general's staff and translated for the Italians; he even had an opportunity to play tennis with a count! He did not talk about Kozara.

His prospects seemed better than ever. In a few days he would officially become a first lieutenant in the reserve. Perhaps before too long he would be able to call himself Reserve First Lieutenant *Doctor* Waldheim. Both Waldheim and his father liked titles, and this one sounded impressive, particularly for a young man still several weeks shy of his twenty-fourth birthday.

Over the next few weeks, Waldheim went looking for former friends from his school days. He managed to locate a few of them, but others had fallen in combat. According to one friend who saw him at the time, he was distressed to learn that his Jewish acquaintances from the old days were now all "in the east." Waldheim, the friend reported, was deeply upset by news of the deportations, murmuring, "It is so terrible! It is so terrible!" On another occasion, Waldheim supposedly told a Dutch friend that he hated his German uniform.

Years later, Waldheim maintained that he never considered himself to be serving the Nazi regime. In "doing my duty," he told me, "I was doing it toward my comrades, so as not to let them down." Whatever his motivation, the German army certainly appreciated his service. A steady string of promotions since 1938, plus four medals, made that clear.

One day late that winter, while visiting the University of Vienna, Waldheim noticed a tall, striking, dark-haired girl of about twenty-one intently studying a bulletin board in the law school building. Her hair was long and thick, her eyes piercing. Instantly smitten, Waldheim politely introduced himself, and they began to talk. Her name was Elizabeth Lieselotte Ritschel; her friends called her Lilo. Like Kurt, she planned to pursue a legal career; indeed, she was currently studying for her law exams, which she would take the following summer. The more they talked, the more Waldheim became convinced that this was the girl for him.

Lilo had been barely sixteen, a student at the Women's High School on the Wenzgasse (one of the best schools in Vienna), when the *Anschluss* took place. Though she was intelligent and hardworking, up to then she had mainly been distinguished by her physical characteristics: her beautiful hair and her tall, womanly figure.

The *Anschluss*, however, changed all that, for Lilo and her father were fervent Nazis. Wilhelm Ritschel had been an Illegal since February 1934; by the time of the *Anschluss*, he had risen to become a cell director of the Austrian Nazi party. Ambitious for himself and his family, Ritschel knew that his political affiliations would help his daughter in Hitler's coming New Order. Thus, while Kurt was receiving his Wehrmacht cavalry training in Berlin and Stockerau, Lilo was renouncing her Catholic faith and being initiated into the League of German Maidens, the female equivalent of the Hitler Youth. In October 1940, Lilo took an even bigger step, applying to join the Nazi party. She was accepted as a member on January 1, 1941.[1]

The encounter by the law school bulletin board marked the beginning of a lifelong passion. Lilo and Kurt made a handsome couple, socially impressive and personally charming. Not only did both of them tower over most of their friends, but each was a perfect complement to the other. She was a beautiful, strong-willed young woman; he was ambitious, yet pliable and tender. What's more, she could help him with his career. Waldheim's military record had made him tolerable to the regime, but he craved more than toleration. He craved advancement, and Lilo's membership in the Nazi party could give him the extra boost he needed. His alliance with her would prove to the Nazis that he had the right kind of friends, those loyal to the regime.

Waldheim established another important relationship that winter. In search of a subject for his doctoral dissertation, he attended a seminar given by Professor Alfred Verdross, one of the best-known members of the University of Vienna's law faculty. Waldheim had been in contact with Verdross for some time, and at this seminar the famous law professor suggested that the young Wehrmacht lieutenant write his dissertation on Konstantin Frantz, a German political theorist of the mid-nineteenth century, whose violently anti-Semitic, pan-German ideas were celebrated by many Nazi writers as having foreshadowed Hitler's Greater German Reich. From a political point of view, it was an astute choice for an upwardly mobile Austrian. But then, Professor Verdross was sensitive to such matters.

Alfred Verdross von Drossberg was a prolific writer and a gifted teacher, with a worldwide reputation as an expert on international law. He was also a shameless opportunist. The son of a distinguished Habsburg military officer and an accomplished diplomat himself, Verdross was only thirty-five when he was appointed a full professor at the University of Vienna in 1925. Soon one of the law faculty's leading lights, a leading expert on war crimes, and a star lecturer at the nearby Consular Academy, he espoused a flexible political and legal philosophy that managed to combine both liberal and Catholic ideas. On the one hand, he had been a strong supporter of the League of Nations. On the other, he embraced the conservative ideology of Engelbert Dollfuss.

The fact was, Verdross never let philosophical conviction interfere with personal advancement. In 1937, as Dollfuss's successor, Kurt von Schuschnigg, weakened and drew closer to the German Reich, Verdross lost his enthusiasm for the corporative state and began to advocate a return to the Habsburg monarchy. His interest was more than academic, for he saw in the political turmoil that gripped Austria an opportunity to enhance his own importance. Convinced that the *Anschluss* was inevitable, he intended to set himself up as the personal mediator between the pretender, Otto of Habsburg, and the Führer. After meeting with Otto, Verdross put out secret feelers to Nazi leaders. He was in a position to do this because he had been saying good things about the Nazis for several years—though only to certain people. (His Jewish friends and colleagues had no idea of his pro-Nazi sentiments.) At the same time, Verdross tried to stay in Schuschnigg's good graces. He would not openly embrace the Nazis until after they had won.

Verdross had first helped the Austrian Nazis after their bloody attempt to seize power in July 1934. When Schuschnigg suppressed the Nazi party following the murder of Dollfuss, Nazi students lost their scholarships—even their subsidized cafeteria tickets. Verdross thereupon organized and led a front group to help "worthy National Socialist and nationalist" law students continue with their studies.

When it became apparent after the *Anschluss* that the Nazis had no interest in restoring Otto to the throne, Verdross dropped that idea and began talking as if he had been an Illegal all along. Despite his groveling opportunism, however, Verdross had not moved fast enough for some of his Nazi colleagues. Ernst Schönbauer, the dean of the University of Vienna law school and a real Illegal, finally told him to tone down his comments; his posture was not appropriate for someone who not only had been a supporter of Dollfuss and the League of Nations but was reputed to be friendly with both Jews and clerics.

While Nazis in the law faculty schemed and plotted to oust Verdross,

Schönbauer tried to protect his distinguished if politically spineless colleague by telling Nazi political authorities that though his star professor lacked courage and conviction, he was well-intentioned. In the end, Verdross was allowed to remain on the law faculty, though he was no longer permitted to teach the philosophy of law. Good National Socialists could better deal with that, men like Schönbauer, who taught law to Lilo Ritschel. Nor was Verdross permitted to continue lecturing at the Consular Academy. Nineteen- and twenty-year-old minds were simply too impressionable to be entrusted to such a politically unreliable teacher. (Verdross was replaced at the academy by his assistant, Dr. Karl Hofbauer, who was reputed to be an agent of the S.D., or security police.)

Instead, Verdross was ordered to limit his teaching to international law, and only in small seminars attended by advanced students. If he watched his step, he might be permitted to supervise doctoral dissertations. Schönbauer assured the authorities that Verdross was no risk to the regime. "He is a soft man," the dean reported, "full of goodwill, and as a consequence of the disappointment he has experienced, he will work doubly hard."[2]

When Waldheim turned up in one of Verdross's seminars, the opportunistic professor quickly spotted the younger man's potential. Intelligent and well-meaning, Waldheim was an Austrian Catholic who yearned for nothing as much as a good career as a lawyer and diplomat. Verdross could identify with that.

Given Waldheim's background and ambitions, Verdross's suggestion that he devote his dissertation to Konstantin Frantz was little short of brilliant. Not only was Frantz politically acceptable to the Nazi regime, but as a federalist who bitterly rejected Otto von Bismarck's Protestant, anti-Austrian Reich, he represented a philosophy completely in accord with Waldheim's conservative upbringing. Waldheim could thus serve his conscience as well as his career by writing about Frantz. His dissertation would both celebrate European federalism and bear on its title page the name of an acknowledged and revered precursor of Hitler.

Early in April 1943, Waldheim returned to active duty in the Balkans. Lilo had promised to write, and the young lieutenant anxiously awaited her letters. Little had changed since the previous fall, though the Twelfth Army was now known as Army Group E. Once again Waldheim received a pleasant assignment, one that led him to recall the halcyon days he had spent in Montenegro with General Esposito and the Pusteria Division the previous spring.

This time he was ordered to report to the German liaison staff in the

Albanian capital of Tirana. Albania, a primitive country that lacked even a single railroad, was an Italian protectorate. The Italian Ninth Army was headquartered in Tirana, while the Italian XIV Army Corps was based just across the border in the Montenegran town of Podgorica.

Waldheim's job was to act as interpreter at meetings between German officers and their Italian counterparts. Because of the mountainous terrain, the terrible roads, and the lack of any rail transport, Waldheim generally had to fly from conference to conference. The meetings usually revolved around two problems: the prospect of possible Allied landings in the Balkans and the widening partisan war.

Waldheim was also responsible for helping to translate all the paperwork turned out by the Italian commands. This was no small task, for that was where the Italians tended to do most of their fighting—on paper.

As a result of his job, Waldheim, whose Italian had improved markedly since the Pusteria days, had the opportunity to meet some of the highest-ranking officers in the Balkans. Among those whose acquaintance he made were General Ercole Roncaglia, commander of XIV Corps and governor of Montenegro, and Roncaglia's chief of staff, Colonel Gaetano Giannuzzi. Waldheim would make small talk with them about his Pusteria days, always being careful to say nice things about General Esposito. He would also recall the friendly Montenegran family he had stayed with in Pljevlje.

The chief of the liaison staff, Waldheim's boss, was Colonel Joachim Macholz, a forty-four-year-old career officer, who had been in uniform since 1917.[3] The son of a Silesian landowner who was himself a reserve officer, Macholz was a self-confident man whose military bearing and sure sense of command reflected his origins. Wounded in 1918, he had served after the First World War in a *Freikorps* unit defending the East Prussian frontier against the Poles. His first love was the cavalry, especially cavalry reconnaissance. Bored with his assignment to a unit defending the Norwegian coast, Macholz managed to obtain a transfer to Reconnaissance Unit 26, which saw action in the Western *Blitzkrieg* as well as in Russia.

The coincidences did not escape Waldheim. Both he and his superior loved the cavalry, had served in reconnaissance units, and had been wounded at the front. Not surprisingly, Macholz took a liking to his young interpreter. Not only was Waldheim pleasant and useful without being intrusive, but he was a real soldier.

The main German concern in the Balkans at the time was what the high command in Arsakli regarded as the war-weariness, corruption, and unwillingness to fight of its Italian allies. In a major antipartisan offensive (known as Operation White) in Bosnia the previous winter, Axis troops had destroyed more than eleven thousand of Tito's partisans. To the Germans' fury, however, the survivors, carrying their sick and wounded, managed to escape across the Neretva River to northern Montenegro, where Tito was now regrouping his forces.

As the Germans saw it, Italian incompetence and disloyalty were to blame for the partisans' escape. A series of conferences held to discuss the situation—often filled with bitter recriminations—kept Macholz and Waldheim busy that March and April.

What particularly irked the Germans was the fact that in the aftermath of Kozara, the partisans had been able to transfer their main base of operations to the Italian-occupied zones in southern and southeastern Croatia. Instead of doing anything about it, the Italians—who were far more interested in annexing large parts, if not all, of Dalmatia, Herzegovina, and Montenegro—had concentrated on suppressing the Croatian police and military forces. When the Germans protested, the Italians explained that "the Croatians are Communists!"[4] The response was a confusing one, since everyone knew that Ante Pavelić's Ustasha regime, which governed the nominally Independent State of Croatia, was rabidly Fascist.

Even worse from the German perspective, the Italians were protecting the Jews in their territories, some of whom had fled there from elsewhere in Croatia. At the same time, they allowed the local Chetnik groups—bands of Serb former officers, bandits, monarchists, and adventurers, who hated the Croatians and Tito's Communist partisans with equal fervor—to kill and plunder the Croatian population. In the quagmire of Balkan politics, the brutality of the Chetniks increased support for Tito's partisans, who offered the local people something the Axis occupiers could not or would not provide—protection. As a result, German officials had been warning for almost a year that "in some areas the Italians have caused the growth rather than the collapse of the partisan movement."[5]

By the spring of 1943, the Germans were fed up with the Italians and tired of their excuses. It wasn't that the Italians lacked mobility. Or that they were holding back their forces in order to defend the coasts. No, the truth was that while the Germans wanted to pursue the partisans, all Mussolini's commanders cared about was annexing and looting as much of Croatia as they could, saving their necks, and going home alive and wealthy.

The Germans refused to entertain the notion that their own behavior might have contributed to the growth of the Communist partisan movement. If Wehrmacht soldiers were brutal to civilians, it was no more than the civilians deserved. The issue simply wasn't worth discussing. (Nor, evidently, were complaints worth investigating. When reports reached General Bader's staff about a German company commander who had ordered the mass shooting of women and children, proceedings against the officer were quashed.)[6]

The Germans were slightly more willing to point a finger at Pavelić's Ustasha forces. Indeed, early in the autumn of 1942, after Ustasha troops murdered 270 Serb noncombatants in reprisal for a partisan attack, the German envoy in the Croatian capital of Zagreb, Siegfried Kasche, complained that something had to be done about Ustasha "excesses."[7]

In the winter of 1942–43, General Alexander Löhr, the commander in chief of Army Group E, came up with what he felt was the solution. As Löhr saw it, Pavelić's Ustasha regime had been a total failure. Its brutality and penchant for atrocities had so far led to the murder of no less than 400,000 Serbs—as a result of which the partisans now controlled large parts of Croatia. Löhr's answer: Close down the German legation in Zagreb and replace Pavelić and his cronies with a German military government. The suggestion was rejected by Hitler.[8]

In May 1943, Macholz and Waldheim learned that yet another major Axis offensive against the partisans was in the works. Called Operation Black (in contrast to the previous winter's Operation White), the campaign was designed to forestall what the German command regarded as a frightening prospect. If the Allies landed in western Albania, Dalmatia, or Greece, it was feared, they would probably have no trouble pushing aside the inept Italians and linking up with the partisans—thereby cutting off the southern commands of Army Group E. Through Operation Black, the Germans hoped to eliminate this possibility by destroying the main body of partisan fighters, currently ensconced in Herzegovina and Montenegro. The plan was to rout the partisans, then annihilate them as they fled south toward Albania.

Operation Black was also meant to safeguard German strategic interests in Herzegovina. The Germans were particularly concerned about the partisan threat to the bauxite mines near Mostar, bauxite being vital to the German war machine. Though the Germans had controlled the mines since the middle of March, they wouldn't feel secure until they also controlled Mostar, its airport, and the adjacent rail links to Sarajevo and Dubrovnik.[9]

In contrast to the Kozara operation, the Germans were eager to enlist Italian help in Operation Black. And the Italians were happy to give it—at least in Montenegro. There, with General Roncaglia's XIV Corps dominating the scene, the Italian command was confident of its ability to maintain control. Herzegovina was a different story. There was a lot at stake here—in addition to rich mines, Herzegovina possessed access to the "Italian" Adriatic through the port of Dubrovnik—and the Italians worried that once they helped the Germans push the partisans out of the region, the Germans might turn around and push *them* out.[10]

On paper, the Axis would be putting more than 120,000 troops into the field in Operation Black—67,000 Germans, 43,000 Italians, and 11,000 Croatians. In addition, the Germans enjoyed complete control of the air and would be deploying great fleets of motorized transport.

To repulse what they called "the fifth enemy offensive," the partisans had a mere 16,000 fighters. They also had some 3,400 sick and wounded to care for. They had virtually no motorized transport, and though there was still snow in the mountains in May, they lacked warm clothing.[11]

Still, the partisans had one big advantage. They were fighting for their homeland, in their homeland. In a wild country filled with rivers and streams that changed course unpredictably, and mountains that suddenly loomed up when one rounded a bend in the road, their knowledge of the terrain was unbeatable. They also knew how to take advantage of the bad weather—it rained constantly—to close in on the enemy without warning. Above all, they knew what fate awaited them if they surrendered or were captured. The memories of what Tito called "heroic Kozara" were still painfully fresh.[12]

The burden of the offensive would be carried by two crack German units—the 1st Mountain Division, which had earned its stripes on the Russian front, and the 7th S.S. Volunteer Mountain Division (known as the Prinz Eugen, after the Italian prince from Savoy who defended the Habsburgs from the Turks in the early eighteenth century). The Prinz Eugen, with a fighting strength at the time of about fourteen thousand men, was made up mainly of *Volksdeutsche,* ethnic Germans from Balkan lands. It was commanded by *Obergruppenführer und General der Waffen S.S.* Artur Phleps, an ethnic German from Rumania who had served the old Austrian empire in the First World War.[13]

The German battle plan was simple. The 1st Mountain Division would march west from Mitrovica early in May and link up with the Prinz Eugen, moving southeast from Banja Luka. The partisans would be crushed between them before they could find refuge in Albania.

That's not how things worked out. As soon as the German forces began to move into Italian-held territory in Herzegovina, they ran into trouble. In addition to the Italian reluctance to allow the Germans too much running room in Herzegovina, there was something in particular about General Phleps and his troops that seemed to rub the Italians the wrong way. Not only did they resent the *Obergruppenführer's* gruff manner; they also regarded the name of his division as an insult. Prinz Eugen was an Italian prince; how dare the Germans appropriate his name! As one of the Italian propaganda brochures put it: "The ashes of [Prinz Eugen] rest today in the Cathedral of St. Stephan's in Vienna. His heart, however, rests in Piedmont."[14]

The Italians' hostile attitude made itself felt in ways large and small. On one occasion, Phleps came to a town in Herzegovina to pay his respects to the local Italian general and negotiate passage for his troops. To his fury, the Italian sentries at the edge of town would not let him pass. It wasn't until he threatened them with execution that he was allowed through. Phleps was also outraged by the armed Chetniks he saw moving around freely through the Italian-occupied territory. The Chetniks, after all, occasionally fought alongside the partisans against the Germans, and Hitler had repeatedly warned Mussolini against helping them. Even more serious, it wasn't until May 20 that the Italians consented to let the Germans use the airfield near Mostar.

Meanwhile, the fighting was raging hot and heavy in northern Montenegro. The partisans, enduring terrible hardships, fell back to the highest mountain peaks. The Prinz Eugen and the 1st Mountain Division followed. There were heavy losses on both sides as the partisans battled desperately to avoid being encircled.

With the outcome of the entire campaign at stake, and the frustrating experience in Herzegovina still unresolved, General Phleps decided he could not afford the risk of any new Italian insolence. He thus demanded that the Germans be given unambiguous control of what was nominally a joint operation in Montenegro.

Citing orders from Rome, General Roncaglia refused.[15]

At his wits' end, Phleps appealed to General Rudolf Lüters, who had replaced General Bader as commander of all German troops in Croatia.

On Saturday, May 22, 1943, Lüters flew to Podgorica to sort things out. Waiting for him at the airport under gray and rainy skies was the choleric Phleps, clutching his dispatch case as if it were a weapon. Alongside him was General Roncaglia, the orders from Rome making him commander of the joint operation tucked securely in his pocket. A few steps behind them were liaison chief Macholz and his interpreter, Lieutenant Waldheim.

After what seemed like an interminable wait, Lüters's plane descended out of the overcast and landed. An honor guard saluted smartly as the general stepped out onto the tarmac.

After some preliminary pleasantries, Phleps made his case. Here he was fighting the toughest campaign of his life, and he could not get the cooperation of his own ally. He felt that the Italians had sabotaged him in Herzegovina. Was he now to be under their command in Montenegro, at the peak of the great battle? Lüters replied that he could not make a decision without orders from Army Group E in Arsakli. And he had no such orders. With Waldheim translating, Roncaglia declared this to be irrelevant. After all, *he* had orders, from the *Comando Supremo* in Rome. Lüters shook his head. Roncaglia could not have overall control of the joint force. Lüters did not state the obvious—namely, that since the Germans were doing all the fighting, they saw absolutely no reason to hand over command to the untested Roncaglia. Phleps was not nearly so tactful. He was more than willing to air his opinion of these lazy "macaronis," these so-called allies. His voice grew harsher, his guttural tones became threatening.

The meeting was on the verge of turning into a brawl. Yet somehow tempers stayed calm enough for Lüters to be able to paper over the disagreement between Phleps and Roncaglia by telling them that there was nothing he could do until he checked with his superiors in Arsakli. In the meantime, Phleps should continue to run his division, while Roncaglia could retain his prerogatives. It was a classic case of settling a sticky question by deciding not to decide. Phleps was not exactly ecstatic, but he accepted the nondecision. For his part, Roncaglia graciously assured Lüters of his cooperation. As a result, Phleps was able to proceed without any further interference from Roncaglia.

What had kept the feuding generals from coming to blows?

A comparison of German and Italian accounts of the meeting in Podgorica reveals an interesting inconsistency. The main German account, written by a confidant of Phleps, describes an angry, explosive confrontation. The Italian documents, on the other hand, make it seem as if the parties indulged in nothing more than that classic of diplomacy, a frank but polite exchange of views.[16]

The discrepancy may be explained by the fact that Waldheim was interpreting for both sides. Did he deliberately tone down the abuse Phleps heaped on the Italians? After all, the history of diplomacy is filled with examples of stormy international conferences that were salvaged by clever translators who kept relations from breaking down by intentionally mistranslating vitriolic language.

When I asked Waldheim about this in 1987, he confirmed that he had done just that. "Phleps was very angry with me," he said, smiling proudly. "At one point, he turned to me angrily and said, 'Listen, Waldheim, I know some Italian, and you are not translating what I am telling this so-and-so!'"

At the age of twenty-four, in the Montenegran town of Podgorica, Kurt Waldheim had achieved his first diplomatic triumph.

CHAPTER SIX

A Cog in the Machine

The final phase of Operation Black took place over the next three weeks. Casualties on both sides were heavy—though as before, the partisans suffered the most. General Löhr later estimated that the Wehrmacht lost over three thousand men in the campaign. The partisans lost four times that many—more than twelve thousand men and women—a third of their total troop strength throughout the country. Tito himself was wounded in the fighting, narrowly escaping capture when German paratroopers descended upon his headquarters near Drvar.

As a result of Operation Black, the Germans began to realize their goal of supplanting the Italians in Herzegovina. German newsreel audiences saw pictures of General Phleps entering Mostar and parading on horseback past Croatian youths.[1]

Still, the German victory was hardly complete. The 1st Mountain Division reported that despite partisan losses, "the enemy has slipped further away." The survivors regrouped, and Tito's forces continued to grow. Eventually, with British and Soviet help, they would drive the Germans out of Yugoslavia entirely.

With Operation Black at an end, Waldheim was now available for a new assignment. Colonel Macholz, greatly impressed by Waldheim's performance, had sent a glowing evaluation of him to his superiors at Army Group E. It was thus decided that the young but increasingly experienced and well-regarded lieutenant would continue to work with the Italians, but at an even higher level and with more responsibility. In the process, Waldheim would also get to realize a childhood dream of his and finally see the Acropolis in Athens.

In Salonika, the high command of Army Group E was growing more and more worried about the possibility of an Allied invasion of Greece. Though partisan activity was intensifying, the Italians, whose Eleventh Army had 188,000 men in Greece, once again seemed to be doing little or nothing about it. As a result, at the beginning of July 1943, the German command decided to send a new, high-level military liaison delegation to the commander of the Eleventh Army, General Carlo Vecchiarelli, at his headquarters in Athens.

The German delegation was headed by newly promoted Major General Heinz von Gyldenfeldt, a highly intelligent, sophisticated officer with strong nerves. Only forty-four, Gyldenfeldt had been picked by the high command to head the German staff in Athens because of his ability to remain calm in a crisis.

Due to manpower shortages, General Gyldenfeldt's entire team consisted of only nine or ten officers, plus several noncoms and translators. Gyldenfeldt's second in command, his chief of operations, was Colonel Bruno Willers, a much-decorated combat veteran who combined a soldier's bravery with an intellectual's interest in military history and the economic aspects of warfare. Despite the burden of a slight stammer, Willers had a strong talent for leadership as well as a reputation for tact and consideration. He drew as his number two a highly recommended young Austrian staff officer fresh from service in Yugoslavia, Lieutenant Kurt Waldheim.[2]

After having served in the cavalry, in the quartermaster's department, and as an interpreter, Waldheim thus assumed yet another role—that of deputy operations officer. He was earning a reputation as a versatile officer who could be trusted with important jobs, especially those in which discretion was required.

Waldheim flew to Athens with Gyldenfeldt and Willers on July 19, 1943. After the primitive conditions he had had to put up with in Tirana and Podgorica, the staff quarters in the Greek capital proved a pleasant surprise. The hospitable Italians had billeted the Germans at the luxurious Hotel Grande Bretagne.

Life was once again pleasant. Though the sweltering July heat bothered him, Waldheim knew it was preferable to the cold winds of the Russian front. The Italians provided wonderful food, and Waldheim came to love the lavish dinners of linguini and spaghetti, washed down with copious quantities of bardolino, hosted nightly by General Vecchiarelli and his chief of staff, General Gandini. Waldheim also found time to study the Hellenic antiquities in the museums of Athens and to take snapshots of the Acropolis with his Leica. He shared his knowledge of Greek history and culture with his less educated superiors, but never in a condescending way. As before, the Italians quickly came to like and trust the smiling young Austrian lieutenant.

Though General Gyldenfeldt liked and respected General Vecchiarelli, he despised the bulk of Vecchiarelli's Eleventh Army.[3] Gyldenfeldt was particularly offended by the prevalence of thievery and black marketeering in the Italian ranks. Not only did Italian soldiers openly hawk army-issue fountain pens for twenty or thirty drachmas each, but Italian weapons often wound up in the hands of ELAS or EDES, the two main Greek partisan groups. So did looted medical supplies. (With one third of the local population suffering from tuberculosis, medicines were as valuable as gold, and Italian soldiers bartered them for precious metals or British pounds.) To add insult to injury, Italian officers ignored their German superiors on the streets of Athens, not even bothering to salute. In fact, the poor discipline and bad behavior of the Italian troops was quite understandable. Italian army rations were so bad that many soldiers were driven to sell army equipment in order to buy food. What's more, the enormous poverty in Athens, exacerbated by runaway inflation, guaranteed the existence of a thriving illegal economy and its concomitant temptations.[4]

Occupied by the vast amount of paperwork that the Italians continued to churn out, Waldheim did not see much of this side of life in Athens. As Colonel Willers's top aide, he was not only in charge of maintaining the staff war diary; he also had to read and initial the large number of reports that came in from Army Group E headquarters in Arsakli as well as from German units in the field, and to make sure they were forwarded to the appropriate German and Italian commands. In addition, Waldheim continued to work as an interpreter. (He was considered the best-qualified Italian translator the Germans had in Athens.)

From his position astride the information flow, Waldheim was well aware that the Italian war effort was flagging. Still, he didn't expect the news that came in on his radio the morning of Monday, July 26, 1943, the beginning of his second week in Athens. To his surprise, Waldheim learned that General Löhr was on his way to Athens for an emergency meeting with General Gyldenfeldt and General Vecchiarelli.

What was surprising was the reason for Löhr's visit. The Fascist Grand Council, Mussolini's own creation, had overthrown the Duce. King Victor Emmanuel III ordered the arrest of Mussolini. Fearing Ger-

man intervention, the new Italian government under Marshal Pietro
Badoglio quickly reassured Hitler that Italy intended to stay in the war.
The Führer, however, didn't trust Badoglio. He was sending General Löhr
to Athens to probe the attitude of the Italians there.[5]

Löhr quickly sized up the situation. If the Italians laid down their
arms, vast stretches of Greece's western coastline would be open to Allied
invasion. What's more, the Greek partisans would certainly become much
more aggressive. Even worse, the Italians, who outnumbered the Germans
in the Athens area by ten to one, might even turn on their old allies.

Löhr's gloomy assessment confirmed Hitler's view of the situation.
The Führer changed the German command structure in the Balkans.
Concerned about the Italians, and frustrated by the failure of the Axis
forces in Operation Black, Hitler was forced to the conclusion that the
problems in Yugoslavia and Greece were simply too big for any one
general. From here on out, he decided, Löhr and his Army Group E would
be responsible only for the Greek mainland, the Greek islands, and parts
of southern Albania. Yugoslavia would become the province (both literally
and figuratively) of a newly created Army Group F, headquartered in
Belgrade and led by the new supreme commander in the Balkans, Field
Marshal Maximilian Freiherr von Weichs. The creation of Army Group
F represented Hitler's tacit admission that Tito's forces required full-time
attention—indeed, that the "bandit" partisans were becoming a bona fide
army capable of tying down twenty German divisions.

One result of the realignment was that Vecchiarelli and his Eleventh
Army were now subordinate to Löhr. Not surprisingly, the Italians greeted
this news with something less than enthusiasm. Still, it could have been
worse. A rumor had gone through the Italian ranks that the Germans were
setting up a new army group, under Field Marshal Erwin Rommel. The
Italians detested the "Desert Fox," as Rommel was known, for the con-
temptuous way he had treated them in Africa. Better Löhr, many Italians
felt, than Rommel.

Counting the Second Army in Yugoslavia, the Italians had a total of
almost 700,000 troops in the Balkans. With Mussolini now gone, partisans throughout the region looked forward to—and the Germans began
to worry about—the prospect of vast amounts of Italian arms falling into
rebel hands. In order to prevent this, German purchasing agents were
authorized to buy as many Italian weapons as they could while relations
between the Axis partners remained (officially, at least) unchanged.[6]

Reflecting German worries about the reliability of their Italian allies,
early in August word came across Waldheim's desk of a top-secret contin-

gency plan called Case Axis. It described how the Germans would seize and disarm Italian forces in the event of an Italian surrender or other form of treachery.[7]

A strange, strained atmosphere settled over the customary evening meals attended by Gyldenfeldt's and Vecchiarelli's staffs at the Hotel Grande Bretagne. Though the delicious dinners continued, complete with numerous toasts to German-Italian solidarity, the pleasantries were subverted by a growing air of mistrust. Publicly, everyone pretended to believe Marshal Badoglio's assurances of Italy's undying loyalty to its beloved German ally. Privately, the German staff was uneasy about the messages Waldheim was receiving. For his part, General Vecchiarelli had decided to obey whatever orders he received from Rome.

Toward the end of August, Waldheim was instructed to inform all German units that were technically subordinate to Vecchiarelli's Eleventh Army to stop sending reports to their nominal Italian commanders. Henceforth, all reports would go directly to Gyldenfeldt, who would decide what Vecchiarelli would hear from "his" German units.[8]

Not surprisingly, as German-Italian relations deteriorated, the partisans grew bolder. The Germans responded with brute force, rounding up and shooting an increasing number of civilian hostages in reprisal for the growing number of partisan attacks. The Germans were particularly concerned that the combination of partisan aggressiveness and Italian weakness (or treachery) might tempt the Allies into invading Greece. Allied bases now ringed much of the Mediterranean (the result of Italian ineptitude, the Germans maintained). To secure the vulnerable Ionnina area in northwest Greece against an Allied landing, the 1st Mountain Division, fresh from Operation Black, had been brought down from Yugoslavia.[9]

Over the next few weeks, as the crisis intensified, Waldheim would witness a remarkable struggle over counterinsurgency tactics between the commander of the 1st Mountain Division and his Italian superiors. Waldheim would describe this struggle in great detail—increasingly aware, as he was doing so, that what he was recording was the collapse of the Axis alliance.

Shortly after the 1st Mountain Division arrived in Greece, its commander, Lieutenant General Walter von Stettner, received a visit from Waldheim's boss, Colonel Willers. Von Stettner was a battle-tested officer who understood his mission to be the ruthless suppression of partisans. Willers, however, brought confusing news. The 1st Mountain Division, he told von Stettner, was now under the command of General Vecchiarelli's

Eleventh Army. To von Stettner, who knew something of the Italian policy (or lack of it) toward the partisans, that made no sense. General Vecchiarelli had just issued an order forbidding massive reprisals and deportations. How could the 1st Mountain Division be expected to destroy the partisans, von Stettner wanted to know, if he had to answer to such a man?

Von Stettner was doubly frustrated, because he also knew that new, no-nonsense German orders concerning counterinsurgency were about to be issued by Berlin. These orders were based on the self-evident if brutal premise that the one sure way to destroy the partisan movement in a particular area was to round up and deport the area's entire male population.

Von Stettner's frustration increased on August 5, when Colonel Willers once again came to see him. This time Willers brought news of Case Axis, the contingency plan for disarming the Italian armies in the event that Rome capitulated to the Allies. Earlier that same day, General Vecchiarelli had repeated his orders, first issued on July 19, limiting the action combat units could take against civilians suspected of supporting the partisans. The situation was ironic, to say the least. On the one hand, von Stettner's superiors were telling him to go against his better judgment and obey the orders of an Italian general even if they hampered his efforts to destroy the partisans. On the other, he was being told to be ready to move against that very same Italian general.

The next day, the 1st Mountain Division engaged in heavy combat against partisan units near the Albanian border. For von Stettner, that was the last straw. Vecchiarelli's strictures notwithstanding, he ordered his men to seize every male between the ages of sixteen and sixty who resided in or near all partisan-infested areas. Those who had actually engaged in partisan activity, or who had helped the partisans, or who were suspected of doing either, were to be shot. All the rest were to be deported to German labor camps.

When word of this reached Vecchiarelli in Athens, the Italian general demanded that von Stettner rescind his order. To placate the German, Vecchiarelli's chief of staff, General Gandini, added that the Italian 26th Army Corps would assist the 1st Mountain Division in vigorously combating the partisans in certain key areas. Von Stettner was not placated.

Indeed, his position hardened two days later, on August 7, when he learned the specifics of Hitler's new policy on counterinsurgency. "According to the new Führer Order," headquarters informed him, "bandits seized in battle are to be shot. All other bandit suspects, etc., are to be seized and deported for labor purposes to Germany." Taking the new policy to heart, von Stettner once again ordered mass arrests.[10]

Once again, Vecchiarelli ordered von Stettner's instructions rescinded.

This time, however, Vecchiarelli gave a little ground. He authorized the shooting of partisan prisoners and said that in certain areas suspected partisans could be deported. But there was to be no mass expulsion of the entire male population. In vain, von Stettner pointed out that Vecchiarelli's attitude made hash of his efforts. When von Stettner's units came to a village, the partisans would flee to the mountains. Unless he could deport entire populations, they would simply return after the Germans moved on.

On August 10, von Stettner finally got what he wanted. Vecchiarelli's German superior, General Löhr, issued orders concerning the partisans that reflected Hitler's new policy. From now on, division and regimental commanders had the authority to order the seizure of an area's entire male population (aged fifteen to sixty) if "it does not have to be shot or hanged on account of participation in [battle] or support of the bandits; insofar as it is capable of work, it is to be brought to prisoner collection centers for deportation to the Reich."[11]

Von Stettner was back in business. Or at least he thought he was.

In fact, General Vecchiarelli continued to sabotage von Stettner's plans. Though he knew nothing of Case Axis, he was nonetheless suspicious of the Germans' intentions, and he decided it might be a good idea to disperse their troops among his numerically superior forces. Accordingly, he ordered that the German forces under his control be scattered for small-scale search-and-destroy operations. The effect of the order was to render massive deportations impossible.

The struggle between von Stettner and Vecchiarelli continued. When von Stettner's troops found munitions in the village of Kuklesi on August 12, they shot ten civilian suspects in reprisal and burned the village down. Vecchiarelli responded by instructing his chief of staff to forward another copy of his July 19 reprisal order to the 1st Mountain Division. When units of the German 68th Army Corps seized six Greek civilians and announced they would be killed in reprisal for partisan attacks carried out in conjunction with an Allied air drop, the Italians tried in vain to free the hostages.[12]

The internecine fighting might have gone on for the rest of the war if Field Marshal von Weichs, the newly appointed supreme commander in the Balkans, hadn't finally stepped in. On August 20, Waldheim received, recorded, and forwarded a new order from von Weichs authorizing the mass deportation of male populations. Vecchiarelli had been finally overruled.

From his vantage point at the Hotel Grande Bretagne in Athens, Lieutenant Waldheim recorded every twist and turn of von Stettner's struggle with Vecchiarelli in the staff war diary. In effect, he was charting the collapse of an alliance. The Germans had trusted Vecchiarelli when he was taking orders from Mussolini's *Comando Supremo.* Now they were no longer so sure about him.

In the midst of all this, a paper crossed Waldheim's desk concerning problems the 1st Mountain Division was having with the Jews of the town of Ionnina. Waldheim processed it with his usual efficiency. Given his abilities and experience, that was hardly surprising. In retrospect, however, the incident would come to take on a special significance, for this particular bit of paperwork represented the first recorded link to something that, forty years later, Kurt Waldheim would deny with particular vehemence—his involvement with the bureaucratic machinery of the Holocaust.

The agony of the Greek Jews began soon after the Germans invaded Greece, in April 1941. Of particular interest to the occupying forces was the Jewish community of the port of Salonika, next door to which the Twelfth Army (the future Army Group E) later established its headquarters. Numbering more than fifty thousand—nearly a third of the city's total population—the Jews of Salonika included descendants of great Sephardic families, who reputedly possessed great wealth. The more prosperous among them fled to Italian-occupied areas ahead of the Germans. The majority who stayed behind soon began to suffer from disease and hunger—as well as from the indignity of having their synagogues and homes looted of priceless books, scrolls, and other religious treasures by Nazi authorities who hoped to use them in anti-Jewish propaganda.

By the summer of 1942, the Jewish population of Salonika had declined to 45,000.

Still, the Germans felt uneasy. They didn't like having so many Jews living so close to Twelfth Army headquarters (Arsakli was just three miles away), and in a strategically important port, to boot. Since S.S. security police were not yet available to organize roundups and deportations, the army decided to move on its own. On the morning of Saturday, July 11, 1942, Lieutenant General Curt von Krenzki, commander of the Salonika/ Aegean region and the man in charge of both the local Wehrmacht security forces and the Greek police, ordered all male Jews aged eighteen to forty-eight to assemble in the city's Liberty Square to be registered for compulsory labor. Between six thousand and nine thousand men showed up.

For the next several hours, the Jews were made to stand at attention in the square under the hot sun. Those who fainted were doused with water and beaten. Anyone who moved, or tried to put on a hat or light a cigarette, was forced to perform difficult and unnatural contortions, a sort of sadistic calisthenics. All the while, German officers and enlisted men stood around the edges of the square, one witness later recalled, "laughing and clapping hands." Many took snapshots so that their comrades on duty elsewhere could enjoy the scene. Some ailing Jews died of their mistreatment in the square. Many of the survivors were shipped off to work in malarial swamps, where a large number soon died of disease.

The public humiliation of Salonika's Jews was a sensation, played up by the German press. The July 26, 1942, issue of *Donauzeitung*, a prominent German newspaper published in Croatia, carried a photograph of the suffering men in Liberty Square, with the caption: "Work Instead of Thievery."

People were still talking about it six weeks later, when Lieutenant Kurt Waldheim, fresh from his service at Kozara, came to Salonika on his way to Twelfth Army headquarters in Arsakli for a new duty assignment.[13]

The following February, while Waldheim was home on study leave, units of the notorious S.D. security police finally arrived in Salonika. The city's Jews, now forced to wear yellow stars of David and collected in ghettos that included the Baron de Hirsch concentration camp, could at last be deported.

The trains began rolling the next month. By May 1943, most of the Jewish population of Salonika had been shipped off to the death camp at Auschwitz. The final trainload of Jews left Salonika in August, just a few weeks after Waldheim came through town on his way to Athens with General Gyldenfeldt.[14]

On August 14, 1943, General von Stettner's 1st Mountain Division telexed a report to Gyldenfeldt's headquarters at the Hotel Grande Bretagne. It described the completion of a so-called cleansing operation in the Paramythia/Parga region. Eighty partisans were killed, another 160 suspects were under arrest. The Germans lost one man. As usual, Lieutenant Waldheim summarized the report in the staff war diary and appended a copy of the telex. He also forwarded copies of the report to General Vecchiarelli's Eleventh Army and to Army Group E in Arsakli.

The next day, August 15, Waldheim received a long radio message from the 1st Mountain Division, containing an expanded, more polished version of the August 14 report. Among other things, it included the following intelligence assessment: "Ionnina and the emerging Jewish committee there to be seen as preparatory center for a revolutionary movement." (A report sent to Waldheim's intelligence counterpart around the same time described the activities of this "Jewish committee" in more detail, reporting that the Jews of Ionnina were supposedly gathering American dollars dropped from Allied planes and converting them into drachmas, which were used to sustain the partisans.)

With characteristic efficiency, Waldheim meticulously transcribed the August 15 radio message, signed the copies, put one in his files, and sent another to the operations department of Army Group E.[15]

Then he did something odd. When he wrote his summary of the message for the staff war diary, he did not include a single word about the Jews and their alleged "revolutionary" activity in Ionnina. Nor did he attach a copy of the full message to the diary.

Why did the usually meticulous Waldheim fail to mention the Jewish threat in the diary? And why did he not append a copy of the full message on which his summary was based? One thing is certain: As a staff officer, Lieutenant Waldheim always played by the rules. In this case, the rules were contained in a document attached to the war diary—the Supreme Command of the Army's "Instructions for Maintaining War Diaries and Activity Reports."[16] According to these instructions, the officer responsible for keeping the war diary was to include summaries of all significant information that crossed his desk. There was one important exception to this routine. The instructions did permit—indeed, they required—the responsible officer to withhold significant information from the war diary if the information concerned an operation that was classified as secret.

By any standard, a report of Jewish "revolutionary" activity certainly constituted significant information—and Waldheim's judgment in such matters was faultless. Assuming, therefore, that Waldheim did not for some unknown reason suddenly decide to depart from his normally impeccable bureaucratic standards and violate diary policy, the inescapable conclusion is that he suppressed any mention of the information about the Jews (as well as a copy of the full message containing the information) because he knew it to be connected to a secret operation.

The secret operation concerning the Jews was, of course, Hitler's Final Solution—the Holocaust. And, indeed, the only people to whom Waldheim disclosed the information he had received about the Jews of Ionnina was a group responsible for implementing this secret policy, the operations department of Army Group E. Seven months later, this same department instigated the deportation of almost two thousand Ionnina Jews.

It is possible, of course, that while Waldheim was aware of the existence of some sort of secret operation concerning the Jews—the knowledge of which led him to leave the Ionnina information out of the diary—he might have had no idea what the operation actually involved. After all, the bureaucracy of the Third Reich operated on a strict "need to know" basis. Hitler himself had spelled it out in an order issued on January 11, 1940:

> No one—no agency, no officer—is permitted to learn more about a matter that is to be kept secret than he absolutely needs to know for official purposes.

Waldheim himself has long maintained that this was in fact the case. "I did not know about these things," he insisted to reporters in March 1986. "They were not handled by the Army; those things, as far as I know, were handled by . . . the secret police and other organizations." He continued: "I swear to you that I did not have the slightest thing to do with the deportation of the Jews. I just learned about these things from recent newspaper reports. . . . I know it sounds improbable, but I did not know about it."[17]

His assertion of ignorance does sound improbable. Waldheim was aware of mass deportations of Jews as early as December 1942, after he returned home from Kozara to find that all his old Jewish acquaintances were now "in the east." What's more, it is hard to believe that when he came back to Arsakli in July 1943 (after his diplomatic triumph in Podgorica), this ambitious young staff officer, whose success had been based in large part on his ability to keep abreast of what was going on, could have failed to notice that most of the Jewish community of Salonika—nearly a third of the city's population—had been shipped off to Auschwitz.

But whether he knew about the Holocaust or not, one fact is indisputable: In properly transmitting information about the disposition of Jews in occupied territories—a task that required at least some understanding of the significance of that information—the deputy operations officer in General Gyldenfeldt's Athens headquarters played a small but necessary role in the smooth execution of Hitler's Final Solution. As that officer, Kurt Waldheim served as an efficient and effective cog in the machinery of genocide.

* * *

Early in September 1943, German intelligence learned that Italy was about to drop out of the war. At the Hotel Grande Bretagne in Athens, the atmosphere grew more strained, more depressing. General Gyldenfeldt knew that Germany's future in the Balkans would in large part be determined by General Vecchiarelli. It was clear that the Italians were readying their ships for the trip home—with their equipment. This was not what the Germans wanted, for who knew who would ultimately wind up with the Italians' weapons? But separating the Italians from their weaponry was not going to be easy. If Vecchiarelli decided to resist, his Eleventh Army could cripple—or even annihilate—the heavily outnumbered German forces in Greece, especially those in the Athens area.

On the evening of Wednesday, September 8, 1943, Gyldenfeldt received the long-expected news from Vecchiarelli. Italian radio had announced that Italy had surrendered to the Allies. Having received no orders from Rome, Vecchiarelli thought the announcement might be a trick, and he assured Gyldenfeldt that his troops would remain in place. They would neither fire on the Germans nor join up with the partisans. If attacked, however, they would fight back.

The Germans were hardly caught by surprise. Anticipating this eventuality, they had already formed a new command unit—Army Group South Greece—consisting of the 68th Army Corps, the 11th Luftwaffe Field Division, S.S. Police *Panzergrenadier* Regiment 2, and a number of other units, including General Gyldenfeldt's Athens staff.

Later that night, Gyldenfeldt issued Vecchiarelli an ultimatum: Either he and his troops ignore Rome's capitulation and continued to fight alongside the Germans, or they turn over all their weapons and equipment to the Wehrmacht. Case Axis was now in effect.

Gyldenfeldt spent an entire hour arguing with Vecchiarelli. Hoping to be able to take his army home to Italy, the Italian general proposed a compromise. The Eleventh Army would give up its heavy weapons but keep its small arms. In return, the Italians promised to help the Germans fight off any partisan attacks.

Confused and demoralized by the continued lack of instructions from Rome, Vecchiarelli was asking to be deceived.

Meanwhile, his troops celebrated in the streets, fraternizing with the local Greek population, convinced that their war was over, that they were all going home.

Early the next morning, September 9, German troops in Athens secured the docks and the train stations, and seized vast amounts of munitions and stores. With the Italians' supplies and ships in their hands, the Germans could now determine the fate of Vecchiarelli's troops. One thing was certain: The Eleventh Army wouldn't be leaving for home anytime soon.

By late morning, Waldheim was able to report that the disarming of Italian troops in the Athens area was proceeding on schedule.

Officially, General Vecchiarelli was informed that he and his men would stay where they were for another fourteen days or so. Then, bearing small arms for self-defense, the Eleventh Army would be allowed to march northwest toward Slovenia. When it reached the German-Italian border, it would give up its remaining weapons and proceed home.

In fact, Army Group South Greece had already ordered the 68th Army Corps to prepare to disarm the Italians completely and "deport them in the direction of Belgrade." The German command had concluded that repatriating the Eleventh Army was too impractical and too risky to be attempted.

Now on the staff of Army Group South Greece, Lieutenant Waldheim was busy translating the message traffic between Vecchiarelli and the German High Command. The task depressed him, for he was well aware of how his superiors were deceiving his former dinner companions and friends.

By September 12, the Eleventh Army had been stripped of its small arms. Still, the Italians were not yet aware that instead of marching to Slovenia (and from there to Italy), or sailing home across the Adriatic on their ships, they would be deported via Belgrade. Fearing resistance if the Italians knew the truth, the Germans had deliberately kept them in the dark.

The Germans had another reason for stalling. The collection camps for the huge Eleventh Army were not yet ready. Once the Italians were in the camps, it would be easy for the Germans to do whatever they wanted with them.

Not surprisingly, Hitler had been enraged by Italy's surrender. Indeed, his first response had been to order the execution of any Italian soldier who let his weapons fall into partisan hands. He followed that with a similar order regarding Italian soldiers found wearing civilian clothing. Then he changed his mind. Why not get some use out of the "traitors" as slave laborers? Indeed, why not conscript all Italian soldiers who laid down their arms? (Italians who wanted to continue fighting for Germany would be allowed to do so, but only in small, auxiliary units.)[18]

On September 13, while Waldheim was translating reassuring messages to Vecchiarelli, German collection camps around Athens began opening their doors. Each day after that, two or three trains rolled in from the Peloponnesus, jammed with several thousand Italian soldiers. Soon trains with similar cargoes began arriving from Attica and Boeotia. Confused, tired, and hot, lacking supplies, many were happy to arrive at the camps. At least there would be food and water, and above all, they would soon be heading home to their loved ones in Italia. They still did not know the truth. (Those who suspected what was in store were quickly whipped into line. General Roncaglia, for whom Waldheim had translated at Podgorica, was told that if he did not march his men northeast to Belgrade, he would be shot.)[19]

With the Italians now under control, the Wehrmacht no longer had any need for Waldheim's linguistic skills. He was given a new assignment, helping to coordinate the deportation of his former colleagues. His specific job was to keep track of the number of Italian internees and relay the information to Arsakli.

His job notwithstanding, Waldheim later insisted that he, too, was kept in the dark about the ultimate fate awaiting the Italians. The Germans always followed Hitler's "need to know" policy when it came to such matters, he told me, and he lacked a need to know. The mass deportation of the Italians was something he learned about only after the war, he said.

The records indicate otherwise. Waldheim's initials appear on a September 17, 1943, report by Army Group South Greece's operations department referring to upcoming deportations. The next day, September 18, five trains, with six thousand Italian troops on board, left Athens. On September 20, five more trains, containing almost eight thousand men, rolled north.

While the Italian Eleventh Army was being dismantled, Waldheim sat at his desk at the Hotel Grande Bretagne, swamped with paperwork. The wonderful pasta dinners were a thing of the past. He would never see Vecchiarelli and Gandini again.

Wednesday, September 22, was a particularly busy day for Waldheim. Figures concerning the Italians were pouring in from the collection camps and railroad depots. He had to keep meticulous records, and he did. Army Group Command and other agencies relied on his statistics to make a number of crucial decisions. They had to know how many trains were needed for the long trip north to Belgrade, and how many slave laborers were being retained in the Athens area.

Waldheim worked far into the night. At 9:30 P.M., his record shows, he telephoned Lieutenant Frey at Army Group operational headquarters to report the arrival in Athens of 23,749 Italian noncoms and enlisted men, with 2,400 more on the way. "Deportation of the Italians from Attica and Boeotia has been concluded," Waldheim told Frey, "with the exception of smaller demobilization units. For performance of labor tasks, 4,598 men remain in Athens."

As of September 30, 108,000 men had been deported. Another 50,000, still in the Greek islands, would soon follow, along with horses and more equipment. By early October, General Gyldenfeldt was able to report that "the Italian Eleventh Army has been liquidated."

Waldheim's job had been to deceive his former allies for as long as possible. More than forty years later, Colonel Willers still recalled him as "an officer who did his duty, a discreet, reticent man. He spoke very good Italian and he transmitted the ongoing discussions with the Italian army leadership."

Some Italians did not go quietly. Those who did not were dealt with harshly. When Italian troops on the island of Cephalonia resisted, the Germans killed 4,000 of them. In the end, about 20,000 Italian soldiers wound up going over to the partisans.

Right up until the end, the men of the Eleventh Army believed that the German trains were taking them home. Few questioned the German officers who told them, as their trains approached western Slovenia, that damage to the rails mandated a detour along the *Reichsbahn* tracks to Innsbruck. Most gladly accepted the assurance that from Innsbruck they would head south to Italy.

In fact, the trains headed east to Vienna. Along the way, German military police got on board and confiscated any remaining weapons. After the police departed, the doors were sealed from the outside. When they were finally opened again, it was to deposit the dazed former soldiers in a German forced-labor camp.

According to German records, by August 1944 there were 427,238 former Italian soldiers at work in such camps throughout the Reich.[20]

CHAPTER SEVEN

Dr. Waldheim

Lieutenant Waldheim was not sorry to leave Athens and fly back to Arsakli at the beginning of October 1943. Though his experience in the Greek capital had given him the kind of broad European perspective that was bound to be useful to a future diplomat, September had been a depressing month. What Waldheim really wanted to do was go home. He yearned to see Lilo and his family, and to get down to the business of writing his doctoral dissertation.

At Army Group E headquarters, he rejoined the Ic/AO intelligence staff, to which he had been briefly assigned the previous autumn. (Ic, to which Waldheim was attached, was military intelligence; AO was the Abwehr, or counterintelligence, section.) The staff consisted of eighteen officers, noncoms, and enlisted men, who worked out of a villa that had once been part of the American college in Arsakli. It was pleasant duty: The furnishings were comfortable, the atmosphere collegial.

The last time Waldheim had worked for Ic/AO he had merely been one of several translators. This time he was given a far more important job, that of intelligence analyst, responsible for evaluating, filing, and forwarding information received from units in the field. Though this largely consisted of routine, sometimes even boring, office work, Waldheim was not about to complain. It was better than the blood and mud of the Russian front, where Waldheim's old cavalry unit was suffering enormous casualties.

The man closest to Waldheim on a daily basis was Lieutenant Colonel

Herbert Warnstorff, the chief of the Ic branch of Ic/AO. Warnstorff was an elegant and attractive officer, only a few years older than Waldheim. He was also ambitious, and rumors circulated that he had powerful friends in the Army Personnel Office in Berlin. If so, they did him no good. Warnstorff had wanted to command a panzer unit and win a German Cross in Gold. When that failed to materialize, he lobbied for an appointment as head of Field Marshal von Weichs's Ic at Army Group F in Belgrade. That, too, fell through.[1]

Having little patience for paperwork, Warnstorff craved a suitable O3 (third *Ordonnanzoffizier*), a top aide who would prepare the morning and evening reports, handle incoming documents, and direct the preparation of maps and charts. A good O3 had to be bright and possessed of a very good memory; it would also help if he was a decorated battle veteran. Waldheim fit the bill perfectly.

In addition to maintaining the files and preparing situation reports about the various fronts, Waldheim was responsible for summarizing all incoming intelligence and passing his analyses along to Colonel Warnstorff, who then briefed the chief of the general staff of Army Group E, Major General August Winter, and participated in conferences with General Löhr, the commander in chief. As usual, Waldheim was diligent and precise, and Warnstorff quickly came to regard the twenty-four-year-old Austrian lieutenant as indispensable. Part analyst, part file clerk, able to combine the latest information with what he had learned in Athens, Waldheim was so good at his job that Warnstorff let him brief General Winter (and his eventual replacement, General Erich Schmidt-Richberg) directly. Occasionally, Warnstorff even sent Waldheim to report on Ic activities to General Löhr himself. Waldheim, Warnstorff recalled recently, did "perfectly correct work."

Waldheim enjoyed this assignment. Warnstorff may have missed the adrenaline-pumping excitement of battle, but Waldheim preferred to have ink on his fingers rather than dirt on his boots.

Among other things, Waldheim's responsibilities included the maintenance of files on prisoner interrogations. As part of its counterintelligence function, the Abwehr side of Ic/AO worked with groups like the Secret Field Police, interrogating—and often torturing—suspected partisans and captured Allied commandos in an effort to find out the enemy's strength and intentions. Waldheim's contact with this sort of activity consisted mainly of receiving reports from his Abwehr counterparts and passing along summaries to his superiors. He has long denied ever performing any interrogations himself, and since his unit's interrogation records did not survive the war, there is no evidence to contradict him.[2]

The reports that crossed Waldheim's desk told a grim story of a new kind of war, partisan war, a never-ending battle against ghosts who struck anywhere, then disappeared into nowhere. When Waldheim had worked for Ic/AO the year before, the Twelfth Army (as Army Group E was then called) reigned supreme in the Balkans, and its Italian allies held substantial territory. Now, in autumn 1943, the Italians were gone (except for a few volunteer auxiliary units), and the partisans were wreaking havoc from Serbia in the north to Epirus in the south.

Reflecting this, the German command structure in the Balkans had been drastically changed. Responsibility for Greece and Yugoslavia was now divided between Löhr's Army Group E in Arsakli and Field Marshal von Weichs's Belgrade-based Army Group F—a tacit recognition of the increasing effectiveness of the partisan forces. Officially, however, the war was still regarded by Berlin as a struggle against primeval hordes of subhuman criminals. Brutal police measures were thus considered both necessary and appropriate. To coordinate them, the Germans established (in August 1943) a third territorial command in the Balkans, one both subordinate and parallel to the two army groups. Known as the Military Commander Southeast, this group had charge of all the police units in the region, including the S.D. and the security police, as well as the Gestapo and various Abwehr troops. Though the group's prime responsibility was security in Serbia, its commander, General Hans Gustav Felber, also had nominal authority over the Athens-based military commander in Greece, Lieutenant General Wilhelm Speidel. (This control was limited by the fact that Löhr's Army Group E worked closely with Speidel's commands and controlled its major activities.)[3]

Through his position as an intelligence analyst, Waldheim quickly became an expert on the partisan war in Greece. As Warnstorff's O3, he was generally the first officer to see every report that came into Ic/AO. It was an excellent vantage point. News came in from far and wide—from the islands, the Peloponnesus, the mainland. The tall young man sat at his ornate wooden desk in Arsakli as if at the summit of a bureaucratic pyramid, part of a small group of officers who had a need to know almost everything about significant German and enemy military activity in the Balkans.[4]

Army Group E, after all, was still a huge and powerful entity. Despite its failure to eradicate the partisans, it continued to dominate the region. (Indeed, its strength may have been one factor in deterring the Allies from invading.) At any one time, General Löhr might have more than 300,000 men under his command; sometimes the figure ranged upwards of 450,000. Beyond that, Löhr's decisions, along with those of his superior,

Field Marshal von Weichs, affected the lives of perhaps thirty million Greeks, Albanians, Bulgarians, and Yugoslavs. General Löhr had to know what was going on, and Colonel Warnstorff was his main source of information. Unless Warnstorff knew, General Löhr could not know; unless Lieutenant Waldheim knew, Colonel Warnstorff could not know.[5]

From his vantage point atop the bureaucratic pyramid, Waldheim knew the war was going badly for the Reich. The Russians were on the march in the Ukraine; the Allies were beginning to dominate the skies over Germany; one no longer heard much about U-boat successes in the North Atlantic. Of particular concern to Army Group E, the Allies now had bomber bases near Bari in southeastern Italy, and there were rumors that Turkey might enter the war on the Allied side. The reports crossing Waldheim's desk indicated that the Greek economy was collapsing, while the Communists were growing stronger every day.

The immediate problem facing the German forces in Greece was the fact that while the local people respected German strength, most Greeks were pro-British. Waldheim's colleagues on the Abwehr side of Ic/AO tried to turn things around through the use of propaganda, organizing a campaign aimed at convincing the Greeks that the British had betrayed them, and that if the Germans lost, the Soviets would take over the Balkans. The campaign also sought to remind everyone that it was the Germans who were feeding the people and maintaining law and order, while it was the Communists who had poked the eyes out of an icon of the Holy Madonna.[6]

But after more than two years of hunger, brutality, and catastrophic inflation, the Greeks were not very receptive to the German message. Waldheim himself soon came to realize that in many ways the Germans were their own worst enemy in Greece, that their harsh way of dealing with even the slightest sign of resistance did more harm than good.

Like many of his colleagues on the Ic/AO staff, Waldheim spent most of his time in Arsakli. Occasionally, he would drive the three miles down to Salonika, usually to attend mass on Sunday. It was not an outing he relished. The once-thriving port was now a grim place, a haven for black marketeers and gamblers. (The Gestapo raked off part of the profits from the town's popular casino.) During the day, a few broken-down trams served the business district. Electricity was available for shops and banks only in the morning. At night, the city was blacked out.[7]

Morale among the German troops was not good. War weariness was spreading. Some soldiers said they no longer cared who won; they just wanted to make it home alive. Waldheim coped with the tedium and frustration by researching his dissertation, reading the works of Konstantin Frantz and taking notes. But he couldn't escape the feeling that he was losing time. His future was in Austria—in the form of Lilo and his doctorate. He hoped desperately to obtain leave in November.

Waldheim did not know it at the time, but his future was also being shaped in Moscow. At the end of October 1943, representatives of the three major Allied powers—Britain, the United States, and the Soviet Union—met in the Soviet capital to discuss how those who had fought for the Axis would be treated after the war. Their decision, announced in what became known as the Moscow Declaration, was uncompromising:

> German officers and men who have been responsible for, or have taken a consenting part in . . . atrocities, massacres, and persecutions will be sent back to the countries in which their abominable deeds were done in order that they may be judged and punished according to the laws of these liberated countries and of the free governments which will be erected therein.

The Moscow Declaration also included a second, equally momentous decision by the Big Three: The *Anschluss* was to be considered null and void. Once Hitler was defeated, Austria would be restored to its former position as a free and independent nation, regarded not as a collaborator in Nazi aggression but as its first victim. Still, that didn't mean Austria would not have to answer for her complicity with the Reich. As the Moscow Declaration put it:

> Austria is reminded . . . that she has a responsibility, which she cannot evade, for participation in the war at the side of Hitlerite Germany, and that in the final settlement account will inevitably be taken of her own contribution to her liberation.[8]

A few months later, the newly established United Nations War Crimes Commission held its first meeting in London. Among other things, the commission began collecting lists of war criminals and suspected war criminals, and assembling and evaluating evidence of war crimes provided by the various Allied governments. Also under its aegis, legal scholars began to study the literature on war crimes, punishment, and extradition. Ironically, among the key sources they consulted were the works of Waldheim's dissertation adviser, Professor Alfred Verdross.

*   *   *

In November 1943, despite the bleak military situation, Waldheim got his wish—he was granted home leave. He returned to a Baden completely transformed by the war. In the old days, Baden had been a fashionable spa, its ancient mineral baths and famous sanitariums and hotels attracting a wealthy[9]—and largely Jewish—clientele as well as the old Emperor Franz Joseph himself. Now the town was ringed with factories, airfields, and underground bomb shelters. The Jews were long since gone.

Though the blackouts made everyone nervous, the area had so far been spared the ravages of the "Allied terror bombers" that were reducing large sections of Hamburg and Berlin to rubble. Still, life was hard and getting harder. Eggs cost the 1988 U.S. equivalent of two dollars each, coffee was the equivalent of forty dollars a kilo, and a pair of men's shoes with artificial rubber soles went for the equivalent of one hundred and seventy-five dollars. The substitute beer was undrinkable. Physical deterioration was evident in everything from the shabby clothes people wore to the broken streetlamps.

Though word of the Moscow Declaration was making the rounds in some circles—primarily conservative, Catholic ones—it didn't have much impact. What mainly concerned most people was simple survival. Few had time to worry about an abstract concept like "Austria"; fewer still gave any thought to the fate of the Jews. "If we win the war, we are Germans," cynics declared. "If we lose, we are Austrians."

In any case, one had to be careful about what one said. The Gestapo and the S.D. listened to everything, and what they missed the ubiquitous Nazi informers picked up. Nonetheless, only about a quarter of the population retained any enthusiasm for the *Anschluss*. The rest told mordant jokes, like the one about how Hitler, Göring, and Goebbels were stopped at the Pearly Gates by St. Peter and told they could enter heaven only if they could keep their heads above water while walking through a swamp. The catch was, the more they had lied while on earth, the deeper into the muck they would sink. Göring stepped in first and immediately sank out of sight. Managing to resurface for a moment, he was shocked to see that Hitler was only submerged up to his neck. "But you have lied as much as me!" the Reich Marshal shrieked. "How come you are not sinking?"

Replied Hitler: "I am standing on Goebbels's head."[10]

Waldheim did not need to hear jokes like this to know that Germany was losing the war. He had attended too many briefings about the Allied advances in southern Italy and the western Ukraine to have much hope. He explained the strategic situation to his family and a few friends. One look at the disposition and balance of forces told the story.

* * *

One of the first people Waldheim sought out when he got home in November 1943 was Lilo. They had been discussing the possibility of marriage in their letters; now was the time to make a decision. Lilo had passed her law exams the previous summer, and Kurt was beginning to think about his—their—life after the war. There was no lack of compatibility or passion. Still, there was a problem: religion. Waldheim and his parents very much wanted a proper Catholic wedding. But Lilo had left the Church before she joined the Nazi party. Would she agree to rejoin the Church for the sake of the marriage?

She would, and she did. (At the same time, she managed to retain her party membership—though she cut her involvement back to a bare minimum.) The wedding would take place as soon as Kurt finished his dissertation and could obtain some extra leave.

To Lilo, Kurt's downbeat predictions about the future sounded more convincing than her family's tirades about inevitable victory. In any case, as the Nazis' fortunes ebbed, Waldheim's continued to advance. The Reich Justice Ministry approved his application for a promotion from junior barrister to assistant judge. The promotion itself seemed likely to come through sometime in the new year. In the meantime, he celebrated his twenty-fifth birthday, and he enlisted Lilo and Professor Verdross's aid in completing the paperwork required for a doctoral degree. He also got them to help him obtain such basic tools of the academic trade as a typewriter and bond paper.

Waldheim returned to his intelligence work with Ic/AO at Arsakli shortly after Christmas. When he had time, he made notes and drew up outlines for his dissertation. He hoped to have the paper finished by spring. The prospect of his doctorate was what kept him going—that and the thought of his impending marriage to Lilo. Those two reinforcing passions, his career and his beloved Fräulein Ritschel, gave Waldheim strength.

He also enjoyed an increasingly personal relationship with Army Group E's commander in chief, General Löhr. The son of an Austrian ship captain, Löhr had been a pioneer in military aviation; he may have been the only man in the army group who had bombed Serbia in both world wars—as an Austrian pilot in the first war and as commander of the Luftwaffe forces in post-*Anschluss* Austria in the second. Hitler greatly admired Löhr and in 1942 personally selected him to lead what was then called the Twelfth Army. Löhr obeyed the orders he received from Berlin—and though some of the commands he carried out would later be regarded as criminal (by the Nüremberg Tribunal as well as by the Yugoslav government), he did not strike the men who served under him as being either a fanatic Nazi or a bloodthirsty martinet. Indeed, he supposedly permitted anti-Nazi satires to circulate in Arsakli, and he is credited with making sure that the local Greek population was inoculated against smallpox and malaria (an action that may have been humanitarian but also protected his own men).[11]

Löhr enjoyed discussing intellectual matters with the young Austrian doctoral candidate on his intelligence staff, and he occasionally took Waldheim along on plane trips to the Greek islands. Waldheim was especially interested in Löhr's experiences as a diplomat (he had represented pre-*Anschluss* Austria at disarmament talks in Switzerland). He was also delighted to discover that the general was familiar with the writings of Professor Verdross and believed that Waldheim had done well to choose such an eminent man as his *Doktorvater,* or doctoral supervisor.

As the weeks went by, Waldheim steadily accumulated more responsibility—but without any increase in rank. Because he had no interest in pursuing a military career, Waldheim had made no long-term commitment to the Wehrmacht. Had he done so, he would have quickly been promoted to captain, and later perhaps to major. Still, on January 30, 1944, the eleventh anniversary of Hitler's seizure of power, Waldheim's appreciative superiors awarded him the War Merit Cross, Second Class, with Swords, a medal given to highly regarded staff officers.[12] As the U.S. War Department's 1943 *Handbook of German Military Forces* notes, "Swords are awarded for especially meritorious service in the zone of enemy action or for exceptional services in furthering the war effort."

By this time, Waldheim had his own service staff. Three noncommissioned officers assisted him in preparing the twice-daily reports he made to his immediate superior, Colonel Warnstorff, while another subordinate kept him abreast of reports from Ic people assigned to field units. Several others drew maps and charts, monitored and reported on foreign broadcasts, collated statements by prisoners of war and deserters, and provided relevant information from Abwehr and Secret Field Police reports. In addition, translators working in seven different languages allowed Waldheim to enjoy a steady flow of documents from both the Balkan and the eastern Mediterranean theaters of war.

As in any close-knit unit, Waldheim and his men did little favors for each other. One of Waldheim's cartographers, Sergeant Markus Hartner, had access to the radio transmitter. Knowing that Waldheim had a young lady at home, Hartner was happy to help his lieutenant send messages to her.

Waldheim and his fellow officers elsewhere at headquarters also helped each other out. When Lieutenant Brendl, who reported on the weather and enemy air activity, was away from his desk, Waldheim covered for him. Waldheim also pooled data with Lieutenant (later Captain) Frey, his counterpart at operations, whose Ia reports often contained the same data as Waldheim's Ic reports.[13]

Such cooperation was vital, for while the headquarters staff was small, the tasks facing it were immense. As elsewhere in Europe, the war was entering a critical phase in Greece at the beginning of 1944. According to a report prepared by Waldheim on January 18, 1944, Army Group E faced as many as 25,000 Greek partisans in the field, plus 4,000 Italians. There were two main partisan forces: the Communist-led ELAS *(Ellinokos Laikos Apeleftherotikos Stratos)*, or Greek Army of Popular Liberation, and the royalist EDES *(Ellinikos Dimokratikos Ethnikos Sindesmos)*, or Greek National Democratic Union. The two groups hated each other more than they hated the Germans. The Communist ELAS forces, which were the stronger of the two, believed that if they didn't crush EDES before the Germans pulled out, the British might intervene and restore the monarchy. The principal leader of EDES, General Napoleon Zervas, felt the same way—as a result of which he tried to conserve his forces, even if it meant coexisting with the Nazis on occasion. For their part, the Germans sometimes collaborated with Zervas, or at least ignored his strongholds, while concentrating their efforts against ELAS.[14]

Waldheim kept tabs on the situation through a noncommissioned officer named Wende, who worked for him in Arsakli. Before the war, Wende had taught in the German School in Athens, and he knew many Greeks. It was from Wende that Waldheim first heard of rumors that the Germans were preparing to pull out of Greece.[15]

Waldheim also had good contacts in the Abwehr. In particular, he cultivated a Major Fuhrmann, the head of Abwehr Troop 311. It wasn't simply that Fuhrmann could provide him with information gleaned from Abwehr interrogations; the major was also a good friend of Waldheim's boss, Colonel Warnstorff.[16]

Though the Greeks were divided, ELAS still managed to take the offensive against the Germans when the terrain and circumstances were favorable. The Germans responded with a wave of terror. According to Allied intelligence, by the end of January 1944 German troops in Greece had destroyed 485 villages and devastated 166 others, leaving 762,000 civilians as homeless refugees. When Waldheim returned to Arsakli at the end of December 1943, everyone there was talking about the massacre at Kalavryta, where German soldiers attached to the 68th Army Corps had run wild, slaughtering nearly seven hundred of the town's men and destroying a monastery. Only the timely—and unwelcome—intervention of a German officer saved Kalavryta's women and children from a similar fate.[17]

General Wilhelm Speidel, the military commander in Greece, was so concerned about the effect that incidents like the one at Kalavryta were having on Greek public opinion that he complained to General Löhr, arguing that such indiscriminate slaughter only weakened the German cause. Though Waldheim privately agreed with Speidel, he was not about to say anything in public—at least not yet.[18]

By the middle of February 1944, Waldheim was no longer his old, energetic self. The winter weather and a recurring thyroid problem had sapped his strength, and he was suffering mysterious flu-like symptoms. As always, his superiors were sympathetic. They could no longer give him any study leave, but he could be sent home, at least temporarily, for health reasons. Well aware that his valued aide wanted to see his fiancée and complete his dissertation, Colonel Warnstorff generously arranged for Waldheim to be granted a twenty-eight-day medical leave starting February 25.

Waldheim was ordered to report to a military hospital in Semmering, near Vienna. After just over a month there, he was told by medical authorities that he needed more therapy—in Baden, which just happened to be where his parents lived.

To be close to Kurt, Lilo took a room in the Hotel Panhans, a pension in Semmering. Her goal was to help her fiancé complete his dissertation as quickly as possible. She had already managed to find him a typewriter and some bond paper. Now she began going through his notes, trying to get everything organized.

Professor Verdross was equally determined to help Waldheim get his doctorate. He liked the conservative, federalist tone of Waldheim's drafts—it mirrored his own political mood of the moment—and he was ready to approve the dissertation as soon as it was complete.

Sensing the shift in the geopolitical wind, Verdross was once again reorienting himself, this time cautiously turning away from his Nazi superiors and colleagues. He was not ready to join the small anti-Nazi Austrian resistance movement; that might get him arrested.[19] But he had begun cultivating a young priest named Franz König, who later went on to become archbishop of Vienna.

Meanwhile, Kurt recuperated and worked on his dissertation, basking in Fräulein Ritschel's loving dedication. He no longer called her Lilo. That nickname belonged to the past, to the National Socialist who had rejected the Church. She assured Kurt that she would talk to a priest about becoming a good Catholic once again. To Kurt, she was now "Cissy."

Everything was changing. Soon Lieutenant Waldheim would be Dr. Waldheim, and the Ostmark would once again be Austria. Verdross the fellow traveler was becoming Verdross the liberal federalist. The Greater German Reich was crumbling; one had to adapt to new circumstances.

Waldheim's dissertation—"The Idea of the Reich in Konstantin Frantz"—was a slim work, not quite a hundred pages long. What made it remarkable was not its intellectual strength but its subtlety. Reading it today, one is often hard put to tell who is speaking, the author or his subject, Kurt Waldheim or Konstantin Frantz.[20]

What Waldheim did was to seize upon one aspect of Frantz's work and use it as a political metaphor for his own (and Verdross's) vision of Europe's future. In the process, he turned Frantz on his head, giving the nineteenth-century anti-Semite[21] what amounted to an anti-Nazi ideology that repudiated the overly centralized modern state. In the end, Waldheim wound up presenting Frantz not as the prophet of the Greater German Reich but as the forefather of European federalist integration. By emphasizing the liberal, individualistic aspect of Frantz's work, Waldheim in some ways anticipated the Allies' vision of the future United Nations.

Though the Nazis celebrated Frantz for opposing Bismarck's "little Germany"—and, hence, foreshadowing Hitler's "Greater Germany"— Waldheim quite naturally sympathized with Austria in its losing struggle against Prussia. He was nostalgic for the Holy Roman Empire and the Habsburgs, whose venerable tradition he felt was best preserved in the German-speaking lands of Austria—which he described in his dissertation as "the living memorial to the old history of the Reich."

The dissertation was thus an intellectual throwback to what the Nazis considered the "reactionary" ideas of the Schuschnigg era—a celebration, as it were, of a Catholic, corporativist Austria. In 1944, of course, such notions were little short of heretical, and so Waldheim concealed them under rhetorical trappings acceptable to the current regime. From Heinrich von Srbik, an honored Nazi professor of history at the University of Vienna, he borrowed the idea of the Third Reich as the final summation of German unity, the reconciliation of Prussian and Austrian, of modern nationalism and medieval imperialism.

Waldheim's experiences in the Balkans strongly influenced his attitude toward Frantz. Watching one ethnic group murder another, while the Germans themselves did no better, he was led to the conclusion that centralized power and extreme nationalism were both evil. What he favored was a federation guided by "principles of autonomy and of free social development"—a kind of idealized portrait of the old Habsburg empire. In one of the few daring statements in the dissertation, Waldheim described Germany as a "nation made up of nations," arguing that because "the Reich from the beginning contained considerable Slavic elements . . . it could not be a closed national body unto itself, but rather a federal common entity with a universal character."

Waldheim has since been criticized for including Belgium, Holland, and Switzerland in his notion of the Reich. In fact, all he was doing was summoning up the pre-1648 Holy Roman Empire. In any case, his vision was one of peaceful federation, not military conquest. "Only those powers rise which dedicate themselves to great purposes," he wrote.

This was yet another implicit criticism of the Nazis, and to protect himself Waldheim again invoked the spirit of Konstantin Frantz, turning the federal idea into the moral and spiritual justification of Hitler's Reich. The final pages of his dissertation were worthy of the agile Professor Verdross, who guided Waldheim through the treacherous terrain of contemporary academia. In them, he somehow made his liberal-sounding "community of peoples" synonymous with the defense of Europe against Asiatic Bolshevism, and he maintained that Germany was bringing Frantz's idea of a European Reich to fruition by "serving all of Europe as a strong heartland." Echoing the logic of Nazi propagandists,[22] he argued it was inevitable that the Third Reich would save Europe in its struggle with the non-European world: "Europe has fallen because of Germany. Through Germany it must rise again."

With the help of Cissy, Verdross, and his father, Waldheim was able to submit his dissertation by early April 1944. A few days later, while enjoying his rest and recuperation in Baden, he received a terse telegram: DISSERTATION ACCEPTED. CONGRATULATIONS. VERDROSS.

Lieutenant Kurt Josef Waldheim was now also Doctor Iuris Waldheim. He received his doctorate officially on April 14, 1944.

Cissy and Walter were overjoyed. Kurt would soon rise to become an assistant judge. Perhaps one day he would be a major diplomat.

It was a rare moment of contentment. Allied bombers were coming closer every day, and there was increasing talk of an invasion in the west. As Waldheim prepared to return to Arsakli, his fiancée and his father embraced him, praying they would see him again soon.

Just before Kurt left on April 15 or 16, Cissy agreed to talk with the priest about the wedding. They decided it would take place in August.

CHAPTER EIGHT

A Changed Man

For the far-flung German armies, the early spring of 1944 was a time of watchful waiting. The eastern front was relatively quiet; the Allies had not yet invaded France; in Italy, the Wehrmacht continued to maintain strongholds southeast of Rome. As he returned to Arsakli in the middle of April, Kurt Waldheim was mainly concerned about the Allied bombing raids that were raining destruction over an ever-widening portion of Europe. The idea that Cissy or his parents might be hurt or killed was almost too much to bear. Yet he could do nothing to protect or help them.

Back at Ic/AO, the political theories of Konstantin Frantz quickly came to seem a dim memory. Waldheim's colleagues were all talking about the latest massacre. On April 4, partisans had fired on a German truck convoy in the nearby village of Clissura. The next day, an S.S. regiment entered Clissura to exact revenge. The partisans having long since fled, the Germans proceeded to slaughter two hundred fifteen innocent villagers, nine of them infants less than a year old.

Outraged by the incident, the German Plenipotentiary for the Southeast, Hermann Neubacher, protested to Hitler's foreign minister, Joachim von Ribbentrop, arguing that this sort of thing only made good propaganda for the Communists.[1] In doing so, Neubacher articulated the growing conviction of many Wehrmacht officers—among them, an increasingly pessimistic Lieutenant Waldheim.

In every way, the German position—in the Balkans in general as well as in Greece in particular—was growing weaker. With four thousand miles of coastline to watch, plus innumerable Aegean islands to defend, Army Group E's forces were being stretched painfully thin. At the same time, the beleaguered Luftwaffe was hard-pressed to protect an air corridor that extended from Albania to Crete and from the Peloponnesus to Thrace.

To make matters worse, Bulgaria's loyalty to the Reich was faltering, the Red Army was approaching Rumania, the situation in Serbia was deteriorating, Croatia was near collapse, and the consensus among Waldheim's superiors was that Albania would do what it had done in 1918 and turn against the Germans the moment the Allies landed.[2] In Greece, the strength of the Communist-led ELAS forces had mushroomed to more than thirty thousand men, and on May 1 Waldheim learned for the first time that Soviet officers were assisting the 9th and 13th ELAS divisions.[3] Meanwhile, the royalist EDES forces, which were often willing to collaborate with the Germans, were losing ground. (Not that it really mattered; when the Allies arrived, EDES was certain to support them.)

As the partisans grew bolder, German units in the field grew ever more vicious, responding to partisan attacks with brutal reprisals against Greek civilians that made the massacre at Clissura look like a mere warm-up. On May 24, 1944, the entire male population of the village of Pogonion was deported to a camp near Ionnina—to be held as hostages who could be shot in retaliation for partisan attacks on German soldiers. Shortly afterward, the 68th Army Corps informed army group headquarters that partisans had attacked the 41st Fortress Division; the Germans responded by shooting 325 civilians.[4]

In strange and hostile territory, far from home, harried by guerrilla fighters who seemed indistinguishable from the surrounding civilian population, the soldiers of Army Group E were hardly the first—or last—occupation troops in history to let their frustration boil over into indiscriminate slaughter. But in this case the killing of civilians was not an aberration—as was the case in Vietnam. It was German policy. The aim, of course, was to destroy the partisans by terrorizing the civilian population into refusing to support them. By themselves, the partisans were no match for Army Group E. The real danger they posed was their ability to distract and harass German forces in the event of an Allied invasion.

In any case, it was becoming increasingly clear that the policy of random reprisals was not having the desired effect. Indeed, a growing number of Wehrmacht officers—including such high-ranking figures as General Speidel, the military commander in Greece—was beginning to regard the policy as self-defeating.

That Kurt Waldheim was one of those officers should come as no surprise. As a well-informed intelligence analyst who had been serving in the Balkans on and off for more than two years, he knew better than most the realities of partisan warfare. What does come as a surprise is the fact that, the day after the male population of Pogonion was taken hostage, the agreeable young Austrian lieutenant who had worked so hard to prove his political reliability to his Nazi masters became one of the first—indeed, one of the only—Wehrmacht critics to put his doubts on record.

The uncharacteristic protest by Waldheim came at the end of a depressing report on enemy activities in Greece that he sent to General Schmidt-Richberg, the chief of the general staff of Army Group E, on Thursday, May 25, 1944.* (Copies also went to the S.S. units that worked with the army group.)

The bulk of the report consisted of a routine summary of intelligence supplied by Ic officers in the field. Near the end, however, Waldheim discarded his usual dry, bureaucratic prose for the following blunt denunciation of the policy of random retaliation against civilians:

> *The reprisal measures imposed in response* to acts of sabotage and ambush *have, despite their severity,* failed to achieve any noteworthy success, since our own measures have been only transitory, so that the punished communities or territories soon have to be abandoned once more to the [partisan] bands. On the contrary, exaggerated reprisal measures undertaken without a more precise examination of the objective situation have only caused embitterment and have been useful to the bands. It can be demonstrated that the population broadly supports the bands and supplies them with excellent information. [The italics are Waldheim's own.][5]

It is something of an understatement to note that Waldheim was not generally given to questioning authority. His recently completed dissertation had been a model of discretion. Indeed, the last time he had gone out on a limb for anything had been in March 1938, when he had campaigned in Tulln and Vienna for a vote against the *Anschluss* in Schuschnigg's ill-fated plebiscite. Yet here he was criticizing—in writing—a policy endorsed not only by his superiors in the Wehrmacht right

*That the report was written by Waldheim is certain. Eager for his superiors to know how hard he was working on their behalf, Waldheim was more diligent about initialing documents than most junior officers. This report bore his usual handwritten "W" at the end of the last sentence.

up through Field Marshal Wilhelm Keitel but by Adolf Hitler himself.

What was behind this uncharacteristic outburst? Clearly, Waldheim had returned to Arsakli in the spring of 1944 something of a changed man. He was now Dr. Waldheim, on the verge of a promising legal career, engaged to be married to the only woman he had ever loved. He also knew that Germany was losing the war, and he was looking forward to a life in a world not dominated by the Nazis. He wanted to live, and everything crossing his desk celebrated death.

Whatever the motivation, Waldheim's criticism of the reprisal policy was a singular gesture. Though many in the Wehrmacht may have felt the same way privately, Waldheim was one of the only junior staff officers willing to put his opposition on record. Indeed, in examining thousands of similar documents produced by the German forces in Greece, I have seen few stronger protests of this kind, and then only from the pens of far more powerful men, such as General Speidel or plenipotentiary Neubacher.

To be sure, Waldheim's critique, though in my view moral in inspiration, was not couched in moral terms. He didn't argue that the German policy of reprisals was evil or criminal, merely that it was counterproductive. And whatever motivated it, there is no evidence that Waldheim ever openly criticized or otherwise protested against Nazi brutality on any other occasion.

The activities (and treatment) of Greek civilians wasn't Ic/AO's only concern. Since the spring of 1943, Britain's Special Operations Executive—which Winston Churchill had established early in the war to "set Europe ablaze" by aiding local partisan movements—had infiltrated more than two hundred commandos on fifty-three separate missions into Greece. They parachuted from the sky or landed in small boats on dark, obscure beaches. By the spring of 1944, as many as four hundred regular Allied soldiers, under the aegis of the Allied Military Mission in Greece, had joined the commandos and their Greek hosts, supplying the partisans with weapons, medical supplies, money, and tactical advice.[6]

The German policy toward such troops was characteristically harsh. On October 18, 1942, two months after Canadian commandos outraged Hitler by attacking the French port of Dieppe, the Führer had issued what became known as his Commando Order. In it, he defined commandos as criminals who, if caught, were to be interrogated and then automatically shot—even if they had been in uniform when captured. As this represented a clear violation of the rules of war, the order was a criminal one.

General Löhr put Hitler's Commando Order into effect in his area of command on October 28, 1942. Equating the commandos with partisan "bandits," he instructed his troops to treat them with the "most brutal hardness." Like many other Wehrmacht commanders, however, Löhr seemed to recognize the criminal nature of the orders, for he decreed that all records of them were "to be recalled by the divisions and destroyed."[7]

Under Army Group E regulations, captured commandos and other Allied troops who might possess important intelligence information were supposed to be sent to Arsakli or Salonika for interrogation by Ic/AO. Such prisoners were generally held in Secret Field Police or Gestapo prisons, and were questioned there by Ic officers such as Waldheim's immediate superior, Colonel Warnstorff. The records of these sessions were then filed by Waldheim, whose reports from the time mention "Interrogations of prisoners of the Anglo-American Military Mission in Greece."[8] Most of the interrogation protocols were destroyed by the Germans before they left Arsakli.

The German military generally cloaked its criminal activities in euphemisms. Thus, the murder of captured commandos was referred to as *Sonderbehandlung,* or "special treatment." In the spring of 1944, Waldheim's unit received a message from Field Marshal von Weichs's Belgrade-based High Command for the Southeast ordering such "special treatment" for a British radioman named Carpenter and a Greek sailor named Lisgaris, both of whom were being held at Arsakli by Ic/AO after having been captured during a raid on the island of Alimnia. The fate of Carpenter and Lisgaris is unknown, for the records dealing with it did not survive the war.[9]

What is known is that after being interrogated by Ic/AO, some prisoners disappeared forever. Indeed, in response to a question in the House of Commons, British foreign secretary Sir Geoffrey Howe reported in August 1986 that the fate of at least half a dozen British commandos who had taken part in operations in areas controlled by Army Group E has never been determined. It is, of course, likely that at least some of these men were murdered by the Germans. If so, the actual executions were carried out by the S.D., but the men of Ic/AO were at least complicit in their criminal treatment. To put it another way, if the disappeared men were killed, the Ic/AO unit of which Waldheim was a member participated in what the Nüremberg Tribunal would call "war crimes."[10]

While no evidence has ever surfaced linking Kurt Waldheim personally to the disappearance of any Allied commandos, his handwritten "W" does appear on a report concerning the interrogations of three commandos who were captured while taking part in an attack on a German communications base on the island of Kalymnos the night of July 1, 1944. It is possible that Waldheim participated in the interrogation of one of the three—an American medic named James Doughty—on July 17, 1944. Since the actual interrogation protocols have not been found, there is no way of knowing for certain. It is no crime to interrogate a prisoner, unless the prisoner is abused. (In this particular case, the rules of war seem to have been observed. Two of the commando prisoners mentioned in Waldheim's report wound up surviving the war, while the third died of wounds suffered at the time of his capture.)[11]

This case aside, however, Waldheim's role regarding Allied commandos generally seems to have been similar to the one he played in connection with the doomed Jews of Ionnina. He kept the operations staff and the S.D. apprised of all relevant intelligence and he kept records of the interrogations and final disposition of Ic/AO's commando prisoners.

As Army Group E's position in Greece deteriorated and the prospect of a pullout grew more and more likely, the Germans grew increasingly determined to complete the elimination of all Jews in the region before it was too late. Though the security police and the S.D. did most of the actual deporting and killing, the cooperation of Army Group E—and, in particular, its Ic/AO section—turned out to be essential in completing this phase of the Holocaust.

The key Ic/AO player in this tragedy was the unit's AO, or Abwehr chief, Major Friedrich Wilhelm Hammer. An older man who walked with a cane, Hammer inaugurated the tragedy a few days after Waldheim returned to Arsakli from Baden. On April 21, 1944, he ordered the military command on Corfu to prepare for a mass deportation by taking a census of all the Jews on the island. Roughly six weeks later, early on the morning of June 9, S.S. troops burst into Corfu's ghetto, screaming that all Jews were to assemble in a public square. While the Jews stood there, the Germans looted their houses, turning over anything they didn't want to the avaricious Greek authorities. By June 17, Corfu's entire Jewish population of nearly two thousand men, women, and children was on its way to the gas chambers at Auschwitz.[12]

At the end of July 1944, Waldheim's superiors at Ic/AO ordered the deportation of all Jews remaining anywhere in Army Group E's territory. Actual responsibility for carrying out the order was left to the S.D., which set up a special unit for the purpose. In all, they managed to deport more than sixty thousand Jews from Greece—of whom more than fifty thousand were eventually murdered.[13]

Waldheim has since claimed that he knew nothing of the mass deportations at the time, learning of them only long after the war had ended. But though it is true that Major Hammer's AO office had more to do with the deportations than Waldheim's Ic section, the fact remains that the two departments were part of the same unit. More to the point, Waldheim prepared numerous reports for Major Hammer, and these were hardly the only bureaucratic contacts he had with the Abwehr.[14]

By July 1944, the tide had turned unmistakably against the Reich. In Poland, Waldheim's old Army Group Center was being overwhelmed by the Red Army. In Italy, Rome had fallen. In France, the Allies were pushing east from Normandy, and Paris seemed likely to come under siege at any time.

Compared to all that, the situation in Greece appeared positively tranquil. Still, the handwriting was on the wall. The resistance movement was stronger than ever, American airplanes controlled the skies, and the morale of German troops was crumbling. Some soldiers considered the German POWs being held in Britain and the United States to be lucky. In Greece, they complained about their rations, and like the Italians a year earlier, many were selling Wehrmacht tires and goods to civilians. There was also a sharp rise in the number of reported cases of venereal disease, mainly because prophylactics and medical assistance were in short supply.[15] The bulk of the Greek population in Salonika talked openly—and eagerly—about the imminent prospect of a German pullout.

Lieutenant Waldheim followed all of this closely.[16] But his mind was on other things. He and Cissy had set the date—they would be married in Baden on Saturday, August 19. Waldheim was painfully aware that the military crisis might easily affect their plans. Indeed, rumors were circulating that the army was about to issue regulations sharply curtailing all leave. Still, he had been in the Wehrmacht long enough to know that no matter what the regulations said, there were always loopholes—especially if your superiors were on your side.

It was a bizarre time to be planning to go off on a honeymoon. On July 20, Hitler had miraculously escaped an assassination attempt when a bomb went off in his command bunker near Rastenburg in East Prussia. In the frenzied aftermath, Heinrich Himmler's secret police were arresting and executing thousands of civilians and military men suspected of anti-Nazi sympathies. In Arsakli, General Schmidt-Richberg called his corps commanders together on July 29 to tell them that it had become "self-evident that more than ever a National Socialist attitude is absolutely necessary in the officer corps." In fact, Schmidt-Richberg's boss, General

Löhr, was beginning to entertain profound doubts about Hitler's military genius. Nonetheless, like all his fellow generals, he proclaimed his continuing loyalty to the Führer, declaring: "My Führer, I have reacted with profound indignation to the accursed attempt against your life. I swear for myself and for the troops under my command in Greece and the Aegean islands that we will prove our unbreakable loyalty through our deeds."

Meanwhile, Waldheim's own reports told him of the accelerating collapse of Germany's Balkan allies. If the Soviets reached Croatia, Army Group E would be cut off and trapped in Greece. As eager as Waldheim was to get home, he did not want disaster to engulf his comrades in Arsakli while he was with Cissy.

As it turned out, Waldheim didn't need to pull any strings to get home. On July 31, word came down that the new rules expressly permitted marital leave.

As a result, he proceeded with his plans, buying a couple of new shirts and having his boots repaired. Exactly where he and Cissy would spend their honeymoon depended on wartime travel restrictions, the state of accommodations, and the vagaries of Allied bombing raids. But all these problems were secondary; like many an eager bridegroom, Waldheim was determined to let nothing get in the way of his wedding. He even managed to get a few days premarital leave in July—time to see Cissy and help finalize their plans.

Back in Arsakli, he wound up working right up through the eve of his departure for home and the wedding. On August 11, he reported substantial partisan activity south of Iraklion on Crete. Three days later, on Monday, August 14, he was able to record the German response: twenty hostages shot, two villages destroyed.

The wedding went off as scheduled on August 19. The honeymoon, however, nearly ended before it began. Though Waldheim was under orders to be back in Arsakli in less than three weeks, he and his bride were looking forward to a romantic idyll in the quaint mountain resort of Mariazell, about seventy miles southwest of Vienna. Unfortunately, as they boarded their train, an Allied bomber fleet was spotted approaching from the west. As a result, the train was not allowed to leave, and they wound up spending their wedding night huddled in the station.

They made it to Mariazell the next day. They were blissfully happy, finally able to give full expression to their youthful passion. They made a striking couple, both of them tall and radiant, the voluptuous Cissy with her long, thick brunette hair, and impressive Kurt, the slim, blond, blue-eyed officer with his sharp features and winsome manner. If they could survive the collapse of Nazi Germany, everything would be wonderful. Cissy was qualified to practice law, and Kurt had earned his doctorate. She was back in the Church, and despite Kurt's fears, the Gestapo had not arrested his father in the massive roundups that had followed the attempt on Hitler's life.

While Kurt and Cissy relaxed in Mariazell, the secret police reported widespread defeatism and rumor-mongering in towns like Baden and especially in Vienna. People were talking about what life would be like when the war was over, about a reborn Austria.

The newlyweds had their own concerns. A few weeks after the honeymoon, Kurt learned that Cissy was expecting his child.[17]

Waldheim returned to Arsakli on September 3, 1944, and immediately discovered that the decision had been made: With the Red Army now in the Balkans, the Germans would soon be abandoning Greece. While he had been away, the military commander had ordered all German women and children (along with all male German civilians in occupations not considered vital to the war effort) out of the country. A few days later, all of Greece had been declared a battle zone.[18]

Army Group E was to be ready to pull out as soon as orders came from the Führer. According to Field Marshal von Weichs, German soldiers would not be allowed to take any non-German women with them, nor would they be able to remove furniture or other large objects. (In this regard, Waldheim was luckier than many of his colleagues at Arsakli: He had no Greek girlfriend, and the few souvenirs he had picked up in the Balkans were small, easily portable items such as an antique pistol and a dagger.)

The situation in the Balkans was growing more desperate by the day. The first week in September, Bulgaria surrendered to the Russians, then declared war on the Reich. In Macedonia, German lines of communication to Greece were being disrupted by partisans. Meanwhile, the Red Army was preparing to move west out of Rumania, massing for an attack on the important Yugoslavian town of Niš. The Soviets were on their way toward Belgrade. If the Russians managed to link up with Tito's divisions in Serbia, Army Group E would be hard-pressed to reach Croatia. As a precaution, Field Marshal von Weichs and the high command of Army Group F evacuated Belgrade, moving their headquarters northwest to Vukovar.

On September 19, Waldheim's Ic/AO reported heavy enemy air activity over the Aegean. The Allies were again bombing Crete. At headquarters in Arsakli, anxiety was increasing. An army group of 300,000 men might be cut off and destroyed.

Poring over his maps in an effort to find a way out for his men, General Löhr quickly realized he had few options. To the east stood newly hostile Bulgaria, its troops armed in part with good German weapons. To the west and northwest were Albania and Montenegro, both hostile, treacherous lands, almost impassable in the winter. Löhr's only decent line of retreat from Greece would be directly north-northwest through a narrow strip of Macedonia. Both he and von Weichs knew that the Macedonian bottleneck would have to be held if Army Group E was to survive.[19]

By late September, German men and equipment were converging on Salonika from all over the Aegean. The Luftwaffe flew transport after transport, bringing in troops from Crete, Rhodes, and other islands. At the same time, Allied air attacks reached record proportions. On September 24, 541 enemy planes harassed the retreating Germans, attacking ships, aircraft, rail lines, and roads. Had bad weather not grounded Allied fighters and bombers for the next week, Army Group E might have been finished off then and there.

Desperate to save as much of his scattered army as he could, Löhr placed severe limitations on baggage weights and fuel consumption. In all, he managed to evacuate some thirty thousand soldiers from the islands. But nearly twenty thousand more had to be left behind—with orders to fight to the last, if attacked.[20]

Löhr was racing against time—and the Red Army. According to a communiqué from Tass, the official Soviet news agency, Tito had agreed to the "temporary entry of Soviet troops into Yugoslav territory which borders on Hungary."[21] The Red Army was clearly driving on Belgrade. That was Löhr's goal as well. He hoped to link up there with von Weichs's Second Panzer Army and form a shield behind which his army could complete its withdrawal from Greece.

On October 2, the long-awaited order finally came—Löhr was to pull Army Group E out of Greece, southern Albania, and southern Macedonia. He was to lead his troops north, living off his own supplies; except for coal for the trains, the army group would be on its own until it reached Skopje in northern Macedonia.[22]

At headquarters in Arsakli, Lieutenant Waldheim and his comrades on Ic/AO began destroying hundreds of secret documents. They also warned Zervas's "nationalist" EDES guerrillas of the army's impending departure, to give them a chance to assume control of the country before their Communist counterparts in ELAS had a chance to react.[23]

The key to the group's retreat was the road between the Macedonian towns of Stip and Kočani. If the Germans managed to keep the road open, Army Group E would be able to make it to Belgrade and safety. But enemy attacks around Kočani could plug up the vital bottleneck. And if Kočani actually fell, Löhr would have no choice but to try to move his troops in winter weather through Albania and Montenegro. With the Allies already holding key islands off the Albanian and Dalmatian coasts, Army Group E could be destroyed in the process.

On the morning of October 12, Waldheim passed along vital news of "strengthened band activity against the Stip-Kočani road." An addendum to the report later that day noted "more band forces on the march toward the Stip-Kočani road." General Löhr knew exactly what that meant: Time was running out for Army Group E. Two days later, in the middle of the afternoon of October 14, 1944, he and his staff, including Lieutenant Waldheim, left Arsakli for the last time.[24]

It was a depressing departure. At the airfield, Löhr inquired about the whereabouts of his adjutant, Major von Schenk—only to be informed several hours later that the man had gone AWOL. Eventually, the staff flew to Pristina, then drove to their new headquarters at Stari Trg, near Mitrovica. By 8 P.M. that night, Waldheim was back at work.

Monsignor Ignaz Seipel, the Christian Social chancellor of Austria from 1922 to 1929. The Waldheims were longtime supporters of the Christian Social party, and they admired Seipel's stern, patriarchal style. UPI/BETTMANN NEWSPHOTOS

Engelbert Dollfuss (in his Patriotic Front uniform, saluting) with his wife and children at a 1934 May Day festival in Vienna. Dollfuss, who succeeded Seipel as chancellor, was murdered by the Nazis less than two months after this photo was taken. UPI/BETTMANN NEWSPHOTOS

Nineteen-year-old cavalry recruit Kurt Waldheim (mounted, third from left) in training with the elite Austrian Dragoon Regiment 1 in 1937. PROFIL

Less than a month after Hitler forced him to put Nazis in his cabinet, Chancellor Kurt Schuschnigg tells parliament that Austria will defend to the death its independence. Six days later, on March 13, 1938, Germany absorbed Austria. UPI/BETTMANN NEWSPHOTOS

In the aftermath of the *Anschluss,* Austrian Nazis poured
into the streets to celebrate—and torment their enemies.
Here, they force Jews to scrub the streets of Vienna.
UPI/BETTMANN NEWSPHOTOS

Lieselotte (Lilo) Ritschel, the future Mrs. Kurt Waldheim, around the time of the *Anschluss*. Just sixteen, she would soon renounce her Catholic faith and join the League of German Maidens, the female equivalent of the Hitler Youth. GERHARD OBERSCHLICK/FORUM

Lilo's Nazi party membership card, showing she applied for membership on October 12, 1940, and was accepted as of January 1, 1941. The lack of any entries on the line marked "Austritt" [Leaving] shows that she never formally left the party before it was officially dissolved in May 1945.

Kurt Waldheim's military record, as of June 2, 1939. He is listed as being a member of two Nazi-affiliated organizations—the S.A. and the National Socialist German Students League.

A Serbian victim of German reprisals hanging from a
lamppost in Belgrade, Yugoslavia. Such scenes were
common when Waldheim arrived there in March 1942.
LIBRARY OF CONGRESS

Raped and murdered Serbian peasants—victims of the
1942 Kozara massacre. ARHIV JUGOSLAVIJE

Survivors of Kozara being marched off to German
concentration camps. Estimates of the number of
Yugoslavs who were killed or deported in the Kozara
"operation" range upwards of 66,000. ARHIV JUGOSLAVIJE

Waldheim at the scene of his first diplomatic triumph—the airfield outside Podgorica in Montenegro on May 22, 1943. From left: General Ercole Roncaglia, commander of the Italian XIV Corps; First Lieutenant Waldheim; Colonel Joachim Macholz, chief of the German Liaison Staff and Waldheim's immediate superior; Waffen S.S. General Artur Phleps, commander of the 7th S.S. Volunteer Mountain Division, also known as the "Prinz Eugen." WORLD JEWISH CONGRESS

General Alexander Löhr, the bespectacled
commander-in-chief of Army Group E, studies his maps at
his Sarajevo headquarters as he plans the group's retreat
northward through Yugoslavia in December 1944. The
young officer looking on at the top of the photo is Kurt
Waldheim.

Kurt and Cissy (he never liked calling her Lilo) shortly after
the end of the war. GERHARD OBERSCHLICK/FORUM

Waldheim's diplomatic mentor, Austrian foreign minister
Karl Gruber (left), with U.S. Secretary of State John Foster
Dulles in November 1952. UPI/BETTMANN NEWSPHOTOS

A beaming Waldheim at the United Nations on December 21, 1971, the day the Security Council voted to recommend that he be appointed secretary-general.

The newly appointed secretary-general meets with
President Richard Nixon at the White House shortly after
taking up his UN post. UPI/BETTMANN NEWSPHOTOS

The Waldheims in a portrait that appeared on a 1986 Austrian presidential campaign brochure. Among other things, the brochure hails Waldheim's "Civil Courage."

A triumphant Waldheim greets supporters in Vienna after beating Socialist candidate Kurt Streyer in the June 8, 1986, run-off election for the presidency of Austria.

Israeli demonstrators in Tel Aviv protesting Waldheim's election. UPI/BETTMANN NEWSPHOTOS

Waldheim at his June 1987 Vatican audience with Pope
John Paul II. The Pope was the first world figure of
consequence to meet with Waldheim after the Reagan
administration barred the Austrian president from entering
the United States. UPI/BETTMANN NEWSPHOTOS

CHAPTER NINE

The Final Retreat

General Löhr's troops managed to hold the Stip-Kočani road. Late in October, however, Niš and Belgrade fell to the Russians.[1]

With that line of retreat gone, Field Marshal von Weichs, who by then had moved his headquarters 250 miles northwest to Zagreb, ordered Army Group E to link up with the Second Panzer Army near Visegrad, east of Sarajevo. The idea was to establish a new "east front" to stop the Soviet advance. At stake were the western Balkans, Croatia, and the road to Vienna.

Though the task seemed impossible, General Löhr managed to pull it off. Three factors made it possible: Löhr's tactical skill, the determination of his soldiers, and a secret agreement between Tito and the Red Army that changed the entire strategic picture. Tito had been properly grateful to the Soviets for liberating the Yugoslavian capital. Nonetheless, he was no more eager to have his country occupied by Russians than by Germans. As a result, he persuaded Moscow to allow his units to take on the forces of von Weichs and Löhr, while the Red Army turned north toward Hungary and Austria. This was a considerable break for the Germans, for while Tito's partisans were fierce fighters, they were not nearly as formidable an enemy as the battle-hardened, better armed, and far more numerous Soviet regulars. Tito himself complained that his fighters found it difficult to adapt to traditional forms of warfare. Eventually, they did adapt, but it took time—providing Löhr and his men with a badly needed respite.

As General Löhr struggled to bring his troops northward, he became concerned about an army of fourteen thousand Chetniks hovering on his right flank in the region between Višegrad and Novi Pazar. The Chetniks were now desperate men. Abandoned by the Allies, they had lost most of the popular support they had once commanded. Still, the Chetnik leader, Draža Mihailović, continued his struggle against Tito's Communist partisans.

Mihailović's chief aim in November of 1944 was to keep his main army strong enough to prevent a complete Communist takeover when Yugoslavia was finally liberated. To that end, he was eager to make contact with the Western Allies, believing that direct talks with their military missions might change their hostile attitude toward his forces. The problem was, he could not reach the Allied lines without crossing through territory controlled by Army Group E—which, despite its plight, was still the most powerful non-Communist force in the area. He thus decided to try to make a deal with General Löhr.

On the face of it, Mihailović's plan made no sense. In effect, he wanted the Germans to help him save his army so he could offer it to the Allies as an anti-German cobelligerent. Nonetheless, Löhr was at least willing to talk. After all, if Mihailović wanted to make trouble, his forces could be an annoying thorn in Army Group E's side.

On November 3, Löhr dispatched three officers to meet with Mihailović's chief of staff, Major Jevdjenijevič. The German delegation consisted of Colonel Warnstorff, Warnstorff's Abwehr friend Major Fuhrmann, and First Lieutenant Waldheim. Just as he had done in the Phleps-Roncaglia talks at the Podgorica airfield in 1943, Waldheim once again found himself enjoying a firsthand view of high-level negotiations in the midst of a crisis. This time he didn't act as an interpreter, though his rudimentary knowledge of Serbo-Croatian did prove useful. Mainly, he took notes and watched.

What the Chetniks wanted was for Löhr to allow three of their emissaries to pass through German lines on their way to the Albanian coast, where they hoped to make contact with the Allies. As a sign of goodwill, the Chetniks were ready to release several hundred German soldiers they had captured. The Chetniks also wanted Löhr to supply them with arms—in return for which they promised to help Army Group E continue its retreat to East Bosnia by engaging Tito's forces once the Red Army pulled out of Serbia.

Löhr did not trust the Chetniks (and for good reason: while Major Jevdjenijević was meeting with Colonel Warnstorff & Co., other Chetnik commanders were holding similar talks with the Red Army). Still, his army group could use all the help it could get. Thus, a deal was struck: The Chetniks released their German prisoners, and Warnstorff gave Jevdjenijević three safe-conduct passes.[2]

This was a particularly difficult period for Waldheim. Not yet twenty-six, he was not only separated from his new (and pregnant) bride but, in the confusion of Army Group E's retreat, he was under the gun (figuratively as well as literally) as never before in the Balkans.

The main problem was that General Löhr's troops in the field were not getting good reconnaissance information. For an army facing partisans on all sides (as well as Bulgarians to the east, Russians to the northeast, and Allied commandos on some of the Dalmatian islands and coastal strips), this was a prescription for disaster. With bad weather on the way, a blind army was a dead army.

To make up for the lack of reconnaissance, Waldheim found himself under intense pressure to analyze and summarize every scrap of captured paper the Germans managed to get their hands on, and to do it quickly. As a result, he spent early November working day and night, with virtually no break.[3]

On November 15, 1944, Army Group E moved its headquarters to the East Bosnian capital of Sarajevo. Waldheim flew there with the high command staff. By 8 P.M. the same evening, the new HQ was set up and in business.[4]

Waldheim had last been in East Bosnia in the spring of 1942. That seemed like another lifetime. Germany had dominated Europe then; the partisan troubles were a minor sideshow, a mere passing annoyance. In those days, Waldheim had sat in the warm sun, playing cards and drinking wine with General Esposito. Now winter was coming, and everything was crumbling around him.

To make matters worse, the news from home was dismal. With the Red Army crossing the Vistula River and approaching Budapest from Warsaw, the relentless Allied bombardment of eastern Austria was coming to seem increasingly like a prelude to a siege of Vienna. Cissy was looking for quarters outside the city, but so far she hadn't found anything. Things were equally uncertain with Waldheim's parents in Baden. The factories at nearby Wiener Neustadt had become a favorite Allied target, and air attacks were increasingly frequent.

The first advance units of Army Group E reached Sarajevo within days after the new staff headquarters was established. With heavy snow and freezing cold making the mountain passes treacherous, the Brod-Sarajevo railroad became the army group's lifeline, carrying more than three hundred tons of clothing, coal, and other supplies to the desperately needy soldiers those final weeks of November.[5]

By December 1, however, that lifeline was choked off as the partisans went after the railway with a vengeance, blowing up as many as twenty separate stretches of track a night. The misery deepened when fifty thousand men of the 21st Army Corps arrived in Sarajevo. (Army Group E consisted of three army corps, 21st, the 34th, and the 91st.) Hardly anyone was prepared for a Bosnian winter, and there were shortages of everything from field caps to coats, from gloves to shoes. Many soldiers still wore tropical uniforms, more suitable to a campaign in Africa or southern Greece. Dressed in ragged clothing and lacking soap, the local population was infested with lice. Before long, a typhus epidemic was raging.[6]

Adding to the confusion, the partisans blew up a key bridge spanning the Drina River at Višegrad, thereby disrupting communications between headquarters and the 34th and 91st Army Corps, which were still retreating northwest toward Sarajevo from Kraljevo. To reestablish contact, Löhr's chief of staff, General Schmidt-Richberg, ordered his Ic chief, Colonel Warnstorff, to fly to Kraljevo with an *Einsatzstab,* or mobile action staff. As usual in such critical situations, Warnstorff made sure he was accompanied on the mission by his calm and methodical O3, Lieutenant Waldheim.

Warnstorff's group quickly restored communications, enabling the massive and complicated retreat to continue in an orderly fashion. Just before Warnstorff and Waldheim left Kraljevo, the Allies bombed the town, causing substantial damage. Waldheim managed to escape injury, and never told his family of his close call. They worried enough as it was.[7]

Despite the immense difficulties, General Löhr was carrying out his mission. The men of Army Group E were completing one of the great retreats in military history, a German Dunkirk, building a defensive wall based around key positions at Mostar, Sarajevo, and Banja Luka that could prevent the partisans from moving in from the east while keeping the Allies from landing in force on the Adriatic coast of Croatia to the west. If their comrades in Army Group South could hold out to the north, a new front would emerge in the northwestern Balkans, with Army Group E, von Weichs's Second Panzer Army, and Army Group South protecting Croatia, Austria, and southwestern Hungary from enemy attack.[8]

Kurt Waldheim was the unofficial historian of this remarkable maneuver, his reports providing a clear picture of Army Group E's changing strategic and tactical position. Day and night, he sat at his desk in Sarajevo, analyzing and summarizing the Red Army's moves in Hungary, the death throes of the Chetniks, the successes of Tito's forces in Serbia. He described how the partisans were building up their strength near Mostar, and he narrated the enemy siege of Mitrovica. His information was culled from a number of sources, the most important of which were the transcripts of prisoner interrogations.[9]

Familiar names from the old days took on new associations for him. Pljevlje, where he had once enjoyed himself in the company of a Montenegran family and an Italian general, was falling to the partisans. There was no time for nostalgia, however. New interrogation protocols had to be processed. Weather reports and aerial reconnaissance information had to be collated. Foreign radio broadcasts required analysis. Everything remotely connected with intelligence seemed to land on Waldheim's desk.[10]

Waldheim's duties included filing documents concerning the army group's propaganda efforts. As the army group retreated and the partisans became bolder, the civilian population grew less cooperative. Propaganda thus took on new urgency. Ic/AO worked with Propaganda Company 690 to produce and distribute enormous numbers of pamphlets and leaflets, as many as eighty thousand copies at a time. Printed in Serbo-Croatian, Russian, and Bulgarian, they contained simple messages: Let the German army pass through unmolested; This is the Jews' war; Stalin intends to take over the Balkans. The language was often primitive, but then, the Germans believed they were dealing with primitive peoples.[11]

With the German army suffering defeat after defeat, German propagandists also made a virtue of necessity and began celebrating Army Group E's successful retreat as if it were another *Anschluss.* On December 3, 1944, the German army newspaper *Die Wacht Im Südosten* (The Watch in the Southeast) ran a front-page feature on General Löhr's achievement. The article included a photograph of the general studying his maps. Clearly visible in the picture, looking over Löhr's left shoulder, was a grim Kurt Waldheim.[12]

Throughout these chaotic times, Waldheim's thoughts were invariably with Cissy and the baby she was carrying. Though he worried about his family incessantly, he knew there was little chance of obtaining leave. His twenty-sixth birthday was fast approaching, soon to be followed by Christmas and New Year's. What would 1945 bring? With the Allied air attacks increasing and the Red Army coming closer, it was clear the war was nearing an end.

During the final weeks of 1944, Lieutenant Waldheim processed intelligence reports about Tito's forces radioed by German agents operating behind partisan lines. With codes names such as Max, Hans, and Franz, these agents provided Waldheim with detailed information about enemy plans, supplies, and morale. Waldheim found it depressing to learn that the Bulgarians—and even some partisans—had warm winter clothing.[13]

Equally depressing was the news that the German columns retreating toward Sarajevo were being attacked by Allied bombers even in bad weather. On Christmas Eve, Waldheim reported that six Allied bombers had hit rail installations in and around Sarajevo. The next day he noted that the Allies had bombed the Mostar area. That sort of thing was bad enough, but Waldheim worried even more on days when the skies seemed to be clear of enemy airplanes. If the Allies weren't bombing Army Group E, they might be attacking the industrial belt around Wiener Neustadt or the rail yards near Vienna.[14]

General Löhr was well aware of how much his men missed their families during this depressing Christmas season, and he warned them not to let down their guard. As an Austrian himself, however, Löhr was hardly devoid of sentimentality. On Christmas Day, he arranged a celebration for his staff in the still-beautiful port of Dubrovnik, appropriating the town theater for a program that, in addition to a salute to the Führer, included works by Schubert and Haydn (good Austrians both), as well as several hymns.[15]

The evening had both Catholic and Austrian overtones, and Waldheim enjoyed it immensely. When he had first come to Arsakli, he had heard Löhr described as a favorite of Hitler and Göring. Now everyone was saying that Löhr was really a patriotic Austrian who hated what the Nazis had done to his homeland.[16]

During the first two weeks of January 1945, Löhr ordered a number of local offensives in Croatia to strengthen German defensive perimeters. Despite some limited success, however, it soon became clear that Sarajevo was no longer secure. As a result, Waldheim and his colleagues on the headquarters staff prepared to move north once again, this time to Cernik Castle near Nova Gradiska.

A few weeks later, Ic/AO learned that the Bulgarians had pulled back from parts of the new Balkan "east front." Overjoyed at the opportunity to stabilize Army Group E's position, Löhr gave the order for an attack along the entire length of the front.

It was one of the last successes the Wehrmacht would enjoy. While Löhr took advantage of the Bulgarian misstep in the Balkans, the long-awaited Ardennes offensive in the west had turned into a German disaster.

As a result, the Allies were preparing to cross the Rhine in strength. In the east, meanwhile, the Red Army had taken Warsaw and was driving on the Oder River, not far from Berlin. And there was still no sign of the secret "miracle weapons" that would turn the tide, as Goebbels and his propagandists had long been promising.

After a brief leave, Waldheim returned to headquarters, more worried about Cissy than ever.

Early in March, Löhr moved his headquarters farther north to Djakovo; shortly thereafter he moved north again, this time to Resetari. On March 23, Hitler retired Field Marshal von Weichs, naming Löhr to replace him as supreme commander in the southeast. Three days later, Löhr established new headquarters in Zagreb; three days after that, Sarajevo fell to the partisans.

Once a bright and cheerful place, "White" Zagreb had long since been corrupted by inflation and black marketeering. Refugees fleeing the partisans crowded in from all over the Balkans—only to find that the presence of Löhr's headquarters made the place a prime target for the Allied air forces. Even the Russians bombed Zagreb, though at night and with little accuracy.[17]

It wasn't long before Löhr learned that he would have to move north yet again. Word that the Germans were planning to abandon the Croatian capital enraged the Ustasha. Though the Croatian dictator Ante Pavelić had been able to flee the city, most of Pavelić's followers knew they would not be so fortunate; unlike their leader, they had nowhere to go. As a result, Löhr warned his staff to be prepared to deal with Croatian sabotage once the orders to evacuate Zagreb became official.[18]

Amid the gloom and chaos, there was some good news. In late March or early April, Waldheim received leave, which he used to move Cissy out of Vienna, finding her refuge in Ramsau, a little town in Upper Styria. Food was scarce in the area, but so were Allied bombs. Waldheim sent word to his sister Gerlinde, who was relatively safe in Haag am Hausruck in Upper Austria, asking if she could help out. Cissy was due to deliver in less than two months. While one world died, another was being born.

The final collapse of Hitler's Greater German Reich began early in April 1945. The Allies had already crossed the Rhine in the west. Now the Soviets launched their final drive on Berlin from the east. At the same time, the Allied noose on Austria was closing. While the American Fifth Army moved northward across Italy's Po Valley toward the Tyrol and Carinthia, and the Seventh Army raced southeast through Bavaria toward Salzburg and Upper Austria, Soviet forces were breaking through German lines in the Burgenland and Lower Austria and soon laying siege to Vienna.

From his bunker deep beneath the rubble of Berlin, Hitler ordered Vienna held to the bitter end. Enraged by the news that Austrians in the capital had raised the old red-and-white flag as a symbol of a new, free Austria, German artillerymen used the spire of St. Stephan's Cathedral as an orientation point to shell the city.

The Soviets entered Vienna on April 13. Once in the great city, they turned almost immediately on the civilian population. Drunken Red Army soldiers methodically looted homes, destroyed property, robbed passersby, and assaulted women. One Viennese physician estimated that as many as seventy thousand women were raped by rampaging Russian troops.[19] Soviet officers soon restored order, but the memory of those anarchic April days was not easily forgotten. Elderly Viennese still refer to the monument to the victorious Red Army in the Schwarzenbergplatz as the "Monument to the Unknown Rapist."

While the Red Army stormed through Vienna, Lieutenant Waldheim received his last German medal and his last Wehrmacht assignment. On the Führer's birthday, April 20, he was awarded the War Merit Cross, First Class, with Swords, in recognition of his staff work for General Löhr. Four days later, he received frightening orders. Having decided that they could no longer afford the luxury of keeping a young, healthy officer like Waldheim off the front lines, his desperate superiors transferred him to the 1st March Regiment of the 438th Infantry Division, a weak reserve unit fighting the partisans in western Slovenia, north of Trieste.

Together with some comrades, Waldheim obediently headed out in search of his new unit. The signs of total collapse were all around him. The roads were a mess, littered with wrecked, overturned vehicles and crowded with long columns of refugees babbling a half-dozen different languages. After a few days, he was forced to detour north. Anxious about Cissy and the baby, who was now due in less than a month, Waldheim was making his way toward Klagenfurt in eastern Carinthia when he heard that the Führer had killed himself, supposedly "fighting to his last breath against Bolshevism."

At the same time, the main body of Army Group E was falling back in much the same direction as Waldheim. As the Soviets advanced from the east, the Tito divisions from the south, and the British from the west, the Klagenfurt area was beginning to resemble what an Allied intelligence report described as "the corner of the sink to which all dregs appeared to drain."[20]

Aware that the German Armed Forces High Command intended to surrender to the Allies on May 7, General Löhr spent the last few days of the war desperately trying to arrange to hand over his army group to the British—rather than the Soviets or, even worse, the Yugoslavs. Löhr knew well just how Tito's partisans felt about Army Group E; he expected no mercy from them.[21]

While negotiating with the British, Löhr made one basic decision. Whatever happened, he would not abandon his troops. Even if he had to surrender to the Yugoslavs, he would accompany his men into captivity. When General Schmidt-Richberg heard of his commander's decision, he asked Löhr if he was aware of what it meant. Löhr replied without hesitation: "Without a doubt, death."

In the end, the British turned down Löhr's appeal that he be allowed to surrender to them. For one thing, they had neither the means nor the desire to feed and police the more than 200,000 men of Army Group E. For another, they saw no reason to offend the Yugoslavs, who were demanding custody of Löhr and his army. (The Yugoslavs were motivated by more than simple revenge; Tito saw all those skilled Germans as a labor force that could help him rebuild his shattered country.)

When the British position became clear, many of Löhr's troops begged him to let them keep fighting rather than surrender to the Yugoslavs, yelling to him, "Father Löhr, give us the order to open fire!" But Löhr knew he had no choice. The only alternative was to continue a hopeless battle on Austrian territory. Not only would more men be killed, but his own homeland would be devastated in the process. Löhr thus ended his negotiations with the British. Urging his personal staff to seek safety in the West, he agreed to hand over Army Group E—and himself—to the Yugoslavs.

Still at large, near Istria, Lieutenant Waldheim had finally—and sensibly—given up trying to reach the 438th Infantry Division. He had a new goal in mind: to get home to Cissy in Ramsau. Exhausted, hitching rides on passing military vehicles, he slowly made his way north through Carinthia and into Styria, at last reaching Ramsau in the second week of May 1945. His overjoyed wife had a surprise for him—their new daughter, Lieselotte. She had been born on May 7.

Though worried about his parents—Baden had been overrun by the Red Army—Waldheim breathed a huge sigh of relief. Not only had he, his wife, and their new daughter all survived the war, but Ramsau was in territory controlled by the Western Allies, not the Russians.

Still, conditions were abysmal. There was precious little food, and the roads were clogged with every type of human being: liberated slave workers (now called "displaced persons") trudging home, thousands of Wehrmacht soldiers heading back to Germany, civilians looking for relatives, Allied military detachments in the early stages of establishing their own authority. Brigandage and looting were widespread.

Waldheim hoped to stay awhile in Ramsau with Cissy and the baby, then head back with them to Baden to find his parents—or if that wasn't possible, to his sister's house in Upper Austria. The first thing he had to do, however, was get his official release from the army. As efficient as ever, the Wehrmacht had established a series of district demobilization offices. Waldheim reported to the one in Ramsau, where he turned in his sidearm and had his paybook stamped. Though he could not shed his uniform until he had identified himself to the local U.S. Army authorities, he was no longer Lieutenant Waldheim.

In the middle of May, the newly demobilized Dr. Waldheim reported to the American processing center in nearby Schladming. He did not expect any problems. After all, he had been nothing more than an obscure reserve first lieutenant in the Wehrmacht, and an Austrian one, at that. At most, he figured, he might have to attend a lecture or two, and perhaps undergo an interrogation.

Waldheim was in for a bitter disappointment. Unbeknownst to him, the Americans were aware that he had served as an intelligence officer under General Löhr. (British military intelligence had learned of his record late in April and shared the information with the American OSS.) Thus, instead of being released after a few simple formalities, he was told to inform his family not to expect him home anytime soon.

The Americans then ordered him to get into a truck filled with former Wehrmacht soldiers. Most of the other men considered themselves lucky. The Americans would treat them decently, they knew, unlike the Russians or the Yugoslavs.

Outside Schladming, Waldheim's truck joined a convoy of similar vehicles. Slowly, the column wound its way toward the west, the bad condition of the roads forcing it to make detour after detour. The traffic—everything from Allied tanks to refugee horse carts—was horrendous. Eventually, the convoy reached its destination in Bavaria. Kurt Waldheim was now an inmate at the POW camp near Bad Tölz.[22]

PART TWO

The Man Without a Past

CHAPTER TEN

To the Ballhausplatz

Kurt Waldheim did not remain a POW for very long. Having endorsed the Moscow Declaration, with its pledge to restore a "free, independent, and democratic Austria," the Americans tried to release Austrian prisoners as quickly as they could process them—generally speaking, within a month or so. In any case, Waldheim came across in his debriefings as an innocuous enough fellow. As far as anyone could tell, he had never been a member of the Nazi party, he had not served in the S.S., and his name wasn't on any war-crimes lists.

Bad Tölz was an interrogation center that specialized in questioning prisoners "of interest" to U.S. military intelligence. What made Waldheim interesting was his knowledge of Communist organizations and partisan tactics, which he had acquired as an Ic officer.

Fortunately for Waldheim, with the Soviets dominating Vienna, the Americans were very nervous about the political situation in newly liberated Austria, and he was precisely the sort of young anti-Communist whom the Americas felt was needed to help rebuild the country. As a result, he was released from Bad Tölz and was able to make it back to Ramsau by the middle of June 1945.

Cissy and baby Lieselotte were fine, but food was in short supply in Styria. Conditions were better in Upper Austria, where Waldheim's sister Gerlinde had settled. Thus, at the end of June, with Gerlinde's help, Kurt moved his family to a peasant's cottage in Obermettenback, near Haag am Hausruck.[1]

While Waldheim looked after his wife and child, the victorious Allies were determining his country's future. The war had left Austria in ruins. Nearly 400,000 of its people had been killed, including 85,000 civilians (mostly Jews) who were murdered by the Nazis. Tens of thousands more remained in Allied prison camps. Much of the country was on the verge of starvation.

Vienna was in particularly bad shape. Though the capital had not suffered the terrible destruction of Warsaw or Dresden, it was nonetheless a grim, shattered city. Almost 21,000 buildings had been destroyed or heavily damaged, including the two great symbols of Viennese grandeur, the opera house and St. Stephan's Cathedral. Much of the city was without gas or electricity. Water had to be trucked in from the suburbs. Forty percent of the tram lines were unusable.

Adding to the misery was the conduct of the 400,000 Russian troops who now controlled the Vienna region, acting more like conquerors than liberators. The Soviet High Command had installed itself in the Hotel Imperial, replacing the portrait of Emperor Franz Joseph with a twenty-five-foot-high likeness of Stalin. The Russians also took over the Grand Hotel, and turned part of the Hofburg complex into a Soviet officers club. While the Soviet generals staged elaborate military parades and held lavish dinners and ornate balls to demonstrate their power, civilian Viennese of all ages found themselves being conscripted by the Russians to clear rubble from the streets. (The unwilling workers received half a loaf of bread for a full day's labor.)[2]

Things were not much better in the Soviet-controlled parts of Lower Austria, Burgenland, and Styria. Despite the Moscow Declaration, which had asserted that Austria had been the Nazis' first victim, the Soviets behaved as if they were occupying a defeated aggressor. Believing themselves entitled to expropriate "German" property in Austria, Stalin's troops systematically looted the areas they controlled. In Styria, Soviet generals disassembled factories and sent them back to Russia—in the process, removing fully 40 percent of eastern Austria's industrial capacity (an amount equal to what had been destroyed by bombing during the war). In Burgenland and Lower Austria, the hungry nation's breadbasket, they seized thousands of hectares of prime farmland, claiming they needed it as training grounds for their soldiers. By the time the Russians were finished, 70 percent of the region's cattle and 93 percent of its swine had been slaughtered or stolen.[3]

To be sure, the Soviets weren't the only ones who behaved barbarically. Western soldiers engaged in looting and raping too, though not nearly on the scale of the Russians. Acting out of ignorance rather than malice, they also destroyed countless irreplaceable documents embodying three centuries of Austrian history, which archivists had carefully removed from the House, Court, and State Archives before the siege of Vienna. At Markhof Castle, British troops threw twenty-five hundred bundles of such documents out of the windows in order to make room for cots. At Güntersdorf Castle, soldiers burned nearly nine hundred similar bundles for fuel. Some documents were even torn up for use as wrapping paper.[4]

The Allied troops were inadvertently continuing a project begun by the Nazis: the obliteration of Austria's national memory. With many Austrians busily burning documents of more recent vintage in an effort to hide their wartime political and military activities from prying Allied eyes, the country was in danger of falling into a kind of collective amnesia.

By early July 1945, the four Allied powers had reached final agreement on the terms of their occupation of Austria. Postwar Austria, they decided, would consist of the lands that lay within the frontiers established in 1937. Inside those borders, the country would be divided into four zones, each controlled by the power whose forces currently occupied it—the Americans in Upper Austria, the British in most of Styria and Carinthia, the French in the Vorarlberg and the Tyrol, and the Russians in Lower Austria, Burgenland, and the non-British part of Styria. To administer Austria as a whole, the four powers established an Allied Council, consisting of the commanders in chief of the four occupying armies, each of whom would also serve as high commissioner of his respective zone; chairmanship of the council would rotate monthly.

Vienna was a separate matter. Recognizing that whoever controlled the capital would inevitably control the entire country, the Allies decided to administer the metropolis jointly under a Vienna Inter-Allied Command. Like the country as a whole, Vienna was divided into four sectors. The heart of the city, which contained all the major government buildings, was declared an International Sector, patrolled by a mixed force of military police drawn from each of the powers (the "four men in a jeep" of Cold War fame).

Not surprisingly, the Soviets, who had liberated Vienna and were now comfortably ensconced there, at first objected to this plan, resisting when the other Allied powers tried to send their own troops and administrative personnel into what were supposed to be their sectors of the city. The Russians quickly relented, however, since they needed Western help to feed the capital and eastern Austria.[5]

* * *

The elaborate Allied administration was meant not to replace the Austrian government but merely to oversee it. In the chaotic aftermath of the war, however, who—or what—was to be that government? The Soviets knew what they wanted. Shortly after the liberation of Vienna in April 1945, they had installed the old Socialist leader Karl Renner as chancellor of a provisional government.

On the face of it, Renner's government seemed a good thing. Renner was a self-confident man (to the point of being something of a garrulous know-it-all), but he was also flexible and clever, and he created a coalition regime that, in addition to Socialists and Communists, included Christian Socials.

Still, the Western Allies were wary, believing Renner's government to be too susceptible to Soviet pressure and not representative enough of the western *Länder*. The United States and Britain were especially put off by Renner's apparent popularity with Stalin. The Soviet leader called the provisional chancellor his "esteemed comrade" and effusively promised him Russian support, assuring him in a letter:

> Please do not doubt that your concern over the independence, integrity, and progress of Austria is my concern as well.
> I am ready to extend any help that Austria might need, to the extent of my ability.

The Western Allies were in a bind. On the one hand, they had real doubts about Renner's coalition. On the other, they were supposed to be in favor of Austrian self-determination. An imperious refusal to recognize the Renner regime would simply confirm what the cynics were saying: that Western promises of a new democratic order amounted to nothing more than yet another naïve dream that was destined to be dashed. The Nazi era had produced a disillusioned generation that regarded all governments as hopelessly corrupt, including the new one. "The same old pigsty," cynics called liberated Austria, "inhabited by new swine." Concerned that such attitudes would make a Soviet takeover of Austria that much easier, the Western Allies wanted to restore faith in democracy. Withholding recognition of Renner's government would have the opposite effect.

At the beginning of May, Renner solved the West's dilemma by including more politicians from western Austria in his government and promising to hold free elections late in November. That, combined with the four-power agreement to administer Vienna jointly, made it possible for the the West to recognize his government.[6]

An equally knotty—and serious—problem remained, however. There were huge gaps in the government infrastructure, created by the departure of Nazi officials who had quit or been fired from their jobs when the Allies took over. Most young people being too cynical or disillusioned about politics to have any interest in participating in public life, the Allies had no choice but to fill the void with figures like Renner, old men who had served the government before the war. The problem was, one could not build a vibrant new democratic order by relying on septuagenarians. The Americans, in particular, wanted reliable young men, whom they had debriefed and vetted, in the new governmental apparatus—nowhere more so than in the foreign ministry. This was clearly a time in which a twenty-six-year-old with a yen for government service—and a clean record—could go far.

After nearly a month in the cottage at Obermettenback, Waldheim decided it was time to take Cissy and the baby home to Baden. Despite the Soviet occupation of the area, his parents seemed to be all right. Walter Waldheim was doing some volunteer work for the Red Cross and helping to reestablish the Lower Austrian school system.

Early in August, Waldheim managed to obtain a place for himself and his family on a freight train heading south. As Waldheim later recalled it, they traveled in a sweltering cattle car jammed with refugees, squeezing themselves between crates of fruits and vegetables. It took them three days to get to Baden, the baby howling incessantly, the train stopping for hours at the demarcation line between the American and Soviet zones.

Though the reunion in Baden was a happy one, Waldheim knew the family was in for a hard autumn and winter. His parents' house had been damaged, and the materials needed to repair it were hard to find.

In addition to building supplies, Waldheim needed to find a job. His first thought was to regain his old post as a junior magistrate at the district court in Baden. Like all adult Austrians, Waldheim would have to fill out a *Fragebogen,* or questionnaire, in order to get work—and as a prospective government employee, he would have to answer more than the usual number of questions about his past. Though he didn't anticipate any problems (after all, he had been cleared by the Americans at Bad Tölz), Waldheim decided to play it safe and secure some strong letters of recommendation from unquestioned anti-Nazis. On August 28, 1945, he obtained an affidavit from Herr Schwanzer, the conservative leader of his old hometown of Tulln. A few days later, he went to see Heinrich Wild, the longtime Christian Social mayor of Tulln. Wild immediately wrote him an enthusiastic endorsement. Waldheim then went to see the leader of the Socialist party in Tulln, a man named Stern. Stern wrote a similarly effusive letter, attesting to the fact that the Waldheims were good anti-Nazis.

Waldheim reported to the court in Baden the next day. Once again an assistant judge, he helped his superiors prepare for cases and write opinions.

In October, he had the letters of recommendation from Wild and Stern formally notarized at the Superior State Court in Baden. By then he had composed a résumé, which discreetly mentioned his military service in the "southeast."[7]

Waldheim had far more on his mind than provincial court cases. He had not forgotten the dream that had sustained him for more than a decade now: to go to the Ballhausplatz in Vienna, the home of the Austrian foreign ministry since the days of the Habsburgs, and there join the foreign service.

As dreams went, this was hardly an unrealistic one. For one thing, the Austrian government desperately needed capable young diplomats. For another, Waldheim could boast excellent credentials: Not only did he have a diploma from the Consular Academy and a doctorate in international law, but he spoke or read at least four foreign languages.

The foreign ministry was currently being run by a dynamic young under secretary of state named Karl Gruber, a thirty-six-year-old *Wunderkind* whose energy and enthusiasm were already becoming legendary in government circles. As soon as his papers were all in order, Waldheim planned to call on Dr. Gruber.

Though its government would not achieve real legitimacy until after the parliamentary elections were held at the end of November, by the early fall Austria was already taking on at least the trappings of a democratic republic. The Allies had permitted the reappearance of trade unions and the reestablishment of a free press (provided, of course, that the newspapers did not question the authority of the occupying powers). They also granted citizens the right to move freely throughout the country (at least in principle). They even gave the government the right to pass its own laws (subject at first to Allied approval).[8]

The political situation was equally encouraging. Taking its cue from Renner, moderate elements of the Socialist party were working harmoniously with the anti-Fascist wing of the old Christian Social movement.

Many left-wingers still hadn't forgiven the Christian Socials for suppressing them in the thirties, but Renner and Socialist party leader Adolf
Schärf had no compunctions about working with conservatives. The past
offered only bitterness; they looked to the future.

For their part, the Christian Socials had rejected the clerical fascism
of the Dollfuss-Schuschnigg era and renamed themselves the *Volkspartei*,
or Austrian People's Party (ÖVP). Their new titular head was Leopold
Kunschak, a seventy-four-year-old Catholic trade unionist who had opposed the suppression of the Socialists in 1933–34, calling instead for a
united front against the Nazi menace. Though the People's party still
reflected the Catholic Church's views on education and cultural issues, it
was more liberal and democratic than the old Christian Social movement.
Kunschak, for example, supported the Church's recent decision to pro-
hibit priests from engaging in political activity.

Despite the Church's diminished role, the Waldheims supported the
new People's party. In part, that was because an old acquaintance of
Walter Waldheim's, Leopold Figl, had emerged as the party's real boss.
The elder Waldheim had gotten to know Figl before the war, when Figl
was an agricultural leader in Lower Austria. A supporter of Dollfuss, Figl
had run afoul of the Nazis and spent nearly six years in the concentration
camp at Dachau. (He was awaiting "trial" on charges of high treason
when the U.S. Army liberated the camp on April 6, 1945.)

Now the leader of the powerful Peasants' League, Figl served in
Renner's provisional government as state secretary without portfolio. He
was not a brilliant man, but he did have good political common sense. In
particular, he had learned the great lesson of the 1930s: that the only
alternative to democracy in Austria was fascism and war. Thus, though
he had no use for socialism, he was willing to join with Renner and Schärf
in the work of national reconstruction.[9]

He was also willing—indeed, eager—to establish good relations with
Ernst Fischer, the brilliant leader of the Austrian Communist party. Karl
Renner did the same, urging Fischer to merge his organization with the
Socialists. Though many Austrians hated the Communists—regarding the
behavior of the Russian troops in Vienna as proof that Hitler had been
right about Bolshevism—Renner and Figl recognized that the four-power
occupation of their country would never end without Soviet agreement.
And the most likely way of obtaining that was to get along with the local
Communists.[10]

For a country that had seen more than its share of charismatic dema-
gogues, Figl was exactly the sort of political leader Austria needed. He was
pleasant and down-to-earth, wily but unthreatening. Completely unpre-

tentious, he resembled nothing so much as a prosperous farmer dressed up for a trip to the big city.

The upcoming parliamentary elections dominated the news in the autumn of 1945. Voter enthusiasm, however, was minimal. Austrians had heard too much political rhetoric over the previous decade. A clear majority seemed to favor the new democratic order, but weariness and cynicism muted their cheers.

Most people expected the Socialists to win. After all, they had been in the desert for thirteen years, and they had the father figure of Karl Renner to boost their image. What's more, they were popularly believed to have the Allies on their side—especially now that a Labor government had taken power in Britain.

When the country finally went to the polls on Sunday, November 25, 1945, the results surprised everyone. Instead of the Socialists, it was the People's party that won—and not simply a plurality of seats but an absolute majority. Renner promptly stepped down as chancellor, yielding the post to Figl. Figl, in turn, named the patriarchal Renner to the largely ceremonial post of president (a post Renner's Socialist party continued to control until Waldheim won it forty-one years later).

The outright victory of the People's party notwithstanding, Figl and Renner knew that the best way to convince the Allies that Austria really could be trusted to govern itself again would be to create a coalition regime. Figl thus invited both Communists and Socialists to join his government, appointing Socialist party chief Schärf as his vice-chancellor. He also filled his cabinet with staunch anti-Fascists; nine of the seventeen ministers he named had been jailed by the Nazis, while four more had been imprisoned during the Dollfuss-Schuschnigg era.[11]

No one was more delighted by the election results than Karl Gruber. The brilliant young under secretary of state for foreign affairs hailed from Innsbruck in the Tyrol, a longtime bastion of the Christian Social movement, now firmly behind the victorious People's party.

Gruber was a political conservative with impeccable anti-Nazi credentials. After the *Anschluss,* he had attempted to emigrate to America, where his wife had secured him a lectureship at Fordham University in New York. The Nazis, however, would not let him leave Austria. Instead, he got a job as an engineer for Siemens and Halsko. (Though he had studied law at the University of Vienna, his principal interest was communications technology.) He wound up spending the war traveling between Vienna and Berlin, taking advantage of his freedom of movement and his exemption from military service to become active in the Austrian resistance, eventually becoming western leader of the Provisional Austrian National Committee. Just before the final collapse, he had returned to Innsbruck, where he distinguished himself (along with about one thousand other resisters) in the struggle to preserve the city from destruction at the hands of the vindictive and fanatical S.S.

A decisive man of action, Gruber quickly impressed the Americans who liberated Innsbruck with his "can do" attitude and perceptive grasp of local politics. As a result, despite his tender years—and the objections of older politicians, who grumbled about this pipsqueak who had come out of nowhere—the Americans appointed him *Landeshauptmann*, or governor, of the province. It was a clever choice. Not only was Gruber young and dynamic, but he provided a Western-oriented counterweight to the elderly Renner, whom the Americans viewed as being too much under Moscow's thumb.

When Renner expanded his provisional government in May 1945, Karl Gruber was one of the western Austrians he added to his cabinet. Though he was nominally only under secretary of state for foreign affairs, Gruber functioned as de facto foreign minister. Working out of the chancellor's office, he saw the opportunity to accomplish three major goals: He could represent the western provinces in Vienna; he could reunite his beloved Tyrol (the southern section of which had been annexed by Italy in 1919); and he could work to liberate Austria from the four-power occupation.[12]

Before Gruber could do anything, however, he had to rebuild the Austrian foreign ministry. In part, that meant physically restoring the place. The famous offices on the Ballhausplatz had been badly damaged in the last weeks of the war. Lacking electricity, the small staff worked by candlelight or the flickering glow of kerosene lamps.

More challenging than reconstructing the physical plant was rebuilding the staff. Gruber had no intention of bringing back the hidebound diplomatic corps of the Dollfuss-Schuschnigg era. Instead, he began to populate the ministry with ambitious, hardworking young men. As his top personal and political aide, he chose Fritz Peter Molden, a glamorous, adventurous figure still in his twenties. A veteran of the resistance, Molden had worked for the American OSS during the war, collecting intelligence about the Wehrmacht and the German war economy in Austria and northern Italy.

Gruber had first met Molden in Innsbruck in the last days of the war. The two young men wound up celebrating the fall of the Reich together. Years later, Molden recalled the sense of euphoria they had shared:

[A]ll that night we sat drinking together and exchanging dreams.
. . . After seven years we had a country of our own once more; Austria
had risen out of the ashes, and we were no longer second-, third-, or
fourth-rate human beings, but just as good as the next man.[13]

Gruber was determined to preserve that feeling. Though the Austrian
underground had been too small and its actions too inconsequential to
justify the creation of an elaborate mythology such as that which glorified
the resistance in France, Russia, or Yugoslavia, Gruber believed that
veterans of the struggle like himself and Molden could still bring something of value to the new government of a reborn Austria.

Both Gruber and Molden had strong ties to U.S. intelligence. Molden
actually wound up marrying the daughter of OSS (later CIA) chief Allen
Dulles, for whom he had worked during the war. For his part, Gruber
began providing information and documents to the 430th Detachment
of the U.S. Counter-Intelligence Corps in the spring of 1945. (He continued doing so until at least the early fifties.) This, after all, was the
American Century, as Henry Luce had called it. Gruber believed what
Luce preached: that with American support, Austria could regain her
liberty and achieve a new prosperity.

As a result, one of Gruber's top priorities was preventing the Soviets
from infiltrating the foreign ministry. That meant finding young men who
were not only capable but also acceptable to U.S. intelligence authorities.[14]

Getting the foreign ministry going again was not an easy task. Vienna
was a violent, anarchic place in the immediate aftermath of the war. It
was the world of Graham Greene's *The Third Man*, where anything was
available for a price. Staggering inflation, overwhelming poverty, and
shortages of everything from food to tires to penicillin had created a black
marketeer's paradise. The city was so dangerous that Gruber and his staff
often slept at the ministry rather than tempt the fates by risking the
streets late at night. Even if a young diplomat managed to avoid being
waylaid by robbers, there was always the chance that he might be grabbed
by Soviet soldiers, handed a shovel, and ordered to start clearing away
rubble.[15]

On the morning of October 8, 1945, Fritz Molden was at his desk in the
ministry, reading letters and reports by candlelight, when he heard someone enter his office. He looked up and saw a very tall young man wearing
an old, once elegant pair of knickerbockers, his dark blond hair combed
straight back. Smiling nervously, the stranger introduced himself as Kurt

Waldheim. "Can you direct me to the personnel office?" he asked in a soft, deferential voice.

Molden motioned toward a door at the other end of the hallway, and Waldheim disappeared down the corridor.

It had taken Waldheim several hours to make the journey from Baden to the Ballhausplatz. He had awakened very early that morning, then walked several miles to Mödling, where he waited for the ramshackle tram that would take him into Vienna. Clutched in his fist were his precious papers—the letters of recommendation from Tulln and his carefully worded résumé—his tickets to what he hoped would be a brighter future.

Later that day, Gruber summoned Molden. He wanted to discuss this tall young man who had just applied for a post. The two men agreed that Waldheim seemed promising. His training at the Consular Academy, his doctorate in international law, his grasp of foreign languages (French, Italian, English, some Serbo-Croatian), his stated desire to become a career diplomat, his willingness to start work immediately—it was all very impressive.

Above all, Waldheim's timing was fortuitous. Gruber's diplomatic secretary was about to leave his post, and Molden himself was becoming restless. When Molden had first joined the foreign ministry staff, he told Gruber he would serve until things had settled down. Now that Austria had a duly elected government, he felt the time had come for him to move on.

Decisive as always, Gruber persuaded Molden to stay on awhile longer. Then he called Waldheim in and told him he was considering hiring him as his new personal diplomatic secretary. But first, he added, some security checks had to be completed. The Allies were determined to prevent any Nazis and other security risks from entering Austrian government service.

Gruber turned the background investigation over to Molden. In turn, Molden asked his friends in American intelligence to check Waldheim out. This was, of course, redundant. Eventually, Molden reported to Gruber that his contacts had "investigated [Waldheim] and found no material on him, nothing, nothing."

Forty years later, Molden recalled that it was clear to him and Gruber at the time that they were dealing with "a man who is not a hero, not the type of guy who goes into the underground." Still, he admitted, "we did not ask [Waldheim] very much [about his background], we didn't put much importance in it, which might have been a mistake."[16]

* * *

As a result of Molden's favorable report, Gruber told Waldheim the job was his. His title would be Provisional Attaché in the chancellor's office, Department of Foreign Affairs. Overjoyed, Waldheim promptly gave notice at the Baden court. His last day there was November 30.

Walter and Cissy were ecstatic. Less than a month short of his twenty-seventh birthday, the would-be diplomat was finally on his way. Modestly, Waldheim pointed out that he was merely an administrative assistant, that he would have to prove himself before he would be allowed even to get close to handling anything of substance.

His first task was to find a place to live, preferably near the Ballhausplatz. In the end, the housing shortage, and his meager means, forced him to rent a small single room in a large apartment. He didn't like having to leave Cissy and Lieselotte with Walter, but he had no choice. Anyway, it was safer for the family in Baden, and food was more readily available in the nearby rural markets. Family was important, but so was his career. He could commute home on weekends.

Though his appointment was formally dated December 1, 1945, Waldheim didn't actually report to work at the foreign ministry until the following Thursday, December 6. A probationary employee on a three-month tryout, he showed Gruber the same modesty, enthusiasm, and dedication that had so impressed his superiors in the Wehrmacht.

Gruber was like no boss Waldheim had ever had before. Brash and impulsive, when he decided it was time for Austria to reestablish her ties to Czechoslovakia, he did not merely send a telegram to his counterpart in the Czech government; he piled into a car with an aide and a chauffeur, and drove to Prague himself, undeterred by either normal protocol or a blinding snowstorm.[17]

While the restless Gruber pursued his often fanciful schemes, Waldheim kept the office functioning, making sure that the telephones worked, that stationery was available, that visitors were treated courteously, and that the right people got in to see the minister promptly. He also listened patiently as Gruber enthusiastically expounded his plans for reclaiming the South Tyrol from Italy or restoring Austria's place in the world. Often, in his meticulous way, Waldheim would correct a mistaken assumption or point out an inconsistency that might cause the young foreign minister to rethink his ideas.[18]

Given his plans for the Tyrol, Gruber was delighted to discover that his new aide understood a lot about negotiating with the Italians. Waldheim also seemed to know something about Yugoslavia, but it was unclear how much. In any case, Gruber was soon soliciting Waldheim's quiet and carefully considered opinions about a wide variety of matters, including personnel decisions. With his energy and quicksilver temperament, Gruber usually burned out his subordinates. Waldheim thrived.[19]

Always agreeable and eager to please, Waldheim delighted in doing favors, not just for his boss but for the people who came to see him, regardless of their politics. One day early in his tenure with Gruber, a short, stocky, intense young man with a ruddy complexion and curly reddish hair appeared in front of his desk. His name was Bruno Kreisky, and he wanted an appointment with Gruber—right away. Though Kreisky was a Socialist who had been imprisoned by the Dollfuss-Schuschnigg regime, Waldheim got him in to see the minister.

Kreisky had sat out the war in exile in Sweden. Now, as Austria's representative in Stockholm, he was assisting Swedish relief agencies in providing badly needed aid to the Austrian people. "When I came to see Gruber, Waldheim was always helpful," Kreisky told me forty years later. "He arranged appointments without delay. I knew that he was a clerical, but that did not cause any difficulties."

Gruber influenced Waldheim in many ways. Among other things, he affected his young aide's opinions about America. While Waldheim's dissertation had demonstrated his ignorance of—and mild hostility toward—the United States, Gruber was endlessly enthusiastic about the Americans. Only the Americans could save Europe, he insisted. If Waldheim was smart, he added, he would perfect his English. Waldheim followed his boss's advice.

In 1946, Gruber visited the United States. He returned to Vienna, to regale Waldheim with his descriptions of the Manhattan skyline, the praise heaped on him by Henry Luce's magazines, and the honorary degree he received from the University of Southern California. He also brought home a new enthusiasm—the importance of the United Nations. Gruber had come away from a talk with UN secretary-general Trygve Lie convinced that Austria would soon be admitted to membership in the world body. The UN, he felt, was an ideal place for a small nation trying to regain its freedom. Besides, his American friends controlled it.

Waldheim listened carefully. He thought Gruber was probably right about the UN. After all, there were strong similarities between the UN concept and the federalist ideals he had described in his 1944 doctoral dissertation. (Just the same, he did not say much about his dissertation to Gruber.)

Gruber and Waldheim spent a lot of their time working on two projects: gaining more foreign aid for Austria and reopening diplomatic relations with as many nations as they could. Waldheim was particularly interested in restoring Austria's foreign ties. Eager to see more of the world, he was hoping to be posted abroad as soon as possible.

Anxious not to lose his capable new attaché, Gruber reassured Waldheim that great things were about to happen in the Ballhausplatz. Gruber felt he was close to persuading the four powers to sign a treaty restoring Austria's sovereignty and independence. He was certain that with Western support he could pull it off. Waldheim might even be present when such a treaty was negotiated. (This treaty would be called a "state treaty" as opposed to a peace treaty, since the Allies regarded Austria as a victim of the Third Reich and not a cobelligerent power.)

As exciting as that prospect was, Waldheim had more immediate concerns. His three-month probationary period would end at the close of February. If he chose, Gruber could give him a second three-month conditional appointment. But that was it. As of June 1, 1946, Waldheim had to be either accepted as a permanent employee of the foreign ministry—or discharged, his career over before it had barely begun.

Which road his future took would depend on the outcome of an Austrian investigation into his political past.

CHAPTER ELEVEN

Denazification

At its height, the Austrian National Socialist party had boasted some 700,000 members. Many of them did not survive the war, and some fled to Germany and elsewhere in the last weeks before the final collapse. Even so, when the Allies took over in May 1945, there were still more than half a million Nazis in Austria—roughly 8 percent of the country's total population.

In an effort to purge the Nazi bacillus from Austrian society, the Allies embarked on a program known as *Entnazifizierung*, or denazification. The party and its affiliates were dissolved, the teaching of National Socialist doctrines was outlawed, and huge numbers of former party members were either arrested or barred from employment. By September 1, 1945, some 55,000 Austrian Nazis had been imprisoned by the Allies; within a year after that, another 110,000 had been dismissed from their jobs.[1]

The main instrument of this massive undertaking was the Allies' Denazification Bureau. The bureau began its work by requiring all former party members to register with the occupation government and fill out lengthy forms detailing their wartime activities. Unfortunately, the bureau lacked the manpower to review—no less actually investigate—more than a third of the 500,000 questionnaires it managed to collect.[2]

As far as some Allied authorities were concerned, that was just as well. While everyone agreed that all vestiges of National Socialism had to be stamped out, denazification wasn't the only Allied priority. There were other, equally important imperatives, some of which actively conflicted with the work of the Denazification Bureau. For one thing, how could the war-torn Austrian economy be restored to health if a large minority of the country's population was ostracized, imprisoned, or otherwise barred from the labor force? For another, shouldn't the Austrians be cleaning their own house? After all, according to the Moscow Declaration, they were just as much victims of Nazi aggression as anyone else.

In the end, the Allies came to agree on a subtle formula. "Good" Austrians would be given broad authority to conduct the denazification program themselves, under the following guidelines: Austrian Nazis who had been important figures in the party would have to leave their jobs (in some cases, their professions); those diehards who had belonged to the party during the "Illegal" period would suffer heavier penalties than the opportunists who joined after March 1938; unimportant, rank-and-file party members (those "less implicated") would be subject to the lightest penalties of all: Though they might lose their right to vote for a few years and have to pay fines, they would be considered rehabilitated after demonstrating good behavior.

Even these relatively modest strictures could be suspended if circumstances warranted. Perhaps the best example of this was seen in the Austrian judiciary. As late as 1946, there were still seventy-two judges on the bench in Vienna (out of a total of 231) who had been members of the Nazi party. Technically, their Nazi backgrounds should have barred them from hearing cases and dispensing justice. But with anarchy threatening, the capital needed courts and judges more than ever. As a result, the questionable judges were declared "denazified."[3]

Kurt Waldheim knew some of these judges, at least by reputation. If they could be forgiven their wartime indiscretions, then he shouldn't have any problems.

On January 10, 1946, the Allied Council formally voted to turn the daily work of denazification over to the government of newly elected Chancellor Leopold Figl. (The Denazification Bureau would, however, retain the authority to intervene if it was felt that the Austrians were slacking.)

The Allies instructed Figl to make his top priority the purging of any and all former Nazis from the "Austrian government machinery." Figl replied that his government had already cleaned house. As proof, he pointed to the fact that a review of all government employees by the Denazification Bureau had so far led to only four dismissals. But the Allies were insistent. The Austrians were to complete a new, broader series of personnel investigations no later than April 17.[4]

To do the job, Figl appointed a Ministerial Committee for Denazification, consisting of himself, Vice-Chancellor Schärf, and four other men, including his de facto foreign minister, Karl Gruber. In turn, the committee authorized the establishment of 173 special commissions to hear whatever cases were deemed worthy of review.

The impact of the new round of investigations was quickly felt throughout the government—even by as junior an aide as Gruber's provisional attaché, Kurt Waldheim. On January 23, as he neared the end of his first three-month probationary period at the foreign ministry, Waldheim learned that he was going to be asked to explain some of his political affiliations—in particular, his membership in the S.A. Cavalry Corps and the National Socialist German Students League. The prospect didn't trouble him overly: He hadn't been an officer of either organization—and anyway, neither group was considered by his inquisitors to have been particularly significant. Perhaps more important, Waldheim knew he could count on Gruber's support.

Waldheim's confidence in his boss was at least partly based on the fact that Gruber was openly critical of the denazification effort, arguing that a National Socialist background shouldn't by itself automatically disqualify anyone from participating in the new democratic order. (With his impressive record of anti-Nazi activism, the young foreign minister could voice such heretical opinions with impunity.) A shrewd, ambitious politician, Gruber was keenly aware that there were huge numbers of former Nazi rank-and-filers in the Tyrol, his home province, as well as in adjoining Styria and Carinthia. As a potential voting bloc, they were too powerful to be ignored.

Nonetheless, Waldheim saw no reason to take any chances. By way of preparing for the inquiry, he had his character references notarized at a court in the inner city and he spent two days writing a statement explaining just how he had come to be enrolled in the two suspect organizations. As he told it, he could not have completed his studies without joining the Students League, nor would he have been permitted to begin his legal career without being part of some Nazi-affiliated body like the S.A. Cavalry Corps. He also claimed that his activity in the S.A. group had been of a "sports-like" character. The tone of the statement was both callow and self-pitying, seeming to suggest that the compromises he had made were more than justified by the overall goal—the advancement of his career.

Waldheim returned to the notary on February 6 to obtain certification of the 1940 Nazi evaluation that had described him as having been "a supporter of the Schuschnigg regime [whose record] boasted ample evidence of his hostility toward our movement." He was convinced that this proof of his pre-*Anschluss* patriotism, plus the laudatory letters he had secured from Schwanzer, Wild, and Stern, would more than make up for any embarrassing associations with Nazi organizations. (He was equally sanguine about his wife's Nazi background. Cissy was neither practicing law nor working for the state, and he could not imagine that Austrian authorities would investigate a twenty-three-year-old housewife and mother.)

Indeed, the impending inquiry notwithstanding, Waldheim was certain enough of his future at the Ballhausplatz to start making plans to move his wife and daughter to Vienna. On February 21, he wrote to the local housing authority requesting preferential treatment in securing an apartment for himself and his family, on the grounds that his work at the foreign ministry made convenient housing "indispensable." Waldheim realized that bringing Cissy and Lieselotte into town would sharply increase his expenses, but he knew he would be in line for a raise when he was made a permanent government employee on June 1.[5]

Denazification Case No. SK 235, in the matter of a twenty-seven-year-old provisional government attaché named Kurt Waldheim, was referred to a special commission on March 28, 1946. Waldheim's dossier contained the statement he had written, his court records, and material from the foreign ministry.[6]

SK 235 was one of more than thirteen thousand similar cases up for review—too many for the overworked, understaffed special commissions to handle by the April 17 deadline the Allies had set. Figl thus asked for an extension, declaring that his Ministerial Committee on Denazification needed more time to complete its work. The Allies were not pleased. Not only did many officials feel the denazification effort was moving far too slowly, but some complained that the Austrians tended to ignore "compromising evidence which is close at hand." The government rejected the charges, insisting that it was "in all its branches [free] of the National Socialist spirit."[7]

The Allies weren't the only ones who were impatient at the slow pace of denazification. Gruber was also in a hurry, but for a different reason. Among other factors, Waldheim was too valuable an aide to be kept dangling.

On April 15, two days before the commissions were scheduled to go out of business, the foreign ministry contacted the unit handling Case No. SK 235 and requested an immediate decision on Waldheim, without further discussion or testimony. The request was ignored. At the last minute, however, the Allies agreed to extend their deadline. The commissions would have an extra six weeks—until June 30, 1946—to complete their work.

By June 29, the special commission had still not taken any action on Case No. SK 235. Its patience exhausted, the foreign ministry retrieved Waldheim's dossier and—even though no finding had been made regarding his background—appointed him a career member of the Austrian foreign service, retroactive to June 1.

In the end, the special commissions managed to resolve only about half the cases presented to them. SK 235 was not one of them. The following November, Waldheim received formal notice that he would not be subject to any penalties arising from having had Nazi affiliations, nor would he be required to register with the government as a former Nazi. He was, in short, officially denazified. No one cared about his military record.[8]

Shortly after he received his permanent appointment, Waldheim moved his family into Vienna. He also redoubled his efforts on behalf of Karl Gruber.

The summer of 1946 was a busy one for Gruber and Waldheim. In six months' time, the deputy foreign ministers of Britain, France, the Soviet Union, and the United States would be meeting in London to discuss the future status of Germany and Austria—and to Gruber's delight, Austria would be invited to send a delegation. Ever the optimist, Gruber took this as a sign that the Allies were at last ready to draft the long-awaited state treaty that would finally end the four-power occupation of his homeland.

Optimism, however, was no justification for complacency, and Gruber, Waldheim, and the rest of the small foreign ministry staff worked hard getting ready for the deputies' conference. In particular, Gruber knew he had to be prepared to debate two big issues in London—the so-called German assets question and Communist Yugoslavia's claim to a sizable chunk of Austrian territory.[9]

The German assets question arose from an agreement, reached at the July 1945 Big Four meeting in Potsdam, that as a victim itself of Nazi aggression, Austria would not be required to pay any war reparations. Instead, Soviet forces in eastern Austria would be allowed to seize so-called *deutsches Eigentum,* or German assets. Unfortunately, the Allies didn't bother to define exactly what they meant by German assets. The West assumed it referred to property that had belonged to the German Reich, its businesses, or its citizens before the *Anschluss.* The Soviets, on the other hand, maintained that "German assets" also consisted of property brought into Austria by the Germans after the *Anschluss*—including factories built with German capital and property purchased by German investors. Under the Soviet definition, Moscow would be entitled to appropriate much of the Austrian economy, including the vital Zistersdorf oil refinery complex. Gruber intended to oppose this extravagant claim, and he expected the West to support him.

The territorial dispute with Yugoslavia was equally significant. Ever since 1942, Marshal Tito had been asserting Yugoslavia's right to what he called "our Carinthia"—specifically, more than three thousand square kilometers of southern Carinthia and Styria, an area that included the strategically important cities of Klagenfurt and Villach. Indeed, if the British hadn't intervened, Tito would have kept those parts of the disputed territory that he had seized around the time of the German surrender.

To rebut Tito's claims, Gruber appointed two experts to his delegation—Hans Piesch, the Socialist governor of Carinthia, who would talk about how well Austria treated the Slovene minority in his province, and Max Hoffinger, a retired diplomat who had helped to negotiate the 1919 armistice with Yugoslavia.[10]

Unbeknownst to him, Gruber had someone on his staff who was also quite familiar with the issue. Kurt Waldheim had spent twelve months in Yugoslavia during the war, including some time in the disputed territory. Waldheim, however, never told Gruber of his special expertise.

The Big Four deputy foreign ministers convened at Lancaster House in London on January 14, 1947. Almost immediately, they agreed to allow both the Yugoslavs and the Austrians to present their cases on the border question.

Gruber and his delegation arrived in London a week later. Among those in the group was an excited Kurt Waldheim. Gruber had named him legation secretary.

Having never been to London before, Waldheim was looking forward to seeing the fabled sights of the British capital. The weather, however, conspired against him. The winter of 1947 was the worst in modern European history, and threadbare postwar London was ill-equipped to cope. Great drifts of snow paralyzed the city. Traffic was a mess, the streets icy and dangerous. Buses ran late or not at all. Coal shortages caused power outages. As a junket, the expedition was a total bust. The hotel was freezing, the food mediocre, the service poor.[11]

As a diplomatic mission, the trip was equally disappointing. Gruber and his colleagues were not prepared for the vehemence of the Yugoslav attacks on Austria. Before the Austrians even arrived, Yugoslav delegate Josef Vilfan delivered a long, emotional harangue in which he accused Austria of having fought on Hitler's side. He also insisted that many of the 200,000 Yugoslavs living in Austria had been forcibly "Germanized" by the Nazis.

Austrian archivists had provided Gruber's delegation with plenty of material to rebut the Yugoslav territorial claims, and Waldheim, Hoffinger, and Piesch made copious use of it as they helped their foreign minister prepare his reply. Hoping that calm, well-supported arguments would carry more sway with the Allies than Vilfan's self-righteous emotionalism, Gruber pointed out that the Allies had already effectively agreed that Austria should resume her 1937 borders—which, not incidentally, included the disputed territories. He also argued that it made neither geographical nor economic sense to split up Carinthia. And he noted that Yugoslavia had never complained about Austria's treatment of her Slovene minority during the interwar period.[12]

Unfortunately for Gruber, it was big-power politics, not debating skills, that decided disputes like this. The Yugoslavs understood that—and they were just getting warmed up.

The very same week the deputies' conference got under way in London, Tito's government arranged for General Alexander Löhr to go on trial for his life before a war-crimes tribunal in Belgrade. Löhr, of course, was the Austrian-born former commander in chief of Army Group E whom Waldheim had served in the Balkans. The Moscow Declaration notwithstanding, Tito had no intention of letting anyone forget that the Austrians had helped the Nazis commit unspeakable atrocities in his homeland—certainly not while the Allies were considering what, if anything, Austria owed Yugoslavia.

On January 30, the Yugoslavians broadened their strategy of Nazi-baiting. They accused Austrian delegate Hans Piesch, the governor of Carinthia, of having collaborated with the Nazis, and they demanded that he be expelled from the conference. Though the British and the Americans declared that Piesch was innocent, the Soviets insisted that the Allied Council officially investigate the charges. The Russians also accused the Austrian government of protecting war criminals and of coddling former Nazis.

Gruber hadn't expected the Soviets to take up the Yugoslav cause with such alacrity. Once again, politics was the reason. As some Western delegates read the tea leaves, the Russians saw siding with Yugoslavia on Carinthia as a way to improve their position on the German assets question. For one thing, they were forcing Gruber to fight a two-front war—

the notion being that the more time and energy he had to spend on the territorial dispute, the less he would have for the assets debate. For another, they were picking up a bargaining chip that might prove useful later; if the assets debate seemed to be going against them, they could always offer to barter concessions on Carinthia in return for a better deal.

For the next few days, the Yugoslavs and the Austrians traded angry charges and denials. While Vilfan berated the Austrians for committing war crimes in the Balkans and accused Piesch of having worked for the Nazis, Gruber cleverly reminded the Allies of the bloody record of Ustasha and other Yugoslav Fascists.

The conference sputtered on until the end of February, the Allies unable to reach agreement on either the dispute over southern Carinthia or the German assets question. (When Western delegates told the Russians that it wasn't fair of them to seize "German" property that had been acquired by the Nazis in Austria through "force or duress," the Soviet representative laconically retorted: "Nobody can rape his own wife"—in effect, alleging that Austria had been a willing ally of the Reich.) Still, Gruber wasn't completely discouraged. The deputies' conference was merely the prelude to a meeting of Big Four foreign ministers, who were scheduled to gather in Moscow at the end of March. Perhaps an Austrian state treaty would come out of that.

In any case, the deputies' conference did yield at least one concrete result. Spurred by the Yugoslavian charges and the Soviet demands for a full inquiry, British investigators eventually established that Hans Piesch *had* been mixed up with the Nazis, working as an official of Himmler's Race and Settlement Office. As a result, Piesch wound up having to resign his post as governor of Carinthia.[13]

There was an important lesson here for both the Yugoslavs and the Austrians. Belgrade could accuse Austrian officials of having collaborated with the Nazis—and no matter how unsupported or blatantly political the charges were, the Allies would have to follow them up. What's more, in the process of looking into even the most ludicrous of accusations, there was always a chance that investigators might come across evidence of real wrongdoing. That was something worth thinking about.

The weather improved slightly in February, allowing Waldheim the chance to see a bit of London and buy Cissy and Lieselotte some souvenirs. The grandeur of Westminster Palace was overwhelming, especially in contrast to the misery in the streets outside. Unfortunately, the House of Commons was not in session. Still, Waldheim and his colleagues were able to attend a hearing in the House of Lords.

The Austrian delegation returned home at the end of February, just in time for Waldheim to read a depressing story in the Vienna newspapers. The Yugoslavs had executed his old commander in chief, General Löhr. (In tacit recognition of his personal honor as a military man, however, they allowed him to be shot rather than hanged.)

Less than a month later, Gruber, Waldheim, and the rest of the small Austrian delegation left Vienna once again—this time for the foreign ministers' meeting in Moscow. On their way to the Soviet capital, they stopped over in the city of Lvov. Gruber was appalled by the place—the filthy accommodations, the loudspeakers blaring out propaganda day and night, the garbage-strewn streets, the overwhelming poverty. Many years later, he recalled wondering at the time if this was a preview of Austria's future in a Soviet-dominated Europe.

Unlike Gruber, Waldheim had been to Russia before. He understood the strength of the country, and he realized there would be no Austrian state treaty without Soviet cooperation.

The Moscow conference of March 1947 was a great opportunity for a young diplomat. The twenty-eight-year-old Waldheim got to observe firsthand some of the most important statesmen of the day: U.S. Secretary of State George Marshall, British Foreign Secretary Ernest Bevin, Soviet Foreign Minister V. M. Molotov, French Foreign Minister Georges Bidault. Waldheim was particularly fascinated by the American negotiators: Robert Murphy, Charles ("Chip") Bohlen, Walter Bedell Smith, and John Foster Dulles. Young diplomats didn't often get the chance to see so much brilliance assembled in one place. Waldheim took in every detail.

His optimism undiminished, Gruber believed that Austria's hour had come. A state treaty had been drafted, he told Waldheim, and there were indications that the Soviets might actually agree to endorse it. Among other things, he claimed to find significance in the fact that while the delegation was dining at the Hotel Moskva one evening, the orchestra had struck up Strauss's "Blue Danube" waltz. To Gruber, the choice of music was an unmistakable omen that the Soviets had decided to give the Austrians what they wanted—even if that meant abandoning their support for Yugoslavia's territorial claims.[14]

Waldheim wasn't so sure the Yugoslav Communists would be sloughed off quite so easily. But Gruber wasn't worried. After all, he argued, without Soviet backing, what could the Yugoslavs possibly do to hurt him or Austria?

CHAPTER TWELVE

Power Politics

While Gruber, Waldheim, and the rest of the Austrian delegation cooled their heels, waiting for the Moscow conference to begin, Josef Stalin was meeting with their counterparts from Belgrade. The Soviet leader listened patiently as the chief Yugoslav delegate, Edvard Kardelj, outlined his government's territorial demands, then assured him: "Your claims are certainly justified and we will support them." As if to emphasize his sincerity, Stalin then turned to V. M. Molotov, his foreign minister. "Vyacheslav," he said, "do everything possible to support the Yugoslavs."

Though Kardelj and his fellow delegates appreciated the sentiment, the Yugoslavs were well aware that the Soviets in general and Stalin in particular were not to be trusted. Stalin, they knew, feared Marshal Tito's independent ways. He preferred the sort of subservient regimes the Red Army had installed throughout the rest of Eastern Europe, and he worried about Tito's Balkan ambitions. The fact that Yugoslavia had largely liberated itself made him uneasy.[1]

Still, when the foreign ministers' conference finally got under way, there were no surprises—at least not at first. The Yugoslavs restated their demand for the return of the Klagenfurt Basin (as well as for cash reparations), and Gruber repeated the Austrian government's categorical rejection of Belgrade's claims. Concerned about the strategic and economic implications of a Yugoslav southern Carinthia, the United States lined up behind the Austrians, while the Soviets called Gruber a liar and officially proclaimed their support for Yugoslavia.[2]

Behind the scenes, however, something was going on. In private, Molotov was telling Gruber to work out a compromise with the Yugoslavs. And he was hinting to the other Allies that Moscow might be willing to sign a state treaty even if Belgrade didn't get the territory it wanted.

As the Yugoslavs had suspected, all Stalin really cared about was a favorable resolution of the German assets question. Despite his assurances, he had no compunctions whatsoever about abandoning Yugoslavia to get what he wanted.

The Soviet strategy became apparent when Molotov rose to address the conference in support of the Yugoslavs. With unprecedented mildness, he merely recommended that Belgrade's territorial claims "be considered in a favorable spirit." It didn't take much sensitivity to diplomatic nuance to be able to read between the lines. As U.S. Secretary of State George Marshall observed, Molotov's surprising restraint represented "some indication" that the Soviets were "reconsidering [their] position." Sensing the same thing, Gruber told his colleagues that the momentum was shifting in their favor.[3]

Realizing that they were now on their own, the Yugoslavs decided to change tack. After repeating the old claims to Carinthia, and once again accusing Austria of repressing the Slovene people, Kardelj linked Yugoslavia's territorial demands to the issue of Austrian war crimes. Hitler's army, he told the conference, had contained more than eighty Austrian generals—one of whom, Alexander Löhr, had run the southeastern theater and bombed helpless Belgrade. "Austria," he said, echoing the Moscow Declaration, "should deliver all war criminals and traitors to the nation which was the victim of their crimes or of their treason."

The Soviets could not disagree. After all, they too had been demanding prompt extradition of all war criminals.

Gruber responded to this new diplomatic thrust with a clever parry, arguing that Kardelj's latest accusation only proved the bankruptcy of Yugoslavia's territorial demands. If there were any merit to its claims, he said, Belgrade wouldn't be so "obviously anxious to give them a political basis." Gruber then made use of the Moscow Declaration, reminding everyone of its finding that "Austria was the first country to lose her freedom and independence as a result of [Nazi] aggression."[4]

Meanwhile, word was reaching Molotov that the West might be willing to yield on the German assets questions in return for a quick settlement of the territorial dispute. The Soviets responded with alacrity, telling Kardelj to come up with a new list, with less ambitious claims. After checking with Belgrade, the Yugoslav complied. Instead of insisting on the return of more than 2,600 square kilometers of Carinthia and Styria,

Kardelj now said his government would be willing to accept a mere 680 square kilometers of Austrian territory.

Not surprisingly, this surrender of three quarters of "our Carinthia" was a bitter pill for the Yugoslavs. In the end, however, they didn't have to swallow it. Despite all the maneuvering, the Allies were unable to agree on the German assets issue, and the Big Four adjourned the conference without making any final decisions on anything. Instead, an Austrian Treaty Commission was established to study the unresolved questions.[5]

Over the next five months, the Austrian Treaty Commission met repeatedly in Vienna, but very little was accomplished. The German assets question remained the primary obstacle.

As far as the Austrian Communists were concerned, the impasse was all Gruber's fault; if only he was more reasonable in dealing with the Soviets, they insisted, an acceptable state treaty could be negotiated. Egged on by Moscow, the Communists accused him of being an "errand boy" for Washington, who sought nothing less than an *Anschluss* with the United States. When his name was mentioned at Communist rallies, the crowds roared, "Hang him! Hang him!"

On May 5, 1947, the Communists staged a violent food riot in Vienna, and President Renner gloomily predicted a winter of despair if Austria failed to regain her sovereignty by year's end. Chancellor Figl, meanwhile, recalled the promises of independence and self-determination enshrined in the Moscow Declaration, and he called on the Allies "to honor your signature and keep faith [with] the Magna Carta of world justice."[6]

As a result of the increasing pressure, Gruber's moods fluctuated constantly. Waldheim was one of the few people who could cope with them. Gruber worked his young aide hard, but Waldheim never complained. On February 14, 1947, Gruber formally named him legation secretary, third class.

Waldheim was not only receiving a remarkable firsthand education in big-power politics; he was also learning about the politics of Austrian powerlessness. The more Waldheim saw, the more he became convinced that Gruber's diplomatic style was inappropriate to the postwar world. He was coming to believe that the new Austria had to be cautious and accommodating to *all* of the big powers, not brash and stubborn in defense of the interests of one of them.

It wasn't just the Communists who blamed Gruber for the lack of a state treaty. Some of Gruber's own cabinet colleagues felt the same way, wondering if he "was too much in the pockets of the Americans." (The British foreign office shared that belief, though it felt that the pro-Western Gruber was still preferable to some unknown quantity.)[7]

Gruber had even alienated his own party leader, Chancellor Figl. In addition to his disappointment over his foreign minister's failure to procure a state treaty, Figl was growing increasingly annoyed by Gruber's penchant for dealing directly with the Allies, his reluctance to channel his high-level contacts through the chancellor's office. Indeed, by June 1947, Figl was so fed up with Gruber that he agreed to meet secretly with Austrian Communist party boss Ernst Fischer. Fischer took advantage of the opportunity to tell Figl there was no chance that Moscow would sign a state treaty as long as the cabinet remained intact. "Above all," he said, "Foreign Minister Gruber has to disappear."[8]

Gruber's dilemma was clear: With everyone blaming him for the lack of a state treaty, he would have to produce something good for Austria— and produce it quickly—if he wanted to retain his position in the government. Fortunately for Gruber, his American friends, who were working on the massive foreign-aid program that would become known as the Marshall Plan, were aware of his precarious situation, and they gave him just what he needed. On June 25, 1947, Figl and Gruber were able to announce that they had signed an agreement with Washington guaranteeing immediate delivery of $85 million in badly needed interim aid to Austria. Though *Pravda* called the Marshall Plan an "enslaving agreement for Austria," news of the interim-aid pact improved morale markedly. Gruber's stock rose even further a few days later, when the United States agreed to start paying its own occupation costs.[9]

In linking Austria to the Marshall Plan, Figl and Gruber were tying their country to the capitalist West. From the Soviet point of view, that was a potent argument for refusing to sign a state treaty that would restore Austrian sovereignty—for in the new context of things, a free Austria would be a pro-Western Austria.

Secretary of State Marshall and General Geoffrey Keyes, the commander of U.S. Forces in Austria (USFA), couldn't argue with the Soviet analysis. The fact was, while the Americans were happy to provide the aid that Austria so desperately needed, their assistance carried a price—the continued presence of Western troops in Austria. If that undermined the chances for a state treaty, so be it.

To the twenty-eight-year-old Waldheim, these developments only reinforced his natural sense of caution. In a world dominated by big powers, he concluded, a diplomat from a small country like Austria had to tread carefully. Gruber's dynamism, his desire to lead, might seem impressive, but these qualities often irritated his superiors and threatened his position. For his part, Waldheim was happy to be regarded as a loyal, useful follower, one who was content simply to serve. An American observer at the time described Waldheim as an "amiable but not especially forceful personality." That was just the attitude he wanted to project. Waldheim, the quiet servant, aspired to become the head of the household someday.[10]

Though his post at Gruber's side gave him an unparalleled view of international events, Waldheim was nonetheless ready to move on. He was eager to gain diplomatic experience abroad, and he had set his sights on a position in the Austrian Legation in Paris. Unfortunately, Gruber was not yet ready to lose his diligent assistant. He thus agreed in principle to the Paris appointment, but asked Waldheim to remain with him at the Ballhausplatz a few months longer.

In July 1947, Waldheim learned that his wife was expecting their second child. Life seemed full indeed. In September, he would take his oath as a foreign service officer, and he expected to be transferred to Paris shortly thereafter.

Gruber was similarly pleased with the progress of things. Not only had his enemies failed to dislodge him from the government, but as a result of the Marshall Plan, Austria might one day be back on its feet. Convinced that the combination of U.S. backing and the restored economy would give him a stronger hand when treaty negotiations resumed in the autumn, Gruber decided to show the Americans that he could be counted on. He thus became an increasingly vocal opponent of communism, a pioneer Cold Warrior.

Austria, he declared, belonged to the West, culturally as well as politically. If she fell to the Eastern bloc, he added, she would be cut off from both her trading partners and her credit. *Pravda* retorted by calling Gruber another Goebbels, who made "dirty insinuations" against the Socialist states. In response, Gruber denounced Austrian Communists as Trojan horses willing to do Moscow's bidding.[11]

This sort of rhetorical brawling made Waldheim uncomfortable. He preferred quiet diplomacy. Paris was looking more and more attractive to him.

In the meantime, life in Vienna had its compensations. For one thing, Waldheim and his wife had become quite popular among the growing American community there. That was hardly surprising. Not only were

Kurt and Cissy young, attractive, and charming, but their English was becoming excellent. This was particularly important, for few American diplomats in Vienna spoke much German.

For all that, Waldheim's attitude toward the Americans remained considerably more standoffish than that of his boss. Unlike Gruber, Waldheim did not try to impress his American contacts with any crusading anti-Bolshevik sentiments. Nor was he particularly willing to reveal Austrian diplomatic business to curious acquaintances from the U.S. Legation. That's not to say he wasn't grateful when an American friend invited him and Cissy to dinner. At the very least, such invitations meant a rich meal filled with delicacies one could not obtain elsewhere. What's more, the considerate "Amis" often gave their Austrian guests nice tidbits to take home with them.

At the beginning of autumn, Gruber informed Waldheim that France would have to wait awhile longer. In late November, the Big Four deputy foreign ministers would be meeting once again in London, and once again Gruber wanted Waldheim to accompany him. Though concerned about leaving his pregnant wife, and disappointed by the postponement of his transfer to Paris, Waldheim knew that attending the conference would help Gruber as well as advance his own career.

The weather in London this time was considerably better than it had been for the last deputies' meeting, and the Austrian delegation received much better care. Among other things, its members were treated to a luncheon in their honor in the House of Commons.[12]

Despite Gruber's optimism, the second London conference got no closer to achieving agreement on a state treaty than any of the previous Big Four meetings. Publicly, the failure of the talks was blamed on Moscow's stubborn refusal to make any concessions on the German assets question. Previously, the Americans had favored an independent Austria, free of foreign troops. However, the recent Communist takeover in Hungary, and the growing threat to democratic Czechoslovakia, had changed Washington's viewpoint. With the division of Europe becoming a fact, Austria would be the easternmost bulwark of George Marshall's European Recovery Program. As such, she could provide an important listening post as well as a vital link between Germany and Italy. Thus, Washington was now determined to continue the occupation of Austria until "safeguards against Soviet domination" could be devised.

Gruber was disappointed by the new American stance, but he quickly fell into line. On balance, he was pleased with the way things had gone over the past year. True, a state treaty now seemed further off than ever, as did a resolution of the German assets question. On the other hand, the Americans had promised Austria $350 million in aid beginning in 1948.[13]

Gruber's only real worry was the growing ferocity of Yugoslavia's diplomatic assault on Austria. The territorial dispute was just one item on Tito's list of grievances. Not only did Belgrade accuse British forces in Carinthia of encouraging guerrilla incursions into Slovenia by Ustasha "refugees"; it also claimed that the Western Allies were providing notorious war criminals with safe havens in their zones of Austria. In addition, Belgrade was enraged by the increasing reluctance of the Western powers to approve—or even respond to—Yugoslavian attempts to extradite alleged war criminals.

The prosecution of war criminals was one of the earliest casualties of the incipient Cold War. In 1945, thousands of Nazi and Ustasha collaborators had fled to Austria and Germany from Yugoslavia. Quite understandably, Tito wanted them returned, so his regime could try them for their heinous crimes. At the same time, however, a series of purges, show trials, and border incidents with Western forces was earning Yugoslavia a reputation as Moscow's most aggressive surrogate—as a result of which the Americans were becoming increasingly suspicious of Tito's motives. After all, these refugees (who claimed that Tito was a liar, leveling trumped-up charges against good Christian men) were anti-Communists. Perhaps more important, some of them were in a position to provide valuable intelligence about Yugoslavia—intelligence that could be crucial in the event that the Third World War, like the Great War of 1914–18, broke out in the Balkans.

By late 1946, it was apparent to Belgrade that the Americans were dragging their feet when it came to extraditing accused war criminals to Yugoslavia. In fact, the U.S. government had considered adopting a blanket policy of turning down *all* Yugoslav extradition requests. When the State Department decided that this would not be appropriate, American occupation authorities simply began to demand more and more proof against accused war criminals before they would approve any requests to extradite them. The effect was nearly the same as a blanket ban. According to Yugoslav acting foreign minister Aleš Bebler, of 950 extradition requests made to Allied authorities in Austria, Germany, and Italy after 1945 only 59 were honored.[14]

The Yugoslavs retaliated early in 1947, when the American Embassy in Belgrade asked the Tito government to permit a team from the U.S. Office of War Crimes to interview General Löhr. The Americans were hoping to obtain evidence that would help the Nüremberg Tribunal prosecute German officers accused of committing war crimes in the Balkans. When the team arrived in Belgrade on March 5, it discovered that Löhr had been executed a week earlier. The Yugoslavs had gotten vast amounts of military information from Löhr—but they had no interest in sharing any of it with their former allies.[15]

A few months later, in the summer of 1947, Austria passed a new law that appeared designed to restrict further the extradition of accused war criminals of Austrian nationality. The law stated that no Austrian could be extradited unless the nation making the request guaranteed that it would, in turn, extradite to Vienna any of its own nationals who might be accused of having committed atrocities in Austria. For its part, the Austrian government insisted that the measure was not aimed at shielding war criminals; rather, it merely represented a return to prewar principles of reciprocity. The implication of the law, however, was both ludicrous and offensive—suggesting that the Austrian government believed there might be Poles or Yugoslavs who had committed war crimes in Austria.

Though, in a rare display of unanimity, the Allied Council vetoed the law, the Yugoslavs nonetheless regarded it as yet another indication of the growing U.S. effort to protect war criminals. Gruber had supported the legislation, and as far as Belgrade was concerned, he represented American interests.[16]

Facing growing outrage at home, the British agreed to let Yugoslav screening teams continue to work in Germany and Austria. The United States, by contrast, hardened its position. After November 1, 1947, General Keyes generally refused to accept any more Yugoslav requests for the surrender of war criminals alleged to be residing in the American zones of Austria. (Not that he and his predecessor, General Mark W. Clark, had approved all that many to begin with. Between the summer of 1945 and October 10, 1947, the Yugoslav government had asked the USFA to extradite 137 alleged war criminals and traitors; the Americans sent them only 19.)[17]

The case of Oskar Turina particularly infuriated the Yugoslavs. Turina had been the Ustasha man in charge of deportations at the time of the Kozara massacre in 1942. During the last days of the war, he had fled into Austria, where he surrendered to American authorities. Soon afterward, Belgrade requested his extradition. As the request was accompanied by a good deal of information, both army intelligence and the USFA Extradition Board okayed it within months. At that point, the Americans should have sent Turina back to Yugoslavia. They didn't. Instead, they claimed they needed more evidence against him.

Coincidentally, this need manifested itself at precisely the point at which Washington's relations with Belgrade collapsed. Clearly, with

Tito's regime now regarded as the enemy, American intelligence had decided that Turina's knowledge of the Yugoslav partisans, plus his ability to work with Western intelligence agencies in recruiting refugees for undercover work in Yugoslavia, made him too valuable to give up.

Yugoslavia, of course, continued to press for Turina's extradition. On October 10, 1947, however, the USFA officially informed the Yugoslav Military Mission that Turina had been "disapproved for extradition and will not be again considered unless more detailed crime description is submitted." Apparently taking the American rejection at face value, the head of the Yugoslav mission informed his superiors back home that they would have to come up with "more extensive evidential materials, including interviews with witnesses, documents," and so forth. The problem was that though the Yugoslavs possessed strong circumstantial evidence of Turina's crimes, they had few if any witnesses. Most were either dead or missing. Nor did they have many documents. The Americans had captured most of the relevant German paperwork—and for the next four years they did their best to keep the Yugoslavs from getting their hands on it.

Two months later, in December 1947, the USFA told the Yugoslavs that they had until February 12, 1948, to provide American authorities with the additional evidence they had requested. If the documentation was not forthcoming by then, the USFA would consider the Turina case closed—and refuse to reconsider its decision not to extradite him.[18] In desperation, the Yugoslavs decided to take their case to the United Nations. There, they introduced a resolution urging member states to facilitate the extradition of accused war criminals. The United States and Britain opposed the resolution, arguing that accuser nations had to provide strong evidence that suspects had indeed committed specific crimes, and it was overwhelmingly defeated.[19]

As the 1947 deputies' conference recessed for the year and Waldheim prepared to return home to Vienna for the Christmas holidays, he was able to look back on what for him had been a very good year. Despite his disappointment over the failure to secure a state treaty, he had received an unparalleled education in big-power politics, observing at first hand the giants of the day. He had also been able to enjoy more than his share of uncommon pleasures. At a time when most Austrians were barely eking out a subsistence living, scrounging for food and other necessities, he had been serenaded in Moscow and been feted at Westminster. He had also been appointed a legation secretary and taken the oath of a foreign service officer.

Waldheim looked forward to a *gemütlich* Christmas in Vienna with his family, perhaps his last for a while. Soon, he hoped, he would take up the post of first secretary in the small but prestigious Austrian Legation in Paris. And not long after that, his wife would give birth to their second child (both hoped it would be a boy). He would prefer to wait until the spring, after the baby had come and the weather improved, to make the move to France. But he served at the pleasure of his superiors, and he never complained.

As Kurt Waldheim packed his bags in a London hotel room, pleased with his progress and excited about his prospects, a war-crimes commission in Belgrade was preparing to indict him on charges of mass murder.

CHAPTER THIRTEEN

Conspiracy in Belgrade

Belgrade had first become aware of the existence of Kurt Waldheim early in 1947, when the Yugoslav Ministry of the Interior launched a massive inquiry into the wartime activities of Waldheim's old Wehrmacht command, Army Group E. At first, investigators had no idea who he was. When they found out, they went after him with a vengeance.

As the timing of General Löhr's trial and execution had demonstrated, Belgrade's interest in Army Group E involved more than a simple desire for justice or revenge. To be sure, the army group had committed terrible atrocities in the Balkans, and the victorious Yugoslavs quite understandably wanted those responsible to pay for their crimes. But there were other, far more urgent motives behind Belgrade's determination to identify those who had done the group's dirty work. For one thing, Belgrade had reason to believe that many Wehrmacht intelligence officers who had served in the Balkans were now working with American and British forces in Austria, lending their expertise to a Western effort aimed at destabilizing Yugoslav border regions. For another, with the dispute over Carinthia raging hot and heavy, Yugoslav propagandists could make good use of the fact that there had been plenty of Austrians in Army Group E—many of whom, like General Löhr, had participated in or been responsible for war crimes.

In the spring of 1947, following the four-power Moscow conference, at which Belgrade found its claims subverted by the Soviets, the Yugoslav Ministry of the Interior began to focus its attention on the intelligence

branch of Army Group E, the Ic/AO unit. Agents attached to the Yugoslav Military Mission in Vienna quickly determined that Ic/AO had
included a number of Austrians on its personnel roster—among them, a
reserve first lieutenant named Kurt Waldheim. By September 1947, the
interior ministry had discovered that this same Kurt Waldheim was now
working as an aide to none other than Austrian foreign minister Karl
Gruber, Yugoslavia's chief nemesis in the continuing border dispute.[1]

The connection to Gruber galvanized Belgrade's interest in Waldheim. For nearly a year, Gruber had tenaciously—and successfully—
opposed every Yugoslav territorial and financial claim against Austria. Not
surprisingly, the Yugoslavs were desperate to discredit him. But they had
been stymied by Gruber's impeccable record of anti-Nazi activism. Now,
however, Gruber appeared to be vulnerable. If it could be shown that his
closest aide had participated in Nazi atrocities, Gruber's own admirable
background would not be enough to keep him from being driven from
office.

The plan was simple. In order to discredit Gruber, the Yugoslav
delegation to the United Nations War Crimes Commission (UNWCC)
in London would get the commission to list Waldheim as an accused war
criminal. It would be hard for the big powers to scream "propaganda"
after their own officials had voted to accuse Gruber's top aide of Nazi war
crimes.

The UN War Crimes Commission was very important to a small, devastated nation like Yugoslavia. It offered Belgrade a chance to bear witness
to the atrocities committed on its soil. It was also a forum for blatantly
political machinations.

The commission owed its existence to an inter-allied conference that
had met at St. James's Palace in London in January 1942. (Kurt Waldheim was in Vienna at the time, recuperating from the leg wound he had
suffered on the Russian front.) At the meeting, representatives of the
Allied powers, including Yugoslavia, resolved that war crimes committed
by the Axis—especially massacres, the executions of hostages, and mass
expulsions—would not go unpunished.[2] Nearly two years later, on October 20, 1943, the UNWCC held its first meeting. The Soviet Union was
conspicuous by its absence. It had refused to participate unless it received
seven seats on the commission, one for each of the Soviet republics—a
concession that was unacceptable to most of the seventeen other Allied
nations that made up the body.[3]

The commission got down to work in earnest early in 1945, under the
energetic chairmanship of the chief Australian delegate, Lord Wright.

From the beginning, the UNWCC was dependent on the good faith and investigative prowess of its member nations. Since Allied Headquarters would not permit the commission to attach its own investigators to military units in the field, the commission was never able to conduct independent inquiries. Instead, it collected information and evidence from the individual war-crimes commissions set up by each of the Allied powers.[4]

The material it gathered was sent to a group known as Committee I, which met weekly. Committee I evaluated the information on the following basis:

1. Did the charges indicate the existence of actual war crimes?

2. Was there sufficient evidence to identify the alleged offender?

3. Was there good reason to assume that if put on trial, the alleged offender would be convicted?[5]

If Committee I was able to answer all these questions in the affirmative, it would recommend that the accused individual be listed by the full commission as an "A"-category alleged war criminal. (There were other categories for suspects and witnesses.) Ultimately, the UNWCC published eighty lists, containing a total of nearly 37,000 names of suspects, witnesses, and alleged war criminals. According to Lord Wright, no one was put on the "A" list lightly; inclusion by the commission implied that there was a prima facie reason to put the accused on trial.[6]

The commission assumed that its member nations were interested in finding and extraditing the accused war criminals whose names they sought to list. After all, why else would they go to the trouble of registering them?

Belgrade's chances of getting the UNWCC to list Kurt Waldheim as an "A"-list war criminal depended on whose standards were applied. As the Yugoslavs well knew, the Western powers defined "evidence" somewhat differently than they did. Western authorities would not brand someone a war criminal simply because he had served in a unit (such as Army Group E's Ic/AO) that was in some general sense known to have been involved in atrocities. A Yugoslav Ministry of the Interior memorandum summed up the situation succinctly, noting: "The investigation cannot be very useful to us until we can establish the [criminal] responsibility of the individual members of the Abwehr or Ic departments."

What the Yugoslavs had on Waldheim did not establish that individual responsibility. While they could make a case against Ic officers in general, or against his Ic/AO unit as a group, they had no evidence implicating Waldheim himself in any specific crime. There was, for example, no doubt that many Ic officers in Army Group E had participated in illegal reprisal actions; the guilty parties, however, invariably operated at the company, battalion, regimental, or divisional level, while Waldheim was attached to the headquarters staff. Similarly, while the Yugoslavs knew that Abwehr officers on the AO side of Waldheim's Ic/AO staff had participated in reprisals and other atrocities, they were also aware that "although they worked together," Ic and AO were separate departments. The most the Yugoslavs could say was that as a member of Ic/AO, Waldheim "took part in retaliatory measures, though it cannot be spelled out which particular ones." And that, they knew, wasn't enough.[7]

In an effort to bolster their case, Yugoslav authorities looked to the tens of thousands of German and Austrian POWs they were holding, hoping that someone who had served at Army Group E headquarters could be found to provide eyewitness evidence against Waldheim.

For a time, they thought they had turned up just such a witness in the person of Johann Mayer, a former clerk in the personnel department of the Army Group E staff, who was being held as a POW in the Kalvarija-Zemun camp. Described by Yugoslav authorities as "opportunistic," Mayer was a model prisoner, serving as the camp *Antifa*, or anti-Fascist agitator and coordinator. He claimed to know all about Waldheim's political past, describing him as "an old and Illegal [i.e., pre-1938] National Socialist," who had been personally responsible for the murder of hostages in the Balkans.

As eager as they were to nail Waldheim, even the Yugoslavs had trouble swallowing Mayer's allegations. For one thing, in order to have been an Illegal, Waldheim would have had to join the Nazi party while he was still in his teens. For another, Gruber would have never knowingly hired someone with an Illegal background—and had Waldheim possessed one, it was inconceivable that he could have hidden it from Gruber. The Yugoslavs needed charges that sounded plausible. Mayer's were considered too absurd to be of any use.

Despite its lofty aims, by 1947 the UNWCC had become another Cold War battleground. Convinced that the smaller countries, such as Yugoslavia, were often using the lists for political reasons, both the Americans and the British—without whose support the UNWCC could not function—secretly agreed that the commission would go out of business by March 31, 1948. That meant that Committee I would examine its last cases in January or February of 1948—which implied that any cases that were submitted by member nations after New Year's Day would probably never be acted on.

On December 12, 1947, Uroš Bjelić, a legal expert at the Yugoslav Ministry of the Interior, sent the following query to the foreign ministry:

> Advise us if it is necessary . . . to make a decision on Gruber's assistant Lieutenant Waldheim, on the basis of which he could be registered by the United Nations War Crimes Commission (keep in mind that the deadline for the registration will expire at the end of this year).[8]

Thus prodded by Bjelić, the Yugoslav State Commission for the Determination of Crimes Committed by the Occupying Forces and Their Collaborators rushed to complete its *Odluka,* or indictment, against Kurt Waldheim.* On December 18, 1947, just after Waldheim had returned to Vienna from London, the *Odluka* was issued. It declared that as an officer on the Ic staff of Army Group E, Lieutenant Waldheim was "responsible for the preparation and issuing of . . . criminal orders while his group operated in Yugoslavia"—orders that resulted in "murders and massacres, execution of hostages, deliberate destruction of property, [and] burning of settlements." As these actions all represented violations of the Hague Agreement of 1907, the *Odluka* concluded, "Lt. Kurt Waldheim is a war criminal."[9]

The *Odluka* cited no documents or other proof that directly implicated Waldheim in any atrocities. It merely provided evidence that Hitler and the German High Command had mandated a deliberate policy of criminal terror in the Balkans, and it quoted the testimony of POWs who had served in Army Group E—the bulk of which was neither relevant nor conclusive.

For example, the *Odluka* referred to the case of Karl-Heinz Egberts-Hilker, the former commander of a panzer reconnaissance unit that had fought to hold the Stip-Kočani road as Army Group E retreated northward out of Greece in October 1944. In June 1947, a Yugoslav tribunal had tried and convicted Egberts-Hilker on charges of having instigated a massacre of civilians near Stip. According to the *Odluka,* "the responsibility for [Egberts-Hilker's war crime] extends to Waldheim."

The Yugoslavs based this assertion on the assumption that the Führer Order on reprisals had been transmitted to Egberts-Hilker by the Ic staff

---

Odluka may also be translated as "finding" or "decision." This particular *Odluka* represented a preliminary finding of guilt—in other words, there was more than enough evidence to justify putting the accused on trial for his life.

of Army Group E. The fact that Waldheim had been a member of that staff, the *Odluka* insisted, "implies Waldheim's responsibility."

In fact, there was no evidence that Egberts-Hilker had ever heard of Kurt Waldheim. What's more, at his trial Egberts-Hilker had specifically rejected the notion that blame for the massacre should be attached to anyone but himself, declaring:

> I have acknowledged this action [the Stip massacre] from the first day of my interrogation. I emphasized that I accept the entire responsibility, and that none of my subordinates and soldiers bear any guilt. Nor have I ever tried to shift the blame to my own superiors or use the . . . "General Order" [regarding reprisals] as an excuse.[10]

The *Odluka* was also based in part on new testimony obtained from Johann Mayer, who claimed knowledge that would implicate Waldheim in mass shootings of hostages and similar atrocities. Mayer did not accuse Waldheim of actually participating in any specific war crimes. Rather, he made him complicit in *all* of his unit's activities, testifying: "I wish to state that most of these [criminal] incidents in Macedonia and in Bosnia took place on direct orders from Section Ic and the responsible officers Waldheim and Warnstorff."

As Mayer told it, Waldheim prepared reprisal orders, his superiors Colonel Warnstorff and General Schmidt-Richberg approved them, and officers in the field carried them out.

This seems highly unlikely. For one thing, officers in the field, from the divisional level to that of unit commanders like Egberts-Hilker, had full authority to order reprisals on their own. For another, to this day no one has ever turned up a copy of any such order prepared by Waldheim.

Mayer's credibility (or, rather, his lack of it) is perhaps best demonstrated by the *Odluka*'s assertion that he "knew Waldheim well because he worked with him in Löhr's command." In fact, Mayer was never attached to the Ic branch.

Such inconsistencies were, of course, beside the point. The *Odluka* wasn't meant to be a brief that would stand up in an American or a British court of law. It was a political document intended to embarrass and destroy Waldheim's boss, Karl Gruber. Containing no names of any alleged victims, nor listing any places where the alleged crimes were supposed to have occurred, the *Odluka* simply and flatly asserted that "Waldheim is a war criminal." As a result, it went on to insist, "Arrest and imprisonment of this defendant is mandatory under Article 4, Paragraph V of the Yugoslav Code on criminal activities against the people and the state, and his extradition to the Yugoslav authorities is obligatory under the terms of the Moscow Agreement of October 30, 1943 [the Moscow Declaration]."

On December 26, 1947, Dr. Dušan Nedeljković, chairman of the state war-crimes commission, informed the Yugoslav foreign ministry that his body had declared Waldheim a war criminal. Noting that Waldheim "is at this time on the staff of the Austrian minister Dr. Gruber," Nedeljković went on to the ask the foreign ministry "to lodge our registration application with the United Nations Commission for War Crimes in London . . . emphasizing the special importance we attach to this registration."[11]

Despite the pro forma legal phrase contained in the *Odluka* demanding Waldheim's arrest and surrender to the Yugoslav authorities, there is no evidence that Belgrade ever seriously sought—or, indeed, even discussed—the extradition of Waldheim. To be sure, any such attempt would have faced enormous problems. As an Austrian government employee who worked in the International District of Vienna, Waldheim was subject to four-power control—meaning all four members of the Allied Council would have had to agree to his extradition. The Americans had already balked at extraditing as notorious a war criminal as Oskar Turina. It was thus extremely unlikely that they would approve a request based on a case as shaky as the one Belgrade had concocted against Waldheim.

Of course, even had Belgrade amassed an airtight case against Waldheim, there was virtually no chance the Western Allies would have approved his extradition. For one thing, they would have been aware of the impact such a move would have on Gruber and the Austrian government. For another, the U.S. forces in Germany and Austria did not extradite anyone in their zones of occupation who was considered "of interest" to their intelligence people—which Waldheim certainly was. By the end of 1947, Army Intelligence had been keeping a file on him for over two years. His position with Gruber gave him access to all sorts of sensitive information—including knowledge of Gruber's cooperation with the U.S. Counter-Intelligence Corps. Under no circumstances could such an individual be allowed to fall into the hands of a hostile country.

The fact was, however, Belgrade had no interest in extraditing Waldheim. What would be the point of bringing him back to Yugoslavia? To put him before a war-crimes tribunal and then hang him? Whatever his culpability, Waldheim was too small a fish to be worth the trouble. No, the Yugoslavs wanted Waldheim to stay right where he was—at Karl

Gruber's side. They had in mind something far more effective than yet another dreary trial. They would get his name on the UNWCC "A" list and then wait for the right moment—preferably in the middle of another international conference in London—at which they could expose him for what he was. Kurt Waldheim was simply a means to an end—the destruction of Karl Gruber.

During the last hectic months of the UNWCC's life, cases poured into its cramped London offices. One hundred and twenty arrived in one week alone. The Yugoslavs expected the deluge to force Committee I to let its review practices grow more slipshod than ever. They hoped that even the shakiest of cases would thus get through.

In the early days of January, the Yugoslav representatives to the UNWCC worked feverishly to translate key portions of the Waldheim *Odluka* into English. The time pressure was intense. Not only would Committee I hear its last cases around February 21, but reports were circulating in Vienna that the Soviets were looking with some favor on a French proposal that could resolve the German assets question. The Big Four deputy foreign ministers were scheduled to convene again in London on February 13, and Belgrade feared the meeting might produce a rapprochement between the Soviets and Gruber, which could kill once and for all Yugoslavia's chances of regaining southern Carinthia.

On January 9, 1948, Belgrade's hope that the Waldheim case could somehow be slipped through received a setback. In a ruling concerning a Yugoslav request to put a former Wehrmacht Ic officer identified as Lieutenant Hanzer on the "A" list of alleged war criminals, Committee I declared that the simple fact that Hanzer had been an intelligence officer could not be "considered as prima facie [proof] of a war crime." Hanzer, the committee continued, "could not be held responsible for war crimes committed by the troops of his unit in the absence of further information which would disclose his actual participation in war crimes."[12]

Despite the time pressure, the American and British cochairmen of Committee I, E. W. Kintner and Sir Robert Craigie, were continuing to impose Western standards of proof. The implications for the Waldheim *Odluka* were obvious. The Yugoslav representative to the UNWCC, Dr. Veljko Milenković, informed his superiors that unless the Ministry of the Interior could provide him with better evidence, the request to list Kurt Waldheim was bound to be rejected.

*   *   *

Desperate to come up with some sort of "smoking gun" that would tie Waldheim directly to a war crime, Ministry of the Interior interrogators in Belgrade turned to POW Markus Hartner, the former Ic cartographer who had actually worked for Waldheim in Arsakli. Hartner provided the Yugoslavs with a good deal of valuable and accurate information about Ic, but none of it implicated Waldheim in anything criminal.

Frustrated, the Yugoslavs returned to Johann Mayer. At some point before February 13, either Mayer or his interrogators amended his earlier testimony. Instead of accusing Waldheim of a general complicity in all of Ic/AO's activities, Mayer now claimed that Waldheim was guilty of specific murders:

> I remember certain persons have been murdered at Sarajevo in November 1944. They were executed according to the order given by Waldheim in retaliation for desertion from the German Army of some other persons.[13]

Milenković now had the "proof" he needed to satisfy the UNWCC that Waldheim had been a war criminal. He would have been even more relieved had he known that the United States was about to relinquish the cochairmanship of Committee I. E. W. Kintner was being eased out of the job—ironically, because his superiors believed he had been too lax about letting unwarranted listings slip through.[14]

In Vienna, tensions were rising. During December, while Gruber and Waldheim were in London, a wave of kidnappings had struck the Austrian capital, as the Soviets began seizing Austrian officials in the Russian sector of the city as well as in the International Sector.[15]

At the same time, the Western Allies were growing increasingly concerned about a Soviet-backed paramilitary force called the Werkschutz, which contained several thousand armed and well-trained Austrian Communists, many of whom had fought under Tito in the Austrian Freedom Battalions. As the West saw it, the Communists could easily provoke an uprising, whereupon the Werkschutz would seize Vienna and, with Soviet support, arrest Gruber and the other Austrian ministers.[16]

Meanwhile, the situation in Carinthia was deteriorating. According to American intelligence, there were some 25,000 former Ustasha and related dissidents operating in the province—and most of them were calling for war against Yugoslavia. Word was that Belgrade was planning to respond with something dramatic in the coming weeks. As a British diplomat noted, "the Yugoslavs . . . consider themselves in a state of latent war with Austria until their territorial demands [are] met." One Vienna newspaper estimated that the Yugoslavs had already abducted 450 Austrians from the province in recent months.[17]

To Western eyes, none of this was coincidental. In particular, the Americans were convinced that there was a direct link between the Soviet kidnappings in Vienna and the Yugoslavs' persistent efforts to put Austrian officials on the war-crimes list. As one American intelligence report noted:

> The victims involved persons who are suspected of espionage, of association with the United States or other Western intelligence activities, of former intelligence activity on behalf of the German army, or of war crimes against the Soviet Union or its satellites.[18]

Kurt Waldheim fit that profile exactly.

What neither the Americans nor their contacts in the Austrian government understood was that the Yugoslavs were not playing the Soviets' game—indeed, that Belgrade and Moscow were increasingly at odds. To be sure, such a split would have been hard to credit at the time. After all, Belgrade was host to the Cominform, the coordinating body of the world Communist movement. Could Tito, supposedly Stalin's loyal henchman, be acting on his own without informing the Kremlin?

In fact, he was. The indictment against Waldheim would embarrass the Soviets as much as the West, for it would call into question Moscow's lackadaisical support for Yugoslavia's territorial claims. At the very least, it would prove a major obstacle to any rapprochement between the Soviets and Gruber.

CHAPTER FOURTEEN

Off the Hook

On February 13, 1948, Yugoslav representative Veljko Milenković officially presented his government's indictment of Kurt Waldheim to Committee I. Six days later, the UNWCC file of charges against Waldheim was ready for perusal by the members of the committee. Four days after that, on February 23, the UNWCC Secretariat registered its receipt of the Waldheim file.

That same week, Sir Alfred Brown of the British mission in Vienna had an interesting conversation with Josef Gerö, the Austrian minister of justice. Observing that Karl Gruber would soon be returning to London to restate the Austrian case at the next Big Four deputies' conference, Gerö told Brown that he hoped Gruber would "not give way in regard to the claims of Yugoslavia." Though Gruber had always been a hard-liner on the territorial dispute, Gerö said he was afraid the foreign minister might now yield to American pressure and reverse himself.[1]

Gerö's concern was—and is—hard to fathom. Gruber was indeed beholden to the Americans, but as Gerö well knew, Washington had no interest in accommodating either Yugoslavia or the Soviet Union on Austrian matters. So why was Gerö, a survivor of Dachau and Buchenwald, who went on to become one of the great Austrian jurists of his day, concerned that Gruber might suddenly give in to Belgrade? As justice minister, Gerö was much involved with extradition requests. Could he have known about the Waldheim problem and surmised its likely effect on Gruber? This is one of the more intriguing aspects of a remarkable series of events that in the end would allow Kurt Waldheim to continue to escape the consequences of his suspect past.

At 10:30 A.M. on Thursday, February 26, 1948, Committee I convened for the last time. The press of business at this final meeting was enormous. The Yugoslavs presented twelve cases; the Greeks, thirty-six; the Dutch, five; the Czechs, thirty-one.

Dr. Milenković did everything he could to bury Waldheim's "strengthened" *Odluka* in the heap of cases. Belgrade wanted no untoward attention focused on this matter—at least not yet. No one was to know who Kurt Waldheim was, or for whom he currently worked. As if to underscore the obscurity of the accused former Wehrmacht lieutenant, the Yugoslavs even put a phony question mark after his first name. His identity was to be a surprise that would be revealed to the world in a more dramatic context.

The committee began its last session by considering the Yugoslav submissions. With so much on the agenda, there was no time for any prolonged debate. Case after case was disposed of in a minute or two. The Waldheim file was no exception. With apparently no discussion and no dissent, the committee—which included representatives of both the British and the American governments—agreed to place the name of Kurt Waldheim on UNWCC list No. 79 as an *Abwehroffizier* wanted for war crimes that included putting hostages to death and other acts of murder.

A month later, the full UN War Crimes Commission routinely approved the final listing.

Now that it was on the UNWCC "A" list, the name of Kurt Waldheim was bound to wind up on another, even more significant roster: the list kept by the Anglo-American-dominated Central Registry of War Criminals and Security Suspects (CROWCASS). Working out of cluttered offices in Berlin under the direction of the Allied Control Council, CROWCASS assisted the various Allied war-crimes groups (but mainly the British and the Americans) in apprehending suspected war criminals. By early 1948, it had amassed an index of some 69,000 wanted war criminals, suspects, and witnesses. What made the CROWCASS list special, in addition to the fact that it carried the endorsement of both American and British intelligence, was that back in May 1945, the Allies had ruled that anyone whose name appeared on it was subject to mandatory extradition.[2]

The Yugoslavs, of course, made no effort to enlist CROWCASS's help in finding Waldheim. In April, CROWCASS received the UN list containing Waldheim's name, and incorporated all its contents in a final consolidated list of war criminals that was put out in June.

When the Yugoslavs had accused Hans Piesch, the Austrian governor of Carinthia, of having a Nazi past, they had run up against a solid wall of Western skepticism and hostility. There would be no such problems, the Yugoslavs believed, when the moment arrived to expose Waldheim. This time they would be able to show that the Western Allies had already endorsed their charges. If the West wasn't impressed by the fact that their own representatives had voted to put Waldheim's name on the UNWCC "A" list, let them try to explain his presence in the CROWCASS index. The British and the Americans might privately scoff at the UNWCC lists, but there was no way they could denigrate their own intelligence registry.

As well prepared as the Yugoslavs were to spring their trap, they would have been in even better shape if they had managed to get their hands on Oskar Turina. Belgrade knew about Turina's role in the Kozara massacre, and had repeatedly tried to convince the Americans to extradite him to Yugoslavia. For a long time, the Americans stalled, demanding that Belgrade provide more evidence against the former Ustasha official. Finally, on April 26, 1948, U.S. authorities informed the Yugoslav mission in Vienna that "Turina had departed from the U.S. Zone of Austria for an unknown destination." If he ever showed up again, the Americans promised, they would be happy to reconsider Yugoslavia's extradition request.

In fact, the Americans had helped Turina to make his way to Italy. From there, he left Europe. Some sources claim he eventually took up residence in Argentina, while others say he settled in the United States.

Had the Americans turned Turina over to Belgrade, not only would a major war criminal have been brought to justice, but the Yugoslavs might have learned something they had no idea of at the time—that Kurt Waldheim had been involved in the notorious Kozara deportations.

The Big Four deputy foreign ministers' conference that convened in London in February 1948 produced some enormous surprises—most of them generated by the Soviets, whose earlier stubbornness now seemed to give way to sweet reason. To begin with, after long insisting that Austria settle the German assets question by paying them $200 million over a two-year period, the Soviets announced that they would accept $150 million spread out over six years. With this one stroke, the Soviets eliminated a major obstacle that had been preventing the Allies from agreeing on an Austrian state treaty.

Shortly afterward, the Soviets offered another significant concession. Worried about the security of Carinthia and Styria after an Allied pull-out—as well as the possibility of a Communist coup—Chancellor Figl's government had been insisting that a 53,000-man *Bundesheer*, or Austrian federal army, be armed and in place before the four powers removed their troops. Early in April, Moscow agreed to this demand.[3]

The Soviets, it seemed, genuinely wanted to bring the treaty negotiations to a successful conclusion. They were ready to withdraw their troops from Austria—as long as the West did the same.

Moscow's sudden appearance of reasonableness put American policymakers in an awkward position. For more than two years, they had been pushing for a state treaty that would end the four-power occupation of Austria. By 1948, however, Poland, Hungary, and Czechoslovakia had fallen to the Communists. With Europe divided, the United States no longer wanted to remove its forces from Austria. General Keyes, the U.S. commander in Austria, reflected the growing consensus when he pointed out that "withdrawal of troops would involve surrender of strategic advantages to the U.S." In particular, Western military planners were becoming convinced that control of Alpine Austria was essential to the defense of Western Europe. As a result, noted one British diplomat, the Western powers were "no longer primarily concerned to achieve a good settlement of the assets problem. Their main objective must be to keep Western Forces in Austria."[4]

The problem was that the Americans could not simply refuse to sign a state treaty. Nor could they argue that Moscow's concessions on the assets question were insufficient. If they did, Austrian outrage would almost certainly bring down the pro-Western Figl government. That would mean new elections, which would likely result in a leftist victory.

Searching for a way out, U.S. diplomats hit upon the idea of using Soviet demands for the Zistersdorf oil-refinery complex as a pretext to end the treaty talks. On April 5, however, the Soviets made major concessions on this issue too. "Today we were hit by a flying saucer," Samuel Reber, the key State Department representative in Europe, cabled his superiors in Washington. Reber concluded that the "Soviets either genuinely desire conclusion of treaty or are willing to take calculated risk that treaty conclusion will be blocked by Western powers and give Soviets propaganda advantage." Somewhat plaintively, Reber asked Washington whether or not the United States wanted a treaty, adding: "If not, what is your advice on best tactics to be employed in breaking off negotiations?"

The State Department reply was quick and unambiguous: "For military reasons, in particular troop withdrawal, Austrian treaty undesirable at this time."[5]

In the end, it was the Yugoslavs who got the United States off the hook.

In the aftermath of the Moscow conference of March 1947, Belgrade had drastically reduced what it was demanding from Austria. All it wanted now was $150 million in reparations and 680 square kilometers of disputed territory. Nonetheless, the Yugoslavs still could not win the backing of any of the Big Four.[6]

In one last attempt to sway the Allies, Yugoslav foreign minister Aleš Bebler decided to present the deputies' meeting with still more evidence of Austrian war crimes in Yugoslavia. On April 26, he began his presentation. The debate raged for several days. At one point Bebler launched into a violent tirade against the new governor of Carinthia, Ferdinand Wedenig, who was sitting next to Gruber. Calling Wedenig a notorious Nazi collaborator, Bebler demanded his immediate dismissal.

As Bebler fulminated, Gruber noticed one of the Soviet delegates pointing to his own head as if to indicate that the Yugoslav was insane. Certainly, as Gruber pointed out in his rebuttal, Bebler's charges made no sense. Wedenig was a Socialist, whose resistance activities against the Nazis had got him sent to Dachau.[7]

In any case, by refusing to drop their territorial demands, the Yugoslavs gave Washington the excuse it needed to terminate the treaty talks. Knowing that Moscow still felt obliged to voice mild, pro forma support for some minor, face-saving concessions to Belgrade, the Americans formally asked the chief Soviet delegate at the London conference if his government still expected the final state treaty to include provisions under which some Austrian territory would be ceded to Yugoslavia. To no one's surprise, the Soviet delegate answered in the affirmative.

That was just what Samuel Reber, the chief American representative, was waiting to hear. "Further discussion seems to be futile," he declared. "I will not bargain over Austria's frontiers."

A few moments later, the conference adjourned *sine die*—without having concluded a state treaty.

Privately, the Soviets told Reber that they were prepared to be flexible "in the interest of agreement." Reber replied that the United States wanted no part of further negotiations "at this time."[8]

Though he was deeply disappointed by the collapse of the treaty talks, Gruber was relieved to have an excuse that he could bring home to Austria. The failure to achieve a state treaty was neither his fault nor that

of the Americans—it was the stubbornness of the Soviets and the Yugoslavs that was to blame.

What had happened to Belgrade's elaborately laid plans to destroy Gruber
by exposing Kurt Waldheim? Bebler could not use the carefully prepared
dossier for one simple reason: For the first time since the Allies had begun
discussing the state treaty, Waldheim was not at Gruber's side in the
Austrian delegation. On January 14, 1948, a full month before the deputies' conference had convened, Gruber had officially transferred Waldheim to the Austrian Legation in Paris.

Had Waldheim been at Gruber's side in London, Bebler would
doubtless have played out a scene of high drama. Following the script he
had used in the Piesch and Wedenig cases, the Yugoslav representative
would have produced the *Odluka* with appended extradition requests and
pointed an accusing finger at the Austrian delegation. That tall, quiet
young man seated behind the Austrian foreign minister, he would have
shouted, Gruber's top aide—he was a mass murderer! Having been
through this sort of thing before, the Western delegates might have rolled
their eyes—perhaps, in order to move things along, agreeing to refer the
charges to the Allied Council in Vienna for investigation. But Bebler
would not have stopped there. When they had accused Piesch and Wedenig, the Yugoslavs had acted alone. This time a triumphant Bebler could
hurl the damning UNWCC list on the felt-covered table in Lancaster
House. These charges could not be ignored. The Western powers themselves had agreed that Waldheim should be tried.

It is difficult to imagine how Waldheim's career, or Gruber's tenure
as foreign minister, could have survived such a scene.

With Waldheim in Paris, however, Bebler had to hold his fire. Denouncing an absent minor official would have smacked of desperation. It
might even have helped Gruber. In any case, the collapse of the conference had left Belgrade's territorial claims intact. The ammunition against
Waldheim could be saved for another time.

Why didn't Gruber bring Waldheim to London with him? He certainly could have used the help of his now-experienced aide at these vital,
complicated talks. Did Gruber know about Waldheim's war record? Had
he been warned by Justice Minister Gerö that the Yugoslavs had something on him? In a recent letter to me, Gruber maintained that he knew
nothing of the Yugoslav *Odluka* or any other threat to Waldheim. The
transfer, he insisted, was routine, the fortuitous timing completely coincidental.

Several facts make this assertion hard to accept. For one thing, it was an extremely inconvenient time for Waldheim to move to Paris. Not only was it the middle of winter, but France was still reeling from a series of strikes that had paralyzed much of the country. To make matters worse, Cissy was almost six months pregnant. Even more significant, there were signs that the Russians were really ready to conclude a state treaty—in which case Gruber would need Waldheim at his side more than ever during the upcoming London talks. The Paris post was hardly a vital one, especially compared to the fate of the state treaty.

Despite all this, the Waldheims abruptly left for the French capital a month before the conference convened. Not only did Gruber fail to summon Waldheim to the London talks; he kept him at arm's length for the next three years.

If the timing of Waldheim's transfer was merely coincidental, it was an enormous stroke of luck for both the foreign minister and his aide. Still, Waldheim remained personally vulnerable—at least until May 1948, when the London conference broke down—his fate held hostage to the state of relations between Yugoslavia and Austria.

As first secretary in Austria's understaffed Paris Legation, Waldheim found himself working hard that May and June at a variety of administrative tasks, many of them exceedingly mundane. Beyond the drudgery, however, he got the chance to carry out his first diplomatic assignments. By September, when the ambassador was ill or away, it was the first secretary who represented Austria. Waldheim gloried in the role.

The press soon began to take notice of the young diplomat. Gracious and friendly, he studied diligently to improve his passable French. He did not dwell on an unhappier time, when his Wehrmacht cavalry unit had taken part in the 1940 *Blitzkrieg.* He never talked about the Balkans.

On April 2, 1948, Cissy gave birth in Paris to their second child, a son, whom they named Gerhard. It was a happy time. Word from home indicated that the tensions of the previous winter had dissipated. Living standards were on the rise. There were no signs that Moscow was about to partition Austria, as it had Germany, nor did the Soviets seem likely to attempt a Berlin-like blockade of Vienna. The Waldheims settled comfortably into their Paris flat, looking forward to what they hoped would be a long and pleasant stay.

His absence from the London conference had saved Waldheim from the Yugoslav conspiracy, but he was by no means out of danger. Even though no one had yet noticed it, his name was still on the UNWCC list. Indeed, by June 1948, it was on the CROWCASS list as well. The Yugoslavs could expose him as a "war criminal" anytime they wanted.

The French set great store by the UN war-crimes list. In the Allied Council in Vienna, they consistently voted with the Soviets in favor of extraditing listed individuals. Certainly, the French government would not have been pleased to be told that it had granted diplomatic immunity to a "war criminal."

Once again, however, Waldheim was lucky. By July 1948, the Yugoslavs had decided that it was no longer in their interest to pursue his case.

What had happened to change Belgrade's mind was nothing less than a major shift in the geopolitical landscape—the opening of a profound rift between Yugoslavia and the Soviet Union.

The trouble had been brewing for some time. Stalin had always been both wary and jealous of Tito, as well as fearful of his Balkan ambitions. In March 1948, he decided to bring the independent-minded Yugoslav leader to heel by crushing the Communist party of Yugoslavia. To that end, he withdrew Soviet advisers from Yugoslavia and began encouraging his Cominform allies to criticize the Tito regime.

The Yugoslav response perplexed and infuriated the Soviets. Instead of debasing themselves and admitting their errors, the Yugoslavs accused Stalin of issuing "a call to civil war, a call to destroy our country." Declaring that "we cannot allow the Soviet intelligence service to spread its net in our country," Tito's party chiefs purged their ranks of all pro-Cominform officials and reminded the nation how the Soviets had subverted Yugoslavia's claims against Austria.

Stalin replied to this effrontery by expelling the Yugoslav party from the Cominform at the end of June and ordering the Communist world to impose an economic blockade on Yugoslavia. With East-bloc military forces threatening their frontier, and their leader the object of a barrage of hate-filled, subversive propaganda, the Yugoslav people rallied behind Tito. They also began to dig trenches and build border fortifications. A poor country, already devastated by a terrible war, was once again mobilizing for conflict.[9]

By the summer, it was clear to the Yugoslav leadership that they had to adapt to new realities. Surrounded by Stalin's bayonets, Yugoslavia now needed to reopen her trade to the West—and to do that, she needed access to the contested cities of Trieste and Villach. For the moment, the desire to regain control of southern Carinthia yielded to the survival instinct. Good relations with Austria were suddenly more important than nationalistic pride. Belgrade thus informed Vienna that all Austrian

POWs currently being held in Yugoslavia would be returned by the end of the year.[10]

Gruber seized the opportunity. "Yugoslavia needs economic aid more urgently than political pseudo-successes," he told Aleš Bebler. "Liquidating these frontier difficulties is of vital importance to you." Before long, an Austrian soccer team was visiting Belgrade, Yugoslav emissaries were making cautious inquiries about securing Marshall Plan aid, and Gruber was conducting secret talks with his old enemies. Though for the record both sides maintained their conflicting boundary claims, Gruber told his American contacts that the dispute should "present no obstacle to the establishment of closer economic ties between the two countries." In turn, the Americans told the Yugoslavs that they should resolve their outstanding differences with Austria. Tito's road to U.S. aid, it seemed, went through the Ballhausplatz in Vienna.[11]

One of the luckiest beneficiaries of this remarkable turnabout was Kurt Waldheim, whose dossier Belgrade now found it prudent to suppress. The Yugoslavs had created the *Odluka* and gotten Waldheim's name on the UNWCC and CROWCASS lists in order to destroy Gruber and embarrass their Western enemies. Now Gruber was Yugoslavia's friend, her conduit to the Western aid that had suddenly become essential to her survival. Against this new backdrop, it was hardly surprising that in July 1948, Belgrade somehow "lost" the Waldheim extradition request as well as the appended war-criminals list that contained his name.

Any chance that the Yugoslavs might one day resume their pursuit of Waldheim disappeared by July 22, 1948, when Belgrade released Johann Mayer, the Austrian POW whose tainted testimony had been at the heart of the Waldheim *Odluka*. With Mayer now free—to recant his testimony as well as undergo interrogation by Allied investigators—the Yugoslav case against Waldheim ceased to exist.[12]

Ever since the trial of General Löhr, Kurt Waldheim had been in mortal danger. Now, through no action of his own, he was safe. The same impersonal, geopolitical forces that in December 1947 had required his destruction mandated his survival six months later.

Was there a lesson to be drawn from any of this? One thing was certain. Although the Yugoslav charges had been politically motivated fabrications, there was no denying that they were based on an unpleasant truth—the indisputable fact that Waldheim had served in the Balkans as a Wehrmacht intelligence officer.

Over the next few years, Waldheim would construct a new persona for himself—that of a man without a Balkan past.

CHAPTER FIFTEEN

The Man Without a Past

The Waldheims prospered in France. The postwar chaos of Vienna now behind them, Kurt and Cissy became a formidable social couple, gracing many a Parisian dinner table. Their main concerns centered around the usual problems that confront an upwardly mobile husband and wife: the children, money, ambition. As far as anyone knew, the young Austrian first secretary had an unblemished past and a bright future. With Karl Gruber, his friend and mentor, still running the foreign ministry, Waldheim could reasonably expect to be rewarded with an ambassadorship at the end of his stint in Paris.

Waldheim was fortunate in another way. As the Cold War reached its height in the late forties, interest in pursuing Nazi war criminals began to abate. The new geopolitical schisms between East and West were of far more pressing concern. By the end of 1948, both CROWCASS and the UN War Crimes Commission had been disbanded, their rosters of alleged war criminals filed away and largely forgotten. The UNWCC's files were brought to New York, where they would gather dust in quiet obscurity for the next thirty-eight years. Until 1986, governments rarely sought access to them, while scholars and researchers were barred from examining individual dossiers—this despite the fact that the UNWCC had originally been founded, among other reasons, in order to provide "a valuable record for future historians."[1]

To the extent that Waldheim's fate was tied to the state of relations between Yugoslavia and Austria, the young diplomat's luck was positively extraordinary. As a result of Belgrade's rift with Moscow, Marshal Tito found himself in the position of having to establish good relations with the Western powers in general and with Austria in particular. To that end, he formally dropped his territorial claims, and in 1951 agreed to exchange ambassadors with Vienna, thus ending the state of war that had legally existed since 1941. In the aftermath, Karl Gruber became the first non-Communist foreign minister to visit postwar Belgrade. He and Tito got along famously.

With Yugoslavia and Austria enjoying full diplomatic relations, it was time to recall Kurt Waldheim to Vienna. After four years and two promotions (from diplomatic secretary second class to diplomatic secretary first class to foreign affairs counselor third class), Waldheim left Paris and returned home with his wife and children late in 1951. Gruber had decided against sending Waldheim to another foreign capital, not because he doubted the younger man's diplomatic skills but because he once again needed him at home. Gruber had always liked the way Waldheim handled confidential documents, and he trusted his judgment, particularly when it came to personnel questions. He also knew that Waldheim was a model of silence and discretion—two characteristics that were not among Gruber's own strong points. In short, Waldheim was the perfect man to fill an important and sensitive position that had just come vacant—that of chief of the personnel division of the Ministry of Foreign Affairs.

    Waldheim assumed his new post in November 1951, just a few weeks shy of his thirty-third birthday. For the first time in his diplomatic career, he had the power to issue significant orders to subordinates. More important, he enjoyed access to, and authority over, every dossier in the foreign ministry's personnel files—including his own. He had achieved every bureaucrat's dream, control of his own vital records.

It was around this time that a vague gray mist began to descend over Kurt Waldheim's past—when the crucial years between 1941 and 1945 seemed to go missing.

    Among other things, it became apparent in the early 1950s that Waldheim's doctoral dissertation on Konstantin Frantz had disappeared from the library of the University of Vienna. Whether someone deliberately removed it or whether it was accidentally lost in the postwar chaos, it was nowhere to be found; as a result, there was no mention of it in a 1954 catalogue that listed every Nazi-era dissertation on file at the university library.[2] Though, for the most part, the dissertation was harmless enough, its last few pages, which glorified Hitler's Third Reich as the culmination of Frantz's idea of European federalism, might have embarrassed the rising young diplomat.

The disappearance of Waldheim's dissertation was consistent with a pattern of omission that was coming to characterize Waldheim's way of dealing with his war years. Waldheim rarely, if ever, actually lied about what he had done during the war; he simply neglected to mention the awkward parts.

This pattern first became evident (in retrospect at least) early in 1952, when the U.S. Department of State sent a routine request to American authorities in Austria, asking for background information on Kurt Waldheim. The acting U.S. high commissioner in Vienna, Walter Dowling, assigned the task to reporting clerk Dorothy L. Ault, who requested a biography of Waldheim from the Austrian foreign ministry. It is likely that Ault's request was forwarded to Waldheim himself, for as chief of the ministry's personnel division, he was the official responsible for supplying such information to representatives of the four Allied powers.

Ault received a Waldheim biography from the foreign ministry the first week in April. On April 8, 1952, she transferred the information onto a U.S. Embassy form, which was then approved by acting high commissioner Dowling and ultimately sent back to Washington. There, it remained hidden from public view until I obtained it under a Freedom of Information Act request some thirty-five years later.

Given Waldheim's meticulous nature, the biographical data his department provided American authorities was surprisingly sloppy and incomplete. Among other things, it contained absolutely no mention of any of Waldheim's military service, either in the Austrian army or in the Wehrmacht, nor did it refer at all to his dissertation on Konstantin Frantz. It also gave the wrong date for Waldheim's doctoral degree. The accompanying report by Dorothy Ault seemed to reflect some awareness of the meagerness of the fare. "As Dr. Waldheim has had little contact with the members of the Embassy," she informed her State Department superiors, "there is no additional biographic data to report at this time. When information does become available, it will be forwarded to the Department."[3]

No such information was ever forthcoming, and the fragmentary data remained the basic source for the State Department's official dossier on Kurt Waldheim. Waldheim's file was updated in future years as his career progressed, but the incomplete account of his life prior to 1952 was never revised.

What is particularly surprising is that no one in either the U.S. Embassy in Vienna or the State Department in Washington appears to have ever questioned the obvious holes in Waldheim's biography. As a healthy Austrian male born in 1918, Waldheim had to have been liable for military service at some point between 1938 and 1945. That much at least would have been obvious to the embassy staff in Vienna. Yet they allowed his dossier to be sent to Washington without correction or amplification. Dowling or some other embassy official had decided not to worry about filling in the gaps in Waldheim's record, that there was no need for the State Department to know about Waldheim's political and military past. It was enough to inform Washington about his personal life and his current career.

Three years later, a brief public biography of Waldheim appeared for the first time in *Who's Who in Austria 1955.*[4] Once again there was no mention of any military service. A similar omission can be found in every succeeding edition of the work, right through the 1971–72 edition, which covers the beginning of Waldheim's decade-long tenure as secretary-general of the United Nations. It is worth noting that most such compendia rely almost entirely on information supplied by the subject. Only a few biographical reference guides employ their own researchers or fact-checkers. And even in these cases, as the publisher of one notes, "the questionnaire filled out by the biographee remains the main source of direct information."[5]

To be sure, Waldheim never denied having been in the Wehrmacht. When questioned, he would reply: "Of course I was in the Wehrmacht. Everyone was. I was a cavalryman in Russia, and I was wounded." To deny the past altogether would not only be impossible; it would raise questions about the really important omissions. Indeed, in private, with fellow Austrians and even with a few selected foreigners, Waldheim did talk about his military service, particularly his experiences on the Russian front. Certainly Fritz Molden had known about it. So had Karl Gruber. The fact was, the vast majority of Waldheim's generation had served the Reich in one way or another; there was no shame attached to the mere fact of having worn a German uniform.

Just the same, Waldheim seems to have made two decisions about revealing his past. He would allow little or nothing about his army days to appear in *print*—and he would never, ever mention having served in the Balkans.

It wasn't that Waldheim felt he had done anything wrong during his six years in the Wehrmacht. However traumatic those missing years may have been for him, they did not seem to inspire in him any feelings of guilt or remorse. It was just that recalling them served no useful purpose.

Why take the risk that someone might get the wrong idea? The past was the past. How much simpler just to wipe it all out of one's mind. If a friend or family member asked him about the war, he would just sigh and say, "My God, those were years!" No details were necessary.

From a careerist standpoint, there was no question that Waldheim had made the right decision. The abortive Yugoslav effort to set him up showed how easily even an incomplete (and largely inaccurate) account of his war record could be used against him. True, by the mid-fifties it was not likely that the soon to be dissolved Allied Council would have had any interest in looking into charges concerning his past, but a chance indiscretion could still do a lot of harm. The French, for example, would have been outraged to learn that the charming young couple who had so recently graced the Austrian legation in Paris had consisted of a former Nazi party member and a former Wehrmacht officer whose name appeared on the UN and CROWCASS lists of alleged war criminals. And the British, who were still trying to find out what had happened to numerous commandos who went missing in Greece in 1944, would have been less than pleased to discover the role Waldheim had played on the intelligence staff at Arsakli.

By 1953, it was clear to Waldheim that Gruber's power was ebbing. The man to watch now was Dr. Bruno Kreisky, the foreign ministry's new state secretary. Waldheim had known Kreisky since the late 1940s, but their contact had been limited. A Jew and a Socialist, the chunky, ruddy-faced Kreisky was a walking advertisement for the new, anti-Nazi, democratic Austria, and his rapid rise was meant to impress the Allies, especially the Americans. Though Kreisky downplayed his Jewishness, thinking of himself solely as an Austrian Socialist, his perspective was not shared by many. "Who is the only person in Austria ignorant of Kreisky's Jewishness?" wags would ask. The answer: "Bruno Kreisky!"

Early in March 1953, Vienna (along with the rest of the world) was stunned by the electrifying news that Stalin had died. The death of the Soviet dictator had enormous implications for Austria. Perhaps Stalin's successors would be more successful in concluding a state treaty to end the four-power occupation of Austria. If so, how would the West—in particular, the United States—react to a Soviet overture? Waldheim and his colleagues debated these and other questions endlessly.

Eight months after Stalin's death, a government shake-up cost Gruber his post as foreign minister. The recently appointed chancellor, former Heimwehr leader Julius Raab, replaced Gruber with Leopold Figl. Gruber's downfall was at least partly his own fault. His sometimes abrupt

style offended people, and his 1953 book, *From Liberation to Liberty,* was
filled with indiscretions that gave his enemies the leverage they needed
to oust him. But most of all, he paid the price for something that was not
really his fault: his inability to bring home a state treaty. Still, he remained
in favor with his American protectors—as a result of which Figl gave him
in 1954 the choice post of ambassador to Washington.

Waldheim learned from his mentor's fall. He would avoid Gruber's
mistakes—his bluntness, his erratic and impulsive decisionmaking, his
overt partisanship, his public identification with one power. He would also
cultivate the foreign ministry's new rising star, Bruno Kreisky.

For his part, Kreisky was not overly enamored of Waldheim. Still, he
valued Waldheim's skills, and he recognized the utility of someone so
pliable, reliable, and—above all—discreet.

Waldheim also cultivated his new boss, Leopold Figl. He liked to
point out that Figl and his father had been friends in Lower Austria before
the war.

As it turned out, the ascension of Raab to the chancellorship was the
first concrete sign that the Soviet attitude toward Austria was indeed
changing. Previously, Moscow had been hostile to Raab, a right-winger
with strong ties to big business. The fact that the Russians now approved
of him as chancellor indicated that they might be ready to offer even
greater concessions than before to secure a state treaty that would establish a fully independent Austria.

That indication hardened into reality in the spring of 1955, when the
new collective leadership in the Kremlin made a momentous decision:
They would sign a state treaty and withdraw their forces from eastern
Austria, provided that the treaty mandated permanent neutrality for
Austria. The Soviet logic was clear: Moscow wanted to prevent the West-
ern Allies from using Austria as a bridge between their armies in Italy and
West Germany. Continued occupation, the Soviets realized, might drive
Austria into the arms of the newly formed NATO alliance. On the other
hand, if Austria was neutral, a non-NATO bloc would stretch from Swit-
zerland down through Yugoslavia.

Though Western hard-liners such as U.S. secretary of state John
Foster Dulles had serious reservations about withdrawing Allied forces
from Austria, the Allies really had no choice. Austria wanted the treaty,
and the Soviets were forthcoming. Soviet Communist party boss Nikita
Khrushchev's "peaceful coexistence" had triumphed over Dulles's Cold
War stance.

The long-awaited treaty was finally signed on May 15, 1955. For most
Austrians, this marked the end of a miserable era that had begun in the

summer of 1914. For the first time in more than twenty years, Austria was once again free and sovereign. Ugly reminders of the past, such as war-crimes trials and denazification programs, could now fade away, scabs on the national consciousness that few Austrians wished to pick open.

No one rejoiced over the state treaty more than Kurt Waldheim. Still a relatively young thirty-six, he knew that his career would advance more rapidly than ever now that Austria was a sovereign nation again. Legations would be upgraded to embassies, and new positions would open up. Waldheim still nurtured the dream of his days at the Consular Academy: He wanted to cut a great figure on the world stage.

He had also grown more than a little bored running the personnel division. To be sure, the information he had gleaned from his access to the files would serve him well in later years. Indeed, it was already helping him. Not only did he enjoy unparalleled insights into the strengths and weaknesses of his colleagues, but he was in a position to do favors for people like Gruber and Kreisky. Nonetheless, it was time to move on, time to begin in earnest the great diplomatic career.

Waldheim's immediate goal was the United Nations in New York. He had long been interested in international organizations, having written of the virtues of European federalism in his dissertation. More to the point, the UN provided an ideal platform for a small nation attempting to establish a place for itself. In particular, it was just the forum in which a rising Austrian diplomat could make a name for himself by demanding better treatment for the German-speaking minority in the Italian-controlled South Tyrol.

With the carefully cultivated support of his peers and superiors, and an impressive dossier of credentials, Waldheim thus arranged to leave the personnel division in 1955 and take up the post of Austrian observer at the UN. Soon after he arrived, Austria became a full member of the world body, with Waldheim her first permanent representative.

The move from Vienna to New York was a happy one for the Waldheims. At first Cissy was worried by the stories of crime and other problems in New York, but she and the rest of the family soon became accustomed to the bustle, traffic, and noise of Manhattan, where they found a small but comfortable apartment. As in Paris, Kurt and Cissy quickly established themselves as a charming and sociable couple. Though their entertainment allowance was limited, they were always ready to play host to a growing circle of well-connected friends, with whom they would play cards and chat well into the night.

The United Nations was an important place in 1955, taken seriously by the big powers. Waldheim had indeed come a long way in a very few years. He cultivated lifelong contacts in the delegates' lounge, his suave, pleasing manner persuading the permanent representatives to listen carefully when he put in a word for the Austrian position on the South Tyrol.

Always smiling, gracious, and helpful, Waldheim made an excellent impression on the UN diplomatic community. His manners were perfect. Peers would receive a brief bow and a handshake. More important people would get a deeper bow, and the assurance that the honor was entirely his. Waldheim's training at the Consular Academy served him well.

After a year at the UN, Waldheim was put in charge of the Austrian Legation in the Canadian capital of Ottawa. As minister to Canada, he was once again a great success. Not only did he speak both English and French, but after his experiences on the Russian front, cold weather held no terror for him. Charmed by the young Austrian envoy with his pretty wife and his love for skiing, the Canadians soon yielded to his entreaties that diplomatic relations between their two governments be upgraded. As a result, in 1958 the Austrian Legation in Ottawa became a full-fledged embassy, and the thirty-nine-year-old minister received the coveted title of ambassador. Waldheim now equaled his former boss Gruber in rank, if not in seniority.

This was a period of profound personal satisfaction for Waldheim. In 1959, he became a father for the third time, when Cissy gave birth to a girl. They named her Christa.

Waldheim took a real interest in his children. He was gratified by their intelligence, made sure they attended the finest schools, and later pulled what strings he could (which were often considerable) to enhance their careers.

His own prospects were better than ever. In 1959, Bruno Kreisky, whom Waldheim had long ago identified as a comer, was named foreign minister. He remained in that post for the next seven years. Though the smiling, diffident "clerical" and the passionate Jewish Socialist made an unlikely couple, the careers of Waldheim and Kreisky were—and would continue to be—linked. Austria was no longer beholden to the big powers, but it was still governed by what was known as the Great Coalition, the Socialist–People's party alliance that had first emerged in 1945. Though he was not a party man, Waldheim was a conservative—and as such he was useful to the left-wing Kreisky, who could mollify right-wing opponents by promoting him.

In 1960, Kreisky brought Waldheim home to Vienna, appointing him to a major foreign ministry post, that of director-general of political affairs. The ultimate civil servant, Waldheim showed Kreisky the same flexibility and dedication that he had lavished on Karl Gruber a dozen years earlier—and on General Löhr four years before that.

Nonetheless, Waldheim did not intend to spend too many years writing memoranda for Kreisky. His first love was diplomacy, and he yearned to go back abroad. ("I always knew I would be a diplomat," he told me in 1987.) Waldheim may have been the model of discretion, but he also loved the fame, pomp, and ceremony of public life. He desired the statesman's life-style without the controversy and anxieties that normally attend political life.

In any case, he convinced Kreisky to send him back to the United Nations in 1962 as Austria's permanent representative. The South Tyrol issue was still unresolved, with terrorism by pro-Austrian radicals on the increase, and Waldheim spent much of his time mastering the arguments in favor of more autonomy for the nearly quarter of a million German-speaking people who lived just across the Austrian border in the Alto Adige region of northern Italy.

The UN had changed since Waldheim was last there. The Third World was beginning to dominate the General Assembly—a trend that Waldheim realized could be good for himself as well as for his country. As a result, he was always ready for a word with some exotic Third World delegate, invariably observing that Austria, too, was neutral in the Cold War.

As the UN's stock fell (at least as far as many in the West were concerned), Waldheim's rose. He was regarded as fair, tenacious, discreet, and pleasant to all. He threatened nobody and charmed nearly everyone. As a result, his fellow delegates elected him to important organizational posts, such as the chairmanship of the Committee on Outer Space.

After six years at the UN, Waldheim's great moment came. In 1968, conservative Chancellor Josef Klaus appointed him foreign minister. At the age of forty-nine, he had attained the highest post in his country's foreign service. Sadly, his parents didn't get to see his great triumph; they had died a few years earlier. At least his old mentor Karl Gruber was still around. Indeed, he was now one of Waldheim's subordinates, a state secretary in the foreign ministry. Gruber didn't stay in that post for long, however. In 1969, Waldheim sent him back to Washington, for a second stint as Austria's ambassador to the United States.

A less ambitious man might have regarded his rise to the top of the foreign ministry as the culmination of a glorious career. Not Kurt Waldheim. He had his eye on even higher peaks. It was looking increasingly likely that U Thant would be retiring as UN secretary-general when his term ended in 1971. Waldheim intended to be ready to take advantage of the opening if and when he did.

That was still three years away, however. In the meantime, Waldheim would have to show he could deal with crises as foreign minister. His first opportunity to do that came rather more quickly than he may have wanted.

In August 1968, Soviet tanks rolled into nearby Czechoslovakia to crush the reformist spirit of what had been hailed as the "Prague spring." Confrontation not being his style, Waldheim took pains to avoid antagonizing Moscow, and ordered the Austrian Embassy in Prague to refrain from granting an excessive number of visas to would-be Czech refugees.

The move later gave rise to speculation that Waldheim was somehow beholden to Moscow—perhaps because the Soviets knew something about his hidden past. This seems unlikely. The fact is, the Soviets were coguarantors of the Austrian state treaty, Austria was a neutral nation, and—perhaps most important—the Red Army was exceedingly powerful. In short, Waldheim was simply exercising his characteristic caution.

In any case, the Austrian ambassador in Prague, Rudolf Kirchschläger, defied Waldheim's orders and issued emergency visas to many desperate Czechs. After the invasion, Waldheim did not attempt to block any of the Czech refugees from entering Austria, nor did he take disciplinary action against his rebellious ambassador.

In the aftermath of the Czech crisis, Waldheim began to court Marshal Tito, who had emerged as one of the leaders of the nonaligned world. Hoping that Tito would use his influence on Austria's behalf, especially in connection with the continuing effort to win some autonomy for the German-speaking residents of the South Tyrol, Waldheim reminded Tito of his close friendship with Gruber. Tito, for his part, cultivated his relationship with Waldheim. He was concerned that the Russians might try to invade Yugoslavia (perhaps through Austria), and he urged Waldheim and his countrymen to be more vigilant than ever.

For all his caution, Waldheim was nonetheless something of a gambler. If he seemed averse to taking risks, it was only because he preferred to try to solve problems with patient behind-the-scenes negotiations, rather than with belligerent public grandstanding. In addition to being a matter of personal style, Waldheim's way also made practical sense, virtually guaranteeing that no matter what the outcome, his personal reputation would remain intact: If he succeeded, he would receive the credit; if he failed, few would be the wiser.

Thus protected, he often saw opportunity where others saw political danger. The rapidly worsening situation in the South Tyrol presented him with just such an opportunity. By the late 1960s, frustrations had reached a point where German-speaking terrorists were threatening the Italians with revolution unless the region received either independence or *Anschluss* with Austria. With bombs going off almost daily, Waldheim decided to try to resolve the issue once and for all by undertaking high-level talks with Rome and mobilizing his contacts at the UN. There was no question that the enterprise was a risky one. If he stumbled, his meteoric rise would come to a shuddering halt.

The South Tyrol issue was an emotional one for many Austrians. Gruber, who hailed from the region himself, had so infuriated his fellow Tyroleans with the unsatisfactory agreement he had negotiated in 1946 that virtually no one lifted a finger to help him when he got into political trouble in the early 1950s. Waldheim, by contrast, had no emotional ties to the region. (Indeed, until 1986, he never showed emotion of any kind in public.) That proved a powerful advantage. Cool and well-informed, always smiling and patient, Waldheim impressed his Italian adversaries.

What few people realized was that Waldheim had considerable experience negotiating with the Italians; indeed, it dated back to April 1942, when he first served in the Balkans with General Esposito. Not only did Waldheim enjoy a fine command of the language; he was also one of the few Austrians the Italians really liked.

Having learned from Gruber's mistakes, Waldheim avoided erratic changes of course and agreed to discuss anything and everything the Italians wanted to put on the table, from bilingualism to political rights, from security questions to educational issues. He also refrained from making rash predictions to the press about imminent triumphs.

Firm but patient, Waldheim finally achieved an agreement with Rome in 1969, persuading the Italians to grant significant linguistic and cultural rights to the disputed region's German-speakers. It was an unalloyed triumph—and he deservedly got most of the credit.

The following year, Bruno Kreisky's narrow electoral victory, and his decision to govern with a minority Socialist cabinet, led Waldheim to resume his old post as Austria's permanent representative to the UN in New York.

It was, of course, all part of a plan, one that had Kreisky's full support. U Thant's term would expire in less than two years, and the consensus was that he would not run again. For someone who hoped to succeed him, now was the time to start seeking votes, to begin calling in old IOUs.

Unfortunately, U Thant did not cooperate with Waldheim's plans. The unpredictable secretary-general refused to reveal his intentions, remaining a remote, enigmatic figure. Waldheim began to grow anxious.

Perhaps U Thant planned to defy the consensus and seek a third term.

Meanwhile, a new possibility arose for Waldheim. The incumbent president of Austria, Franz Jonas, was elderly and ill, and the conservative Austrian People's Party (ÖVP), the postwar successor to the old Christian Social movement, which the Waldheim family had long supported, was looking for a candidate to carry its standard in the 1971 race. Though Waldheim had always avoided partisan politics, the conservatives—particularly in Lower Austria—knew he was one of them. Impressed by his success in resolving the South Tyrol issue, the ÖVP began to try to persuade Waldheim to accept its nomination for the largely ceremonial post—which the Socialists had held without interruption since the war.

At first Waldheim was coy, reluctant to temporarily vacate his seat at the UN. Then he relented, for on reflection the timing seemed fortuitous. If U Thant did decide to attempt one more stint in office before he retired, Waldheim could happily sit out the period in the Hofburg Palace in Vienna as president of Austria, with a term that would conveniently end in 1977—just a few months after the UN job would once again come open.

With that in mind, he permitted the ÖVP to nominate him for president in 1971. He was hardly a backslapping, baby-kissing candidate. Still, his dignity and competence impressed his countrymen. In the first election he ever fought, representing a party that had never won the presidency, Waldheim pulled in a surprising and impressive 47 percent of the vote.

As it turned out, it was fortunate for Waldheim that he lost the election, for the gossip from the UN was that U Thant was out. His own intentions had turned out to be less important than those of the Western powers—most of which had apparently had enough of him. Waldheim quickly returned to New York, once again taking up his old post as Austria's permanent representative to the UN. Not long afterward, U Thant confirmed the rumors, announcing that because of ill health he would not be seeking another term as secretary-general.

Waldheim was ready. With Cissy at his side, he entertained at a dizzying pace, hosting bridge parties, dinners, and receptions. Having cultivated the Third World since the mid-1960s, he was now in a position to reap the dividends. The Western pressure on U Thant had antagonized many African and Asian delegates. Waldheim was able to tell them of his regard for the Burmese secretary-general. In addition, he pointed to his ties to Marshal Tito and to India's late revered leader, Jawaharlal Nehru. He also had the full backing of Chancellor Kreisky, who mobilized his international Socialist contacts on Waldheim's behalf.

At the same time, he made sure he had the support of the big powers, the five permanent members of the Security Council—Britain, China, France, the Soviet Union, and the United States—whose backing (or at least toleration) he would need to win the job. Waldheim was keenly aware that the great powers were looking for a discreet administrator, a workaholic who could manage the UN's bloated bureaucracy, not another moralist who would use the UN as a forum to lecture them, offering alternative policies and generally meddling in their business.

The Soviets were evidently behind Waldheim, believing he had behaved responsibly during the Czech invasion. They also were wary of his main rival, Finland's Max Jakobson, who was not only a would-be policymaker but pro-Western and pro-Israeli to boot. The Americans were a bit less enthusiastic; still, as U.S. delegate George Bush observed, Waldheim was "ideally equipped" for the job. Only the recently admitted delegation from mainland China refused to support him—at least at first. The Peking government wanted the job to go to a Third World delegate.

In the end, Waldheim's careful preparation paid off. On December 21, 1971, by a vote of eleven for, one against, and three abstaining, the Security Council passed a resolution recommending to the General Assembly "that Mr. Kurt Waldheim be appointed Secretary-General of the United Nations."

As the years passed, Waldheim had slowly and cautiously begun to fill in some of the more harmless gaps in his history. Still, the record remained murky, filled with half-truths and distortions. For example, while a 1971 campaign brochure put out on his behalf during the Austrian presidential race mentioned that Waldheim was familiar with Slavic languages, it did not specifically say that he knew some Serbo-Croatian.[6] Nor did it describe the circumstances under which he had gained his familiarity. And though the brochure also allowed as how he had fought in the Wehrmacht, it claimed that after being wounded in 1942, he had resumed his law studies, adding vaguely that he returned to Austria at the end of the war from some unnamed front.

Later in 1971, *The New York Times* noted in a "Man in the News" profile that Waldheim had been in the infantry during World War II, "reportedly seeing service on both the Italian and Russian fronts before a wound in 1942 ended his active duty and he resumed his law studies." Out of six facts concerning his war record, the *Times* got four wrong.[7]

After Waldheim was elected UN secretary-general, a 1972 biography based on information presumably supplied by him contained a similar mixture of truth, half-truth, and outright falsehood. It noted (accurately) that his father had been imprisoned by the Nazis and that Waldheim himself had been wounded while serving on the Russian front. But it also (inaccurately) placed the date of the injury in 1942 and said that "after his recuperation he was discharged from military service." The same year, the German newsmagazine *Der Spiegel* quoted Waldheim to similarly misleading effect; according to the magazine, the new UN secretary-general claimed that the wounds he suffered on the Russian front had effectively ended his wartime service.

Anyone, of course, can get a date wrong. The fact that Waldheim may have repeatedly ascribed a 1942 date to a wound he actually suffered in December 1941 hardly implies the existence of a deliberate pattern of deception. What is less innocuous, however, is the consistent lack of any reference by Waldheim to his service in the Balkans. The three-year period from the beginning of 1942 to the early spring of 1945 is simply missing from his résumé.

In an autobiographical essay he wrote in 1978, for example, Waldheim summed up his war years by noting that after recuperating from his wounds, he was recalled to service and found himself in the Trieste region. The account provided no dates, nor did it contain any mention of Bosnia, Montenegro, Athens, or Arsakli. The English-language edition of Waldheim's 1984 memoir, *In the Eye of the Storm,* was even less forthcoming. His defenders later maintained that this was because a crucial paragraph that appeared in the German-language edition of the book—a paragraph that supposedly told the truth about the missing years—was inadvertently omitted. In fact, the missing passage is just as misleading and uninformative as the 1978 essay, consisting in its entirety of the following:

> Upon termination of my study leave, and after recovering from my leg injury, I was recalled to army service. Shortly before the end of the war, I was in the area of Trieste.[8]

Waldheim continued to stick to his carefully edited story as late as 1986, when he mounted his second race for the presidency of Austria. His official campaign biography maintained that he had been drafted into the army and wounded on the eastern front, after which he returned home, studied law, and met his future wife. He gave a similar account in personal conversations with supporters, adding that after a long recuperation from his leg wound, he was assigned to some unspecified staff unit and ended the war in the Trieste region.[9]

It wasn't until the spring of 1986, after I uncovered documentary evidence of his service in the Balkans, that Waldheim finally began to confront—however hesitantly—the numerous untold truths about his past.

Could the story of Waldheim's missing years have been revealed before the mid-1980s? The answer, I think, is an unequivocal yes.[10]

In 1945, the Western Allies captured huge amounts of German military and political documents—one hundred tons of the material in northern Germany alone! By 1947, one hundred fifty separate German documentary collections had been established, with several tons of papers arriving in Washington each week. In the United States, legal authorities used these materials to prepare for war-crimes trials, while military men analyzed them for intelligence purposes. At the same time, the U.S. Army's German Military Documents Section was readying the vast hoard of data for future archival use. By 1954, the Department of the Army had developed a plan to photograph the records, collaborating with the American Historical Association in making the resulting microfilms available to researchers. Four years later, the National Archives boasted more than five thousand linear feet of microfilmed German documents. Amid that mass were large numbers of documents that either mentioned Kurt Waldheim or bore his signature.[11]

In the mid-1960s, as part of a historical inquiry into the partisan campaigns of World War II, the Yugoslav government purchased many reels of these microfilmed German documents from the U.S. government. As historian Venčeslav Glisić has since acknowledged, Yugoslav researchers quickly discovered materials relating to Waldheim. As a result, Belgrade updated its Waldheim file in 1967.

Though the new information about Waldheim was interesting, it did not prove that he had been a war criminal. In any case, the Tito regime decided that it was more important to maintain good relations with neutral Austria than to set the historical record straight—especially after the Russians invaded Czechoslovakia in August 1968. Indeed, when Waldheim later visited Belgrade, Marshal Tito personally bestowed on him the Order of the Grand Cross of the Yugoslav Flag. (Waldheim had now been decorated by the Fascist Pavelić and the Communist Tito; he was indeed a flexible man.)[12]

Austrian authorities learned of Waldheim's service in the Balkans a few years later. In the autumn of 1971, as Waldheim mounted his campaign to succeed U Thant as UN secretary-general, disquieting rumors about his past began to circulate. Some gossip had it that Waldheim had been in the S.S. As a result, word soon reached Karl Gruber that American support for Waldheim's candidacy was wavering. In order to provide

Austrian diplomats with evidence to refute the rumors, the Austrian Army Intelligence Service (HND) was ordered to investigate Waldheim's military record.

As it turned out, it wasn't until after Waldheim was appointed secretary-general that the HND managed to obtain the relevant records and discover that he had served in the Balkans for three years. Not surprisingly, the decision was made to suppress the discovery. Nonetheless, by 1973 allegations about Waldheim's missing years were common knowledge in Austrian intelligence circles. One nonadmirer of his used to laugh: "That Watzlawik [Waldheim] was a bureaucratic perpetrator!" Still, no one went public.[13] After all, Waldheim was now something of a national treasure; his international stature was proof that Austria had overcome his past.

Western disenchantment with the UN mounted throughout Waldheim's tenure as secretary-general—the result, mainly, of the Third World's increasing domination of the General Assembly. One outgrowth of this development that particularly bothered the United States was the growing isolation of Israel. It was during Waldheim's tenure that Third World and Eastern bloc delegates both welcomed an armed Yasir Arafat to the speaker's podium and passed the notorious resolution that equated Zionism with racism.

Though Waldheim did not endear himself to Western leaders when he questioned the legality of Israel's daring rescue of the Entebbe airport hostages in 1976, by and large he managed to distance himself from the more outrageous actions and speeches of the UN membership. His bureaucratic professionalism, and his good personal relations with Western ambassadors, guaranteed his survival. So did his cultivation of the Soviets and the Chinese, though he had more luck with the former than with the latter.

The Israelis, on the other hand, were increasingly suspicious of Waldheim. Late in 1978, they contacted Simon Wiesenthal to see if the famed Nazi-hunter could confirm the old rumors about Waldheim's past. Wiesenthal immediately made inquiries through a French contact, who in turn consulted two archives in West Berlin: the U.S.-controlled Berlin Document Center (BDC) and a French-controlled archive known as WAST, which housed Wehrmacht records.

On March 20, 1979, the Berlin Document Center issued a report on Waldheim to Wiesenthal's contact. The report consisted of a standard inquiry form that listed sixteen Nazi organizations, with a space for a positive or negative check mark next to each. All the check marks were negative—there was no record in the BDC of Waldheim's having ever been a member of either the S.S., the Nazi party, or any of the other groups listed on the form. (There *was* a record of Waldheim's wife having been a Nazi party member, but no one had thought to check on her.) The next day, WAST issued a similar report, though this one showed that after recuperating from the wounds he had received on the Russian front, Waldheim had been certified as fit for service on March 6, 1942, and had served in the Balkans after March 14, 1942.[14]

After carefully studying the reports, Wiesenthal accurately informed the Israelis that there was nothing incriminating in Waldheim's BDC record. What Wiesenthal could not know was that Waldheim *had* been a member of two Nazi-affiliated organizations, the S.A. Cavalry Corps and the National Socialist German Students League. The reason he didn't know this was that neither group was among the sixteen listed on the Berlin Document Center's standard report form. Wiesenthal was also unaware of the significance of the French report that Waldheim had served in the Balkans, for he was not familiar with Waldheim's history— specifically, with Waldheim's consistent assertion that for all intents and purposes his military career had ended in Russia. Wiesenthal had no reason to be suspicious, since there was nothing in his own voluminous files on Waldheim.

Once again Kurt Waldheim had been the beneficiary of coincidence and old-fashioned luck.

Still, the rumors about Waldheim's past persisted. By 1980, they had made their way from Berlin, Paris, Vienna, and Tel Aviv to the offices of Brooklyn congressman Stephen Solarz, a young Democratic member of the U.S. House of Representatives. In January 1980, in an article in *The New Republic* magazine, the writer Shirley Hazzard, who had worked at the UN and whose book *Defeat of an Ideal* was highly critical of its management and attitudes, had stated that Waldheim had "taken part in the Nazi youth movement and served in Hitler's army in various campaigns including the Eastern front." Spurred by the article, Solarz wrote to Waldheim on November 26, 1980, asking him about his wartime record. Three weeks later Waldheim replied, assuring Solarz in a letter that the "slanderous" rumors of a Nazi past were nothing more than a "McCarthyesque lie." Wrote Waldheim: "I myself was wounded on the eastern front and, being incapacitated for further service on the front, resumed my law studies at Vienna University, where I graduated in 1944."[15] Despite the clear—and false—implication that his Wehrmacht service had ended in Russia, Waldheim later insisted to me that he had not meant to mislead Solarz. "All I said was that after my wound I was no longer fit for service at the front," he told me in Vienna in 1987. "I meant to say that I could not be sent back to the Russian front."

Solarz also asked the Central Intelligence Agency what it knew about Waldheim's past. On December 31, 1980, he received a reply from Frederick P. Hitz, legislative counsel to the director of Central Intelligence. It was just as misleading and incomplete as Waldheim's response. Indeed, it read like a copy of the secretary-general's letter. Reported Hitz: "We believe that Waldheim was not a member of the Nazi Youth Movement, nor was he involved in anti-Jewish activities."

The first part of that judgment was accurate as far as it went. The second part showed that Hitz was unaware of Ic/AO's work in the Balkans. According to the CIA, Waldheim had been drafted into the army and wounded in Russia. "[F]ollowing his recovery he returned to study law in Vienna," the CIA account continued. "He received his doctorate in law in 1944 . . ." There was not a word about his service in the Balkans.[16]

Waldheim's amazing good fortune continued. On January 2, 1980, while he was in Teheran attempting to negotiate the liberation of the American hostages, the Khomeini regime foiled a plot to assassinate him. On the same trip, he narrowly escaped from an enraged mob while visiting a cemetery containing the remains of revolutionary martyrs. (He was later infuriated by rumors that he had panicked. One thing he had shown in his life was that he was no coward in the face of hostile fire.)

Waldheim loved being UN secretary-general, though he called it "the toughest job in the world." He adored the spectacular view from his palatial office atop the UN building on Manhattan's East Side. He enjoyed the formal ceremonies during which he bestowed or received decorations. He relished the fact that wherever he went (except for Iran), he was greeted with the respect befitting the world's leading diplomat.

As secretary-general, Waldheim worked hard to find peaceful solutions to the world's many conflicts. "I must be the conscience of the world," he often remarked.[17] In addition to conscience, he was also motivated by a desire for prestige—in particular, he was desperate to win the Nobel Peace Prize. And though he rejects the notion, it is hard not to see his efforts at least partly as a form of *Trauerarbeit*, an attempt to make up for his role during World War II.

Toward the end of his second five-year term as UN secretary-general, it became clear to Waldheim that his friends in the Third World—particularly China—would not support his bid for a third term. They wanted a non-European to hold the top UN post. Waldheim thus withdrew from consideration, and the job went to Peru's Javier Pérez de Cuéllar.

Waldheim returned to Austria in 1982; two years later he formally retired from the Austrian foreign ministry. He was sixty-five, but his ambition was still thriving. He desired one more honor, one appropriate for the most famous Austrian diplomat since Prince Metternich. Waldheim coveted his nation's highest elective office, the trophy that had eluded him in 1971. The Hofburg Palace would be a consolation prize for the man who had failed to win the Nobel Peace Prize.

The president of Austria, elected by the people for a six-year term, is the head of state, the living symbol of the nation. The Austrian flag flies over the Hofburg only when the president is working inside. Though the post is largely ceremonial, the president can play an important role in the delicate task of forming new governments.

Waldheim believed that both major parties—the ÖVP and the Socialists—would nominate him. There would be no partisan unpleasantness, no politically motivated inquiries into his past. He was wrong, of course. Nonetheless, it is just as well that he sought the presidency, for had he not, he might well have taken his secrets with him to the grave.

CHAPTER SIXTEEN

The Return of
Lieutenant Waldheim

The good luck that had smoothed Kurt Waldheim's path ever since his brush with death on the Russian front in 1941 continued into the 1980s—only to desert him in 1985.

In the spring of 1985, the People's party turned to Waldheim once again, asking him to be its standard-bearer in the 1986 Austrian presidential race. With the nation tiring of the "Kreisky Era," the conservatives were convinced that this time they finally had a real chance of winning the presidency. Mismanagement, overregulation, mounting unemployment, and a scandal involving the use of antifreeze in wine exports had undermined the popularity of Kreisky's protégé and successor, Socialist chancellor Fred Sinowatz. As the conservatives saw it, politics were trending to the right throughout the industrialized world, in Thatcher's Britain, Kohl's West Germany, and Reagan's America. A Waldheim victory, they believed, might well result in an Austrian *Wende*, a turning point in the country's history that could lead to their capturing outright control of the government in the parliamentary elections that would surely follow such a precedent-shattering upset.

The Socialists, who complacently viewed the presidency as their exclusive property, were unprepared for the challenge posed by Waldheim. They decided to keep the office in their own ranks. Underestimating Waldheim's appeal, and failing to perceive that they would also lose votes to a new environmentalist party, they nominated a decent but weak candidate, Dr. Kurt Steyrer. By the late summer of 1985, however, Chancellor Sinowatz and his cabinet chief, Hans Pusch, realized they were in for a real fight.

Increasingly concerned about the ÖVP's chances, Sinowatz and his supporters began to focus on the rumors about Waldheim's past that had been circulating in Vienna since at least 1971. In 1985, a new story was making the rounds, inspired by the dedication of a controversial plaque at the War Academy. The plaque memorialized General Löhr, the former commander of Army Group E, whom the Yugoslavs had executed for war crimes in 1947. According to the latest gossip, Waldheim had been Löhr's personal adjutant, his 03. Though the story wasn't true, it was embraced by the Socialists as well as by right-wing defenders of Löhr, who claimed that it exonerated the former Wehrmacht general. After all, they argued, how could someone who had employed an aide as respectable as Kurt Waldheim possibly have been a war criminal?

More substantively, some Socialists—among them, historian Georg Tidl—had begun to rummage through the archives. Early in 1986, they discovered parts of Waldheim's *Wehrstammkarte,* or military career file. The material was quickly leaked to the magazine *Profil,* which soon began to publish sensational, albeit incomplete, facts about Waldheim's hidden past.[1]

In New York, officials of the World Jewish Congress watched the developments in Austria with profound interest and growing concern. The WJC had been founded in 1936, three years after Hitler seized power in Germany. Its original aim was to warn the world about Nazism and to prevent the persecution of the Jews. A half-century later, the WJC's secretary-general, Israel Singer, viewed the prospect of a Waldheim victory with undisguised horror. Of Austrian origin himself, Singer believed that for Austria to elect as its president a man with a tainted past would be tantamount to giving him—and all other former servants of the Reich—an "amnesty for the Holocaust." Singer's views were shared by WJC president Edgar Bronfman.

As a result, the WJC, which today has branches in Jewish communities throughout the world (including Austria), sent a representative to Vienna to establish contact with the Austrian journalists and historians who were already looking into the Waldheim case. Despite the outrage of many Austrians, who regarded the charges against Waldheim as a smear on their entire country, the journalists of *Profil,* led by editor Peter Michael Lingens and writer Hubertus Czernin, launched a full-scale investigation into the former secretary-general's past. For their part, the Socialists planned to use the results to try to persuade their countrymen that the election of Waldheim would tarnish Austria's reputation internationally; for its part, the WJC decided to publicize the disclosures in the United States.

There was a problem, however. The information about Waldheim was spotty and ambiguous. More coherent, archival research would be necessary if the world was to be persuaded that Waldheim had in fact concealed a compromised past. However much sensational charges might erode Waldheim's credibility, in the long run they would redound to the detriment of those who had made them if they could not be proved.

With that in mind, the WJC contacted me in the middle of March 1986, asking if I would examine the files in the Captured German Records section of the Modern Military Branch of the National Archives in Washington. In particular, the WJC wanted me to look for evidence of Waldheim's possible involvement in the deportation of more than forty thousand Jews from the Greek port of Salonika to the Nazi death camp at Auschwitz between March and August of 1943. I agreed to accept the assignment, though I advised the WJC that I would not be able to devote more than ten days or so to it.

What I wound up doing that March could have been done at any time since the mid-1960s. Any qualified researcher could have walked into the National Archives in Washington, as I did, obtained an identification card, and proceeded to the fourth floor, where the microfilms of German records captured during and after World War II are stored. Indeed, it is entirely possible that I *had* been preceded by others, who for reasons of their own decided not to make public what they found.

Having had nearly seventeen years' worth of experience working with captured German military records, I was confident that if Waldheim was in the records somewhere, I would find him. And I knew where to start looking. Information from Vienna placed Waldheim in the Balkans during the war. If true, that meant he must have been attached to a unit or units under the command of Army Group E, Army Group F, or the Twelfth Army.

The WJC had sent me some general guidelines, drawn up on legal paper, indicating that Waldheim might be mentioned in various particular documents contained in certain rolls of microfilm. The problem was that the guidelines did not give specific frame numbers—and a roll of microfilm can contain a thousand or more separate frames of poorly reproduced papers. The deterioration of my eyesight over the years is due in no small measure to this research problem.

Fortunately, the Modern Military Branch of the National Archives boasts some of the most knowledgeable archivists in the world, and when

I arrived at the archives on Pennsylvania Avenue I turned to two profes-
sionals whom I had known and worked with for many years: Robert
Wolfe, chief of the Modern Military Branch, and John Mendelsohn, a
senior archivist in the same branch. Both men were interested in the
Waldheim case, and over endless cups of coffee in their musty, over-
crowded offices and in the utilitarian cafeteria in the basement of the
archives building, we would discuss the best places for me to look. "Have
you checked the records of the *Reichsführer* S.S. for anything on
Greece?" Wolfe might ask. "I wonder if there are extant records on the
German liaison staff with the Italian Eleventh Army," I might respond.

The historian needs the archivist in order to carry out his research.
The archivist, in turn, looks to the historian to give value and meaning
to his own work. It is the archivist who authenticates, catalogues, and
maintains collections of historical documents. What he doesn't do is find
or interpret the documents; that is the job of the historian.

Archivists also occasionally help out a historian by providing him with
information from sources not normally open to public scrutiny. John
Mendelsohn did me just such a service at the end of my first week on the
Waldheim case.

Shortly after I first arrived at the archives, I had asked him if Kurt
Waldheim was on any war-crimes lists. As far as I was aware, those lists
were not then publicly available, but I knew that Mendelsohn had access
to them.* In the late afternoon of Friday, March 21, 1986, John found
Waldheim's name on the June 1948 CROWCASS list, charged by the
Yugoslavs with murder. Of course, I later learned that this specific charge
was based on the politically motivated *Odluka* drawn up by the Yugoslav
government in an effort to discredit Karl Gruber in 1947. At the time,
however, it seemed a stunning revelation. (Sadly, John Mendelsohn's
contributions to the search for Waldheim's missing years were the last he
was to make to historical research; he died·shortly afterward.)

In the ten days or so I spent in the archives that March, I uncovered no
evidence that Waldheim had been involved in the mass deportation of
the Jews of Salonika. Indeed, it soon became clear to me that Waldheim
had not even been in Salonika for much of the time in question. I did,
however, come across numerous documents indicating that rather than
having spent the bulk of the war studying law in Vienna, as he had

---

*As it turned out, some war-crimes lists were available to researchers at the time, but not
in the Modern Military Branch or under their proper titles. They were scattered among
other collections, such as those of the Diplomatic Branch.

claimed, Waldheim had returned to active duty after being wounded on the Russian front and had served as a highly valued Wehrmacht staff officer in the Balkans.

I had assumed that if Waldheim was no longer fit for front-line combat after being wounded in Russia, as he had claimed in his memoirs, then he would probably have been assigned to a Ic unit handling intelligence and other related tasks when he returned to active duty. Given the fact that he was a talented linguist who had studied international law, it was likely that he might have been a translator or liaison officer, perhaps with some Italian unit.

At first I wondered if I would find anything with Waldheim's signature on it. Before long, however, I was overwhelmed by the number of documents bearing the now-famous name. It turned out that Waldheim had often worked at the *Oberkommando* (or high command) level, right in the middle of a vast paper flow. He was a diligent desk officer who put his name, number, or initial on a large quantity of important documents.

On March 23, 1986, I turned my tentative findings over to the WJC. Among other things, I had discovered that in August of 1942, Waldheim had evidently played a significant enough role on the West Bosnian staff of General Friedrich Stahl, commander of the Wehrmacht's 714th Infantry Division, to have had his name inscribed on a divisional roll of honor for his contributions to what later became known as the Kozara battle and massacre. I also discovered documents linking Waldheim to the brutal antipartisan campaigns the Germans waged in Montenegro in 1943 and in eastern Macedonia in 1944.

On March 25, at a crowded press conference held in its cramped Manhattan headquarters, the WJC announced my findings to the world. The result was an international uproar that has yet to die down. The Waldheim campaign had led to the Waldheim scandal.

I had accepted the assignment from the WJC because I believed that it was important to learn the truth about an important public figure. In the process, I discovered in a most personal way what differentiates historians from other investigators.

The Austrian presidential campaign was well under way when the news broke of my discoveries about Waldheim's presence at Kozara. Waldheim responded at first by insisting that while it was true that he had been on General Stahl's staff at Kozara, the battle group had merely engaged in a "fierce battle" there. Talk about massacres, he insisted, was nonsense.

A week later, after it became clear that the Yugoslav government had been upset by his denial of the tragedy of "heroic Kozara," he claimed that he hadn't been there; he had reported to Stahl's staff, he said, only to be sent back to General Esposito's Pusteria regiment, southeast of Kozara. When I pointed out that Esposito's forces were not southeast of Kozara at the time, but 120 miles away in Montenegro, Waldheim suddenly remembered that Montenegro was where he had been sent. Finally, after I reminded him that his liaison command with the Italians had been dissolved two months earlier, at the end of May 1942, Waldheim amended his recollection once again: He *had* been with Stahl and he *had* served at Kozara, he conceded, but in an innocuous supply capacity.

In the midst of all this, Waldheim decided to dispatch his son Gerhard to Washington to defend his rapidly unraveling reputation. A Harvard-educated banker who spoke perfect English, Gerhard Waldheim would show that I had misinterpreted the documents that I had discovered in the National Archives.

Shortly before Gerhard arrived in America, I received a telephone call from a man who identified himself as an official of the Austrian Embassy in Washington. "You would like to meet with young Waldheim, yes?" he asked me in thickly accented English. He then invited me to come to the embassy, where Gerhard and I could discuss my findings. I responded that I would prefer to meet Gerhard on more neutral ground. Since correspondent John Martin of ABC News had already told me about Gerhard's impending visit, I suggested that "young Waldheim" and I meet at the ABC News studios in Washington. The Austrian official readily agreed.

Our meeting took place in April 1986. Gerhard was already at the studio when I arrived. Tall, balding, and bespectacled, he looked like a nonacademic's idea of a college professor. Though highly intelligent, Gerhard was trained as a banker, not as a historian, and he seemed unprepared to refute my analysis of the documents. Instead, he brandished a briefcase bulging with affidavits that he and his father had collected from elderly Germans and Austrians, who were willing to attest to Kurt Waldheim's anti-Nazi innocence in the old days. Regardless of the evidence in the archives, he insisted, the testimony of these old acquaintances, collected more than forty years after the fact, demonstrated that his father's record was clean. In any case, he added, his father had not lied about his service in the Balkans; he had simply never talked about it.

John Martin taped our lengthy dialogue—one minute of which appeared on the ABC evening news as a "debate." Viewers at home saw Gerhard denying the charges that had been leveled against his father, insisting that he had not been in Kozara but had merely been placed on the staff list of General Stahl's battle group "for payroll purposes." I responded that this did not strike me as being characteristic of Wehrmacht procedures, nor was it credible that Lieutenant Waldheim would have been awarded the Zvonimir medal if he had been in a "no show" job. I concluded by telling Gerhard that unless he could offer me documentation from the time that contradicted what I had been saying, I would have no choice but to continue to believe that Kurt Waldheim had served on Stahl's staff at Kozara.

After the taping, I told Gerhard in a friendly way that even if I was totally wrong (which was certainly possible, though not likely), he would need the assistance of a professional historian who was familiar with the archives in order to refute me. Our meeting was entirely civil. In the end, I agreed to meet him at the National Archives and personally show him how to find the documents I had uncovered.

At the appointed hour, I waited at the archives until well past the time we had agreed to meet. Gerhard never turned up. I think I understand why. He was not an impartial scholar but a son defending his father. I don't think he was ready then to look at the evidence.

The media's handling of our encounter, and of the continuing debate that followed, reflected the public's misunderstanding of how the facts of history are established. As far as the press was concerned, Gerhard and I were adversaries with an equal claim to the truth. After all, we both had our "documents"—he with his affidavits, I with my copies of old Wehrmacht records. I tried in vain to point out that to be of significant historical interest, a document must have originated in the era to which it pertains. An affidavit or other reminiscence, no matter how deeply felt or accurate it may seem to be, is not a legitimate historical document. Memoirs are always suspect, especially if they are written forty or fifty years after the fact—and doubly so when they concern a controversial case. Waldheim's own memoirs are a good case in point. Yet to much of the media, Gerhard and I were simply arguing about two perplexing piles of paper, one from 1942, the other from 1986.

I met Gerhard again, more than a year later. By then he had acquired a more substantial knowledge of the documentation. Still, his investigatory efforts remained suspect. His problem, which he shared with many people on both sides of the controversy, was that he was mainly interested in finding documents that bolstered his case. Documents that didn't were considered to be irrelevant. This was hardly surprising, for Gerhard quite understandably loved and revered his father, and wanted desperately to clear his name.

As a historian, I had a different task. I had to analyze the records in their own, proper context. I could not disregard a document simply because it contradicted my preconceptions. The historical account must conform to the documents, not the other way around.

Then again, how many of us are called upon to defend our own fathers against these kinds of charges?

The reactions to the results of my early research on Waldheim were varied. Some Jews urged me to stay away from the subject. If Waldheim is exposed, they argued, the Jews will be blamed. Others told me to leave an old man alone. Still another group wanted me to press on, as long as I eventually "nailed [part of Waldheim's anatomy] to the wall."

On April 8, 1986, I published an op-ed piece in *The New York Times* in which I summarized some of my findings and called for research into Waldheim's postwar career. I also listed some unanswered questions about his war record and speculated that the Yugoslav government could probably provide some answers.

The column enraged the Austrian Embassy in Washington. In newspaper interviews, the same official who had arranged my meeting with Gerhard Waldheim now accused me of being "filled with hatred." The phrase struck me as a curious one. As something of an expert on Nazi propaganda, I recognized it as a stock formulation that I had seen repeated over and over again in innumerable anti-Semitic tracts; the Jew, it was always claimed, was "filled with hatred."

The embassy man's reaction was not unusual. Among Austrians, the controversy over Waldheim seemed generally to inspire outrage—not over the possibility that the man who would be president might have concealed a tainted past, but over what many regarded as an international conspiracy designed to discredit Austria as a nation.

This reluctance to deal honestly with the past was not a new phenomenon. Ever since the Moscow Declaration of 1943 had proclaimed that Austria was a victim of German aggression, Austrians had been trying to convince themselves and the world that the Nazi bacillus had been a foreign germ. They ignored the part of the Moscow Declaration that spoke of Austrian complicity in Nazi crimes. Austria wasn't the country of racists like Schönerer and Hitler; it saw itself as the land of *The Sound of Music*, of Sacher tortes and Strauss waltzes, of quaint rococo churches and splendid mountains.[2]

Then came the Waldheim revelations. In one fell swoop, the roof caved in on the Austrian paradise. The innocent land of Mozart was suddenly being pilloried as a refuge for unrepentant Nazis. *Der Spiegel,* the influential German weekly magazine, devoted a cover story to what it called "Austria's quiet fascism," denouncing the "living lie" that was Austria. Among other things, the magazine claimed that a disproportionate number of Nazis and concentration-camp guards had been Austrian. Some Germans followed the controversy with malicious glee, genuine *Schadenfreude*. It was, perhaps, understandable. They had had to put up with a divided country, continuing war-crimes trials, and a long-tattered image, while their neighbors to the southeast convinced the world that Hitler had been a German—and Beethoven an Austrian.[3]

It was all very unsettling. The incumbent Austrian president, Rudolf Kirchschläger (who as ambassador to Prague in 1968 had defied Waldheim's instructions to limit the issuance of visas to Czech refugees), told his countrymen that the Waldheim scandal "affected all of Austria, including our position in the world, which is inseparable from our economic position in the long run."[4]

In general, the Austrian reaction reflected the sheltered provincialism of the country. Many Austrians struck back by attacking the messengers—*Profil* magazine, or the World Jewish Congress, or even me. Their comments often had a distinctly anti-Semitic tone. "It is a shame that these criminals weren't gassed by Hitler," one Austrian told *Newsweek* magazine. "The Jews were and are once again alien bodies in our people," said another. Some even compared Waldheim to Christ, observing that both had been crucified by the Jews.[5]

For his part, Waldheim neither endorsed such sentiments nor denounced them.

On May 4, 1986, the Austrian people went to the polls and gave Waldheim 49.6 percent of their votes. His nearest challenger, the Socialist candidate, Kurt Steyrer, received 43.7 percent. On June 8, Waldheim faced Steyrer again in a two-man runoff election. He won it handily, with a convincing 53.9 percent majority, thus becoming the first conservative ever to be elected president of Austria.

The next day, the government of Chancellor Fred Sinowatz resigned. New parliamentary elections would take place in several months.

In the meantime, Waldheim went to work carrying out a realignment of Austrian politics, steering the nation away from the Socialist-Liberal coalition that had been fashioned by Bruno Kreisky to a grand alliance between younger moderate Socialists and ÖVP pragmatists. In the process, Waldheim skillfully negotiated the creation of a new government, led by moderate Socialist Franz Vranitzky, who had replaced Sinowatz as chancellor, and conservative Alois Mock, who had served as vice-chancellor and foreign minister. The far-right Liberals, some of whom had tainted Nazi pasts, were squeezed out of the government entirely, just as Waldheim had intended.

Mock became Waldheim's fiercest defender in the government, someone who could be counted upon to manipulate every power lever in the foreign ministry on the president's behalf. Vranitsky, on the other hand, viewed Waldheim as an albatross, but he dared not say so, for the Socialists were too weak to govern on their own. Without the support of Mock and his conservatives, Vranitsky's fragile coalition would quickly collapse. Once again, patriotism and self-interest were one and the same for Kurt Waldheim.

Waldheim's election did not end the controversy about his past, as most Austrians had hoped. If anything, it fanned the flames.

New revelations continued to make headlines. In the United States, the World Jewish Congress was pressuring the Justice Department to place Waldheim's name on the Immigration and Naturalization Service's "Watch List" of undesirable aliens prohibited from entering the country.

The WJC's efforts were based on a 1978 amendment to the Immigration and Nationality Act sponsored by Congresswoman Elizabeth Holtzman, a Democrat from Brooklyn. Under the Holtzman amendment, as it became known, the borders of the United States were to be closed to any and all alleged war criminals and former Nazi collaborators—specifically, any alien who, in the view of the attorney general, had "ordered, incited, assisted, or otherwise participated in the persecution of any person because of race, religion, national origin, or political opinion" between March 23, 1933, and May 9, 1945.

Holtzman had been horrified by the number of murderers and other war criminals who had come to the United States after World War II—many of whom arrived on American shores with the full connivance of the U.S. government. She was also concerned about the tendency of Americans to forget the Holocaust. The Watch List, she felt, should act as an automatic antiamnesiac.

Due in large part to the efforts of people like Congresswoman Holtzman and Simon Wiesenthal, Congress also created a unit called the Office of Special Investigations. Eventually placed under the jurisdiction of the Criminal Division of the Department of Justice, the OSI became the Nazi-hunting arm of the U.S. government.

The OSI had two main tasks. It would identify ex-Nazis, collaborators, and accused war criminals who had obtained U.S. citizenship fraudulently (by neglecting to list their suspect affiliations and activities on their citizenship applications) and then take them to court to have them denaturalized, after which they could be deported or extradited. It would also make recommendations to the attorney general about particular aliens with Nazi backgrounds who should be put on the Watch List.

In the spring of 1986, OSI chief Neal Sher recommended to U.S. Attorney General Edwin Meese III that Kurt Waldheim be placed on the Watch List.

Meese's decision would be a momentous one. Waldheim was on the verge of being elected president of Austria. No head of state—no less a democratically elected one—had ever been barred from entering the United States by means of the Watch List. The diplomatic implications were profound.

It seemed clear to me in the spring and summer of 1986 that Yugoslavia held one of the keys to Waldheim's missing years. It was Belgrade, after all, that had charged him with murder in 1947. The evidence that lay behind that charge, if any existed, had to be in the Yugoslav archives.

As the Waldheim controversy burgeoned, however, the Yugoslavs reacted uncertainly and with confusion. The official Yugoslav press agency, Tanjug, did run stories linking Waldheim to the Zvonimir medal and the Kozara deportations, but they provided no specific data. Meanwhile, the Yugoslav government declared that it would not intervene in neighboring Austria's elections.

Simon Wiesenthal called upon the Yugoslavs to release information from their archives in the interest of justice and historical truth. There was no response from Belgrade. The government hunkered down even more when stories surfaced indicating that the Yugoslavs had indicted Waldheim for murder but had evidently not pursued him—and, worse, that even though he knew the case against him, Marshal Tito had actually received and decorated Waldheim when he was foreign minister of Austria and secretary-general of the UN.

Yugoslavs who recalled German and Ustasha wartime atrocities reacted angrily to their government's silence. Old partisan Vladimir Dedijer began to talk and write about a "pro-Waldheim" lobby in Belgrade.

Survivors of Kozara were even angrier. To say the name Kozara to a West Bosnian who lived through the war is like saying the name Auschwitz to a Polish Jew. They couldn't believe that their government was reacting so ambiguously to the charges against Waldheim.

In fact, Belgrade was caught between a rock and a hard place. On the one hand, the Yugoslav government had no wish to alienate Austria, a fellow neutralist nation as well as their neighbor to the northwest. On the other, having just begun exporting a new economy car called the Yugo to the United States, Belgrade was eager to cultivate a favorable image in the American media. To the Yugoslavs, that meant perceiving Waldheim through Jewish eyes.

By the end of 1986, the Yugoslavs were still hesitating. Austrian researchers acting for Waldheim would be permitted quick looks at the Belgrade archives. The same was true of American investigators from the OSI (though Yugoslav officials assured the Austrian ambassador at the end of 1986 that they only showed the Americans documents that had been previously certified as harmless).

The Yugoslav press displayed a similar ambivalence.[6] On the one hand, it published a string of lurid stories about wartime atrocities committed by units in which Waldheim had served. On the other, the leading daily newspapers all avoided addressing the key question: How could Waldheim have been indicted but never pursued, condemned but later invited as an honored guest?

Belgrade had apparently reached a high-level decision. The government would encourage people to believe there was a link between Waldheim and the atrocities ascribed to his old units. But it would not say so itself, at least not publicly. Nor would it comment on the *Odluka* or on the apparent abandonment of the hunt for Waldheim, though a government spokesman did say that the extradition list with Waldheim's name on it had been "lost."

The strategy worked—for a time. As long as people thought that Waldheim had managed to escape justice on his own, Belgrade did not look too bad. In August 1986, however, I discovered that the Yugoslavs had never applied to either the Austrian government or the Allied Council in Vienna for Waldheim's extradition. That suggested two things to me: that the *Odluka* had been a politically motivated fabrication, and that the pursuit of Waldheim had been dropped in the summer of 1948 for equally political reasons.

The only way to find out for sure would be to go to Belgrade and try to locate the relevant documents in the Yugoslav archives. The following month, I went to the Yugoslav Embassy in Washington and submitted a formal request to the government. I asked for unrestricted access to those archives, emphasizing that I was interested in both the military and the war-crimes files. I also made it clear that I had proof that Belgrade had never sought Waldheim's extradition.

Normally, I wouldn't have expected the Yugoslavs to approve my request. But I suspected that this might be one of those rare cases in which public controversy and the distortions of media coverage would actually work in a historian's favor. As it turned out, I was right. Because of the way in which the press had reported on my findings, Yugoslav officials regarded me as a Waldheim critic rather than a disinterested scholar. As a result, they saw my request to use the archives as offering them an opportunity to restore the public-relations balance that was tilting against them both in the United States and at home. After all, how could they be accused of trying to protect Waldheim if they were willing to give such a notorious Waldheim critic as myself unprecedented access to the archives? Even if I managed to uncover still more compromising material, they would come out ahead. They could trumpet whatever new findings I came up with as proof of their willingness to let the chips fall where they may, while telling the Austrians, "Look, it was Herzstein who found the stuff and made the charges, not us!"

I received permission to visit the Yugoslav archives at the end of the year.

In the meantime, however, I had work to do at the Public Records Office in London. As a result, I was unable to get to Belgrade until March 1987. I arrived in the Yugoslav capital on a freezing Saturday night. The city had a grim look; it was clear that economic conditions were not good.

My first stop was the Military History Archive. Colonel Antun Miletić, the distinguished scholar who presides over the collection, is perhaps the premier living historian of the Yugoslav partisan movement as well as the author of a definitive, three-volume documentary history of Jasenovac concentration camp. With his help, I was able to look through many gruesome Wehrmacht Ic documents concerning deportations and interrogations during the Kozara operation. Miletić eventually permitted me to range freely through his archive's voluminous card catalogues and select any document I wanted, including the history of Army Group E written by General Löhr himself just before his execution.

After a few days at the Military History Archive, I made my way to the Arhiv Jugoslavije. This archive, housed in an impressive villa in the Vase Pelagica, a park in the southern part of Belgrade, contains war-crimes records. In this incongruously beautiful setting, I had a long conversation with Dr. Bogdan Lekić, the archive director, in which I candidly summarized my assumptions about the political nature of the *Odluka*. A bit later, I was taken to the research room, where I was given a thick folder marked "Waldheim."

The documents in the folder did more than prove my hunch about the political nature of the *Odluka.* They established beyond doubt the nature and aims of the abortive Yugoslav conspiracy against Waldheim in 1947 and 1948.

Even though I was in the midst of proving that the Yugoslav case against Waldheim had been a specious one, the Austrian government continued its efforts to discredit me. No sooner had I left Belgrade than the Austrian Embassy there issued an angry statement accusing me of "distortion of fact and false interpretations which in no way agree with the facts."

The embassy was referring to an interview I had given to the widely read Yugoslav newspaper *Vecernje Novosti.* The interview, conducted by Jovan Kesar, a distinguished Yugoslav journalist who happens to be one of the few child survivors of Kozara, consisted of a review of my findings to date plus some comments about my future research plans. Among the topics I touched on in the interview was Waldheim's role in the deportation of the Italian Eleventh Army from Greece to forced-labor camps in the Reich. In its statement, the Austrian Embassy insisted that this was a smear. Waldheim, the embassy declared, had helped to *repatriate* the Italians, not deport them. The statement was patently absurd. Even Waldheim himself, in the conversation we had the following summer, did not claim that he had helped to send the troops of the Eleventh Army home to Italy.

This was part of a pattern that had begun late in 1986, when I attended the annual national meeting of the German Studies Association in Albuquerque, New Mexico. According to a major figure in the association, Austrian officials had telephoned him, waxing indignant over the fact that I had been selected to participate in one of the conference's panel discussions. The fact that the panel had absolutely nothing to do with Waldheim or Austria was irrelevant. The Austrians demanded that I be thrown off it. Needless to say, I wasn't.

Waldheim's name did come up at that meeting. Because of the intense interest in the controversy, a member of the UNM faculty asked me to take part in a press conference for the local media. I agreed, and answered questions about my research from an audience that I understood to consist of reporters, university people, and members of the association. One gentleman, who never introduced himself, asked a question about the partisan war in the Balkans. He then left. I later learned that he was a lawyer representing President Waldheim.

Whatever he was doing, whether spying or trying to harass me or merely gathering information, it had no place in an academic setting. I was not mollified to be told later that he had gone away convinced of my "fairness" and "objectivity."

My colleagues in the German Studies Association were even more outraged than I was. The use of academics for political purposes may be endemic in Austria, but it is not considered acceptable in the United States. Unfortunately, some Austrian officials seem to have had a difficult time understanding this.

As the evidence against Waldheim mounted, his defenders became increasingly vicious, and anti-Jewish outpourings grew more common. Many Austrians saw the move to put Waldheim on the Watch List as a Jewish plot. After all, not only was the World Jewish Congress behind the idea, but Congresswoman Holtzman, whose legislation had created the "war crimes" aspect of the Watch List, was herself Jewish. For his part, Waldheim added fuel to the fire by denouncing incomprehensible international conspiracies. Some Austrians—and a few Americans as well—thought he was talking about the Jews.

In July 1987, Carl Hödl, the vice-mayor of Linz, wrote to WJC president Edgar Bronfman, comparing Bronfman's attacks on Waldheim to "those of your fellow believers, who two thousand years ago had Jesus Christ convicted in a show trial, because he did not accommodate the views of the lords of Jersusalem. . . . It remained for you, and for those like you, to bring such a Talmudic concept into the world." Hödl, a pillar of the Linz establishment and a leader of the party that nominated Waldheim for the presidency, went on to defend his letter by arguing that "Eye for eye, tooth for a tooth, is not a European concept."

Waldheim also attracted the support of such far-right publications as the neo-Nazi *National-Zeitung,* which denounced what it called the "hate campaign against the German Wehrmacht."[7] This was a bit awkward for Waldheim, for he had never been a *guter Kamerad,* one of those heavyset, elderly Austrians who wore a Tyrolean hunter's hat, dangled an Iron Cross around his neck, and enjoyed drinking beer with old friends from the war. Indeed, the last thing Waldheim wanted was for anyone to get the impression that he had fond memories of his days in uniform. After all, his story was that he had been a persecuted anti-Nazi who had reluctantly served on the Russian front.

Still, while Waldheim might have been embarrassed by extremist support, he never publicly rejected it. The upwardly mobile, sophisticated Austrian diplomat had become a *guter Kamerad,* after all.

CHAPTER SEVENTEEN

Facing the Truth

The Waldheim affair cannot be understood outside of its Austrian political context.

The Austrian establishment, which maintains a tight hold on public opinion, does not like Austrians who question the great consensus, the view that says, "We were victims of the Nazis, and we are democratic now." Austrians who dispute this notion are invariably accused of committing the worst possible sin—of "hurting Austria's reputation in the world."

This is why, against the backdrop of the 1986 presidential race, Austrian Socialists and other domestic opponents of Waldheim wanted his past to be exposed by foreign organizations. International opposition to Waldheim, his foes reasoned, would spare them the unpleasant and potentially unpopular necessity of becoming entangled in a murky, finger-pointing debate over whether or not he had been complicit in war crimes. Rather than having to argue about the truth of the allegations against Waldheim, they could simply maintain that he should be denied the presidency because he was clearly a controversial figure whose election would tarnish Austria's standing abroad.

In the end, however, the belief that an attack from the outside would doom Waldheim turned out to be a major miscalculation. It backfired because of another essential facet of the great consensus, one that took precedence over concern for Austria's international reputation—the tendency of Austrians (like many other national groups) to draw together regardless of political differences when confronted with a challenge from the outside. As Simon Wiesenthal has asked, if the bulk of the attacks on President Richard M. Nixon over Watergate had come from abroad, would American public opinion have turned against him?

The dilemma facing Waldheim's opponents at home was probably felt most keenly by Bruno Kreisky, the former chancellor who had been Austria's leading political figure for more than a decade.

Kreisky had begun his political career in the 1930s as a revolutionary Socialist. Imprisoned by the Dollfuss-Schuschnigg regime, he had escaped from Austria and survived the Second World War in neutral Sweden. Kreisky was clever and ambitious, and in later years he used Austria's neutrality and strategic geographic position as a platform for gaining worldwide recognition. As a leading figure in the Socialist International (along with West Germany's Willy Brandt), he cultivated Austria's ties with the Soviet bloc and became a kind of European spokesman for the Third World. And though he was an anti-Zionist (he described Zionism to me as a "nationalism of the most unnatural type"), he permitted Austria to serve as a transit point for Jews emigrating from the Soviet Union.

During the first twenty years of the postwar era, the Austrian Socialist party had shared power with the People's party. Kreisky, however, despised the ÖVP, which he regarded as a church-bound group of what he called "clericals." In any case, by the mid-1970s he did not need them, for under his leadership in what came to be known as the Kreisky Era, the Socialists enjoyed an absolute majority in parliament. The country was prosperous, and Kreisky took good care of the workers as well as those dependent on state-run industries and government pensions.

After it began to look as if the Socialists' majority was eroding, Kreisky refused to reestablish the old alliance with the ÖVP. Instead, the wily chancellor turned to the far-right Liberal party, a refuge of former Nazis and other ideological extremists, which was liberal only in its anticlericalism. In order to secure his majority, Kreisky brought four former Nazis into his government, as well as S.S. veteran Friedrich Peter, who became vice-chancellor. Kreisky defended this somewhat unholy alliance with the argument that by bringing extremists into the Austrian political mainstream, he was preventing the potentially dangerous alienation of a sizable segment of the population. When Simon Wiesenthal pointed out that Peter had served as an officer in an S.S. unit that murdered thousands of civilians, an outraged Kreisky accused the distinguished Nazi-hunter of being a "Jewish fascist" and a "mafioso." Later he threatened to close down Wiesenthal's Documentation Center for the League of the Jewish Victims of the Nazi Regime.

The Waldheim controversy put Kreisky in a real bind. On the one hand, he had good reason to applaud the scandal, for a Waldheim victory in the presidential race would mark the beginning of the end of the Socialist-Liberal coalition that Kreisky had worked so hard to build—the end, in short, of the Kreisky Era. On the other hand, he couldn't very well abandon his old foreign ministry colleague. Not to defend Waldheim would not only anger his far-right coalition partners; it might even result in Kreisky's patriotism being questioned.

In the beginning, national unity took precedence. When the scandal first broke, Kreisky defended Waldheim, arguing angrily that the charges made by the World Jewish Congress amounted to an attempted "intervention in Austrian internal politics." What the WJC was doing, he declared, was "an infamy." A gratified Waldheim thereupon embarrassed Kreisky by publicly thanking him for his support.

Then Socialist sources quietly but urgently informed Kreisky that his protégé and successor as chancellor, Fred Sinowatz, had played a key role in exposing Waldheim. Suddenly, Kreisky didn't have much to say.

In the end, Waldheim's victory left Kreisky distraught—the "ruination of my life's work," he called it. That may not have been an overstatement. Waldheim was on record, after all, as favoring the reestablishment of the Great Coalition between the Socialists and the ÖVP. And that's just what happened. In the process, Waldheim isolated the Liberals, pulled the Socialist party to the right, and put the conservatives back into the government. As president, he was far more than a ceremonial figure.

Once Waldheim moved into the Hofburg Palace, the focus of the controversy inside Austria began to shift. The question was no longer "What is the truth about Waldheim's past?" but "Who went after him and why?" The old consensus had reemerged in the form of the uneasy governing coalition. Once again, a miserable past was swept away in favor of a tolerable (if no longer happy) present.

What made this possible in large-part was a growing perception in Austria that the Waldheim issue was really a "Jewish affair." Instead of confronting the difficult questions of complicity and concealment—of not just Waldheim's but their country's real role in the war—Austrians began increasingly to dismiss the matter as an irrelevant controversy that would have died out long ago had it not been for the efforts of a few media-wise, Holocaust-obsessed American Jews. This was an ironic turn of events, for the fact was that Waldheim's personal involvement with the Holocaust was minimal. Many of the victims of the Wehrmacht units in which he served were Russians, Serbs, Bosnians, Croatians, Macedonians, Greeks, and Italians.

On one level, this mistaken perception was quite understandable. When the issue of Nazi war crimes is raised, people naturally think of the Holocaust. Indeed, the first question the WJC wanted me to explore was whether Waldheim had been involved in the deportation of the Jews of Salonika. (To the WJC's credit, it did not lose interest in the case when it turned out that Waldheim's activities seemed mainly to involve non-Jews.)

There is also a sense in which the Waldheim affair became a Jewish issue by default. If there are such organizations as a West Bosnian Anti-Defamation League or a World Serb Congress, they certainly possess neither the resources, the clout, nor the ready access to the media of prominent Jewish organizations such as the WJC. As a result, it was to the Jewish groups that the press invariably turned for comment each time a new revelation about Waldheim surfaced. An interesting dialectic soon unfolded. The more the Jewish groups called for further investigations, the more Waldheim's defenders would claim that the uproar was due to the efforts of a few American Jews. This assertion would enrage other American Jews, who would become involved as a result—making the issue seem even more Jewish. As Congressman Joseph J. DioGuardi of New York observed on May 14, 1986: "It is very interesting to note recent findings that Kurt Waldheim may have played a major role in transporting Italian prisoners of war to labor camps near the end of World War II. Where is the Italian community expressing its outrage?"[1]

Waldheim's evasions, coupled with the outburst of Austrian anti-Semitism that he refused to denounce, completed the process. The more unrepentant Waldheim seemed, the more his accusers came to view him as evil incarnate. The more they viewed him as evil incarnate, the more outrageous their attacks on him became ("He was in the S.S.!")—and the less likely he was to admit that there might be anything to the accusations. A few thoughtful observers tried to oppose this tendency, but their cause was hopeless.

By the spring of 1987, it was Waldheim and Austria against the Jews and the memory of the Holocaust.

In Washington, meanwhile, pressure was mounting on Attorney General Meese to make a decision on Neal Sher's recommendation that Waldheim's name be placed on the Watch List. For diplomatic reasons—

mainly, the desire to avoid offending Austria—the Reagan administration was hoping to find a way to table the whole matter permanently. In the end, it proved impossible. On April 28, 1987, Meese put Waldheim on the Watch List.[2]

Domestic American politics played a role in Meese's decision. Not only was the U.S. government still recovering from the bad press it had received as a result of a clumsy attempt to avoid deporting war criminal Karl Linnas to the Soviet Union, but with the Iran-Contra scandal blooming, and Meese's own problems with the Wedtech influence-peddling case beginning to mount, there was little sentiment in the Reagan administration for a move that would anger Jewish voters. In the midst of all this, the television broadcast of *Shoah,* a powerful documentary film about the Holocaust, inspired an outpouring of anti-Waldheim sentiment.

As far as the average American citizen was concerned, Waldheim appeared to be an accused war criminal. This, in my opinion, was not an accurate perception.

After World War II, the International Military Tribunal (the so-called Nüremberg Tribunal) and the Allied Control Council in Germany defined a war criminal as anyone who had ordered, incited, or committed any of a number of specific criminal acts set out in the Nüremberg Charter. There were two general categories of these acts: war crimes and crimes against humanity. War crimes, the Nüremberg Charter said, were "violations of the laws or customs of war." The charter went on to specify just what that meant:

> Such violations shall include, but not be limited to, murder, ill-treatment, or deportation to slave labor or for any other purpose of civilian population of or in occupied territory, murder or ill-treatment of prisoners of war or persons on the seas, killing of hostages, plunder of public or private property, wanton destruction of cities, towns or villages, or devastation not justified by military necessity . . .

Crimes against humanity, on the other hand, included:

> . . . murder, extermination, enslavement, deportation, and other inhumane acts committed against any civilian population, before or during the war, or persecutions on political, racial, or religious grounds in execution of or in connection with any crimes within the jurisdiction of the Tribunal . . .

Given what we know now, it is fair to say that while Waldheim assisted many individuals who fell into the war-criminal category, he was not a war criminal himself. Rather, he was a bureaucratic accessory to both the criminal and the legitimate military activities of Ic/AO. Waldheim was a facilitator. The Western Allies did not generally prosecute such individuals after the war. Even the Yugoslavs, when they indioted Waldheim, based their charge upon the Hague Convention and the Moscow Declaration, not upon the Nüremberg Tribunal's language, which provides us with the commonly accepted definitions of war crimes and crimes against humanity.

Waldheim's role as a facilitator is precisely why his name belonged on the Watch List. The documentary evidence against him was conclusive. While there was no proof that he had actually committed what is commonly called a "war crime," there seemed little doubt that his activities in Yugoslavia in 1942 and in Greece in 1943 were more than sufficient to qualify him for the conditions of the Holtzman amendment. As a young first lieutenant, he may not have ordered or incited anything, but there was plenty of evidence that as an aide to General Stahl, General Löhr, Colonel Willers, Colonel Warnstorff, and others, he had certainly "assisted, or otherwise participated in the persecution of" Yugoslavs, Greeks, Italians, and Jews.

Though Waldheim tried to make light of his exclusion from the United States, it was a severe blow to his—and Austria's—prestige. For a time it looked as if he might become something of an international pariah. Then, in June 1987, Pope John Paul II agreed to receive him at the Vatican.

The Pope's decision revived the old debate over the Catholic Church's record on anti-Semitism and the Holocaust. In the process, Waldheim's actions somehow became linked to Pope Pius XII's silence on the Holocaust. Eventually, however, some good came out of it all—though not for Waldheim. Responding to the outrage of American Jews, who threatened to boycott a meeting with the Pontiff that had been scheduled as part of his upcoming visit to the United States, John Paul II issued several unprecedented personal statements on the Holocaust—statements that threw Waldheim's continued silence and evasions into even sharper relief.[3]

In the aftermath of the American decision to put Waldheim on the Watch List, word began circulating that supporters of Waldheim, led by his son Gerhard, were preparing a "multi-language" *Weissbuch,* or White Book, a documentary collection that would vindicate the Austrian president by clearing up all the misunderstandings about his missing years. The plan, evidently, was to distribute the White Book as a kind of foreign ministry encyclical to Austrian diplomats abroad, who could use it to rehabilitate Waldheim's tattered image.

The book failed to appear. Supposedly, "technical difficulties" had prevented its publication. In fact, Chancellor Vranitsky had suppressed it, reportedly believing that its self-righteous tone and disorganized structure would do more harm than good to Waldheim's case.

Late in the spring of 1987, the foreign ministry leaked the White Book to *Wochenspresse,* a Vienna magazine friendly to Waldheim. Though *Wochenspresse* trumpeted its scoop, the excerpts the magazine published had little impact. Vranitsky, it seemed, had been right.

Some weeks later, with the assistance of President Waldheim, I obtained a complete draft copy of the White Book from the Austrian Embassy in Washington. I quickly discovered that as a defense brief, its weaknesses far outnumbered its strengths. The book contained Waldheim's usual protestations of innocence and ignorance—supported by a disturbing number of misleading statements and evasions. For example, in an effort to bolster the contention that Waldheim was an anti-Fascist, it quoted the 1940 Nazi party personnel appraisal of Waldheim that spoke of "his hateful attitude to our movement"—while neglecting to note the appraisal's conclusion: that having "proven his worth as a soldier of the German Army," Waldheim was politically reliable enough to be admitted to the judicial service. Similarly, the White Book maintained that the Berlin Document Center contained no evidence that Waldheim ever belonged to any Nazi-affiliated organizations. This was true, of course—but only because the S.A. Cavalry Corps and the National Socialist German Students League were not part of the BDC's standard checklist.

Perhaps most disappointing, the White Book offered nothing regarding Waldheim's view on what he thought the Germans were doing in the Balkans. One would have liked to have Waldheim's own analysis of the documents that crossed his desk in Athens and Arsakli. What did he understand them to be about, with their references to deportations, burned villages, and executions?

In the spring of 1987, I finally got the chance to meet the man whose paper trail I had been pursuing for the previous fourteen months. After several exchanges of letters with Waldheim's staff, on June 9, 1987, I found myself sitting in the former bedchamber of the Empress Maria Theresa in Vienna's Hofburg Palace. A few minutes after three, a side door opened, and a tall, slightly stooped, graying figure strode over to me.

"I am sorry I am a few minutes late, Professor Herzstein," he said in a firm voice. "Please come in."

Offering me a smile and a firm handshake, Kurt Waldheim ushered me into his private office, a cheerful and airy room with large windows, which adjoins the Maria Theresa room.

I genuinely wanted to get his side of the story. I had heard from his critics—indeed, I was considered to be one of them. Now I needed to hear his views on Kozara, on the Italian deportations, on his duties with Army Group E's Ic/AO, on his personal tribulations since the controversy had exploded in the winter and spring of 1986.

Over the next four hours, we discussed all these questions. On certain topics—most notably Kozara—Waldheim drew a complete blank, apparently having suppressed his memories completely. On others, he was amazingly anecdotal and forthcoming. Beneath his relaxed demeanor, I could sense the tension he felt. "God has given me a strong constitution and a resilient spirit," he said, "but this has all been a great strain."

Waldheim insisted that his war record was entirely honorable. "I have a clean conscience," he told me. "I did not do anything wrong." In particular, he insisted that he "had no reason to hide anything" about his service in the Balkans. "I had nothing to do with deportations, I assure you. My function was a minor one."

In any case, he said, he was no Nazi. "I came to the conclusion during the war that the [Nazi] system would never last." This made him smile. "I know that there are some doubts about my political attitude," he added with a chuckle, "but I had no doubts that this system would not succeed."

The insignificance of his role in the German army was a major theme of our conversation. His unimportance was, he said, the reason why his memories of his wartime service were so vague. "If my function on Kozara had been important," he argued, "I would have remembered." In this sense, he argued, his military career really did end on the Eastern Front in December 1941. "For me, the trauma was being wounded in Russia. After that, being an *Ordonnanzoffizer* or an interpreter was not so impressive."

Immediately after Attorney General Meese put his name on the U.S. Watch List, Waldheim addressed the Austrian nation on television. It was an unparalleled opportunity to confront the past with courage and candor. Waldheim did not take advantage of it.

The closest he came to admitting that he had done anything wrong was in a section of the speech in which he discussed what he characterized as "the incapacity of my generation to make a free decision . . . the impotence imposed by superior force." With uncharacteristic bluntness, Waldheim went on to acknowledge what may well be the central fact of the modern Austrian historical experience. "Only very few people were able to tear off the chains imposed by this compulsion, with the risk of paying with their lives for it," he said. "I was not one of them."[4]

That, however, was as far as he was willing to go. The essence of his speech was the same dangerous message he had been preaching ever since the scandal first broke. "Yes," he said, in effect, "I did my duty in a German uniform. So did most everyone else of my generation. In any case, no one can prove that I ever personally committed anything that could be called a crime. So let us forget about the past and get on with our careers." As far as Waldheim was concerned, it had been a bad war, he was sorry about the atrocities that had been committed by both sides, but he had done nothing wrong, and that was that.

As the controversy unfolded in 1986 and early 1987, Waldheim's calm self-assurance was nothing short of remarkable. Only when the U.S. government put his name on the Watch List did he display any real agitation. How could Waldheim have been so serene in the face of so many devastating accusations? And why was he so surprised by his placement on the Watch List? My reading of the documentary evidence, plus interviews with many of the principals, led me to the following explanation: Throughout the postwar period, including his tenure as UN secretary-general, Kurt Waldheim was a U.S. intelligence asset who expected to be—and always was—protected by his friends in the American intelligence community.

Waldheim's relationship with American intelligence began in May 1945 when he was shipped off to the POW camp at Bad Tölz for debriefing by G-2 (U.S. military intelligence). The previous month the OSS had provided G-2 with a list of German officers considered to be "of interest" to the United States. Having served as a Wehrmacht intelligence officer in Yugoslavia, Waldheim would no doubt have been on that list, for the OSS was hungry for information about the "Yugoslavs' secret intentions and methods."[5]

After Waldheim's debriefing at Bad Tölz, he and his family stayed at his sister's house in the U.S.-controlled Linz region until after Western military forces entered Vienna. It was only then that Waldheim returned home to Soviet-occupied Lower Austria. Similarly, he did not apply for a position at the foriegn ministry until it was clear that Western Allies were going to recognize Karl Renner's coalition government.

The foreign ministry, of course, was run by Karl Gruber and his assistant, Fritz Molden—both of whom worked for American 430th Counter-Intelligence Corps. Among their main concerns was keeping Communists from taking control of the newly reorganized ministry. They were also under instructions to provide their American friends with information about the Soviets and the Yugoslavs. In such an enviroment it would have been unthinkable to employ anyone—particularly a personal secretary—whom the Americans didn't trust. The fact that Gruber and Molden hired Waldheim with only the most cursory investigation into his background could mean only one thing: He had already been vetted by U.S. authorities.

In the early years of the Cold War, Waldheim's firsthand knowledge of Tito's partisan army—which at the time was considered to be the main East Bloc threat to Austria and the West—made him increasingly valuable to the Americans. Certianly he was too valuable to be allowed to fall into Communist hands. After all, in addition to his Balkan expertise, there was his undoubted knowledge of Gruber's and Molden's activities on behalf of the U.S. Counter-Intelligence Corps. Viewed in this light, Waldheim's sudden transfer to Paris in January 1948, which foiled the Yugoslav plot to discredit Gruber by publicly accusing his young aide of war crimes, seems more than just a lucky coincidence. Most likely, U.S. intelligence agents—who were intercepting Belgrade's messages to the Yugoslav embassy in London—warned Gruber about the threat to Waldheim.

When Tito broke with Stalin six months later, the Americans helped Waldheim once again. In return for economic aid, they not only forced Yugoslavia to drop its border claims, they also got Belgrade to agree to stop harassing Gruber. Shortly thereafter, in a show of good faith, the Yugoslavs released their main "witness" against Waldheim, the opportunistic POW Johann Mayer.

Waldheim owed a lot to the Americans. After debriefing him at Bad Tölz, they had put him in touch with Molden and Gruber, and found him work. They then warned him about the *Odluka* in the winter of 1947–48 and apparently got him off the hook for good the following July. All this obligated Waldheim to the Americans.

Still, Waldheim remained vulnerable to the Yugoslavs. According to Fritz Molden, Yugoslav diplomat Vladimir Velebit, a confidant of Tito, coyly asked him in late 1951 or early 1952 "whether or not this Waldheim had relatives living in Yugoslavia." The clear implication was that Belgrade had something on the rising young foriegn service officer, some means of pressuring him or his superiors.

The point of Velebit's oblique warning was to let the Austrians know that if Gruber and his American protectors made use of their lingering ties to anti-Tito activists, they—and Waldheim—would pay a price. Of course, as long as Belgrade feared the Soviets more than the West, Waldheim was safe. Waldheim, however, took nothing for granted, and over the next decade he carefully cultivated Tito.

He also began sanitizing his past. And once again, his American friends came to his aid. Not long after Velebit delivered his veiled warning to Molden, the U.S. State Department solicited and accepted without question a selectively edited biography of Waldheim that made it seem as if he had no military record at all. On the face of it, this account of Waldheim's life was absurd; there was simply no way a young Austrian like Waldheim could have avoided military service during the war. In any case, as the successor organization to the OSS, the CIA had records documenting Waldheim's service as a staff officer in the Balkans. Nonetheless, the State Department stuck by Waldheim's incomplete and misleading résumé, using it two decades later as the basis for an official biography that helped quell doubts about his fitness to serve as UN secretary-general. (It also gave Waldheim the opportunity to "correct" the record by telling the press about his service on the Russian front.) In 1980, the CIA compounded the deception when it responded to Congressman Solarz's inquiries by echoing Waldheim's by then familiar assertion that his career as a soldier in the Wehrmacht effectively ended when he was wounded in Russia in 1941.

Given all this, it is hardly surprising that Waldheim seemed so unruffled when the scandal about his war record first broke—and so surprised when Attorney General Meese finally bowed to public pressure and put his name on the Watch List. After all, at virtually every turn in his postwar career, his American friends had intervened to protect him. Why should this time be different? And indeed, for a time it seemed as if his confidence was justified; despite the fact that both the State Department and the Office of Special Investigations insisted that Waldheim's name belonged on the Watch List, it was a full year before the Reagan administration could be persuaded to take any action against him.

To a remarkable extent, Kurt Waldheim *is* postwar Austria. Like most of his generation, though he was not a member of the Nazi party, he collaborated with the Nazi regime. Though he may have inwardly opposed National Socialism, he and men like him helped it to survive until 1945.

So far as I have been able to determine, Kurt Waldheim did not in fact order, incite, or personally commit what is commonly called a war crime. But this nonguilt must not be confused with innocence. The fact that Waldheim played a significant role in military units that unquestionably committed war crimes makes him at the very least morally complicit in those crimes. Lawyers and judges can debate the legal niceties. The historian sees Waldheim as having served as a small but very real cog in a large, murderous machine.

As a historian, I am willing to accept Waldheim's claim that he felt he had no choice but to serve as he did. I reject, however, his protestations of ignorance and innocence. The records that he so meticulously kept as a staff officer both demonstrate his knowledge of and document his bureaucratic participation in the Kozara operation, the identification of troublemaking Jews in Ionnina, the betrayal of the Italian Eleventh Army in Greece, and the brutal antipartisan reprisals that characterized the German campaign throughout the Balkans.

Waldheim was clearly not a psychopath like Dr. Josef Mengele nor a hate-filled racist like Adolf Hitler. He was—and remains—like many others, a well-meaning, ambitious man who simply wanted to get on with his career and his life.

His very ordinariness, in fact, may be the most important thing about him. For if history teaches us anything, it is that the Hitlers and the Mengeles could never have accomplished their atrocious deeds by themselves. It took hundreds of thousands of ordinary men—well-meaning but ambitious men like Kurt Waldheim—to make the Third Reich possible.

After the war, Waldheim was able to build a useful career, a distinguished career in which he contributed to the cause of world peace. He was able to do this by burying his memory of war, of that fateful and troubling period from 1942 through 1945. There is little question that he would never have succeeded in this effort had it not been in the political interest of the United States, Yugoslavia, Austria, and the Soviet Union for him to do so. For political reasons, the West opposed the extradition to Eastern bloc countries of many alleged war criminals. For political reasons, the Yugoslavs first created, then suppressed, a murder indictment against Waldheim. For political reasons, the Austrian government hid what it had learned about his past. For political reasons, the Soviets supported his career. And for political and intelligence reasons, American authorities protected Kurt Waldheim and helped him conceal his past.

The ultimate question of our time concerns moral responsibility. In an era of vast bureaucracies, both military and political, how can the individual cope with his role in history?

Some people rebel against evil. We call them saints or heroes. Few of us belong to this elite group.

Others eagerly join the powers that be, serving them faithfully, committing whatever atrocities the state, the party, or the religion orders. We call these people criminals.

Kurt Waldheim belongs to the third, most numerous class—those who retain some sense of ethical autonomy while still serving evil institutions more or less willingly.

Waldheim and thousands of others like him made the German occupation of the Balkans possible. He was a drop of clean oil in a well-functioning machine, no more—and certainly no less.

Perhaps I am too optimistic, but I still believe that it is in President Waldheim's power to deal with his past in a way that would make a lasting, positive contribution to his nation and to the world.

On May 8, 1985, President Richard von Weizsäcker of the Federal Republic of Germany delivered a historic speech to the Bundestag. The German people, Weizsäcker insisted, had a special responsibility. The horrors committed in their name made amnesia a moral failing. Yet it was not enough for them to resolve never to forget the crimes of the past. They had a responsibility to understand how it all happened. And they had a responsibility to acknowledge that claiming ignorance was no defense—they could have known what was going on had they wished to.

Austria has never had to confront these issues. The Moscow Declaration of 1943 saw to that. What Kurt Waldheim can do, it seems to me, is use the scandal that has been swirling around him to help his country finally shed its self-serving sense of having been a victim and come to grips with its moral responsibility as a collaborator. Instead of defending or covering up, he could make a speech that is long overdue. I suggest the following as a working draft:

> My fellow Austrians! For the past two years, I have been at the center of an international controversy. Grave charges have been leveled against me. I have responded by declaring that I never committed a war crime. At the same time, however, I have refused to examine the past, except to discover evidence of my innocence. I have also seized upon the fact that some of my adversaries, in collusion with foreign organizations and the media, have manipulated historical evidence in order to hurt me politically, exploiting your resentment of such tactics to avoid having to confront that evidence. In short, I have cloaked

myself in the Austrian flag in an effort to place myself above and beyond all criticism.

I have now decided that such evasions can only, in the long run, do more damage to our national interest.

My life has been marked by service and ambition. As you know, I was never a Nazi. I did, however, permit myself to be enrolled in two National Socialist organizations. I did so in order to protect my family and to advance my career. I was not an activist in these groups, and rarely attended their meetings. Nor did I denounce or shun those friends of mine who were being persecuted by the Nazis.

When I was conscripted into the German army, I had little choice but to serve. The alternative was death. On the Russian front, I participated in a war of brutal reprisals and mass exterminations. None of this was my concern, however. The only thing that mattered to us in the front lines was survival. In this sense, the shrapnel that wounded my leg came as a blessing. I was glad to get out of Russia alive.

As I recuperated at home near Vienna, I did not expect to have to return to the army. Instead, I planned for the day when I would have a diplomatic career in an Austria free of the Nazis. I was not, however, among those heroes who worked for the destruction of the regime. To the contrary, I did what I needed to do to secure the regime's approval of my plans.

When I look back now, I see that the turning point of my life came in the summer of 1942. That spring, I had been sent to Yugoslavia as a staff officer attached to the German High Command in Belgrade. That summer, while carrying out my duties in a quartermaster's unit, I learned through the work of the unit about the mass deportations and executions that were taking place at Kozara.

I was then assigned to Army Group E headquarters outside Salonika, where I heard about the mass deportation of the Jewish community there. Though I did not then know about the death camps, I knew that the fate of the Jews would be a bad one.

In the late summer of 1943, I found myself in Athens helping to arrange the deportation of the Italian Eleventh Army. It was depressing beyond belief. Though I tried to convince myself that these former comrades of mine were being sent home to Italy, I knew that the trains on which we were putting them were headed for forced-labor camps in Germany.

In 1944, as an intelligence officer at the headquarters of General Löhr's Army Group E, I received daily reports about the progress of the war against the partisans in Greece and Yugoslavia. I heard how the insurgents were maiming and killing my comrades. I also read how my comrades retaliated out of all proportion to what had been done to them. I was horrified by the mass reprisals, the execution of hostages. On one occasion, I protested this practice in writing, and I am proud that this document has been found. Still, for the most part, I simply filed my reports and went about my business.

My concerns were simple. I wanted to survive, to marry, and to have a career.

As the war ended, I realized that my service in the Balkans might prove a hindrance to my career. Indeed, in 1947 I learned that the Yugoslavs were bringing war-crimes indictments against former officers with backgrounds similar to mine, and I realized why Karl Gruber sent me to Paris in such a hurry. As a result, I resolved never to speak of or otherwise refer to the time I had spent in the Balkans. I preserved this silence until the spring of 1986.

In this, I was representative of the new Austria. Like many of you, I helped to perpetuate the image that we had been victims of, not participants in, the Nazi calamity. The real victims—the Jews, the Slavs, the Austrian Catholics, the Communists, and many others— they were a problem for Germany's conscience, not ours. Yet I knew full well that seven hundred thousand of us had joined the Nazi party, that the Wehrmacht army group to which I had been attached in the Balkans was filled with Austrian generals and officers. Perhaps I hadn't yet heard of Adolf Eichmann and Ernst Kaltenbrunner, but no one had to tell me where Hitler had been born.

Like many of you, I seized upon the Moscow Declaration. It was Germany, not Austria, that needed to confront its past. We were not on trial. There was nothing like the Nuremberg Tribunal in Austria. All we needed to concern ourselves with was the democracy we were building for the future.

With the help of the Allies, we succeeded in creating that democracy. We now need to make it sturdier by placing it in its historic context. This is, in many ways, a personal task. I can only do it for myself, as you can do it only for yourself.

My fellow Austrians: Though I never gave a criminal order myself, I recorded many such orders and facilitated their execution. My greatest failing, however, then and now, was my silence. I suppressed the truth in order to help my family, my country, and myself.

To set the record straight, I have decided to write and publish a frank account of my recollections of the years 1938–48. I have also

decided to turn over all my personal papers from those years to
responsible archivists, who I trust will make them available to interested scholars.

When I assumed the office of president, I vowed to serve as your
head of state for six years. I still intend to do so. If you feel that this
is no longer appropriate, I trust you will make your feelings known to
the national parliament and the federal government.

These past two years have been hard ones for me. Fortunately,
God has given me a strong body and a resilient spirit.

I would like to believe that some good may come out of this affair.
Perhaps the hand of Providence can be divined in the pain we have
suffered. Perhaps I have become the symbol of a defect in our national
consciousness. Perhaps I have been given the chance to begin the
repair of that fault.

May God bless you all! May God bless Austria!

How likely is it that Kurt Waldheim will ever give such a speech? That
is not for a historian to say. What does seem clear is that the Waldheim
affair has raised historical consciousness. An increasing number of young
Austrians are reexamining their nation's past. The Pope has offered important new insights into the Holocaust. Jewish groups are preserving the
heritage of remembrance. Only Kurt Waldheim remains silent.

POSTSCRIPT:

The Waldheim Affair
Three Years Later

What have we learned since the publication of *The Missing Years* more than a year and a half ago? What do we need to investigate further?

I can summarize the first part of my answer in three words: Central Intelligence Agency. Kurt Waldheim was, and perhaps still is "of operational interest" to the Agency.

In a recent letter to me, the CIA defined this term as follows: "[It] means interest in any individual, anywhere in the world, who may be involved in activities or have access to information that the United States Government should be aware of to enhance the security of our country against all threats."

In addition, we have gained new insight into the Waldheim affair, and the nature of Kurt Waldheim's psyche.

Waldheim and the CIA

I began to correspond with high officials of the CIA in 1986; I made clear to the Agency that I had no intention of causing it any embarrassment. I respect its intelligence and information-gathering efforts as highly professional, and deem them to be essential to the national interest of the United States. At the same time, as a professional historian I require access to materials concerning an issue of compelling public importance. I made clear to the CIA that I did not care about the identity of agents in contact with Waldheim, and was willing to accept reasonably sanitized documents. I obtained some, but far from all of these files.

I have learned that in late 1971 the CIA routinely received State Department cables relevant to Waldheim's candidacy for the post of Secretary-General of the United Nations.[1] The Department of State viewed Waldheim as highly acceptable, though he was its second choice (the first choice being the Finn, Max Jakobson). The United States was, however, playing a double game in December, 1971. The U.S. Embassy told Austrians that it would be happy if Waldheim was selected. It did not, it said, want to hurt his chances by endorsing him. This was a strange comment. It becomes meaningful only in the light of fears expressed by powerful Austrians, such as Waldheim's old patron, former Foreign Minister Karl Gruber. They anticipated opposition to Waldheim in the United States. But why? Because rumors about his past might surface if the Americans became *publicly* active on Waldheim's behalf. After Waldheim won, with discreet American support, Foreign Minister Rudolf Kirchschläger offered profuse (and private) thanks to the Americans.

The rumors did not go away, however. They now circulated in the corridors and delegate lounges at the U.N. building. Someone in authority asked the CIA to investigate, according to information I have obtained from the Agency.

Working with Congressman Stephen J. Solarz and his able aide Bob Hathaway, I have discovered that the CIA investigated Waldheim in 1972, soon after he became Secretary-General.[2] Writing to Solarz, the CIA admitted that Waldheim had been an individual of "operational interest under criminal investigation." This research into his past seems to have been a kind of preemptive strike, a research expedition which would enable Waldheim and his sponsors to deny that he had a suspect past. The investigation was thus botched, or left intentionally incomplete.

The CIA claims that it did not research Waldheim's military record, part of which is stored in the French WAST archives in West Berlin. This is peculiar, since all investigative bodies, including the Wiesenthal Documentation Center in Vienna, routinely check WAST in cases of individuals accused of criminal conduct on behalf of the Nazi regime.[3] In Waldheim's case, such research would have uncovered a really explosive truth: Kurt Waldheim had served in the Balkans during a time of repression, atrocities, and deportations. This information would have awakened the suspicions of expert investigators.

Only recently, in late December, 1971, Waldheim had described his military record to the widely read *New York Times*. In his interview, Waldheim forgot to mention his three years in the Balkans.

After the 1972 flap, Waldheim was safe, perhaps because of sloppiness. The CIA could truthfully assure anyone raising questions about the Secretary-General that the Nazi party records housed in West Berlin contained nothing about Waldheim's membership in the party. In this instance Waldheim was lucky, as usual. He had belonged to two Nazi organizations (relatively minor ones), but their names did not figure on the standard Berlin Document Center checklist!

No charges surfaced until 1980; they were inaccurate, but the Agency was prepared.

In 1980 the CIA told Congressman Solarz that Waldheim incurred a leg wound in 1941, received his discharge about a year later, then pursued his legal studies in Vienna. The CIA thus provided Solarz with a virtual copy of what the Brooklyn Democrat later described as Waldheim's own "self-serving disinformation."[4]

There was one slip-up, however. According to the Agency's legislative counsel, Waldheim had been a staff intelligence officer in Russia.[5] This information, wrote the CIA, was "gleaned" from "open source materials." Why did the CIA, in its 1980 report, identify Waldheim as an intelligence officer, since according to all open source materials he had served in a cavalry reconnaisance unit in Russia? How did the CIA know about Waldheim's status as an intelligence officer? What were the open source materials referred to in counsel's letter to Solarz of 31 December 1980? At no point did the Agency inform Solarz of its 1972 investigation (which did not depend upon "open source materials"). Why would the CIA have a record of its 1972 investigation in 1988, but not in 1980?

Within the last two years the public has learned of an OSS-related 1945 document, which makes Waldheim out to be an intelligence officer. We now know of the 1972 inquiry into the State Department's Berlin archive. To admit that the 1980 cover-up circumvented the Agency's own dossiers would be most embarrassing.

Consider this. If the CIA had uncovered the WAST holding— which placed law student Waldheim in the Balkans—it would have subsequently lied to, rather than merely deceived, a Congressman. "I am very sorry if our answers on Mr. Waldheim have caused confusion . . . ," wrote the CIA to Rep. Solarz in 1988. So in 1987 the CIA's Director of Congressional Affairs informed me that "we are not able to identify open source materials the researcher may have used to prepare his 1980 response [to Rep. Solarz]."

The "open source" material appears to have consisted of Waldheim's own account, published earlier that year, with possible addenda taken from documents stored in various collections. Two explanations emerge, assuming that the Agency did not "lose" its research notes after 1980. Both would be embarrassing to the CIA: 1) Waldheim himself may have provided the "open source material" (as he did to the State Department in 1952); or, 2) the Agency based its description of Waldheim as an intelligence officer upon its prior access to closed files, at the U.N. War Crimes Commission Archive,[6] the WAST archives, and its own OSS holdings.

The Agency's protection of President Waldheim appears to have the support of the White House. The CIA's "criminal investigation" took place in 1972, soon after George Bush, U.S. Permanent Representative at the U.N., acting on State Department instructions, cast a vote for Waldheim's candidacy (among other "acceptables") for Secretary-General. Apparently, the CIA found nothing amiss in Waldheim's past, for less than five years later the Austrian received the support of the United States in his re-election bid. At that time Mr. Bush headed the CIA, and had access to information indicating that Waldheim had been investigated, and was "of operational interest."

Did we support Waldheim because he had been cleared (!), or because he was of "operational interest"—despite his murky past. At any rate, the CIA, now headed by Admiral Stansfield Turner, saved Waldheim from exposure in late 1980.

I later corresponded with then Vice President Bush through his national security aide, Donald Gregg, and his counsel, C. Boyden Grey. Mr. Grey, currently White House Counsel and a Bush confidant, assured me two years ago that "the Vice President is unable to add any additional information to that which you have found through your review of United Nations' files."[7] This strikes me as disingenuous. A man who voted for Waldheim, served with him at the U.N., then headed the CIA when the Austrian campaigned for his second term can surely tell us something.

Was Waldheim subject to American (and perhaps other) pressures due to his compromised past? Certainly, Waldheim appears to have resisted KGB attempts at infiltrating the U.N. Secretariat. He went out of his way, at great personal risk, attempting to free the American diplomats and intelligence officers held hostage in Teheran. Waldheim's shock and rage in April, 1987 at being barred from entering the United States makes more sense in the light of his past relationships with American intelligence operatives.

My correspondence with the CIA,[8] and my study of the Waldheim matter convinces me that relevant dossiers, reports, and memoranda on Kurt Waldheim are to be found in the CIA's operational files. They are subsumed under one or more of the following categories:

Counterintelligence operations;
Intelligence operations;
Security liaison arrangements;
Information exchanges with foreign governments or their intelligence or security services; and
Office of Security files documenting investigations of potential foreign intelligence or counterintelligence sources.

Some of these files are "operational," that is, they are active. Further, these files "document the conduct of foreign intelligence or counter-intelligence or security liaison arrangements or information exchanges with foreign governments or their intelligence or security services." Waldheim-related materials may also involve "investigations to determine the suitability of potential foreign intelligence or counterintelligence sources . . ."

Such files fall under the provisions of the CIA Information Act, 50 U.S.C., par. 431., which makes them exempt from FOIA requests. Nor is the legislative branch the only impediment to further research. Under Executive Order 12356, classified confidential information can be exempted from public disclosure if it damages national security, concerns intelligence methods or sources, or compromises information classified confidential by a foreign government. Perhaps President Waldheim draws some satisfaction from the irony of the situation. He is barred from entry into the United States, but American researchers are barred from studying some of their own government's files on Mr. Waldheim.

The present FOIA/CIA law is the problem, and that it needs to be amended so as to close the Waldheim loophole. The public has a right to know about this man's past, and his possible service to the U.S. government. Those of us who have been critical of Mr. Waldheim and of "Austrian amnesia" need to press our own government for the truth.

I do not believe that the Congress intended that the CIA use its operational exemption in order to prevent the public from learning about the concealed past of individuals whose actions during the war led to their placement on our Watch List.

We need a strong CIA, but not one that engages in the protection of a highly public, and gravely compromised individual. Had the Agency not protected Mr. Waldheim, it is unlikely that he would have become head of the United Nations. Later, in the Freedom of Information age, the CIA had its operational exemption, so concealment prevailed as the order of the day. It still does.

I suggest that a revision of 50 U.S.C., par. 431 might read as follows:

"Nothing in this act shall be interpreted to mean that any agency of the U.S. government has the authority to deny Freedom of Information requests about individuals who have been excluded from entry into the United States by reason of their involvement in crimes or persecutions undertaken on behalf of powers at war with the United States between 1941 and 1945."

Just as the Congressional oversight committee monitors covert actions, it might from time to time act to ensure that the CIA abides by the language of the proposed amendment.[9]

The Commission of Historians

In superficial ways, nothing has changed since I committed myself to writing a book about Kurt Waldheim's hidden past. He sits in splendor amidst the rococo trappings of the Hofburg Palace; I prepare classroom lectures, and spend most of my time discussing exams, grades, and writing assignments with college students.

In other, more profound ways, nothing is the same. Delving into Kurt Waldheim's past is like entering a tunnel containing many dimly lit, formerly inhabited caves. Each insight yields more perplexity; each dead-end, if followed to its terminus, suddenly offers a nugget of valuable information.

Rarely has the profession of history become so involved in a contemporary political controversy as in the Waldheim affair. Since the spring of 1986 other historians have joined me in the quest for the truth about Waldheim and his coverup.

A distinguished Historians Commission has portrayed Mr. Waldheim as a knowledgeable bureaucratic cog in the German war machine, fully aware of and contributing to the commission of illegal acts. The Commission, chaired by Swiss jurist Hans-Rudolf Kurz, came into being as a result of an initiative undertaken by Foreign Minister Alois Mock, a fervent Waldheim apologist. The group, which contained historians from several nations, including the United States, met for a total of twenty-eight days. Charged with the task of deciding if Waldheim had incurred personal culpability or guilt during his wartime service, the Commission went far beyond its mandate. Though its work was spotty at times, and often of questionable relevance, the body came up with some startling, and rather harsh findings.

In its report, released early in 1988,[10] Mock's Commission concluded that Kurt Waldheim had voluntarily joined two Nazi organizations; that as 03 he was "an important worker in a central leadership situation" in the Ic department of Army Group E, in fact, that he was the third most important officer in the thirty man strong IC/AO group; that Waldheim had played a role in the interrogation process involving captured Allied commandos, by reason of the fact that he prepared interrogation protocols. Further, the Commission decided that Waldheim had probably helped to deport prisoners and refugees after the bloody Kozara campaign in West Bosnia during the summer of 1942.

The Commission also showed that in September and early October, 1943, Waldheim worked to deport members of the Italian Eleventh Army, an illegal act, since no state of war existed between Italy and Germany at that time. Despite his low rank, the Commission noted, Waldheim knew a great deal about various questionable actions undertaken by his comrades at the orders of their superiors.

In a stunning rebuke to Waldheim, the Commission rejected his defense, which rests upon an Austrian doctrine called *Pflichterfüllung*, or "fulfilment of one's duty." Using harsh terms such as *mitschuldig* (sharing in guilt) in the commission of *Unrecht* (illegal and unjust acts), the Commission rejected this "I had to follow orders" explanation. Those orders, observed the Commission, violated the norms of right.

Waldheim angrily rejected these findings. He felt betrayed by a Commission forced upon him by his own staff and advocates. Perhaps he knew that a body of professional historians would reach embarrassing conclusions about his work as the second-ranking staff transport officer during the Kozara deportations. In a conclusion that smacked of the obvious, but added humiliation to its list of accusations, the Commission criticized Waldheim for covering up his military past. Waldheim's howl of rage left most publics unimpressed. Former Foreign Minister Karl Gruber voiced the desperation that now engulfed the Waldheim camp. Jews on the Commission, he declared, plus a West German socialist, had brought about the debacle. The Hofburg staff, led by Waldheim's chief protector, Dr. Ralph Scheide, acted as if was under siege.

No one, not even in Austria, could accuse the Commission of

parroting the publicity surrounding my research, nor of being "out to get Waldheim." Nor did groups like the World Jewish Congress (which denounced the Commission when its formation first surfaced in the media) have any influence upon its negative findings. The body consisted of some well known historians; they obtained copies of documents first unearthed by myself and other researchers, but its members did their own work.

Barring further revelations, Waldheim can best be described as a bureaucratic accomplice in various military units. He has tried to evade historical judgment; he has certainly maintained a solid degree of political support within his own country. Waldheim's ability to survive the demise of his own credibility reflects broader, unhealthy currents in Western societies.

Waldheim and Holocaust Denial

Looking back to 1986, we can see that a new, "revisionist" attitude to the Holocaust was beginning to turn the whistle-blowers into the real villains. To much of Austria, the World Jewish Congress was the evil-doer, while Waldheim was its victim. Revisionism is a broad term, but in the Waldheim context it has meaning in the sense of revising one's view of the war. By the spring of 1986 public opinion was turning against Israel in much of the West. Lebanon, the Palestinian issue, and relentless "anti-Zionist" propaganda (often anti-semitism without the swastika) had changed many minds. If Israel was no longer the victim, then maybe the Jews had *never* been victims. Pseudo-historians had gained audiences for obscene theories about the phony nature of the Holocaust. The economic dislocations of major sectors of the Western economies led to an upsurge in anti-semitism. Many people had tired of the hunt for alleged war criminals, feeling that decent old men were being hounded by vengeful, Jewish-supported bureaucrats. And in Central Europe, newly prosperous West Germans and Austrians, fearful of more economic turmoil, asked how long they would have to apologize for sins committed by other people, in a time long past.

The Waldheim defense was related to other "revisionist" events of the era, such as President Ronald Reagan's 1985 visit to Bitburg.

Bigburg did not originally cause controversy. It was, as one friend of mine put it, a *schöne Geste*, a generous tribute to the war dead of a former foe. Chancellor Helmut Kohl saw Reagan's visit as politically useful to West Germany's governing coalition. President Reagan wanted to help a powerful ally. Then came revelations about *Waffen SS* graves, and two bizarre defenses emerged. Defense Number One rested upon the fact that Americans stationed in the Bitburg area had long been in the habit of honoring those German war dead. Thus, a presidential visit was nothing extraordinary, at least in moral terms. Defense Number Two emerged after the press learned of the SS graves. It argued that the SS men and boys buried there were also "victims." Indeed they were, but they were victims with some element of choice, serving a nihilistic ideology. By a strange twist, those Holocaust survivers who opposed Bitburg were now put in the position of trying to prevent a President from honoring victims! How selfish and cruel! *Macht und Stimme der Juden!* ("Power and Influence of the Jews!") cursed a popular West German magazine. The language was changing, as convention and current politics corrupted words and attempted to alter historical perceptions. Publications in both West Germany and Austria produced photographs of sinister Jews, plotting to block Reagan's visit to the Bitburg cemetary, or conspiring to destroy Kurt Waldheim.[11]

History had to be distorted or forgotten, so as to justify the existing order of things. Chancellor Kohl, by contrast, the architect of Bitburg, now praised Waldheim as a "great patriot"—for which country, he did not say. We can now see, better than we could three years ago, that Kurt Waldheim had been rehearsing his newly assumed part for several decades. By the 1970s his own, "revised" role was that of the victim of war.

When this disguise was torn from Waldheim, he donned the garb of the martyr.

In his own writings, Kurt Waldheim had been careful to ignore the Jewish presence in, and contribution to Austrian history, culture, and economy before 1938. Yet he appears to have felt compelled to expel any feelings of complicity in the Holocaust from within himself. Strange to tell, Kurt Waldheim sees himself as a kind of Holocaust survivor. The memories of Jewish deportation become the setting for the Waldheim family's return to Lower Austria, amidst horrifying conditions.[12]

Writing in the late 1970s Waldheim spoke of his trip back to Baden, near Vienna, in the company of his wife and young child. "We made the journey," notes Waldheim, "in a cattle car chock-a-block with produce, poultry, freight of every kind, and as many other passengers as could be squeezed aboard. We were crammed against the baby's cradle, and her carriage sat atop the trunks and baggage that held everything we owned. Elisabeth, who was not well, rested on a pile of straw. I . . . perched on an apple crate. Every now and then she and I exchanged places to keep our limbs from getting cramped. . . . It was impossible to sleep and there was no room to stretch our legs. . . . The trip, which ordinarily took three hours, lasted two-and-a-half days. . . . We stopped for hours at interminable places . . . , whose names we couldn't even ascertain because our cattle car had no windows, and they seldom let us leave the train. We were hungry and, above all, thirsty. Liselotte never stopped crying. By the third and final night all the passengers were showing signs of strain. One of them, vexed beyond endurance, threatened to smash the baby's cradle to give himself more room." Waldheim concludes this story on another somber note. Having arrived home in Baden, he finds that his parents' bombed house was nearly uninhabitable, so "we nearly froze to death that winter." There was not much food. Waldheim survived, however, as he always has, and the next paragraph takes us from the train nightmare to the inauguration of a brilliant career.[13]

The fact that he recalls the train ride in such detail, and forgets Kozara is more important than the degree of Waldheim's anecdotal veracity. And what do we have here? We are reading of a Holocaust experience—not enough air, a cramped cattle car, screaming children, asocial behavior, a sick young mother, maddening thirst, an endless ride, guards preventing one from leaving the train, and finally, arrival at the destination, which one expected to be a moment of delight, but which turns into a kind of shocked visit to an ersatz concentration camp. So Waldheim becomes the Holocaust victim, and forty years later who will question the victim about his role as a perpetrator? Waldheim seems to see himself precisely as Austria sees itself in the Moscow Declaration—like the unfortunate Jews, a victim. Like Reagan's *Waffen SS*, everyone becomes a victim.

Waldheim the guiltless accomplice thus became an amnesiac Holocaust victim. His political culture supported the President, his peers did not often question him; his family endorses his "history." While acknowledging that he was no resister, no hero, Waldheim falls back upon his protean concept of *Pflichterfüllung,* "I did my duty to my comrades." A middle course—telling the truth about what he thought he was doing in 1942–1945—does not seem to occur to the President.

An "As If" Personality?

Psychoanalysis may yield some insights into this strange personality. The analyst Helene Deutsch published an important essay in the year

1942, at about the time Lt. Waldheim was busy in the Kozara region.[14] She is writing about the "as if" personality, a marginal type of individual whose main characteristics are outward adaptibility and inner emotional hollowness. Such people, Deutsch notes, accommodate themselves to new theory and technique with "striking ease and speed," but the outcome is "always a spasmodic, if skilled, repetition of a prototype without the slightest trace of originality." She adds that "It is like the performance of an actor who is technically well trained but who lacks the necessary spark to make his impersonations true to life." Is this not a series of portraits of Kurt Waldheim, the Austrian patriot, turned German collaborator, turned diplomat, turned democratic leader, turned crusader for world peace, turned Austrian patriot fighting the evil world? More frightening still is Deutsch's portrait of a man who conducts his life as "if he possessed a complete and sensitive emotional capacity. To him there is no difference between his empty forms and what others actually experience." This blindness explains how Waldheim could confront his accusers with such great indignation; how he could express surprise and shock at his mistreatment at the hands of the Americans and the Jews; how he could be outraged that anyone would question his apparent (or transparent) sincerity. As if she had interviewed Waldheim in the Hofburg, Deutsch concluded that the "as if" personality combines "a completely passive attitude to the environment with a highly plastic readiness to pick up signals from the outer world and to mold oneself and one's behavior accordingly. The identification with what other people are thinking and feeling is the expression of this passive plasticity and thus renders the person capable of the greatest fidelity and the basest perfidy."

One thinks here of Waldheim's relationship to General Löhr, to Karl Gruber, to the United Nations, to the Austrian electorate—but also, to the Jews, to the war, to the truth.

Deutsch portrays her "as if" personalities in devastating terms. "Attaching themselves with great ease to social, ethical, and religious groups," she writes, as-if types "seek, by adhering to a group, to give content and reality to their inner emptiness and establish the validity of their existence by identification. Overenthusiastic adherence to one philosophy can be quickly and completely replaced by another contradictory one without the slightest trace of inward transformation—simply as a result of some accidental regrouping of the circle of acquaintances or the like." Waldheim, the accommodating time-server knew how to disguise his ambition as service. Of such a type Deutsch wrote nearly fifty years ago: ". . . aggressive tendencies are almost completely masked by passivity, lending an air of negative goodness, of mild amiability which, however, is readily convertible to evil."

"Mild amiability" in the service of evil, quickly forgotten—that too is Kurt Waldheim. As Deutsch observes, "Thus it can come about that the individual can be seduced into asocial or criminal acts by a change in his identifications, and it may well be that some of the asocial are recruited from the group of 'as if' personalities who are adapted to reality in this restricted way." Such personalities, Deutsch believes, are narcissistic, lack deep personal ties to others, identify with the authority of the moment, and evade conflict with conscience, which is submerged or underdeveloped. The authority of the moment in 1986 was the Austrian electorate; and Waldheim's conscience never seemed to surface. The development of this kind of personality must date back to childhood. What produced this outcome is unclear, but in Kurt Waldheim family and history combined to create a disturbing, perhaps universal phenomenon.

The gap between Kurt Waldheim's account of his past, and its reality and fact of its exposure, presents humanity with a cautionary tale. Knowing the evil that men do is important, but revealing the evil that they conceal (even where they have not done it), and why they hid that past, may be even more instructive. When will Kurt Waldheim, along with his Austrian defenders and American helpers, confront this past?

Robert Edwin Herzstein
June 16, 1989

Archival Sources

Arhiv Jugoslavije (Belgrade, Yugoslavia). Records of the Yugoslav State Commission on War Crimes Committed by the Occupying Forces and Their Collaborators; files on Kurt Waldheim and Oskar Turina.

Auswärtiges Amt [German Foreign Ministry] (Bonn, West Germany). Politisches Archiv, Inland II geheim, Griechenland [Greece] 1941–44.

The Citadel Archives (Charleston, S.C.). Mark Clark Papers, Austria 1945–47.

Harry S Truman Library (Independence, Mo.). Papers of John M. Cabot; records of the Allied Council, Austria.

Institut für Zeitgeschichte (Munich, West Germany). Eichmann-Prozess [trial of Adolf Eichmann], testimony of Ludwig Teichmann; Feindnachrichten-Blatter (1043/53).

Militärchiv des Bundesarchivs (Freiburg, West Germany). Records of the 714th Infantry Division, Ib, 1942.

National Archives and Records Administration (Washington, D.C., and Suitland, Md.). Record Group 59: general records of the U.S. Department of State. Record Group 84: records of the Foreign Service Posts of the Department of State (Belgrade, Vienna, Zagreb, 1947–48); records of the U.S. High Commissioner for Austria (1946–49); signed minutes of the meetings of the Allied Council; papers of the Allied Council; agendas of the executive committee; correspondence between the Chancellor of Austria and the U.S. forces in Austria; correspondence between various Austrian ministries and the U.S. forces in Austria; correspondence between the Soviet element and the U.S. forces in Austria. Record Group 153: records of the Office of the Judge Advocate General (U.S. Army). Record Group 165: records of the U.S. Department of War, general and special staffs; Record Group 226: records of the OSS. Record Group 238: National Archives Collection of World War II War Crimes Records. Record Group 242: National Archives Collection of Foreign Records Seized, 1941–   ; records of Headquarters of the German Army High Command; records of the Reich Leader of the S.S. and Chief of the German Police; records of German Field Commands, Armies; records of German Field Commands, Rear Areas, Occupied Territories, and Others; records of German Field Commands, Army Groups; records of German Field Commands, Divisions; records of German Field Commands, Corps; miscellaneous S.S. records, Waffen-S.S.; records of the Italian Armed Forces; records of the German Foreign Office; files of the German Army Personnel Office. Record Group 260: records of the United States Occupation Headquarters, World War II. Record Group 319: records of the Army Staff. Records Group 331: records of Allied Operational and Occupation Headquarters, World War II. Record Group 332: records of U.S. Theaters of War, World War II.

Public Record Office (Kew and London, England). Records of the Foreign Office (371 and 1020); records of the War Office.

United Nations Archives (New York). Records of the United Nations War Crimes Commission, Predecessor Archives Group.

Vojnoistoriski [Military History] Institut Arhiv (Belgrade, Yugoslavia). Records of the Pusteria Division; records of the Independent State of Croatia; records of Battle Group West Bosnia, Ic; records of the Regional Police Administration, Banja Luka.

Notes

Part One
A Young Man with a Future

Chapter One
Walter Watzlawik's Son

1. Kurt Waldheim, *In the Eye of the Storm* (Bethesda, MD: 1986), Chapter 2. Additional biographical information about Dr. Waldheim's parents was supplied to the author by Dr. Ralph Scheide of the Präsidentschaftskanzlei, Vienna, and by Ferdinand Trauttmansdorff of the Austrian Embassy, Washington, DC.

2. On Czech-German antagonisms, see R. W. Seton-Watson, *A History of the Czechs and Slovaks* (London: 1943), Chapter XIII; S. Harrison Thompson, *Czechoslovakia in European History* (Princeton: 1943), Chapter IX; Oskar Jaszi, *The Dissolution of the Habsburg Monarchy* (Chicago: 1929), p. 385 ff.; and Arthur J. May, *The Hapsburg Monarchy 1867–1914* (Cambridge, MA: 1951), p. 325 ff.

3. Andrew G. Whiteside, *Austrian National Socialism Before 1918* (The Hague: 1962).

4. William A. Jenks, *Vienna and the Young Hitler* (New York: 1960), pp. 40–67, 113–142; Bradley F. Smith, *Adolf Hitler: His Family, Childhood and Youth* (Stanford: 1967), chapters 6–7.

5. On Austrian anti-Semitism: Salo Wittmayer Baron, *A Social and Religious History of the Jews*, Vol. XI (New York: 1967), pp. 267–277, 417 (note 93), and 420 (note 100); Peter Pulzer, *The Rise of Political Anti-Semitism in Germany and Austria* (New York: 1964), chapters 14–20; Josef Fraenkel, ed., *The Jews of Austria: Essays on Their Life, History and Destruction* (London: 1967); F. L. Carsten, *The Rise of Fascism* (Berkeley: 1967), p. 33 ff.; and Karl R. Stadler, *Austria* (New York: 1971), pp. 134–137.

6. Adolf Hitler, *Mein Kampf* (Boston: 1962), pp. 57–65 et passim.

7. Andrew G. Whiteside, *The Socialism of Fools* (Berkeley: 1975), pp. 52, 104, 209, and 243 ff. Hitler's evaluation of von Schönerer appears in *Mein Kampf*, p. 98 et passim.

8. F. L. Carsten, *Fascist Movements in Austria: From Schönerer to Hitler* (Beverly Hills: 1977), pp. 20–21.

9. Carl E. Schorske, *Fin-de-Siecle Vienna: Politics and Culture* (New York: 1979); and Arthur J. May, *Vienna in the Age of Franz Josef* (Norman, OK: 1966).

10. Eugene Bagger, *Francis Joseph: Emperor of Austria—King of Hungary* (New York: 1927), pp. 493–557; E. M. Kienast and Robert Rie, eds., *The Incredible Friendship: The Letters of Emperor Franz Joseph to Frau Katherina Schratt* (New York: 1966).

11. For a good analysis of the Austrian situation during this period, see the report prepared by the Foreign Affairs Research Department in Whitehall, RG 226/OSS/C.I.D./ 142045.

12. Karl Gutkas, "Niederösterreich," in Erika Weinzierl and Kurt Skalnik, *Österreich 1918–1938: Geschichte der Ersten Republik*, Vol. II (Vienna: 1983), p. 841 ff.

13. Richard Olechowski, "Schulpolitik," in Weinzierl and Skalnik, *Österreich*, II, p. 590 ff.

14. The best account of the Seipel era is Klemens von Klemperer's *Ignaz Seipel: Christian Statesman in a Time of Crisis* (Princeton: 1972).

15. Stadler, *Austria*, p. 140 et passim.

16. Ludwig Jedlicka, "The Austrian Heimwehr," in Walter Laqueur and George L. Mosse, eds., *International Fascism 1920–1945* (New York: 1966); C. Earl Edmondson, *The Heimwehr and Austrian Politics 1918–1936* (Athens, GA: 1978); Carsten, *Fascist Movements in Austria*, pp. 105–228; and Adam Wandruszka, "Austrofaschismus: Anmerkungen zur politischen Bedeutung der 'Heimwehr' in Österreich," in M. Funke, et al., *Demokratie und Diktatur: Geist und Gestalt Politischer Herrschaft in Deutschland und Europa* (Düsseldorf: 1987), pp. 216–222.

17. For Waldheim's analysis of Austrian history during this period, see his book *The Austrian Example* (London: 1973), pp. 18–31.

18. Two highly useful works on the rise of right-wing political violence are Gerhard Botz, *Gewalt in der Politik: Attentate, Zusammenstösse, Putschversuche, Unruhen in Österreich 1918 bis 1934* (Munich: 1976), and Bruce Pauley, *Hitler and the Forgotten Nazis: A History of Austrian National Socialism* (Chapel Hill: 1981).

19. Elisabeth Barker, *Austria 1918–1972* (London: 1973), p. 74 ff.; for a more detailed (and highly sympathetic view), see J. D. Gregory, *Dollfuss and His Times* (London: 1935). G.E.R. Gedye, *Fallen Bastions: The Central European Tragedy* (London: 1939) is unremittingly hostile to Dollfuss. A good guide to Austrian political conflict during this period is Martin Kitchen, *The Coming of Austrian Fascism* (London: 1980).

20. Irmgard Bärnthaler, *Die Vaterländische Front* (Vienna: 1971), pp. 165–173.

21. Jedlicka, "Heimwehr," pp. 138–142.

22. On the role of the Bundesheer, see Ludwig Jedlicka, *Ein Heer im Schatten der Parteien: Die Militärpolitische Lage Österreichs 1918–1938* (Graz: 1955), especially pp. 111–143.

23. The papal encyclical *Quadragesimo Anno* greatly influenced Dollfuss. See R. E. Herzstein, "Pius XI and the Crisis of Liberal Capitalism: *Quadragesimo Anno,*" *Bucknell Review* (December, 1967), pp. 39–46.

24. Charles A. Gulick, *Austria from Habsburg to Hitler,* Vol. II (Berkeley: 1948), chapters XXV–XXVI.

25. In a conversation with me in June 1987, former chancellor Dr. Bruno Kreisky recalled that "one gets to know someone on a human level when one shares a small cell with him."

26. Hitler quoted by Carsten, *The First Austrian Republic 1918–1938* (London: 1986), p. 190.

27. On the role, strategy, and morale of the Austrian Federal Army around the time of Kurt Waldheim's service in the Bundesheer, see T-120/2498/1404–1730. The German military attaché in Vienna had good intelligence sources, probably located inside the Bundesheer.

Chapter Two
In Hitler's Ostmark

1. Alfred D. Low, *The Anschluss Movement, 1931–1938, and the Great Powers* (New York: 1985), p. 190 et passim.

2. See Ludwig Jedlicka, *Ein Heer im Schatten der Parteien: Die Militärpolitische Lage Österreichs 1918–1938,* p. 143, concerning Schuschnigg's geostrategic concepts.

3. U.S. Department of State, *Documents on German Foreign Policy 1918–1945,* C, V (Washington, DC: 1966), pp. 755–761; Waldheim, *The Austrian Example* (London, 1973), p. 40; and G. Schmidt, Aufzeichnungen, in RG 226/X133359.

4. Gerhard L. Weinberg explores the international context of these decisions in *The Foreign Policy of Hitler's Germany: Starting World War II 1937–1939* (Chicago: 1980), pp. 267–269.

5. Karl R. Stadler, *Austria* (New York: 1971), pp. 133–134.

6. One of the best accounts of the Austrian situation during the Schuschnigg era is that of F. L. Carsten, *The First Austrian Republic 1918–1938: A Study Based on British and Austrian Documents* (Aldershot: 1986), pp. 201–284. Carsten makes use of the some of the shrewdest British diplomatic insights into the Austrian tragedy.

7. On the Consular Academy, see "Austria's Schools and Universities," Survey of Foreign Experts, OSS Confidential C.I.D., #122194 (March 16–28, 1945), pp. 20, 32 (RG 226).

8. Schuschnigg offered one account of the meeting in *Austrian Requiem* (New York: 1946), pp. 3–27; Weinberg deals with the Berchtesgaden encounter and its consequences in *Foreign Policy,* p. 291 ff.

9. Report of the German legation in Vienna, to the AA, T-120/2498/271730; on the growing appeal of Nazism, see Carsten, *First Austrian Republic,* p. 268.

10. On the Waldheims' political attitudes during this time, see the affidavits reproduced in Waldheim's so-called White Book: *Kurt Waldheim's Wartime Years: A Documentation* (Vienna: 1987), pp. 101–107. Useful in this context is Edda Pfeifer, *Die Widerstands-bewegung des Konservativen Lagers 1939–1940. Die Gruppen Karl Roman Scholz, Dr. Karl Lederer und Dr. Jakob Kastelic* (Ph.D. dissertation, University of Vienna: 1963), p. 10 ff. Relevant public statements made by Anton Geiger, Otto Vicenzi, Hans Uteschill, and others, seem born out by later Nazi references to the Waldheims' "hatred" for the Nazi movement, that is, hatred before the *Anschluss* took place.

11. Apologists for the Dollfuss-Schuschnigg regime have wrongly used this abandonment as a justification for the policies of the *Ständestaat*. The "abandonment" represents a fact, not a vindication. On foreign attitudes to the *Anschluss*, see Carsten, *First Austrian Republic*, p. 274; Weinberg, *Foreign Policy*, p. 295 et passim; and Low, *Anschluss Movement*, chapters 14–15. On Hitler's expression of thanks to Italy, see Hitler's phone message to Prince Philipp von Hessen, March 11, 1938, in Office of the U.S. Chief of Counsel for the Prosecution of Axis Criminalty, *Nazi Conspiracy and Aggression* (Washington: 1946), Vol. I, 497–498.

12. G.E.R. Gedye tells harrowing stories about the sadistic indignities inflicted upon Viennese Jews in *Fallen Bastions: The Central European Tragedy* (London: 1939), pp. 306–310 and 354–356. The *Völkischer Beobachter* of April 27, 1938, cited by Gedye, p. 357, gloated about the fact that the Jews were trapped.

13. Hitler's Reich press chief, Otto Dietrich, later recalled that "I have seen Hitler the recipient of a great deal of popular enthusiasm. But the demonstrations when he entered Linz and Vienna were, I believe, the most genuine I have ever witnessed." Otto Dietrich, *Hitler* (Chicago: 1955), p. 37. See also Gedye, *Fallen Bastions*, p. 356; Max Domarus, *Hitler: Reden und Proklamationen 1932–1945* (Wiesbaden: 1973) I, ii, pp. 823–825; and Gordon Craig, "The Waldheim File," *The New York Review of Books*, October 9, 1986, p. 3.

14. See Stadler, *Austria*, pp. 195–196.

15. On the administrative "reunion" of Austria with the Reich: SHAEF, Internal Affairs Branch (G-5/1024), "Administrative System of Austria," in RG 331, entry 47/box 32.

16. On the persecution of the church, see Radomir Luza, *Austro-German Relations in the Anschluss Era* (Princeton: 1975), pp. 182–191, and Stadler, *Austria*, p. 196.

17. See Hubertus Czernin, *Profil*, March 3, 1986, and Gruppe "Neues Osterreich," *Pflichterfüllung* (Vienna: 1986), p. 6 et passim, for analyses of young Waldheim's actions during and after the Anschluss. *Kurt Waldheim's Wartime Years*, p. 101 ff., gives Waldheim's account of his family's fate under the Nazis. Also useful was a letter to the author by Dr. Otto Vicenzi, April 8, 1987, and a public statement by Anton Geiger, March 12, 1986. Comm. Ing. Hans Uteschill shared his views with the author in a letter dated March 30, 1987.

18. Der Reichsorganisationsleiter der NSDAP, *Organisationsbuch der NSDAP* (Munich: 1936), pp. 262–265. Both Waldheim's military record from 1939 and his Justice Ministry file (1944) list him as a full member of the Studentenbund. On the "coordination" of the university, see Franz Gall, *Alma Mater Rudolphina 1365–1965* (Vienna: 1965), pp. 31–35.

19. Waldheim's Soldbuch and Wehrstammkarte provided the researcher with information about his military career in the reserves and the Wehrmacht.

20. Karl A. Schleunes, *The Twisted Road to Auschwitz* (Urbana, 1970), p. 229 ff.; Hannah Arendt, *Eichmann in Jerusalem* (New York: 1965), pp. 31–44; and Peter R. Black, *Ernst Kaltenbrunner: Ideological Soldier of the Third Reich* (Princeton: 1984), p. 109. Gerhard Botz, "Stufen der Ausgliederung der Juden aus der Gesellschaft. Die österreichischen Juden vom 'Anschluss' zum 'Holocaust,'" *Zeitgeschichte* (June/July, 1987) is of great value (see pp. 359–369).

21. *Organisationsbuch der NSDAP*, pp. 358–392.

22. See *Der Spiegel* (16/1986), "Gespräch mit Waldheim."

Chapter Three
Wehrmacht Hero

1. Kurt Waldheim, *The Challenge of Peace* (New York: 1980), p. 23. The French edition of this book appeared in 1977, the German edition in 1978. Despite allegations to the contrary, none of the editions contributes important factual data about the missing years.

2. See the citation from the Fragebogen of April 24, 1940, in the Tagebuch in dem Verfahren zur Beurteilung des Rechtsanwaltsanwärters Dr. Kurt Waldheim, SK 235 (1946).

3. NSDAP, Gauleitung Niederdonau, Personalamt, as quoted in the Tagebuch cited in note 2.

4. Nürnberg Red Series, VI, 421, testimony on Himmler's policy in Russia, recorded on November 26, 1945. See also *Unsere Ehre Heisst Treue* (Vienna: 1965), which contains the activity reports of the 1st and 2nd infantry brigades, and of the Sonderkommandos of the SS. These units operated for a time in the sector adjacent to Waldheim's army unit.

5. On the operations of the 45th I.D., see NAM T-315/916/0881–0947 ff., as well as roll 919. Also important is Rudolf Geschöpf, *Mein Weg mit der 45. Infanteriedivision* (Linz: 1955).

6. Friederice Beyer, "Leutnant Waldheim gen Osten," *Forum* (March 1987), p. 24 ff., and "Waldheims Schwadronfuhrer kann ausschliessen," ibid., July 1987.

7. Erich Kern, *General von Pannwitz und Seine Kossaken* (Göttingen: 1963). See also Jürgen Thorwald, *The Illusion: Soviet Soldiers in Hitler's Armies* (New York: 1974), p. 316.

8. For Waldheim's account, see *In the Eye of the Storm*, pp. 16–18. The president told me at some length about his "traumatic" experience in Russia, about what it was like to be young, far from home, and at death's door. He argues that his later experiences in the Balkans paled in comparison, hence he paid little attention to them in his memoirs.

9. Waldheim's wartime medical record is under French control, at the WAST center in West Berlin. I obtained a French translation of the record from Simon Wiesenthal.

10. Aktennotizen und Anlagen, February 2, 1942, T-312/465/3271; KTB des Kommandierenden Generals und Befehlshaber in Serbien (March 1942), T-501/247/895–913.

11. Hitler's policy mandated support for the genocidal, fascist regime of Ante Pavelić: see Norman Rich, *Hitler's War Aims: The Establishment of the New Order* (New York: 1974), pp. 275–280. The Germans were well informed about Ustasha atrocities. See, for example, 714 I.D., Ia, report for March 1942, T-315/2258/416 ff.; ibid., Ia, TB for April 1942, frame 501 ff.; and Zagreb to AA, June 19, 1942, T-120/5800/311477. A retired German army captain, Arthur Häffner, was one of the few Wehrmacht officials who understood the multiethnic nature of Croatia. He realized, and reported to German military officials in Zagreb, that the Ustasha policy was self-destructive. See his report of April 23, 1941, T-501/265/365–366, and of April 26, 1942, ibid., 259–265. An unidentified report dating from September 1, 1942, expressed similar sentiments: T-501/267/554–558. German staff officers were particularly knowledgeable in regard to Ustasha (and German) atrocities.

12. Zagreb to AA, probably January 24, 1942, T-120/5800/311509.

13. WB-2615-1 (WBHSO to Bader, February 7, 1942); WBHSO Ia, TB, March 1, 1942, T-312/465/286; T-501/207/470–485 (concerning Axis discussions commencing on March 2, 1942); NOKW-1797 (March 3, 1942); Kampfgruppe Bader, Ia, March 22, 1942, T-501/250/410 ff. Bader received instructions from the Twelfth Army mandating the use of "brutal police and secret police methods." WBHSO to Bader, March 23, 1942, NOKW-943; and Bader's statement of policy, March 25, 1942, WB-865. On the military planning and history of the East Bosnian operation, see Paul N. Hehn, *The German Struggle Against Yugoslav Guerrillas in World War II: German Counter-insurgency in Yugoslavia* (New York: 1979), p. 120 ff.

14. Aktennotiz über die Chefbesprechung am 13.4.42, T-311/175/0474 ff.

15. WB-1004c, Twelfth Army, Ia, TB for April 1942 (dated April 30, 1942); see also WB-1004d.

16. Higher German officials did not share Waldheim's attitude. A constant stream of complaints about Italian lassitude and corruption flowed into the German foreign ministry. See Woermann to Rome, April 2, 1942, T-120/2479/437 ff.; AA, Pol. IV, to Rome, and to plenipotentiary in Belgrade, April 30, 1942, ibid., 258548 ff.; AA to Rome, May 15, 1942, ibid., 258615 ff.; Zagreb to AA, May 15, 1942, T-120/2480/258656 ff.

17. Ministero della difesa, stato maggiore dell' esercito, ufficio storico, *Le Operazioni della Unita in Jugoslavia 1941–1943* (Rome: 1978); and Commando della divisione alpina "Pusteria" Ufficio del Capo di S.M., Sezione Operazioni e Servizi, "Esperienze tratte dall'ultimo ciclo di operazioni 22 Aprile–27 Maggio 1942—XX, in Vojnoistoriski Institut Arhiv, Br. Reg. 7/3, K. 93 (Belgrade).

18. Gen. Bader, Aufruf, May 30, 1942, T-120/5800/311487.

19. Führungsstab Westbosnien to 718 I.D., May 29, 1942, T-315/2268/776–785.

Chapter Four
A Place Called Kozara

1. Summary by the Missione militare italiana in croazia, 22 Iuglio 1942—XX, "Operazioni tedesco-croate nella Kozara Planina"; Zagreb to AA, May 15, 1942, T-120/2480/258661; Deutscher General in Agram to Gen. Bader, May 23, 1942, T-501/249/1260; WBHSO,

Ia, TB for May 1942, WB-1004d; and Komm. Gen. in Serbien, Lagebericht for June 1–10, 1942, T-315/2258/677–686.

2. Komm. Gen. in Serbien, Ia, Nr. 263/42 Gen. Kdos., T-315/2262/737 ff.; Gen. Oxilia to Comando Supremo, June 9, 1942, T-821/60/723–737. For a good description of the type of challenge confronting Stahl, see the interrogation of Field Marshal von Weichs, RG 332/108. Tito's proclamations on partisan warfare as they relate to Kozara may be consulted in The Military History Institute of the Yugoslav People's Army, *The National Liberation War and Revolution in Yugoslavia (1941–1945)* (Belgrade: 1982), pp. 291–319 et passim.

3. Much of the documentation concerning Stahl, his staff, and the West Bosnia operation may be found in T-315/2258. Stahl's army personnel file (the so-called "201" file, on microfilm) may be consulted in the National Archives (I obtained access under a Freedom of Information Act request). In addition to the affidavit by Ernst Wiesinger, in Wald-heim's "White Book" (*Kurt Waldheim's Wartime Years: A Documentation* [Vienna: 1987]) one may consult the TB of the 714 I.D., Ia, for February 1942, T-315/2258/342 ff.; report of the Ic, March 4, 1942, ibid., 0425; Führungsstab Kampfgruppe Westbosnien to 718 I.D., May 29, 1942, T-315/2268/776–785; and discussion between Major Gehm and the Croatian General Staff, May 26–27, 1942, T-501/267/459–460. Gen. Stahl's career went steadily downhill after Kozara. His symptoms reflected psychological distress. Stahl found himself in both personal and political difficulty following the plot on Hitler's life in 1944. After the war Stahl drew a blank when he was asked about Kozara by American interrogators: See Office of the U.S. Chief of Counsel for War Crimes, Affidavit by Gen. Stahl, June 13, 1947, NOKW-1714; and the interrogation summary No. 2402, based on the Stahl interrogation of June 10, 1947 (RG 238).

4. I obtained Funke's 201 file under an FOIA request in 1986.

5. Ib records of the 714 I.D., summer of 1942, RH 26-114/48–49, Nr. 27960/13, Militärarchiv des Bundesarchiv, Freiburg, West Germany.

6. T-821/443/697–700; and KTB of the 718 I.D., July 8, 1942, T-315/2266/691 ff. The records of the Croatian 1st Aviation Group, which bombed villages on Kozara, are stored in the Vojnoistoriski Institut Arhiv in Belgrade; the report of July 6, 1942, is particularly important.

7. Missione italiana-Zagrebia, July 4, 1942, T-821/60/460–474; Missione militare italiana, July 9, 1942, ibid., 501–507; report by Bader's Ic, July 10, 1942, T-315/2258/755–762; Missione militare italiana, July 16, 1942, T-821/443/608–610; and WBHSO, July 18, 1942, T-78/329/6138 ff. Developments in West Bosnia can be followed from T-78/329/6127–6165.

8. On the growing appeal of the partisans, see the report by Envoy Kasche, July 3, 1942, T-120/2480/258796 ff., and the Aktenvermerk of September 1, 1942, T-501/267/554–558. See also Dr. Ivo Gromeš to Dr. Oskar Turina, July 17, 1942, Br. Reg. 31/1, F45B K. 87 (Belgrade), and Deutscher General Agram, August 7, 1942, T-120/5800/312057 ff. Bader's Ia issued his report on July 1, 1942 (NOKW-1440).

9. These policies were premeditated, and antedated the Kozara operation. They implicate the WBHSO, the Commanding General in Serbia, the staff of the Battle Group West Bosnia, and the Croatian General Staff. See T-501/267/0040; T-501/249/755; T-501/267/459–460 (documents on reprisals covering the period March 19–May 27, 1942).

10. The conclusion of the *Divisionsgeschichte* of the 714 I.D. may be consulted in T-315/2258. The Kozara deportations were the work of many German agencies. Ample documentation exists: Office of the Commissioner for the Four Year Plan in Belgrade to Legation in Agram, June 15, 1942, T-120/5798/310373. On the coordination of arrests between Stahl's Ic unit and the Croatians, see Br. Reg. 16/1–14, K. 11 (VIIA, Belgrade). On the involvement of the Twelfth Army High Command: Überblick of July 8, 1942, NOKW-1138; and WBHSO, Ia, TB of July 31, 1942, T-311/175/0312. On the role of the German Envoy and the German General, Zagreb, Kasche to Glaise-Horstenau, July 10, 1942, T-501/250/114–118; Glaise-Horstenau's Ia to Legation in Agram, July 11, 1942, T-120/5798/310371; police attaché in legation to Kasche, July 13, 1942, ibid., 370; Kasche to AA, July 21, 1942, T-120/2480/258870 ff.; Helm's report to AA, July 23, 1942, T-120/380/274569–70; and Troll of Zagreb legation to AA, September 5, 1942, T-120/5799/311333. The notorious Samjiste camp was "used for purposes of the Wehrmacht, when the action on the Kozara was in progress": Testimony of Ludwig Teichmann, September 17, 1946, Eichmann-Prozess, BD, Nr. 1437, IfZ, G 01. On deportations to Norway, and the fate of these prisoners, see WBSO, Ia, TB of July 31, 1942, T-311/175/0312; and Gen. Kdo. 71st Corps, Ic, September 1, 1943, T-501/316/176. On reports concerning prisoners, booty, and deportations carried out by the Kampfgruppe, see T-501/351/1079–1166. For an overview of the operation, see Duško Doder, *The Washington Post*, November 7, 1986, pp. 1, A32.

11. T-315/2258, divisional history, contains the relevant pages, and citation list, fr. 1471 et passim.

12. The documents relating to the award of the Zvonimir Medal can be consulted in Belgrade, in the Vojnoistoriski Institut Arhiv. The specific diploma is missing in Waldheim's case, but judging by those that survive, it would not yield much information. Relevant to this award are 714 I.D., Ia, TB for June 1942, T-315/2258/646; the Aktenvermerke for staff conferences held in Belgrade and Banja Luka, July 13–15, 1942, T-501/267/454–458; and Twelfth Army High Command, IIa, October 27, 1942, T-312/468/8157 (the latter summarizing German policy on foreign medals). General Stahl signed the Verleihungsliste Nr. 3 (with Waldheim's name on it) on August 6, 1942; Waldheim's *Urkunde* was sent to the military attaché for transmission to the recipient on December 1, 1942, along with seventy others. Waldheim says he does not recall receiving the medal itself.

13. Waldheim's statements, and those of his spokesman, between April 6 and October 29, 1986, are hard to reconcile. Some of them are alluded to in *Kurt Waldheim's Wartime Years*, Chapter VII.

14. Mr. L. Kadelburg and Col. Antun Miletić of Belgrade kindly discussed the deportation, and referred me to sources on the Jasenovac camp. It is clear to me that the presence of Gen. Stahl and his staff in Banja accelerated, and perhaps even caused the deportation of the Jews by the Croatians. This is especially true of German and Austrian refugees. Indeed, Gen. Stahl's Ic actively participated in the persecution of Jewish individuals. I obtained documentation about the Banja Luka deportation that supports this view: Regional Police Administration, April 8, 1942, T. 497/42, Br. Reg. 38/2 Fl K. 161a, and May 9, 1942, Br. Reg. 10/3-2 K. 162; and the command of the Second Domobranen Unit, July 20, 1942, #7344, Br. Reg. 51/3-1-2 K. 71 (Belgrade). Other documents detail the

entire process, which exactly coincided with the two Axis military operations in East and West Bosnia.

Chapter Five
Lilo, Kurt, and Professor Verdross

1. Ritschel's party membership number was 9027854. Joining the party at such a tender age was unusual, especially for a young woman. Such a move usually reflected fanatical commitment and ambition. Gerhard Oberschlick of *Forum* magazine, Vienna, conducted much of the research on Ritschel. See "Mag. Waldheim-Die Frau an seiner Seite," *Forum*, January/February 1987.

2. Alfred Verdross, *Die Völkerrechtswidrige Kriegshandlung und der Strafanspruch der Staaten* (Berlin: 1920). ["The Conduct of War Contrary to the Norms of International Law and the Punitive Recourse of States"] After World War II, Verdross resumed his illustrious career, once again contributing to international codification of war-crimes agreements. For biographical information on Verdross and on Dean Ernst Schönbauer, see Brigitte Pakes, *Beiträge zur Geschichte des Lehrkörpers der Juridischen Fakultät der Universität Wien Zwischen 1918 und 1938* (Vienna: 1981), pp. 237–239 and 211–213. Dr. Elisabeth Fechter-Petter, a former assistant to Verdross, recalled her encounter with Waldheim during the winter semester: letter to editor of the *Kurier* (Vienna), March 12, 1986.

3. Macholz's army personnel file was made available to me in the National Archives under a Freedom of Information Act request. This biographical information is based on that file.

4. A typical complaint about the Italians was the Reisebericht (signed Kühn) for the Zagreb legation, covering the late winter of 1942, T-120/2479/258851.

5. Kasche to AA, May 4, 1942, ibid., 258604.

6. Correspondence between Gen. Stahl and Bader's Ia, September 5–September 23, 1942, WB-2619.

7. T-315/2258/1478–1479; and Kasche to Glaise, October 20, 1942, T-120/5798/310542.

8. Rich, *Hitler's War Aims: The Establishment of the New Order* (New York: 1974), II, pp. 280–281.

9. On operations "White" and "Black," see Jozo Tomasevich, *The Chetniks: War and Revolution in Yugoslavia 1941–1945* (Stanford: 1975), pp. 243–252 et passim. On the German interest in this region, see the Reisebericht (signed Kühn) done for the Zagreb legation, T-120/2479/258551 ff.; Kasche's memorandum on the *Aufstandsbewegung*, dated May 4, 1942, ibid., 8604; and the unsigned report, dated June 2, 1943 (for Kasche, reporting on a trip through Bosnia and Herzegovina), T-120/5792/589123 ff.

10. See also Franz Schraml, *Kriegsschauplatz Kroatien* (Neckargemünd: 1962), p. 47 ff.

11. Some reports put the Axis forces at 127,000 men. See Fabijan Trgo, *Cetvrta i Peta Neprijatekjska Ofansiva* (Belgrade: 1968), pp. 84–86.

12. A report of the 1st Mountain Division reflects these grim realities: T-78/332/6289986.

13. On "Prinz Eugen," see Georg Tessin, *Verbände und Truppen der Deutschen Wehrmacht und Waffen SS im Zweiten Weltkrieg 1939–1945* (Frankfurt: n.d.), p. 7 ff.; Paul Hausser, *Waffen-SS im Einsatz* (Göttingen: 1953); and Heinz Höhne, *The Order of the Death's Head* (New York: 1966), pp. 527–531. There is a thick file on Phleps stored in the Berlin Document Center, West Berlin, which I obtained while researching his division. On the composition and strength of the division, see T-354/146/6905.

14. Alessandro Tassoni, *Prince Eugene of Savoy: An Italian Prince,* in T-120/2480/258638 ff.

15. On the course of the battle and the difficulties with the Italians: Tagesmeldungen des OBSO an das OKW, T-311/175/1394–1412. Also relevant is Governatorato del Montenegro, Ufficio Militare, T-821/250/16, 35–37.

16. Verbale della riunione tenuta a Podgorica . . . , Br. Reg. 37/3 K. 102 (Belgrade). For a reliable German view, see Otto Kumm's memoir, *Vorwärts Prinz Eugen* (Osnabruck: 1978), p. 76: "There then occurred a confrontation with the Italian army general, who demanded that he direct the entire operation, which was rejected by Gen. Lüters. It took a while to smooth over the waves, but forceful support from the Italians is not to be counted upon." Kumm was extremely close to Phleps.

Chapter Six
A Cog in the Machine

1. German overoptimism was reflected in diplomatic reports: see T-120/5792/589123 ff. On the newsreel: "Kroatische Jugend im Aufmarsch," Deutsche Wochenschau #671 (30/32), Library of Congress.

2. HRGE, Ia, TB (covering the period July 1–December 31, 1943), T-311/186/363–364; and T-501/33/129. Copies of Gyldenfeldt's and Willers's "201" personnel files are stored in the National Archives.

3. Gyldenfeldt to OBSO, T-311/119/1361–1370.

4. Information from the POW Military Intelligence Division, W.D.G.S., obtained by the OSS, June 3, 1943, RG 226/37382.

5. KTB and other documents of the Deutscher Generalstab bei der ital. 11 AOK, T-501/330–331 are major sources for information on this crisis. For the staff roster, see T-501/331/129.

6. T-821/24/645 ff.; and Howard M. Smythe, *Secrets of the Fascist Era* (Carbondale, IL: 1975), p. 138 et passim.

7. Message transcribed by Lt. Waldheim, August 4, 1943, T-314/670/257–258.

8. Ia (with Waldheim initial) to 11th Luftwaffe Field Division, August 22, 1943, T-501/330/1212.

9. BH Saloniki-Ägäis, TB for January 1–June 30, 1943, T-501/252/1116 ff.; and T-311/176/009.

10. NOKW-1887.

11. Order of August 10, 1943, NOKW-155.

12. Divisional report from Greece, August 12, 1943, T-315/66/456. Allied reports claimed that in September the Germans burned down forty villages in the Ionnina prefecture, rendering thirty-eight thousand people homeless: J.I.C.A.M.E. intelligence report of March 2, 1944, RG 226/62677. See also the testimony of General Napoleon Zervas in Athens, May 8, 1947, RG 238/5/5. On problems with the Italians over methods: 68th AK, KTB Nr. 3, July 1–December 31, 1943, WB-1509/1, and T-314/1539/180 ff.; and 1st Mountain Division to German liaison staff in Athens, August 14, 1943, T-501/331/16–17.

13. The DNB or German News Bureau circulated a report about the Salonika event in its Nr. 192 Eigendienst report of July 11, 1942. On July 14 the *Donauzeitung* ran an article that used this material: "Arbeit statt Diebstahl." A prominent photo of the "Juden-Musterung in Saloniki" appeared in the *Donauzeitung*, July 26, 1942, p. 3. The paper was widely read by German soldiers in Croatia and Serbia.

14. On the deportation policy: Police d'Israel, Quartier General, 6e Bureau/245 (IfZ); 12 AOK, Ia, Chefbesprechung am 30.11.42, T-312/468/204 ff.; and T-120/2721/421210–1. For an eyewitness account of the deportation process, see the testimony of Samuel Arrary, September 1946, YIVO Salonique. Raúl Hilberg, *The Destruction of the European Jews* (Chicago: 1967), p. 442 ff.; Gerald Reitlinger, *The Final Solution: The Attempt to Eliminate the Jews of Europe 1939–1945* (New York: 1953), p. 372 ff.; John Louis Hondros, *Occupation and Resistance: The Greek Agony 1941–1944* (New York: 1983), pp. 91–92; Michael Molho, *In Memoriam: Hommage aux Victimes Juives des Nazis en Grece* (Salonika: 1973), pp. 53–58; and Molho and Joseph Nehama, *The Destruction of Greek Jewry 1941–1944* (Jerusalem: 1965).

15. 1. Geb.-Div., monatliche Beurteilung, 15.8.43, T-311/179/1409–1411. The message of August 14 arrived in Athens at 5:25 P.M., and bears Waldheim's initial ("W").

16. Bestimmungen für die Führung von Kriegstagebüchern und Tätigkeitsberichten, OKH, Berlin, April 23, 1940.

17. *The Washington Post*, March 6, 1986. The OBSO assumed that all German liaison officers knew the policy on the Jewish question: T-501/259/99–104.

18. The relevant documentation may be consulted in T-501/330/1121–1141; T-501/331/313–314; and T-311/176/177–197 et passim.

19. An official Italian history of this process is Ministero della difesa, Le Operazioni della Unita italiane nel Settembre–Ottobre 1943 (Rome: 1975). Unfortunately, few records of the Italian 11th Army have survived.

20. Report by Abwehr Troop 390, T-501/259/642. On the labor mobilization: numerical estimates drawn up by the General Staff of the Army, December 10, 1943, contained in Walther Hubatsch, ed., *Kriegstagebuch des Oberkommandos der Wehrmacht* (Frankfurt: 1963), Vol. III, p. 1474 ff.; and Jochen August et al., *Herrenmensch und Arbeitsvölker: Ausländische Arbeiter und Deutsche 1939–1945* (Berlin: 1986). Waldheim's claim that he did not know that he was deporting the Italians flies in the face of the documents with his name or initial on them. The term *Abtransport* is constantly used, and it refers to sending away or deporting; the German equivalents for repatriation *(Heimbeförderung, Heimsendung,* and *Repatriierung)* never occur.

Chapter Seven
Dr. Waldheim

1. Warnstorff became Ic on August 8, 1943: T-311/186/363–364. Biographical information comes from his "201" file, obtained under a Freedom of Information Act request, and from postwar testimony by his fellow soldiers (Waldheim dossier, *Arhiv Jugoslavije*, Belgrade).

2. OSS materials in the National Archives contain a wealth of material on German procedures in Greece: see C.S.D.I.C. Interrogation Report on Greece, December 28, 1943, RG 226/57132. Ic interrogators and personnel, including Warnstorff and Lt. Helmut Poliza, worked closely with Abwehr Troops and Secret Field Police units. They visited their prisons, presumably in search of military intelligence from prisoners: Ic/AO to 22nd Mountain Corps, September 13, 1943, T-314/671/261; and Besprechung des Ic of December 14–15, 1943, T-311/178/347 ff.

3. WBHSO, 12 AOK, Ia, TB for January 1943 (entry for January 1, 1943), WB-1005a. On the new command structure, and its rationale: T-311/176/020 ff.; T-501/258/473; T-501/330/1213–1214; OKW, KTB, III, 1453–1454 ("Neugliederung im Südosten," August 18, 1943), and Kriegsgliederung 26.12.43, 1402–1403; and MBHSO, Vorläufige Dienstanweisung, T-78/332/9838.

4. Arbeitseinteilung, Stand 1. December 1943, Ausfertigung Nr. 45, T-311/181/003 et passim.

5. On the tasks, supply problems, and strength of the army group: Notizen zum Vortrag, HGE, December 6, 1943, T-311/175/0909; T-311/174/97 ff.; and Iststärkemeldung 1.5.44, T-311/180/092–094. The wide variations in numbers resulted from fluctuations in the strength (or even the presence) of Allied troop units, such as Italians or Bulgarians, as well as from German displacements or reinforcements.

6. Ic Lagebericht for October and November, 1943 (November 15, and December 5, 1943), T-311/178/370–393; and propaganda guidelines of September 3, and November 18, 1943, T-311/178/344–350.

7. WO 204/8850 contains information based on interrogations of escapees from Salonika. The reports made use of information assembled in July and August 1943.

8. Statement signed by President Franklin D. Roosevelt, Prime Minister Winston S. Churchill, and Premier J. V. Stalin (Mark Clark Papers, the Citadel Archives, Charleston, SC).

9. Karl Lechner, ed., *Donauländer und Burgenland* (Stuttgart: 1970), 2 vols.

10. OSS report no. NOI/80, May 19, 1943, 226/37294 and 71884. On Austrian life during this period, see Walter B. Maass, *Country Without a Name: Austria Under Nazi Rule 1938–1945* (New York: 1979).

11. This evaluation of Löhr rests in part on his own "Beantwortung der an mich gerichteten kriegsgeschichtlichen Fragen," composed in a Belgrade prison after the war (Arhiv Jugoslavije, Belgrade), and the file on Löhr in the Berlin Document Center. D. J. Diakow,

assist Lohr or the army group, he failed. On the other hand, it was during these last weeks that Western intelligence became aware of Kurt Waldheim, and this explains his subsequent stay in Bad Tölz.

Part Two
The Man Without a Past

Chapter Ten
To the Ballhausplatz

1. Waldheim, *In the Eye of the Storm,* p. 19; I have also used information supplied by Dr. Waldheim, and his personal secretary, Dr. Ralph Scheide (letter to the author, April 9, 1987). On the activities of the OSS in Austria during this period, see Monthly Report, OSS Austria, 13 September 1945, William Donovan Papers, Box 16C, U.S. Army Military History Institute Archives, Carlisle Military Barracks, Carlyle, PA. The OSS supplied "well over ninety percent of all but CI intelligence put out G-2."

2. Martin F. Herz, "Allied Occupation of Austria: The Early Years," in Robert A. Bauer, ed., *The Austrian Solution: International Conflict and Cooperation* (Charlottesville, VA: 1982), pp. 20–40.

3. F.S.V. Donnison, *Civil Affairs and Military Government North-west Europe, 1944–1946* (London: 1961). Karl Gruber, *Between Liberation and Liberty* (London: 1955), p. 35; Marie-Émile Béthouart, *La Bataille pour l'Autriche* (Paris: 1966), p. 75. By late 1946 the Soviets had seized about seventy thousand hectares of land, claiming that they consisted of "former German property": FO 371/55116.

4. FO 1020/2011.

5. Heinrich Siegler, *Austria: Problems and Achievements Since 1945* (Bonn: 1969), p. 8.

6. On the Western position in regard to Austria, see the Civil Affairs Guide on the Administrative Separation of Austria from Germany, War Department Pamphlet No. 31-229 (Washington: 1945). For an analysis of the Renner government, see U.S. Group, Control Council Austria, May 2, 1945, 226/X1 (OSS papers); and the Report on the Provisional Government of Austria, May 5, 1945, p. 23 (OSS #3091), Carlyle Military Barracks, Carlyle, PA On the new Austrian government, see the memorandum of Edgar N. Johnson, 17 July, 1945, and the OSS Research and Analysis Report No. 3, "The Question of Recognizing the Renner Government," in the Paul Sweet Collection, Modern Military Branch, National Archives. The Mark Clark Papers at the Citadel Archives, dealing with Austria 1945–1947, are important. Particularly noteworthy is Reinhold Wagnleitner, ed., *Understanding Austria: The Political Reports and Analyses of Martin F. Herz* (Salzburg: 1984). Herz was a brilliant, German-speaking foreign-service officer active in the Vienna legation. His analyses of Austrian politics during the postwar period are superb. On the Länderkonferenz and the Renner government: Wilfried Aichinger, *Sowjetische Österreichpolitik 1943–1945* (Vienna: 1977).

7. Some of these documents are reproduced in the "White Book," *Kurt Waldheim's Wartime Years: A Documentation,* pp. 111, 126 et passim.

8. Allied Council decisions of September 11, September 20, October 1, October 8, and November 10, RG 84/Vienna Security 1945/33/360.

9. RG 226/136462; U.S. Group, Control Council Austria, May 2, 1945, RG 226/X1 9513; RG 59/740.00119 Control (Austria), 10-2645; and memorandum by M. F. Herz to the Senior Military Officer, Political Division, USACA, in Wagnleitner, *Understanding Austria,* p. 40.

10. U.S. Group, Control Council Austria, May 2, 1945, 226/X1 9513; and memoranda by Herz, in Wagnleitner, *Understanding Austria,* pp, 32, 66 et passim. For Fischer's account, see *Das Ende Einer Illusion* (Vienna: 1973).

11. Mack to Bevin, January 12, 1946, FO 371/55135. See Radomir V. Luza, *The Resistance in Austria, 1938–1945* (Minneapolis: 1984), p. 184 et passim.

12. OSS reports on Gruber: RG 226/134356; 142257C; X1 28035; and 13408C (R&A Report No. 10).

13. Luza, *Resistance,* p. 210 ff.; Joseph E. Persico, *Piercing the Reich* (New York: 1979), p. 94 ff.; and Fritz Molden, *Exploding Star: A Young Austrian Against Hitler* (New York: 1979), pp. 263–269.

14. The Department of the Army controls many of the files on Gruber. Under a Freedom of Information Act request I obtained all or parts of XA 161 171; XA 161 471 I5 C056; 430th C.I.C., Box 39; 66th, Box 204; XA 115 435 I5A023. For examples of the type of information Gruber supplied to the Americans, see RG 59/863.918/12–745.

15. Karl Gruber, *Ein Politisches Leben: Österreichs Weg Zwischen den Diktatoren* (Vienna: 1976).

16. Karl Gruber cited by *The New York Times,* April 25, 1986; and Fritz Molden, cited by the same paper, April 26, 1986. It is interesting that in 1948 an American report on Molden advised, "Use him for contacts and pleasure, but never use any intelligence from him without checking": Memorandum on Political Contacts, U.S. legation, Vienna, December 6, 1948, RG 84/Vienna Security 1948/20/800.

17. Mack to Bevin, January 3, 1946, FO 371/55141; and Gruber, *Liberation,* p. 39.

18. For Gruber's policy on the South Tyrol: Fonoff minute, January 4, 1946, FO 371/55135, and minute of June 4, 1946, FO 371/55122. The British were less enthusiastic about Gruber than were the Americans. They knew he was tied to U.S. intelligence, and the Foreign Office also resented his blatant attempts to push the Allies into a confrontation with Italy over the South Tyrol issue.

19. For a good overview of Gruber's aims, policies, and enthusiasms: Polad to Secstate, July 12, 1945, 59/740.00119 Control (Austria)/7–1245; evaluation of Gruber for State Department, October 26, 1945, ibid., 10-2645; Fonoff to Mack, January 29, 1946, FO 371/55135; and Vienna legation to Secstate, November 27, 1946, RG 59/763.00/11-2746. See also Gruber, *Liberation,* pp. 80–83.

17. Waldheim, *In the Eye of the Storm,* p. 19. The best guide to Waldheim's whereabouts during the war is his Soldbuch, though it, too, may not always be accurate to the day.

18. Von Weichs to commanders in his sector, August 27, 1944, T-311/185/821–825.

19. Aktennotiz, detailing the high-level intelligence Lt. Waldheim received about the new Bulgarian government, T-311/180/056; Beckerle to AA, September 6, 1944, T-120/764/ 358036–037; and Ia, KTB, Aktennotiz über die Chefbesprechung, September 19, 1944, T-311/179/425–426. See Gerhard Hümmelchen, "Balkanräumung 1944," *Wehrwissenschaftliche Rundschau* (1959).

20. One of the most impressive, large-scale strategic retreats in history was now under way, and Waldheim was a participant and chronicler: T-311/179/437; Waldheim f.d.R. to OBSO, September 28, 1944, T-311/179/108; T-311/185/9–14; T-311/186/ 1050–1051; T-311/183/005 ff.; T-311/183/020–021. On the dissolution of the territorial command in Greece: Auflösung Mil. Bfh. Griechenland, T-311/184/ 1010–1011.

21. Cited by Stephen Clissold, ed., *Yugoslavia and the Soviet Union 1939–1973, a Documentary Survey* (London: 1975), p. 161.

22. T-77/1419/640–646.

23. KTB of the Ninety-first Army Corps, T-314/1630/002 ff.; and Hammer's order of October 18, 1944, T-311/186/031. The interrogation of von Weichs is a useful guide to the German attitude toward Zervas: RG 332/108.

24. See especially the Zusatz, October 12, 1944, T-311/183/630; and KTB for October 14, 1944, T-311/183/68–69.

Chapter Nine
The Final Retreat

1. Karl Hnilicka, *Das Ende auf dem Balkan 1944/45* (Göttingen: 1970), provides a good narrative history of the retreat. Schmidt-Richberg's memoir is useful, but lacks detail: *Der Endkampf auf dem Balkan* (Heidelberg: 1955).

2. Warnstorff's report, signed by Schmidt-Richberg, November 3, 1944, T-311/184/681; and report of November 10, 1944, ibid., 541.

3. For examples of the type of intelligence processed by Waldheim, and required by Warnstorff: Zusatz Ic/AO zur Tagemeldung, November 5, 1944, T-311/184/638–639; Zusatz, November 7, 1944, T-311/184/0582; and Warnstorff's Fernschreiben, November 12, 1944, T-311/184/437.

4. KTB, November 15, 1944, T-311/183/208.

5. Heeresgruppenintendant E, November 16, 1944 (Bericht), T-311/184/370 ff.

6. RG 226/GB 4000, Box 81, Entry 108.

7. On the Warnstorff special staff, see T-311/184/311–353, and T-311/185/584. For a geographical orientation on the retreat: T-311/184/0520.

8. Hammer to corps chiefs, November 28, 1944, T-311/184/101.

9. For example: T-311/184/228–262, et passim, and ibid., 116–117.

10. Morgenmeldung, November 29, 1944, T-311/184/083; and Morgenmeldung, November 25, 1944, ibid., 161. Dr. Otto Vicenzi supplied the author with further information about Waldheim's duties toward the end of the war: letter to the author, April 8, 1987.

11. T-311/186/381–383, 415, 639. Waldheim initialed the covering letter on one batch of propaganda pamphlets on November 28, 1944. On December 26 propaganda company 690 was made directly subordinate to the army group Ic/Ao: T-311/185/152.

12. On *Die Wacht im Südosten*, see T-311/178/0343–0359. This newspaper was widely read by German soldiers in the Balkans: T-311/178/343–359.

13. See Waldheim's report of December 22, 1944, where he speaks of "Max" and "Franz": T-311/185/70.

14. Morgenmeldung, December 21, 1944, T-311/185/47–48; Feindeseelagebericht usw, December 24, 1944, ibid., 130–138; Morgenmeldung, December 20, 1944, ibid., 35–36; 91st AK, Ia, to HRGE, Ia, January 1, 1945, T-314/1630/761–764.

15. Löhr's message to his commanders, December 23, 1944, T-311/185/80–81; and ibid., 120–122.

16. Löhr continued to use National Socialist rhetoric in his appeals to his troops: Order of the Day, December 27, 1944, T-311/185/163: The army group had prevailed in "hard and victorious battle against treacherous bands, treasonous former allies and the Bolshevik mortal enemy. . . . Forward over graves! Long live the Führer!"

17. See also "Agram in the Winter of 1945," *Donauzeitung*, February 9, 1945.

18. Stephen Clissold, *Whirlwind: An Account of Marshal Tito's Rise to Power* (New York: 1949), p. 224 ff. German intelligence had warned as early as December 21 that rumors about the evacuation of Croatia by the Wehrmacht were spreading among the population: Warnstorff directive of December 21, 1944, T-311/185/50. On the final battles and collapse of the army group, see Manfried Rauchensteiner, *Krieg in Österreich 1945* (Vienna: 1970), pp. 320–363.

19. OSS report, transmitted by U.S. Political Advisor on Austrian Affairs, July 14, 1945, RG 59/740.00119 Control (Austria)/7-1445.

20. Notes prepared by the Headquarters of the British Army, FO 1020/19.

21. Löhr hoped that reestablished Austria, under Western control, would continue to be a bulwark against Bolshevism. See also Manfried Rauchensteiner, *Der Sonderfall: Die Besatzungszeit in Österreich 1945 bis 1955* (Graz: 1979), p. 58 ff.

22. Waldheim's Soldbuch is the source for his whereabouts (or purported whereabouts) during these last days. There is a good possibility that Löhr sent Waldheim due west toward the British army nearing Trieste, but that Waldheim did not get through, whereupon he headed north toward Klagenfurt. As an English-speaking, non-Nazi intelligence officer, Waldheim may have been on a mission to the Western Allies. Löhr was desperately trying to avoid having to surrender to the Communists. If Waldheim's mission was to

Generaloberst Alexander Löhr (Freiburg: 1964), p. 42 et passim, is highly favorable to the general. On the "liberal" atmosphere permitted by Löhr, see the letter of Dr. Med. Kurt Groeschel to Gerhard Waldheim, March 1986 (Groeschel was the Ia/Org. in the IV/b [medical department] in Arsakli). Gerhard Waldheim supplied me with one of the (mildly) anti-Nazi poetic satires that presumably circulated among Löhr's staff.

12. Information about these medals and decorations comes from Waldheim's own pay-book.

13. Yugoslav interrogations of Robert Voigt and Markus Hartner, Waldheim dossier, Arhiv Jugoslavije, Belgrade.

14. Ic/AO Feind-Nachrichtenblatt Nr. 3 (December 1943), IfZ Archive, 1043/53.

15. Wende's report "Bericht über meinen Aufenthalt in Athen vom 2.4. bis 6 (illegible)" 1944, IfZ, 1043/53.

16. On the important information concerning intelligence, propaganda, and Abwehr available to Waldheim: Hammer on Abwehr and propaganda, T-311/175/955–956; Abwehrtrupp 376 to HRGE, Ic/AO, T-311/284/0218; HRGE, Ia, to OBSO, July 8, 1944, T-311/284/0115; T-311/284/027–132 et passim; T-311/179/887; and Hubatsch, KTB des OKW, IV, i, 665 ff.

17. J.I.C.A.M.E. Intelligence Report, March 2, 1944, RG 226/62677; and *Trials of War Criminals Before the Nürnberg Military Tribunal* (Washington: 1950), X, 1030 ff.

18. Speidel (MBH Griechenland) to Löhr, January 18, 1944, T-311/179/1256–1258.

19. Interview with Fritz P. Molden, Vienna, June 10, 1987.

20. Kurt Waldheim, *Die Reichsidee bei Konstantin Frantz. Inaugural—Dissertation zur Erlangung des Doktorgrades der Rechts—und Staatswissenschaftlichen Fakultät der Universität Wien* (Vienna: 1944).

21. Léon Poliakov, *The Aryan Myth: A History of Racist and Nationalist Ideas in Europe* (New York: 1977), p. 306 ff. On Frantz's anti-Semitism: Hans Kohn, *The Mind of Germany* (New York: 1960), p. 276.

22. Robert E. Herzstein, *When Nazi Dreams Come True* (London: 1982), treats the "European Idea" as promulgated by Nazi theoreticians and propagandists. For insights into Verdross's basic ideas and his attitudes toward his work: Alfred Verdross, "On the Concept of International Law," *American Journal of International Law* (1949), p. 435 ff., and L. Adamovich, "Alfred Verdross—ein Lebensbild," in *Jus Humanitatis, Festschrift zum 90. Geburtstag von Alfred Verdross* (Vienna: 1980).

Chapter Eight
A Changed Man

1. Neubacher to Ribbentrop, May 15, 1944; Altenburg to Wagner, May 18, 1944; Leiter Inland II to Ritter, June 26, 1944; memorandum by von Thadden on the OKW's dilatory response, July 13, 1944: AA, Politisches Archiv, Inland II geheim (Griechenland 1941–1944).

2. Chef Vortrag, T-311/175/0922; T-311/177/1363.

3. Feind-Nachrichtenblatt Nr. 8 (March/April 1944), May 1, 1944, IfZ 1043/53. Waldheim initialed this report (p. 1, top right).

4. Report of May 24, 1944, T-314/1458/066.

5. Feind-Nachrichtenblatt Nr. 9 (April/May 1944), May 25, 1944, IfZ 1043/53. For an expression of similar doubts (by another individual), see T-311/175/0922. Many German staff officers realized that indiscriminate killing created recruits for the bands. Few said so on a typed page intended for their superiors.

6. Bradley F. Smith, *The Shadow Warriors* (New York: 1983), pp. 234–235.

7. NOKW-2009.

8. Ic/AO, TB for July 1944 (August 1, 1944), T-311/186/0341.

9. T-311/285/1183–1185; NOKW-227; NOKW-1791. Several interrogation protocols drawn up by German commands in Greece survived the war, as part of the files of Army Group F. We thus know a good deal about Carpenter, Lisgaris, and others: T-311/285/1094–1107 et passim.

10. Letter of foreign secretary Sir Geoffrey Howe to Greville Janner, M.P., August 1, 1986. Ic/AO's shortage of English translators makes Waldheim's service as an interpreter during interrogations likely: report of Ic conference, T-311/189/357.

11. James Doughty, an American medic captured on the island of Kalymnos during the night of July 1, 1944, was interrogated in Salonika on July 17. Doughty survived the war in a POW camp in Germany. Waldheim drew up the report on his interrogation: WB-2623.

12. Relevant documentation deeply implicates Ic/AO of the army group in these deportations: Abstransport Juden (March 15, 1944), WB-921; WB-917; NOKW-885; Korpsgruppe Ionnina, Ic, to HRGE Ic/AO, April 28, 1944, T-1119/26/0424; T-314/1458/062–063; BH der Sipo und des SD für Griechenland, Aussenstelle Ionnina, to Gen. Kdos. XXII Geb. AK, June 17, 1944, T-314/1458/069. See also Michael Molho, *In Memoriam: Homage aux Victimes Juives des Nazis en Grèce* (Salonika: 1973), p. 226, and Raúl Hilberg, *The Destruction of the European Jews* (New York: 1953), pp. 450–452.

13. John Louis Hondros, *Occupation and Resistance*, p. 93.

14. TB for July–September 1944, T-311/186/337 ff. For obvious reasons, Waldheim's defenders have built a high wall between Ic and AO. They rest their shaky case in part on the postwar testimony of POW Markus Hartner—who, an Ic man himself, wanted to make sure that his Yugoslav captors did not implicate him in the Abwehr's dirty work.

15. Korpsgruppe Saloniki, Ic, "Zusammenfassende Stellungnahme," July 17, 1944, IfZ, 1043/53; OSS Dissemination No. a-27764, May 22, 1944; Dissemination No. a-31177, June 29, 1944, RG 226/72859; and IVb, Beitrag zur Besprechung, May 20, 1944, T-311/177/1185–1186.

16. For example, on August 4 and August 9, 1944, Waldheim reported on the situation in France, Italy, the Balkans, and the Far East: T-311/175/0975 et passim.

Chapter Eleven
Denazification

1. Statement by the Austrian ministry of the interior, for 1946, FO 1020/168. See also Dieter Stiefel, *Entnazifizierung in Österreich* (Vienna: 1981); Oliver Rathkolb, "U.S.-Entnazifizierung in Österreich zwischen kontrollierter Revolution und Elitenrestauration (1945–1949), *Zeitgeschichte*, XI, 9/10, 302 ff. According to Rathkolb, 8.1 percent of the Austrian population had been members of the NSDAP. See also Robert Knight, "Britische Entnazifizierungspolitik 1945–1949," ibid., 287 ff. 270,000 former Nazis had lost their jobs by July 4, 1946, some temporarily.

2. Donald R. Whitnah and Edgar L. Erickson, *The American Occupation of Austria: Planning and Early Years* (Westport, CN: 1985), pp. 219–221.

3. Stiefel, *Entnazifizierung*, p. 152 et passim.

4. Substitute paragraph 2 (to ALCO/P (46) 27), FO 1020/167/107998; Figl to Allied Commission for Austria, Ref #665-Pr/1946, FO 1020/107998; and Allied Commission, Excomm, February 13, 1946, loc. cit.

5. Kurt Waldheim an das Wohnungsamt der Stadt Wien (received February 21, 1946), Haus-, Hof- u. Staatsarchiv, BKA, AA, Kabinettsakten Gruber 1946, Zl. 169.

6. Tagebuch in dem Verfahren zur Beurteilung . . . Dr. Kurt Waldheim, Aktenzeichen VD 235/SK 235.

7. Denazification Bureau of Allied Council to Quadripartite Internal Affairs Division, July 5, 1946, FO 1020/168; and Excomm draft resolution of July 6, 1946, in response to the Austrian government, loc. cit.

8. Stiefel, *Entnazifizierung*, p. 95; "White Book," *Kurt Waldheim's Wartime Years: A Documentation*, p. 84 ff.

9. See *Foreign Relations of the United States 1947, II, Council of Foreign Ministers for Germany and Austria*, 112 ff.

10. "Austrian personalities," FO 371/63944.

11. *Wiener Zeitung*, January 26, 1947; FO 371/6569.

12. *Wiener Zeitung*, January 22–February 2, 1947. On the Yugoslav claims, see Rear Hqrs. 37th Military Mission, re Signal CO/912, March 15, 1945, in the Mark Clark Papers; Karl Gruber, *Liberation*, p. 96; *Wiener Zeitung*, January 22, 1947; CFM, U.S. Delegation, Minutes of the 4th Meeting of the Deputies for Austria, January 22, 1947, in the Mark Clark Papers (Austria/1947). The Yugoslavs circulated a pamphlet entitled *Slovene Carinthia and the Burgenland Croats: The Question of 200,000 Yugoslavs in Austria* (Belgrade: 1947). See also CFM/D/47/A/9 (January 20, 1947), in the Mark Clark Papers, Citadel Archives.

13. Piesch had allegedly signed a letter in 1942, produced by the Nazi teachers' union in Villach, calling for the collection of salvage materials for the war effort. On the conference, see *Wiener Zeitung*, February 15–16, 1947; Clark to Secstate, February 17, 1947, FRUS, II, 132; Gruber, *Liberation*, pp. 93–94; and Manfried Rauchensteiner, *Der Sonderfall: Die Besatzungszeit in Österreich 1945 bis 1955*, pp. 88, 199.

14. For a good summary of the negotiations, see *Keesing's Contemporary Archives* [1947], pp. 8583–8584; and Gruber, *Liberation,* pp. 98–109.

Chapter Twelve
Power Politics

1. Edward Kardelj, *Der Übermacht zum Trotz* (Klagenfurt: 1984), p. 77 et passim.

2. U.S. Delegation Working Paper on Slovene Carinthia, Draft No. 1, 4 April 1947, Mark Clark Papers/Moscow Conference/1947; and interview with General Mark W. Clark, Charleston, SC, September 27, 1965, John Foster Dulles Oral History Project, Princeton University Library. Of special use are Thomas M. Barker, *The Slovene Minority of Carinthia* (New York: 1984), p. 203 ff.; and Robert Knight, "Die Kärnthner Grenzfrage und der kalte Krieg," *Carinthia I,* Jg. 175, 323 ff., and "British Policy towards Occupied Austria 1945–1955" (thesis, U. of London, 1986), Chapter 4.

3. Marshall via Acheson, April 22, 1947, RG 59/740.00119 (Council) Austria/4-2227. See Audrey K. Cronin, *Great Power Politics and the Struggle over Austria 1945–1955* (London: 1986), pp. 45–46.

4. Kardelj, supported by his colleagues Vilfan and Vladimir Dedijer, head of the Yugoslav Information Bureau, spoke on April 17; Gruber gave his reply the next day.

5. Comment by Burrows, June 6, 1947, concerning a telegram from Mack dated June 3, 1947, FO 371/64047. See also: the papers of Walter Wodak, in R. Wagnleitner, *Diplomatie Zwischen Parteiproporz und Weltpolitik* (Salzburg: 1980), p. 942 ff.; and Manfried Rauchensteiner, *Der Sonderfall: Die Besatzungszeit in Österreich 1945 bis 1955,* p. 200. After the break between Tito and Stalin, the debate over who double-crossed whom over Carinthia became intense: see Margaret Carlyle, ed., *Documents on International Affairs 1949–1950* (London: 1953), p. 453 ff. Ambassador Walter Bedell Smith had this to say about the Moscow Conference: "it was clear that the Soviet Union would abandon its advocacy of Yugoslav claims at once if the Kremlin's definition of what constituted 'German assets' in Austria . . . was accepted by the Western Allies": W. B. Smith, *My Three Years in Moscow* (Philadelphia: 1950), p. 226. The Yugoslavs were becoming more strident and desperate; they now connected their Carinthian demands to the war-crimes question: Yugoslav War Crimes Commission, *Report on the Crimes of Austria and the Austrians Against Yugoslavia and Her Peoples* (Belgrade: 1947).

6. FRUS, 1947, II, 587–675; Adolf Schärf, *Österreichs Erneurung 1945–1955* (Vienna: n.d.), p. 166; and *The Times* (London), May 8, 1947.

7. FO 371/63974.

8. H. E. Pomeroy to Figl, May 2, 1946, FO 1020/349, and British Element, Deputy Commissioner's Conference, December 10, 1947, FO 371/70390, contain examples of Figl's problems; see also Rankin to Secstate, June 7, 1947, FRUS 1947, II, 1182 ff., and Charge to Secstate, June 27, 1947, RG 59/863.00/6-2747; and Karl Gruber, *Liberation,* p. 137.

9. FRUS, 1947, II, 580–585 et passim.; and Erhardt to Secstate, June 26, 1947, FRUS, 1947, II, 1185. See also Patricia B. Eggleston, *The Marshall Plan in Austria: A Study in American Containment of the Soviet Union in the Cold War* (U. of Alabama, Ph.D. dissertation: 1980), pp. 132–133; and Cronin, *Great Power Politics,* p. 53.

10. American legation to Secstate, July 9, 1947, on the reorganization of the Austrian foreign ministry, RG 84/Vienna Security/9/800.2.

11. American legation to Secstate, November 17, 1947, RG 59/863.00/11-1747; and Gruber, *Liberation*, p. 77.

12. See the Fonoff note of November 3, 1947, on the Austrian delegation, FO 371/64146; and *The Times* (London), December 11, 1947.

13. Summary of the London negotiations by the U.S. Forces in Austria, December 29, 1947, RG 84/Polad/USCOA/2/711. Gruber justified his policy in the *Wiener Kurier*, December 13, 1947.

14. Erhardt to Secstate, February 28, 1947, RG 59/740.00116EW/2-2847; minute by H. Freeman Matthews, March 1, 1947, ibid., 1-647; Heath in Berlin to Secstate, April 12, 1947, ibid., 4-1247; and Belgrade to Secstate, April 26, 1947, ibid., 4-2647. On internal British and American debate over the wisdom of their extradition policies, see Cabot memorandum of February 25, 1947, FRUS, 1947, IV, 765 ff.; legation to Fonoff, May 5, 1947, FO 371/67376; Cabot to Secstate, May 15, 1947, FRUS, 1947, IV, 799–800; and Walworth Barbour to Peter Solly-Flood, May 19, 1947, RG 59/740.00116/EW/5-547 (5-247 is also relevant).

15. Belgrade to Secstate, March 13, 1947, ibid., 3-1347.

16. Col. P.L.M. Carolet to Figl, November 5, 1947, RG 84/USCOA/Excomm Proceedings/1945–1955/16; and Austrian Ministry of Justice to the Allied Council, December 2, 1947, FO 371/63997.

17. Fonoff to Vienna legation, June 16, 1947, and Draft Agreement between Britain and Yugoslavia on the latter's liaison mission, July 15, 1947, FO 1020/2011; RG 165/Civil Affairs Division/250.401 War Crimes, section xvi (July 11, 1947 to July 31, 1947), and ibid., C.A.D. files, box 304/entry 463; and for extradition figures, RG 59/740.00116/EW/10-2647, and RG 84/Vienna Security/1947/4/200.

18. Yugoslav allegations against, and indictment, of Oskar Turina are contained in the records of the Arhiv Hrvatske, in Zagreb, as well as in the Arhiv Jugoslavije, Belgrade. See Odluka 13.458; war-crimes documentation in the files of the State Commission of War Crimes; and correspondence with the U.S. authorities in Austria, covering the period October 1947 through April 1948. The extradition board records of the U.S. Forces in Austria may be consulted at the National Archives, in Suitland, MD. See also Secstate to Vienna, June 9, 1947, RG 84/Polad/ALCOA/1947/7. Some American diplomats, such as John M. Cabot in Belgrade, protested the shameful policy of protecting fugitive war criminals: Cabot to Secstate, June 12, 1947, RG 59/740.00116 EW/6-1147 ("we are apparently conniving with Vatican and Argentina to get guilty people [to safe havens]." See also Papers of John M. Cabot, Microfilm Reel #6 (1947), Harry S Truman Library, Independence, MO.

19. United Nations General Assembly, 1947, A/425, on the Yugoslavs' draft resolution.

Chapter Thirteen
Conspiracy in Belgrade

1. Undated memorandum (signature illegible) to the chairman of the legal department, Secret No. 3939/47, A.J.

2. See the resolution in FO 1020/200.

3. *History of the United Nations War Crimes Commission and the Development of the Laws of War,* compiled by the commission (London: 1948), p. 158.

4. *History of the UNWCC,* p. 119. On dispatching commission representatives to Allied Headquarters, April/May 1945: FO 1020/200. The commission never became an investigatory body: Brown in the Department of State to Fahy, January 6, 1947, RG 59/740.-00116 EW/1-647. In rare cases Committee I itself initiated and filed charges: *History of the UNWCC,* p. 122. Relevant records of the UNWCC are in the Predecessor Archive Group, UNWCC, 1943–1949, PAG-3.

5. Ibid., p. 482.

6. On prima facie cause: UNWCC memoranda of March 29 and August 1, 1945, WO 219/3585.

7. Löhr's notorious order of August 10, 1943, on deportations and reprisals, specifically granted field commanders the right to order reprisals: NOKW-155.

8. Bjelić to the ministry of foreign affairs, December 12, 1947, Secret 3939/47. At this time there were over ten thousand Austrians in Yugoslav captivity, so the search for more evidence against Waldheim continued. See K. W. Böhme, *Die Deutschen Kriegsgefangenen in Jugoslawien 1941–1949* (Munich: 1962), p. 278.

9. Odluka on "Waldheim (Kurt?)," F number 25572, Arhiv Jugoslavije, Belgrade.

10. "White Book," *Kurt Waldheim's Wartime Years: A Documentation,* p. 55, note 32. The massacre in question cost 114 Macedonians their lives. For survivors' testimony, see Andrew Nagorski, *Newsweek,* April 21, 1986, p. 33.

11. Dr. Dušan Nedeljković to the ministry of foreign affairs, December 26, 1947, Top Secret No. 3939/47.

12. On Committee I's work in January, see the UNWCC report of March 3, 1948, RG 153/1650/150-4b.

13. Hartner's statements are preserved in the Waldheim "Odluka" dossier in the Arhiv Jugoslavije, Belgrade.

14. Springer to Secstate, January 13, 1948, RG 59/740.00116 EW/1-1348.

15. Neale to Bevin, January 14, 1948, FO 371/70408; Vienna to Fonoff, April 3, 1948, ibid.; Erhardt's summary of these threats and incidents, written on June 4, 1948, is contained in RG 84/Polad/USCOA/1948/22.

16. Galloway to Bevin, March 25, 1948, FO 1020/453. U.S. summary of the security situation in Austria, July 1, 1948, RG 84/Vienna Security/1948/20/800.

17. Neale to Bevin, January 14, 1948, FO 371/70408; legation to Secstate, January 19, 1948, RG 59/740.00119/Control (Austria)/1-174; Ward to Fonoff, March 11, 1948, FO 371/70452; and the *Arbeiter-Zeitung,* January 20, 1948.

18. Summary in Vienna legation to secstate, June 4, 1948, RG 59/740.00119/Control (Austria)/6-448. See also Ulrike Metz, *Geschichte der Wiener Polizei-Direktion vom Jahre 1945 bis zum Jahre 1955 mit Berücksichtigung der Zeit vor 1945* (Ph.D. dissertation, Vienna: 1971), pp. 563–565.

Chapter Fourteen
Off the Hook

1. Sir Alfred Brown, minute of conversation with Josef Gerö, February 22, 1948, FO 1020/3460.

2. RG 59/740.00116 EW/8-2147; and *History of the UNWCC,* pp. 364–379.

3. Vienna to Secstate, February 15, 1948, RG 59/740.00119 Control (Austria)/2-1448; Vienna to Secstate, February 26, 1948, RG 84/Vienna Security/1948/20/800; minute by M. F. Cullis, April 7, 1948, FO 371/70408; Vienna to Secstate, April 15, 1948, RG 59/740.00119 Control (Austria)/4-1548; and Erhardt to Secstate, April 21, 1948, loc. cit. See also *The Times* (London), March 6, 1948, quoting Karl Gruber, and Rauchensteiner, *Der Sonderfall: Die Besatzungszeit in Österreich 1945 bis 1955,* pp. 227–229.

4. Minute by R. C. Foy, January 9, 1948, FO 371/70411.

5. Reber to Secstate, April 5, 1948, FRUS, 1948, II (Washington: 1973), 1488–1490; and Marshall to Reber, April 30, 1948, ibid., 1501.

6. See *Neues Österreich,* April 27–30, 1948, for interesting analyses of the Yugoslav proposals.

7. Report by Martin F. Herz, July 30, 1948, in Wagnleitner, *Understanding Austria,* p. 448; and Gruber, *Liberation,* pp. 149–155.

8. Reber to Secstate, Secstate to Reber, both on May 6, 1948, and Reber to Secstate, May 8, 1948, FRUS, 1948, II, 1502–1505 et passim.; and Yost to Erhardt, May 21, 1948, RG 84/Vienna Security/1948/20/800.

9. C.I.C. report (Braunau), July 15, 1948, IRR file/02/004145 (Yugoslav crisis, box 1). Useful are Vladimir Dedijer, *The Battle That Stalin Lost: Memoirs of Yugoslavia 1948–1953* (New York: 1971); Stephen Clissold, ed., *Yugoslavia and the Soviet Union 1939–1973, A Documentary Survey* (London: 1975); Adam B. Ulam, *Titoism and the Cominform* (Cambridge, MA: 1952); and Robert Bass and Elizabeth Murray, *The Soviet and Yugoslav Controversy, 1948–1958: A Documentary Record* (New York: 1959).

10. *Wiener Tageszeitung,* August 4, 1948; and *Wiener Kurier,* August 11, 1948.

11. Cables concerning Yugoslavia, Vienna legation and Secstate, June 29–July 21, 1948, in RG 84/Vienna Security/1948/22/800 (Yugoslavia); conference with Gruber at the American legation, Vienna, reported on October 25, 1948, in RG 84/USCOA/Polad/1948/19; British legation to Fonoff, September 8, 1948, FO 371/70466; and Fonoff to Cheetham, September 27, 1948, FO 371/70452. See also Gruber, *Liberation,* pp. 157–161.

12. On Mayer's character, testimony, and subsequent career, see the affidavits by Rosa Mayer and Franz Kaupe, "White Book," *Kurt Waldheim's Wartime Years,* pp. 253–259. This was neither the first nor the last time that the Yugoslavs used the UNWCC lists for political purposes. After the war Belgrade had listed al-Hajj Amin, the Grand Mufti of Jerusalem, "for inciting brutalities and for pro-German activities among the Bosnian Moslems." Belgrade dropped the case as a result of pressure from the Arab League: J. C. Hurewitz, *The Struggle for Palestine* (New York: 1950), pp. 234–235.

Chapter Fifteen
The Man Without a Past

1. *History of the UNWCC*, p. 6.

2. Lisl Alker, *Verzeichnis der an der Universität Wien Approbierten Dissertationen 1937–1944* (Vienna: 1954).

3. Confidential-Security Information, Biographic Data, A-18, Dr. Kurt Waldheim, declassification date February 5, 1987. Waldheim himself has stated that "To mention the fact of one's military service is all that is expected [in Austria, on official forms]": see United States Congress, 99th Congress, Second Session, April 22, 1986, p. 49.

4. *Who's Who in Austria* (Zürich: 1955), entry "Waldheim, Kurt."

5. *Current Biography Yearbook*, 1972.

6. "Ein Präsident neuen Stils," Waldheim-Pressedienst, February 1, 1971 (proprietor, editor, and publisher: Dr. Kurt Waldheim. Responsible for the contents: Johann Ellinger).

7. *The New York Times*, "The new UN Secretary-General, Kurt Waldheim," December 22, 1971.

8. The "White Book" (*Kurt Waldheim's Wartime Years: A Documentation*) contains correspondence and statements concerning the alleged deletions omitted from the English-language edition of the memoir, p. 269.

9. "Lebenslauf" Dr. Kurt Waldheim.

10. Waldheim and his supporters turn this question around, and ask how he could have served in such high positions if burdened with a suspicious past. Statement by Dr. Kurt Waldheim, February 23, 1986.

11. Seymour J. Pomrenze, "Policies and Procedures for the Protection, Use, and Return of Captured German Records," in Robert Wolfe, ed., *Captured German and Related Records: A National Archives Conference* (Athens, OH: 1974).

12. Kurt Waldheim, *In the Eye of the Storm*, p. 125, discusses his good relations with Marshal Tito.

13. *Profil*, June 30, 1986.

14. Berlin Document Center, report on Kurt Waldheim, #20044798; Gouvernement militaire français, *WAST*, March 21, 1979, report on Kurt Waldheim.

15. Kurt Waldheim to Rep. Stephen Solarz, December 9, 1980.

16. Legal Counsel Frederick P. Hitz to Rep. Stephen Solarz, December 31, 1980.

17. See, for example, Alan Levy, "A Weekend with Waldheim of the UN," *The New York Sunday News Magazine*, April 21, 1974, p. 17 ff.

Chapter Sixteen
The Return of Lieutenant Waldheim

1. *Profil,* March 3, 1986; and August 24, 1987.

2. On Austria's self-image: William T. Bluhm, *Building an Austrian Nation: The Political Integration of a Western State* (New Haven, CT: 1973), pp. 238–239.

3. *Profil,* June 9, 1987.

4. Televised address by Federal President Rudolf Kirchschläger, April 22, 1986.

5. *Newsweek,* May 5, 1986; "Mit Waldheim leben," *Die Zeit,* July 17, 1987; and a perceptive speech by journalist Alan Levy, "An American Jew in Vienna," before the Catholic Students Association Norica, October 21, 1986. The recent Austrian debate over anti-Semitism antedated the Waldheim scandal, and continued during his presidency. See Heinz Kienzl, "Ausgeheilt?," *Zukunft,* November 1985, p. 33 ff.; and Prof. Gerhard Botz's comments in *Die Gemeinde,* June 1, 1987, p. 5. *Der Spiegel* savaged Waldheim and Austria in its title story, 16/1986, referring to "Austria's quiet fascism," its "living lie," etc.

6. For example, Tanjug wire report of March 5, 1986. The report linked Waldheim to Gen. Stahl and the Kozara massacres. For Wiesenthal's views on the Waldheim matter, see S. Wiesenthal, "Waldheims Wahl und die Folgen," *Ausweg,* June 1986, pp. 2–4; and his "My personal comments on the case of Dr. Kurt Waldheim," Bulletin of Information No. 27 (January 31, 1987), Dokumentationszentrum. On the controversy surrounding these views, see James Markham, *The New York Times,* May 17, 1986.

7. "Ist Waldheim vogelfrei . . . ," *National-Zeitung,* June 5, 1987.

Chapter Seventeen
Facing the Truth

1. Hon. Joseph J. DioGuardi, *Congressional Record,* May 14, 1986.

2. Leslie M. Werner, "Inquiry studied data Waldheim gave in rebuttal," *The New York Times,* April 29, 1987.

3. "Address by Representative of U.S. Jews, and the Pope's Reply," *The New York Times,* September 12, 1987.

4. Fernsehansprache des Bundespräsident Dr. Kurt Waldheim, am Dienstag, 19. Mai 1987.

5. See summary of OSS Activities During May 1945, RG 226/99/95/127 and 130.

Postscript
The Waldheim Affair Three Years Later

1. I obtained some of these documents from the Department of State under a Freedom of Information Act request. See Dept. of State to American Embassy, Vienna, 12/17/71, which concludes with the phrase "We are concerned that Austrians should not rpt [repeat] not get impression that we are in any way disinclined to see Waldheim become Secretary General." See also Memorandum of Conversation, December 21, 1971, UN 8-3; Department of State telegrams USUN5185 (12/21/71); UN 8-3 (Deputy Under Secretary

of State for Economic Affairs, December 22, 1971); USUN N 05193 220617Z (December 22, 1971); and Vienna 8122 (December 23, 1971).

2. John L. Helgerson to Stephen J. Solarz, 3 June 1988.

3. Simon Wiesenthal supplied this information to the author in June, 1987.

4. Congressman Solarz used this phrase during an interview on Granada Television's "World in Action" series. The production "The Man Who Lived a Lie," made use of the Solarz interview.

5. While Waldheim had not been an intelligence officer in Russia, he had indeed served in that capacity in the Balkans. If anyone could connect the "intelligence officer" admission to the Balkan locale, he would be halfway towards solving the riddle of the "missing years."

6. The U.N. War Crimes Commission records were not fully available to researchers until November, 1987. They were, however, accessible to representatives of member states, acting for "United Nations purposes."

7. C. Boyden Grey to Robert E. Herzstein, July 14, 1987.

8. Most of this correspondence dates back to 1987–1988. It is quite lengthy, but the most valuable parts of it reveal *why* the Agency claims exemptions under the C.I.A. Information Act.

9. Agent contacts and other security classified information may have to be deleted before the public gains access to the Waldheim files.

10. "Historikerkommission Bericht vom 8. Februar 1988 über den Kriegsdienst des ehem. Oberleutnant Dr. Kurt Waldheim."

11. For other examples of the new revisionism, see Professor Ernst Nolte's observations (1980–1987) in "Zwischen Geschictslegende und Revisionismus?"; "Vergangenheit, die nicht vergegen will"; "Leserbrief an »DIE ZEIT«, 1. August 1986"; and "Anmerkung zum ›Historikerstreit‹." These essays appear in the book *»Historikerstreit«: Die Dokumentation der Kontroverse um die Einzigartigkeit der nationalsocialistischen Judenvernichtung* (Munich: 1987). Some of these observations are based upon my paper "National and Psychological Aspects of the Waldheim Case: A Study of an *Unbewältigte Vergangenheit*," at the GDR/USA Symposium on Nazi Terror and Resistance, sponsored by IREX and held at Princeton University, Princeton, N.J., May 4–6, 1989.

12. Some of these arguments are based upon my essay "Accommodation to the Present as Prelude to Rewriting History: The Example of Dr. Kurt Waldheim, 1938–1986," a paper prepared for presentation at a conference on "The Rise of Adolf Hitler and Other Genocidal Leaders: Psychoanalytic and Historical Symposium," St. Mary's Hospital and Medical Center, San Francisco, CA, April 21–21, 1989.

13. Kurt Waldheim, "Coming of Age," in *The Challenge of Peace* (New York: 1980), p. 18. Waldheim, *In the Eye of the Storm* (New York: 1985), repeats much of the story, which he first recounted in his earlier memoir.

14. Helene Deutsch, "Some Forms of Emotional Disturbance and Their Relationship to Schizophrenia" (1942), in her book *Neuroses and Character Types: Clinical Psychoanalytic Studies* (New York: International Universities Press, 1965), pp. 262–278. I am grateful to Dr. Peter Loewenberg of UCLA for his suggestion that I refer to Deutsch's writing in the Waldheim context.

Abbreviations

AA	Auswärtiges Amt (German or Austrian foreign ministry)
AK	Armeekorps (army corps)
AO	Abwehr-Offizier, counter-intelligence officer
AOK	Armeeoberkommando (high command of an army)
BDC	Berlin Document Center
Befehlshaber–	Commander (usually a territorial command)
CAD	Civil Affairs Division (of the U.S. War Department)
CFM	Council of Foreign Ministers
CIC	Counter-Intelligence Corps of the U.S. Army
CROWCASS	Central Registry of War Criminals and Security Suspects
C.S.D.I.C.	Combined Services Detail Interrogation Center
f.d.R.	für die Richtigkeit (following a signature, attesting to the accuracy of the enclosed material)
f.d.R.d.A	für die Richtigkeit der Ausfertigung (following a signature, attesting to the accuracy of the draft)
FO	(British) Foreign Office, referring to documents stored in the Public Record Office, Kew, U.K.
Fonoff	Foreign Office of Great Britain
FRUS	FOREIGN RELATIONS OF THE UNITED STATES (documents published by the U.S. Department of State)

Geb.-Div.	Gebirgs-Division (mountain division)
Gen.Kdo	General command
HRGE	Heeresgruppe E (Army Group E)
Ia	Operations department (of a division, corps, battle group, army, or army group)
Ib	Quartermaster/supply department
Ic	Intelligence department (of a division, corps, battle group, army, or army group); also, the third general staff officer, in charge of intelligence
Ic/AO	Combined intelligence and counter-intelligence unit of an army group, under the command of the Ic officer
IIa, IIb	Adjutant's department, dealing with personnel
I.D.	Infanterie-Division
IfZ	Institut für Zeitgeschichte (Institut for Contemporary History, Munich)
IRR	Investigative Records Repository
J.I.C.A.M.E.	Joint Intelligence Collecting Agency, Middle East
KTB	Kriegstagebuch (war diary)
M-	National Archives designation for microfilmed records of war-crimes trials
MBH	Militärbefehlshaber (Military Commander)
MBHSO	Militärbefehlshaber Südost (Military Commander, Southeast)
N.A.	National Archives
NAM	National Archives Microcopy (usually Record Group 242)
NOKW, WB	Designation of documents used in war-crimes trials; originals or microcopies of them may generally be found in the M800 or RG 242 collections in the National Archives
NSDAP	Nationalsozialistische Deutsche Arbeiterpartei (National Socialist German Workers Party)
OBSO	Oberbefehlshaber Südost (Supreme Commander Southeast)
OSS	(U.S.) Office of Strategic Services
OKH	Oberkommando des Heeres (Supreme Command of the Army)
OKW	Oberkommando der Wehrmacht (Supreme Command of the Wehrmacht)
Polad	Political Advisor (to the U.S. High Commissioner in Austria)
RG	Record Group (referring to the National Archives)
SD	Sicherheitsdienst (Security Service)
Secstate	U.S. Secretary of State

SHAEF	Supreme Headquarters, Allied Expeditionary Force
Sipo	Sicherheitspolizei (Security Police)
T-	National Archives Microcopy series, in Record Group 242, for example, T-120
TB	Tätigkeitsbericht (activity report)
UNWCC	United Nations War Crimes Commission
USACA	U.S. Element Allied Commission Austria
USCOA	U.S. Commanding Officer Austria
WBHSO	Wehrmachtbefehlshaber Südost (Wehrmacht Commander, Southeast)
W.D.G.S.	War Department General Staff
WO	War Office records, stored in the Public Record Office, Kew and London, U.K.

INDEX

ABC World News Tonight, 238–239
Albania, 84, 120, 128–129
Allied Control Council, 204, 208, 210, 244,
    253
Anschluss, 33, 38–39, 55, 61, 81–82,
    179–180
  Austrian plebiscite on, 52–53, 54, 121
  Moscow Declaration on, 111–112
Arafat, Yasir, 228
Arhiv Jugoslavije, 245
Army, U.S., German Military Documents
    Section of, 227
Army Intelligence, U.S., 199, 257
Arsakli, Waldheim's assignments in, 77, 107,
    109–110, 113, 115, 118, 119, 122,
    124–129, 201, 217, 255
Athens:
  Italian presence in, 92–95, 102–103
  Waldheim in, 92–95, 98, 101, 103–105,
    107, 255, 262
Ault, Dorothy L., 215
Auschwitz, 99, 124, 235

Austria:
  Allied Council administration of, 161–
    167, 172, 173–174, 176, 179, 199
  anti-Semitism in, 29–30, 34–35, 49,
    52–54, 57, 112, 240–241, 247, 252
  Army Intelligence Service of (HND),
    227–228
  Christian Social movement in, 30, 32–35,
    37–39, 52–54, 164–165, 224
  civil war in, 42
  Communist party of, 32–33, 165–166,
    185–186, 187, 201
  crackdown on Catholics in, 54–55, 56
  Czech nationalism and, 28–31, 34
  denazification of, 173–177
  end of four-power occupation of, 172,
    177, 180–181, 184–186, 188–189,
    205–209, 217–219, 222
  German invasion of, 53–54
  during Great Depression, 38–39, 49
  improving relations between Yugoslavia
    and, 210–211, 213–214, 227, 258

Austria (continued)
  Liberal party of, 242, 250–251
  national plebiscite in, 52–53, 54, 121
  Nazis in, 39, 43, 45, 47–49, 51–54,
    81–83, 113, 173–174, 240
  1945 elections in, 166
  1986 elections in, 233–235, 237, 241–242,
    249, 251
  People's Party of (ÖVP), 165–166, 224,
    231, 233, 241, 250–251
  post-World War I, 27, 32–35, 37–38
  post-World War II, 160–165, 168,
    173–174, 176–181, 183–186,
    188–189, 194, 200–202, 203,
    205–211
  pre-World War I, 27–31
  public opinion on Waldheim in, 249–252,
    263–264
  rearmament of, 206
  Red-Black coalition in, 33
  right-wing authoritarian domination of,
    39–44
  school system in, 34–35, 38
  Serbian war with, 31
  Social Democrats of, 31, 32, 34, 37–38,
    41
  Socialist movement in, 33, 37–40, 42, 47,
    164–166, 231, 233–235, 241–242,
    249–251
  Soviet and Yugoslav claims on, 177–181,
    183–185, 188–189, 194, 200–202,
    203, 205–208, 211, 214, 258
  U.S. aid to, 186, 188–189
  war crimes accusations against, 179–180,
    184, 207, 240
  war criminal extradition laws of, 190
  during World War I, 27, 31–32
Austrian Treaty Commission, 185

Baden, 112, 149, 155, 163–164
Bader, Paul:
  Kozara pacification and, 74, 76
  in Operation Trio, 68–70
Badoglio, Pietro, 93–94, 95
Bad Tölz, 156, 159, 257, 258
Banja Luka, Jews deported from, 77
Baron de Hirsch concentration camp, 99
Bauer, Otto, 32–33, 38
Bebler, Aleš, 189, 207–208
Beethoven, Ludwig van, 51, 241
Belgrade, Waldheim's assignment to, 66–68,
  74, 262
Berlin Document Center (BDC), 228–229,
  255
Bevin, Ernest, 181
Bidault, Georges, 181
Bismarck, Otto von, 83, 117
Bjelić, Uroš, 197
Black, Operation, 86–90, 91, 94

Bohlen, Charles "Chip," 181
Bronfman, Edgar, 234, 247
Brown, Sir Alfred, 203
Buchenwald, 57, 203
Bulgaria, 120, 128, 152
  German counterinsurgency operations in,
    109–110
Bush, George, 225

Canada, Austrian Legation to, 220
Carinthia:
  dissident groups operating in, 201
  Yugoslav claims on, 178–180, 183–185,
    200–202
Carr, E. H., 48
Case Axis, 94–95, 97, 102
Catholics, Nazi crackdown on, 54–55, 56
Central Intelligence Agency (CIA), U.S.,
  229–230, 259
Central Office for Jewish Emigration, 57
Central Registry of War Criminals and
  Security Suspects (CROWCASS),
  204–205, 209–211, 213, 217, 236
Chetnik groups, 88, 151
  Tito opposed by, 85, 148–149
China, People's Republic of, 225, 230
Churchill, Winston, 122
Clissura, massacre at, 119–120
Communism, Communists:
  of Austria, 32–33, 165–166, 185–186,
    187, 201
  in Balkans, 67–68, 71, 85–86, 110, 115,
    119–120, 129, 148, 210
  Gruber's opposition to, 187, 258
Consular Academy:
  Verdross as lecturer at, 82–83
  Waldheim's enrollment at, 50, 53, 55–56,
    57–58, 164, 169, 219–220
Corfu, deportation of Jews from, 124–125
Counter-Intelligence Corps, U.S., 168, 199,
  258
Craigie, Sir Robert, 200
Credit-Anstalt bank, collapse of, 38
Czechoslovakia, 56–57
  Soviet invasion of, 222, 225, 227
Czech people, 28–31, 34
Czernin, Hubertus, 234

Dachau, 57, 165, 203, 207
Dedijer, Vladimir, 67, 243
Denazification Bureau, 173–174
Depression, Great, 38, 39, 49
DioGuardi, Joseph J., 252
Documentation Center for the League of
  the Jewish Victims of the Nazi
  Regime, 250–251
Dollfuss, Engelbert, 54, 165
  attempt to abolish political parties by, 40
  death of, 43, 44, 45, 51, 82

Heimwehren supportive of, 39–42
Schuschnigg compared with, 43–44
Socialists suppressed by, 43–44, 47
Ständestaat notion of, 41–42
Verdross and, 82–83
Doughty, James, 124
Dowling, Walter, 215–216
Dulles, Allen, 168
Dulles, John Foster, 181, 218

East Bosnia, Operation Trio in, 68–70
EDES *(Ellinikos Dimokratikos Ethnikos Sindesmos)*, 93, 115, 120, 129
Egberts-Hilker, Karl-Heinz, 197–198
Eichmann, Adolf, 57, 263
ELAS *(Ellinokos Laikos Apeleftherotikos Stratos)*, 93, 115, 120, 129
Esposito, Giovanni, 68–70, 83–84, 149, 223, 237–238
Ethiopia, Italian aggression against, 47–48

Felber, Hans Gustav, 109
Figl, Leopold, 185–186, 217
    as chancellor, 166, 174, 206
    denazification and, 174, 176
    description of, 165–166
    Waldheim's relationship with, 218
Fischer, Ernst, 165, 186
Foreign Affairs Department, Austrian, 170
Foreign Affairs Ministry, Austrian, 214–215
45th Reconnaissance Unit, German, 58, 61–63
    on Soviet front, 64–65
Fourteen Points, 31
France, 62, 161, 210, 217
Frantz, Konstantin, 81, 83, 110–111, 117–118, 119, 214–215
Franz Ferdinand, archduke of Austria, 31
Franz Joseph, emperor of Austria, 28, 30–31, 36, 112, 160
Freedom of Information Act, 215
Freud, Sigmund, 30
Frey, Lieutenant, 104–105, 115
From Liberation to Liberty (Gruber), 217–218
Fuhrmann, Major, 115, 148
Funke, Hermann, 72–73

Gandini, General, 92–93, 96, 104
German people, moral responsibility of, 260–261
German Studies Association, 246–247
Germany, Nazi, 21–22
    Allied invasion of, 153–154
    anti-Semitic actions of, 57, 98–101, 124–125, 235–236

atrocities committed by, 23, 67, 74–75, 77, 97–101, 115–116, 119–125, 179, 190, 197–198, 205
Austria invaded by, 53–54
Balkan operations of, 67–70, 71–77, 85–90, 91, 95–102, 108–110, 113–116, 119–129, 147–152, 154, 179
collapse of, 153–156
disarming and deportation of Italian soldiers by, 102–105, 246, 252, 260, 262
France invaded by, 62
Italian relations with, 85–86, 88–90, 93–98, 101–102
military and political documents of, 227–229, 235–239
retreat from Balkans by, 127–129, 147–153
Schuschnigg's policy toward, 47–48
Soviet counteroffensive against, 65–67, 77–78, 107
Soviet Union invaded by, 63–65
Waldheim's dissertation and, 117–118, 214–215
Germany, Weimar Republic of, 32–33, 38–39
Gerö, Josef, 203, 208
Giannuzzi, Gaetano, 84
Glisić, Venčeslav, 227
Glöckel, Otto, 34, 42
Goebbels, Paul Joseph, 57, 79, 112, 153, 187
Göring, Hermann, 112, 152
Great Britain, 178, 180, 191, 206, 217
    Austria occupied by, 161–162, 166
    German collapse and, 154–155
    Greek partisans and, 110, 115, 122
    Special Operations Executive of, 122
    UNWCC and, 196, 200, 204–205
Greece:
    Allied Military Mission in, 122
    Axis counterinsurgency tactics in, 95–101, 109–110, 113–116
    deportation of Italian army from, 102–105, 246, 252, 260, 262
    deportation of Jews from, 98–99, 101, 124, 235–236, 252, 260, 262
    German terror in, 115–116, 119–125
    German withdrawal from, 127–129
    Italian occupation of, 92–94
    partisan groups in, 93, 94–96, 115, 119–123, 125–127, 129, 263
    Waldheim's expertise on, 109, 115
Greene, Graham, 168
Gruber, Karl, 164, 201
    Austrian sovereignty sought by, 172, 177, 180–181, 184, 188–189, 202, 207–208

Gruber, Karl (*continued*)
  background of, 166–167
  denazification and, 174–176
  foreign ministry rebuilt by, 167–172, 257
  Molden and, 167–169, 258
  on Soviet and Yugoslav claims, 178–180,
    183–184, 194, 202, 203
  Tito and, 214, 222
  Waldheim's relationship with, 170–172,
    175–178, 185–187, 194, 196,
    208–209, 213, 216, 219–221, 227,
    263
  war criminal prosecution and, 190, 207
  Yugoslav attempts at discrediting of, 194,
    198–200, 208, 211, 236, 258
Gyldenfeldt, Heinz von, 92, 93, 95
  Greek cleansing operation and, 99, 101
  Italian surrender and, 102, 104

Hague Agreement (1907), 197, 254
Hammer, Friedrich Wilhelm, 124–125
Handbook of German Military Forces, 114
Hanzer, Lieutenant, 200
Hartner, Markus, 114, 201
Haydn, Franz Joseph, 152
Hazzard, Shirley, 229
Heimwehren, 53
  Dollfuss supported by, 39–42
  Schuschnigg and, 47–49, 52
Herzegovina, 86–87, 91
Himmler, Heinrich, 64, 125, 180
Hitler, Adolf, 39, 44–45, 81, 118, 165, 179,
    241, 263
  anti-Semitism of, 29, 57, 64, 100–101
  attempted assassination of, 125–126
  Austrian plans of, 50–53
  on Austrian plebiscite, 52–53, 54
  Austrian regime attacked by, 42–43
  Badoglio and, 93–94
  Balkan operations and, 86, 88, 94, 96–97,
    119, 121–123, 127, 153
  Commando Order of, 122–123
  Dollfuss criticized by, 42
  Frantz and, 83, 117
  Italian surrender and, 103
  Löhr and, 113, 152
  Mussolini's ties to, 47, 51
  racist ideology of, 64–65, 240, 260
  Schuschnigg and, 48–49, 50–51
  secrecy policy of, 101, 104
  Soviet obsession of, 63–64, 66
  suicide of, 154
Hitler Youth, 53, 55, 79, 81, 229
Hitz, Frederick P., 230
Hlavec von Rechtwall, Friedrich, 50, 55–56
Hödl, Carl, 247
Hoffinger, Max, 178–179
Holocaust:
  John Paul II on, 254, 264

Waldheim's involvement in, 98–101, 125,
    251–252, 260–261
Waldheim's units involved in, 124–125,
    252, 260
Holtzman, Elizabeth, 242, 247, 254
Howe, Sir Geoffrey, 123

"Idea of the Reich in Konstantin Frantz,
    The" (Waldheim), 117–118
Immigration and Nationality Act, U.S., 242
Immigration and Naturalization Service,
    U.S., Watch List of, 242–243, 247,
    252–256, 257, 259
Independent State of Croatia (ISC), 67–68,
    85
  deportation of prisoners from, 74–76
  see also Yugoslavia
Innitzer, Theodor, 54–55
Interior Ministry, Yugoslav, 193–194, 195,
    197, 200–201
In the Eye of the Storm (Waldheim), 226
Ionnina, Jews of, 98, 100–101, 124, 260
Israel, Waldheim's past and, 228–229
Italy, 39, 84
  Balkan operations of, 67–70, 71–72,
    85–90, 91, 94–98, 109, 246
  Ethiopia attacked by, 47–48
  German relations with, 85–86, 88–90,
    93–98, 101–102
  Greek occupation of, 92–94
  surrender of, 102–105

Jakobson, Max, 225
Jasenovac concentration camp, 77, 245
Jevdjenijević, Major, 148–149
Jews, 63
  Austrian expulsion of, 57, 112
  Austrian prejudice against, 29–30, 34–35,
    49, 52–54, 57, 112, 240–241, 247,
    252
  of Croatia, 77, 85
  of Germany, 57
  of Greece, 98–101, 124–125, 235–236,
    252, 260, 262
  of U.S., 251–252
  Verdross friendly with, 82–83
  of Vienna, 30, 52–54, 57
  Waldheim's acquaintance with, 80, 101
John Paul II, pope, 254, 264
Jonas, Franz, 224
Justice Department, U.S., 242–243

Kalavryta, massacre at, 115–116
Kaltenbrunner, Ernst, 263
Kalvarija-Zemun POW camp, 196
Kardelj, Edvard, 183–185
Karl I, emperor of Austria, 31
Kasche, Siegfried, 86
Keitel, Wilhelm, 121–122

Kesar, Jovan, 246
Keyes, Geoffrey, 186, 190, 206
Khomeini, Ayatollah Ruhollah, 230
Khrushchev, Nikita, 218
Kintner, E. W., 200–201
Kirchschläger, Rudolf, 222, 241
Klaus, Josef, 221
Klosterneuburg, 37–38, 43–44
Kohl, Helmut, 233
König, Franz, 116
Korneuberg Oath, 40–41
Kozara:
  casualties in, 73, 75
  German pacification of, 72–76, 190, 205,
    237–239, 243, 245, 260, 262
  partisan withdrawal to, 71–72
  Waldheim's statements about, 77, 256
Kreisky, Bruno, 38, 233, 241
  political career of, 250–251
  Waldheim controversy and, 251
  Waldheim described by, 171
  Waldheim's relationship with, 217–221,
    223–224
Krenzki, Curt von, 98–99
Kunschak, Leopold, 165
Kwisda, Hans-Georg, 65

League of German Maidens, 81
League of Nations, 82–83
Lekić, Bogdan, 245
Lenin, V. I., 32
Lie, Trygve, 171
Lingens, Michael, 234
Löhr, Alexander, 86, 91
  Balkan command of, 94, 97, 109–110,
    113–114, 116, 123, 126, 128–129,
    147–152, 154–155, 179, 198, 245,
    262
  execution of, 181, 190, 193, 234
  overthrow of Mussolini and, 93–94
  surrender negotiated by, 155
  Waldheim's relationship with, 108,
    113–114, 220–221, 234, 254
  war crimes trial of, 179, 184, 189–190,
    193, 211
London deputy foreign ministers'
  conferences, 178–180, 188–191, 200,
    203, 205–209
Luce, Henry, 168
Lueger, Karl, 30, 34
Lüters, Rudolf, 88–89

Macholz, Joachim, 85
  Operation Black and, 86, 89
  Waldheim's relationship with, 84, 91
Mahler, Gustav, 30
Marshall, George C., 181, 184, 186
Marshall Plan, 186, 188, 211
Martin, John, 238

Mayer, Johann, 196, 198, 201, 211, 258
Meese, Edwin, III, 243, 252–253, 256, 259
Mendelsohn, John, 21, 236
Mengele, Josef, 260
Metternich, Clemens von, 231
Mihailović, Draža, 148
Milenković, Veljko, 200–201, 203
Miletić, Antun, 245
Military History Archive, Yugoslav, 245
Ministerial Committee for Denazification,
    174–176
Mock, Alois, 241–242
Molden, Fritz Peter:
  Gruber and, 167–169, 258
  Waldheim's background investigated by,
    169–170, 216, 258
  Waldheim's meeting with, 168–169
Molotov, Vyacheslav M., 181, 183–184
Montenegro, 88–89
  German withdrawal through, 128–129
Moscow Declaration, 111–112, 159–160,
    174, 179, 184–185, 189–199, 240,
    254, 261, 263
Moscow foreign ministers' conference, 181,
    183–185, 193–194, 207
Mostar bauxite mines, 86–87
Murphy, Robert, 181
Mussolini, Benito, 22, 38, 44–45
  Balkan operations and, 85–86, 88, 98
  Dollfuss and, 39, 41, 43, 47
  German ties of, 47–48, 51
  overthrow of, 93–94

National Archives, U.S., 21–23, 227
  Modern Military Branch of, 235–239
National Socialist German Students League,
    55–56, 58, 175, 229, 255
National-Zeitung, 247
Nedeljković, Dušan, 199
Nehru, Jawaharlal, 224
Neubacher, Hermann, 119, 122
New Republic, 229
Newsweek, 241
New York Times, 225, 240
Nixon, Richard M., 250
North Atlantic Treaty Organization
  (NATO), 218
Nüremberg Charter, war crimes defined by,
    253–254
Nüremberg Tribunal, 123, 189–190,
    253–254, 263

Office of Special Investigations (OSI), U.S.,
    242–243, 244, 259
Office of Strategic Services (OSS), U.S.,
    167, 168, 257, 258
Office of War Crimes, U.S., 189–190
Organization Book, Nazi party, 55, 57
Otto of Habsburg, 51–52, 82

Pannwitz, Helmut von, 65
Paramythia/Parga region, cleansing
    operation in, 99–101
Paris, Austrian Legation in, 187, 208–209,
    213–214, 217
Patriotic Front, 40, 42, 44, 48–49
Pavelić, Ante, 75–76, 85–86, 153
Pérez de Cuéllar, Javier, 231
Peter, Friedrich, 250
Phleps, Artur, 91
    Operation Black commanded by, 87–90
Piesch, Hans, 178
    war crimes accusations against, 179–180,
        205, 208
Pius XI, pope, 41
Podgorica, Waldheim's diplomatic triumph
    at, 89–90
Pogonion, deportations from, 120–121
Potsdam, Big Four meeting in, 177
Prague spring, 222
Pravda, 186–187
"Press and Propaganda" (Waldheim), 56
Profil, 234, 241
Provisional Austrian National Committee,
    166–167
Pusch, Hans, 233–234
Pusteria, 68–70, 83–84, 237–238

Raab, Julius, 217
Race and Settlement Office, 180
Radetzky, Joseph, 36
"Radetzky March" (Strauss), 36
Reagan, Ronald, 233
Reber, Samuel, 206–207
Reichskristallnacht, 57
Renner, Karl, 54
    on Austrian sovereignty, 185
    provisional government of, 162–167, 257
Republican Defense League, 37–38, 40–41
Ribbentrop, Joachim von, 119
Roncaglia, Ercole, 84, 87–89
Roosevelt, Franklin D., 75
Rosenbaum, Eli, 22
Rumania, 127

St.-Germain, Treaty of (1919), 33
Salonika, 110, 125
    Jewish community of, 98–99, 101,
        235–236, 252, 262
Sarajevo, Waldheim's assignments in, 149,
    150–152, 201
Schärf, Adolf, 162, 174–175
Schenk, Major von, 129
Schmidt-Richberg, General, 121, 125–126,
    150, 198
Scholz, Roman, 44
Schönbauer, Ernst, 82–83
Schönerer, Georg Ritter von, 30, 240
Schubert, Franz, 36, 152

Schuschnigg, Kurt von, 45, 54, 117, 121
    Dollfuss compared with, 43–44
    German policy of, 47–48
    growth of Nazism under, 47–49, 51–52
    Hitler and, 48–49, 50–51
    Patriotic Front and, 48–49
    resignation of, 53
    Verdross and, 82
    Waldheim as supporter of, 52–53, 121,
        175
Schutzbund, 37–38, 40–42
Schwanzer, Herr, 163–164, 175–176
Seipel, Ignaz, 33–34, 38–39
Semlin concentration camp, 67
Serbia, Austrian war with, 31
Seyss-Inquart, Artur, 51, 53
Sher, Neal, 243, 252
Singer, Israel, 22, 234
Sinowatz, Fred, 233–234, 241–242, 251
Smith, Walter Bedell, 181
Solarz, Stephen, 229–230, 259
South Tyrol, Austrian position on, 219–224
Soviet Union:
    on Austrian sovereignty, 181, 184, 186,
        188, 200, 202, 206–209, 218, 222
    Austria occupied by, 159–163, 165,
        201–202
    Balkans threatened by, 110, 120, 126–128,
        147–148, 151, 154–155
    claims on Austria by, 177–180, 184–185,
        188–189, 200, 202, 203, 205–207
    counteroffensive of, 65–67, 77–78, 107
    Czechoslovakia invaded by, 222, 225, 227
    German collapse and, 154–155
    German invasion of, 63–65
    Germany invaded by, 153–154
    Gruber's opposition to, 168
    Marshall Plan criticized by, 186
    UNWCC and, 194
    Waldheim supported by, 225, 260
    Yugoslav break with, 210, 214
    Yugoslav claims supported by, 179, 183,
        207
Speidel, Wilhelm, 109, 116, 120
Spiegel, 226, 240–241
Srbik, Heinrich von, 117
Stahl, Friedrich, 71, 254
    in Kozara pacification, 72–74, 76,
        237–239
Stalin, Joseph, 63, 151, 160
    death of, 217
    Renner and, 162
    Tito's relationship with, 183, 202, 210
    Yugoslav claims and, 183–184
Stalingrad, battle of, 77–78
State Department, U.S., 189
    on Austrian treaty negotiations, 206–207
    Waldheim's background investigated by,
        215–216, 259

Stern, Herr, 164, 175–176
Stettner, Walter von:
  in counterinsurgency operations, 95–98
  Greek cleansing operation and, 99
Steyrer, Kurt, 233, 241
Stip massacre, 197–198
Stockerau, 49, 56, 58
Storm Troop movement (S.A.), 39, 53, 55
  Waldheim's membership in, 57–58, 175,
    229, 255
Strauss, Johann, 36, 181, 240
Sudetenland, 56–57

Tanjug, 243
Tass, 128
Thant, U, 221–222, 223–224
Thatcher, Margaret, 233
Third Man, The (Greene), 168
Tidl, Georg, 234
Tirana, Waldheim's assignment to, 84
Tito (Josip Broz), 71, 73, 151, 201
  Austrians accused of war crimes by, 179
  Chetnik opposition to, 85, 148–149
  Hitler's respect for, 94
  Operation Black and, 87, 91
  Soviet alliance with, 127–128, 147
  Stalin's relationship with, 183, 202, 210
  successes of, 151–152, 154–155
  territorial claims made by, 178, 189, 214
  U.S. aid sought by, 211
  U.S. opposition to, 190–191
  Waldheim's relationship with, 222, 224,
    227, 243, 259
  war criminal extradition and, 189–190
Trio, Operation, 68–70
Tulln, 27, 30, 35, 38, 50, 55, 121
  description of, 36
  Waldheim's youth in, 37
Turina, Oskar, 76, 190–191, 199, 205

United Nations, 22, 117, 171
  extradition of accused war criminals and,
    191
  General Assembly of, 221, 225, 228
  Outer Space Committee of, 221
  Security Council of, 225
  Waldheim as Austrian representative to,
    219–221, 223–224
  Waldheim as secretary-general of, 216,
    225–230, 257, 259
  Western disenchantment with, 228
United Nations War Crimes Commission
    (UNWCC), 57, 111
  background of, 194–195
  Committee I of, 195, 196–197, 200–201,
    203–204
  disbanding of, 213
  listing of Waldheim by, 194–202,
    203–205, 208–211, 217

United States:
  Austrian sovereignty and, 206–208, 218
  Austria occupied by, 161–163, 167
  Gruber's relationship with, 167–168,
    185–186, 187, 199, 218, 257–258
  treatment of POWs by, 159
  UNWCC and, 196, 200–201, 204–205
  Waldheim placed on Watch List of,
    242–243, 252–256, 257, 259
  Waldheim supported by, 225, 227,
    257–259
  war criminal extradition and, 189–191,
    199, 205, 260
  Yugoslav claims and, 183

Vecchiarelli, Carlo, 92–94
  in counterinsurgency operations, 95–98
  Greek cleansing operation and, 99
  Italian surrender and, 102–104
Večernje Novosti, 246
Velebit, Vladimir, 258–259
Verdross von Drossberg, Alfred, 79,
    117
  Nazi dissatisfaction with, 82–83
  opportunism of, 82, 83
  Waldheim's relationship with, 81–82, 83,
    113–114, 116, 118
Victor Emmanuel III, king of Italy, 93
Vienna, 29, 39
  Allied bombardment of, 149, 152
  anti-Semitic activities in, 52–54, 57
  as cosmopolitan, 32–33, 36–37
  fin de siècle, 30
  Inter-Allied Command administration of,
    161–163, 167
  legitimist rallies in, 51
  Nazi popularity in, 52
  post-World War I, 32–34, 36–37
  Socialist administration of, 32–33, 37–39,
    41–43
  Soviet kidnappings in, 201–202
  Soviet occupation of, 159–162, 165, 168
  Soviet siege of, 153–154
  during World War II, 79–80
Vienna, University of, 22, 56, 79, 117
  disappearance of Waldheim's dissertation
    from, 214–215
  Waldheim's acquaintances at, 80–83
Vilfan, Josef, 179–180
Vranitsky, Franz, 241–242, 255

Wacht Im Südosten, 151
Waldheim, Christa (daughter), 220
Waldheim, Elizabeth Lieselotte Ritschel
    (Cissy; Lilo) (wife), 111, 156, 159,
    163
  honeymoon of, 126–127
  husband's concerns for, 119, 149, 151,
    153–155

Waldheim, Elizabeth (*continued*)
    husband's correspondence with, 83, 113,
        114
    husband's dissertation and, 115, 118
    husband's foreign ministry position and,
        170, 176, 180
    husband's UN mission and, 219, 224
    law studies of, 80, 83, 113, 127
    marriage of, 113, 118, 125–126
    Nazi party membership of, 81, 113
    nicknames of, 116–117
    physical appearance of, 80–81, 127,
        187–188
    popularity of, 187–188
    pregnancies of, 127, 151, 153–154,
        187–188, 192, 209, 220
Waldheim, Gerhard (son), 209, 238
    father's reputation defended by, 238–240,
        254–255
Waldheim, Gerlinde (sister), 35, 153,
    159
Waldheim, Josefine Petrasch (mother), 27
Waldheim, Kurt Josef:
    academic background of, 22, 37, 39,
        43–45, 50, 53, 55–56, 57–58, 61,
        62–63, 66, 79, 81–82, 83, 107,
        110–111, 113–114, 116–118, 127,
        164, 169
    as ambitious, 23, 36, 58–59, 66, 77, 81,
        83, 101, 175, 187–188, 219,
        221–222, 223, 230–231, 260, 262
    Americans courted by, 187–188
    as American intelligence asset, 257–259
    assertions of ignorance by, 101, 104, 125,
        255, 260
    attempted assassination of, 230
    Austrian moral responsibility and,
        260–264
    Austrian presidency of, 241–243, 247,
        252–257, 264
    autobiographical essay of, 226, 229–230
    Axis collapse witnessed by, 93–95, 98
    background investigations of, 169–170,
        172, 175–177, 193–202, 203–205,
        208–211, 214–216, 227–230,
        234–241, 255, 258, 259
    Balkans assignments of, 66–72, 74–77,
        83–86, 89–90, 91–95, 97–101,
        103–105, 107–111, 113–118, 119,
        121–129, 148–152, 154, 179, 211,
        223, 226–227, 229–230, 235–237,
        255–260, 263
    battle wound of, 65–66, 216, 225–226,
        229–230, 236–237, 256
    birth of, 27, 32
    cavalry unit postings of, 49–50, 56–58, 66
    denazification of, 163–164, 169, 175–177
    in deportation of Italian soldiers, 104–105,
        246, 252, 260, 262

diligence of, 50, 108, 170, 237
diplomatic skills of, 62, 76, 89–90, 107,
    219–220, 222–223, 228
diplomatic training of, 50, 53, 55–56,
    57–58, 164, 169, 219–220
doctoral dissertation of, 81–82, 83, 107,
    110–111, 113–114, 116–118, 171,
    214–215
early political activity of, 52–53, 83, 121,
    175–176
as facilitator, 254
in foreign ministry, 170–172, 175–181,
    183, 185–188, 191–192, 194,
    214–215, 217, 219–223
in foreign service, 187, 191, 208–209,
    213–214, 217, 219–222
foreign service ambitions of, 164,
    168–169, 187
German intelligence activities of, 69–70,
    107–111, 113–115, 119, 121–126,
    128–129, 148–152, 156, 159,
    197–198, 211, 217, 237, 257, 262
health problems of, 116
in Holocaust bureaucratic machinery,
    98–101, 125, 251–252, 260–261
honeymoon of, 126–127
honorary degrees awarded to, 22
intelligence staff of, 114–115, 196
international reputation of, 238–240,
    242–243, 252–256
Jewish acquaintances of, 80, 101
in Kozara pacification, 72, 74–77, 205,
    237–239, 243, 256, 260, 262
language skills of, 37, 62, 76, 77, 89–90,
    93, 103–105, 107, 169, 187–188,
    209, 220, 223, 225, 237
law studies pursued by, 58–59, 61, 62–63,
    66, 79, 81–82, 83, 164, 225, 230,
    236–237
London missions of, 178–180, 188, 191
luck of, 208–209, 213–214, 229–230, 233
marriage of, 113, 118, 125–126
memoirs of, 226, 237, 239
meticulous nature of, 215, 256
military awards of, 64, 65, 75–76, 77, 80,
    114, 154, 227, 237, 239, 243
military career file of, 234
Moscow mission of, 181, 183
Nazi affiliations denied by, 230, 255–256
Nazi organization memberships of, 55–56,
    58, 175–177, 217, 229, 255, 263
Nazi party evaluations of, 175–176
Nazism rejected by, 116–117, 256
as officer candidate, 58
omissions from biographies of, 215–217,
    225–231, 259
as "one-year" army volunteer, 44–45, 47,
    49–50
Operation Black and, 86, 89–90, 91

in Operation Trio, 68–70
ordinariness of, 260
in Ostmark reserve, 54
Paris mission of, 187, 208–209, 213–214, 217
physical appearance of, 35–36, 44, 50, 81, 109, 127, 168–169, 208, 255–256
political campaigns of, 224, 225–226, 231, 233–234, 237, 241–242, 249
popularity of, 187–188, 224, 233
as POW, 156, 159, 257, 258
prewar Nazi background of, 22
prisoner interrogation files maintained by, 108, 115, 123–124, 151
in propaganda efforts, 151
reactions to revelations about, 240–243, 246–247, 251–255, 257, 259, 263
reprisals against Greek civilians denounced by, 121–122
romances of, 69, 80–81, 83, 111, 114, 116, 119
secrecy maintained by, 100–101, 259
on Soviet front, 64–66, 107, 216, 225–226, 229–230, 236–237, 256
titles and honors enjoyed by, 37, 80, 230
UN mission of, 219–221, 223–224
as UN secretary-general, 216, 225–230, 257, 259
war crimes committed by military unit of, 123–125, 252
war crimes indictment against, 21, 192, 193–202, 203–205, 208–211, 217, 236, 243–246, 254, 260, 263
in Wehrmacht, 61–77, 80, 83–86, 89–90, 91–95, 97–101, 103–105, 107–118, 119, 121–129, 148–152, 154–156, 179, 204, 211, 215–217, 225, 237, 257, 263
wrongdoing denied by, 256–257
Waldheim, Lieselotte (daughter), 155, 159, 176, 180
Waldheim, Walter (father), 44, 50, 118, 170
as educator, 34–35, 38, 42, 49, 163
name changed by, 34
political affiliation of, 30, 34, 38–39, 40, 42, 52, 165
political problems of, 52, 55, 62–63
in World War I, 27, 31–32
youth of, 27–30
Waldheim, Walther (brother), 35
War Department, U.S., 114
Warnstorff, Herbert, 114, 198
Chetnik negotiations of, 148–149
Waldheim's relationship with, 107–110, 115–116, 123, 150, 254
War That Hitler Won, The (Herzstein), 21
WAST, 228–229

Wedenig, Ferdinand, 207–208
Weichs, Maximilian Freiherr von, 108
Balkan command of, 94, 97–98, 109–110, 123, 127–128, 148, 150, 153
Weizsäcker, Richard von, 258–259
Werkschutz, 201
White Book, 254–255
Who's Who in Austria 1955, 216
Wiesenthal, Simon, 228–229, 242
Kreisky's criticisms of, 250–251
Wild, Heinrich, 164, 175–176
Willers, Bruno, 92–93, 254
counterinsurgency operations and, 95–96
Waldheim described by, 105
Wilson, Woodrow, 31
Winter, August, 108
Wolfe, Robert, 235–236
World Jewish Congress (WJC), 242, 247, 251
Waldheim investigated by, 22–23, 234–235, 241, 252
World War I, 27, 31–32
Wright, Lord, 194–195

Yugoslavia, 68, 227
attempts to extradite war criminals by, 189–191, 198–199
claims on Austria by, 177–181, 183–185, 189, 194, 200–202, 203, 207–208, 211, 214, 258
German atrocities in, 67, 74–75, 77, 86, 179, 190, 197–198, 205
German withdrawal through, 127–128, 147–150
improving relations between Austria and, 210–211, 213–214, 227, 258
partisan operations in, 69–70, 71–76, 85–88, 91, 94, 108–110, 147–148, 150–155, 237–238, 263
reactions to Waldheim revelations in, 243–244
Soviet break with, 210, 214, 258
State Commission for the Determination of Crimes Committed by the Occupying Forces and Their Collaborators, 197
Waldheim's expertise on, 159, 170, 178, 257, 258
war crimes indictment against Waldheim by, 192, 193–202, 203–205, 208–211, 217, 236, 243–246, 254, 258, 260, 263
war crimes trials in, 179, 181, 184, 193, 197–198, 211, 234

Zervas, Napoleon, 115, 129
Zistersdorf oil refinery, 178, 206